HISTORY OF IMPERIAL CHINA

Timothy Brook, General Editor

CHINA'S COSMOPOLITAN EMPIRE

THE TANG DYNASTY

Mark Edward Lewis

THE BELKNAP PRESS OF
HARVARD UNIVERSITY PRESS
Cambridge, Massachusetts
London, England

First Harvard University Press paperback edition, 2012

Library of Congress Cataloging-in-Publication Data
Lewis, Mark Edward, 1954–
China's cosmopolitan empire : the Tang dynasty / Mark Edward Lewis.
p.   cm.
Includes bibliographical references and index.
ISBN 978-0-674-03306-1 (cloth : alk. paper)
ISBN 978-0-674-06401-0 (pbk.)
1. China—History—Tang dynasty, 618-907.   I. Title.   II. Title: Tang dynasty.
S749.3.L47 2009
951′.017—dc22   2008041337

CONTENTS

MAPS

FIGURES

CHINA'S COSMOPOLITAN EMPIRE

The Tang Dynasty

INTRODUCTION

MOST Chinese regard the Tang dynasty (618–907) as the highpoint of imperial China, both politically and culturally. The empire reached its greatest size prior to the Manchu Qing dynasty, becoming the center of an East Asian world linked by religion, script, and many economic and political institutions. Moreover, Tang writers produced the finest poetry in China's great lyric tradition, which has remained the most prestigious literary genre throughout Chinese history. But like most other dynasties that endured for centuries, this was also an age of transformation. The world at the end of the Tang was quite different from what it had been at the beginning, and the dynasty's historical importance is a consequence of the changes that took place during that time.

The military conquests and brilliant poetry that Chinese have traditionally celebrated occurred in the first half of the Tang dynasty. The imperial court never recovered from a cataclysmic rebellion in the middle of the eighth century, and within a few decades Chinese statesmen and authors were already writing of a golden age in whose shadow they now dwelled. Glorification of the Tang's early achievements in politics and art increased in later dynasties. With all of China or its northern half controlled by non-Chinese peoples for most of the empire's subsequent history, the Tang became the last great "Chinese" dynasty. This idea (which dismissed the militarily weak Ming dynasty) ignores the fact that the Tang ruling house was—both genealogically and culturally—a product of the frontier "barbarian" culture that dominated northern China in the fifth and sixth centuries.

For historians, especially in the West, the second half of the Tang is in many ways more interesting than the first. The break marked by the An Lushan rebellion in 756 was a pivotal moment not only in the fortunes of the dynasty but in the entire trajectory of China's development. The Japanese historian Naitō Torajirō argued that the long transition from the Tang to the Song that began in the mid-eighth century marked the shift from "medieval" to "early modern" China. While it is dangerous to impose Western periodization on Chinese history, substantial scholarship since Naitō has confirmed his essential hypothesis. The Tang dynasty's abandonment of key economic, military, and social institutions after the An Lushan rebellion, its reconfiguration of the empire's cultural geography, the expansion of trade relations with the outside world, and the invention of new artistic forms to deal with this changing world were the initial steps that began to distinguish later imperial China from what had come before.

The first element in the transition was the abandonment of institutions whose origins could be traced back to the collapse of the Han dynasty, in A.D. 220. At the beginning of the Tang, the official landholding pattern, at least in the north, was the equal-field system, which periodically redistributed state-owned land to families who held and worked it. Associated with this landholding system were levies in grain, cloth, and labor service exacted according to a fixed standard from all households that received land. The military system inherited by the Tang combined foreign nomadic forces and professional soldiers at the frontier with elite military households organized into a regimental army concentrated around the capital, Chang'an. The capital itself, as well as other major cities, was divided into walled residential wards, with trade largely restricted to specified markets. Society was dominated by a small number of families at the highest level who had enjoyed empire-wide prestige for centuries, as well as a lower level of regionally eminent households. All of these inherited institutions were eliminated during the second half of the dynasty, except for the dominance of the great families, which ended with the fall of the Tang itself, at the beginning of the tenth century.

The overarching pattern of these changes was the loss of state control over property and subjects, coupled with rising commercialization and urbanization. After the An Lushan rebellion, the state abandoned its early efforts to regulate land ownership, and it largely replaced its family-based military system with professional soldiers. As spatial restrictions on trade in cities broke down, urban life shifted toward the late imperial model in which commercial establishments intermingled with residences along noisy city streets. New market towns grew up throughout the countryside to facilitate an increasingly commercialized system of agriculture dominated by a new class of brokers and tradesmen. Meanwhile, elite families linked their status and livelihood to the fortunes of the state through its examination system for imperial office, only to disappear when the Tang collapsed. The examination system itself, however, survived and prospered under subsequent dynasties.

A second step that differentiated the late Tang from the dynasties that preceded it was the emergence of a new cultural geography. In the centuries between the collapse of the Han and the rise of the Sui in 589, a succession of states had opened up the Yangzi River's drainage basin on a large scale, as well as regions farther south. After the marshy lowlands were drained, this newly developed region, with its reliable rainfall, began to achieve higher agricultural productivity than the Yellow River basin in the north, which had been the heartland of ancient China. The Yangzi region also boasted better water transport for shipping bulk commodities, which facilitated interregional trade and, consequently, local specialization. The Grand Canal—the crowning achievement of the short-lived Sui dynasty—transported grain, principally rice, all the way from the south to Chang'an in the northwest. While the population of the south in the late Tang was still somewhat lower than that of the north, the government's loss of control in much of the Yellow River basin after the An Lushan rebellion resulted in the Yangzi valley becoming the economic and fiscal center of the empire. This prototype of a demographically, culturally, and economically dominant south that was controlled—for strategic reasons—from a capital in the north lasted for the rest of imperial Chinese history.

In a third shift toward the pattern of later imperial China, Tang merchants restructured trade relations with the outside world. To the north and west, Tang China continued to deal politically with nomadic confederacies and city-states, and overland trade proceeded intermittently along the ancient "silk roads" when these routes were not disrupted by the rise of the Tibetan state. But it was the numerous natural harbors of the fertile south that facilitated overseas trade in the late Tang. Much trade went eastward to Korea and Japan, as it had in the preceding centuries, but substantial new commerce developed with maritime Southeast Asia, India, and the Persian Gulf. This sea-based trade in bulk commodities tied China to an emerging world economic system—a pattern that would continue throughout later imperial China despite the Ming dynasty's abandonment of state-sponsored maritime expeditions. New commercial opportunities induced many foreign merchants to settle in major Chinese cities and also initiated a Chinese diaspora across Southeast Asia and far beyond.

Increased trade and the commercialization of cities encouraged the fourth transformative step in the Tang, the emergence of major new literary genres. The first half of the dynasty culminated in the High Tang golden age of lyric verse, as epitomized in the writings of Wang Wei, Li Bo (Bai), and Du Fu. The greater freedom and moral seriousness of these early Tang writers was facilitated by a shift of the center of artistic production away from the court—which emphasized a decorous, artificial style of composition—out into the greater capital and other major cities. This expansion of poetry's geographic range continued in the later Tang, when new genres of verse dealing with the joys and sorrows of urban life emerged in the brothels and pleasure quarters of Chang'an and beyond.

In the same period, several authors developed the critical prose essay into a major literary form. The most notable examples were produced by writers associated with the Confucian scholar and philosopher Han Yu, who spent much of their careers exiled from the capital to local administrative centers. And in the last century of the dynasty, authors who would become recognized as part of China's literati tradition first crafted fictional narratives as a means to explore the relationships and interior lives of Tang men and women, as they made their way through an increasingly complex world.

I

THE GEOGRAPHY OF EMPIRE

ONE OF the greatest changes during the Tang dynasty was the spatial redefinition of the Chinese empire. For its first century and a half (from 618 to 756), when the Tang was expanding outward from its base in Chang'an and its secondary capital in Luoyang, the majority of the population lived in the drainage basin of China's great northern waterway, the Yellow River, and along its principal tributaries, the Wei and Fen. The Yellow River's course from the Ordos Plateau in the northwest, through the fertile central plain east of the Hangu Pass, and on to the coastal floodplain in the northeast delineated China's most productive and most populous regions, as it had since the early empires Qin and Han (Map 1).

By the end of the Tang dynasty all that had changed. The old metropolises were once again in ruins, and neither city would ever regain its former status as an imperial capital. China's traditional stronghold in the northwest had begun its long economic and ecological decline into its present condition as an impoverished, semi-desert hinterland. The central plain had lost its luster as the epitome of Chinese culture, along with its demographic and economic dominance. The northeast (modern Hebei and Shandong; Map 2) had become a semi-barbarized frontier, and some parts of that region would not be reunited with China for centuries. The rest would remain the home base of non-Han "conquest dynasties" throughout the late imperial period. Gradually replacing the Yellow River basin as China's demographic and economic center was the lower Yangzi valley to the south, with its abundant rainfall, lush vegetation, and water transport. This region, having steadily developed under the

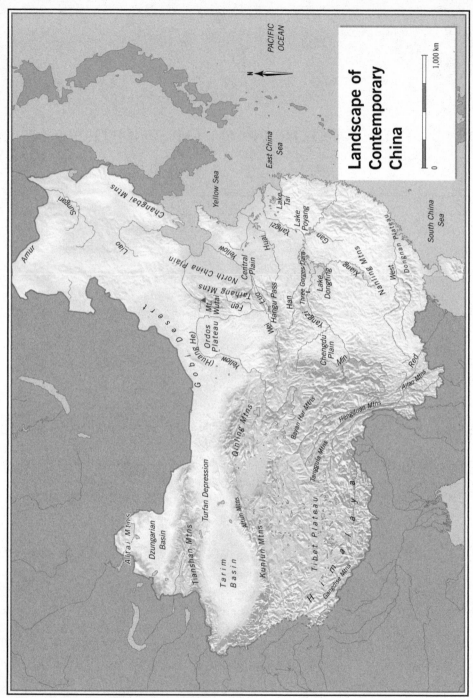

Landscape of
Contemporary
China

MAP I

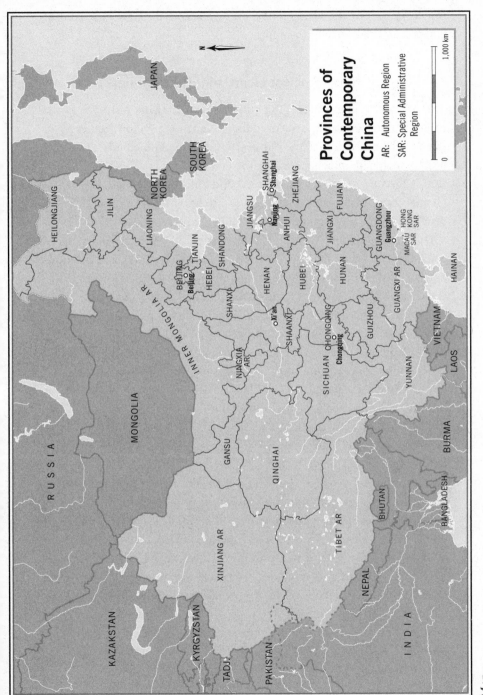

Provinces of
Contemporary
China

AR: Autonomous Region

SAR: Special Administrative
Region

0   1,000 km

MAP 2

four centuries of the southern dynasties, became the new heartland of China over the course of the Tang.[1]

China's Ancient Heartland, Guanzhong

The political center of the Tang empire throughout its history was the capital Chang'an and the surrounding Guanzhong region (centered on the Wei River). This was the old heartland of the Qin empire (221–206 B.C.), which had unified China for the first time, and of the Western Han (B.C. 206–A.D. 8), the Qin's political and cultural successor. The name Guanzhong ("inside the passes") called attention to the natural defenses provided by the mountain ranges and hills that surrounded it.

During the Qin and Western Han dynasties, the court in Chang'an enacted laws and economic policies that favored Guanzhong and discriminated against the vast plain beyond the mountains, a region known in ancient times as Guandong ("east of the [Hangu] pass"). The court used legal pretexts to suppress leading families in distant parts of the empire. Many large families were forcibly resettled near the capital, and money drawn from across the empire was invested to maximize the economic productivity of the region, often by improving water control.[2] During the Qin dynasty, the Zhengguo Canal had turned the northwest into one of the most fertile agricultural areas of China.

The Western Han continued to shape the empire's infrastructure in ways that favored Guanzhong. When the region's agricultural yield eventually proved inadequate to meet the needs of the court, the Han government shipped grain to the capital from the richer floodplain to the northeast. This was an important development in the history of the empire because it marked the first time that China's political and economic centers clearly diverged. The shipping of bulk commodities could be achieved only with water transport, however, which was impossible along much of the Yellow River in the dry season and very inefficient along the treacherous Wei River that linked the Yellow River with Chang'an. The Han Emperor Wu (r. 140–87 B.C.) expended considerable cash and labor to build a canal connecting Chang'an directly to the Yellow River, bypassing the Wei. This was followed by another canal to facilitate the shipment of grain from the fertile Fen River valley.[3]

While the main function of these waterways was to transport grain into the capital from productive regions to its northeast and east, both of these canals also improved irrigation. In 111 B.C. Emperor Wu cut six supplementary irrigation canals into the lands just above the Zhengguo Canal, and the next year he attempted to improve irrigation in the valley of the Luo River, a tributary of the Yellow River near Luoyang. After this project failed, the emperor belatedly turned his attention to the suffering among his subjects on the eastern floodplain, where a major break in a dike of the Yellow River had led to massive flooding for several years. After finally sealing the break and containing the river, Emperor Wu wrote a poem to congratulate himself on his achievement, before refocusing his attention almost exclusively on Guanzhong. There, he restored the deteriorating Zhengguo Canal (renamed the Bo Canal), built three new irrigation canals in the vicinity of Chang'an, connected the capital to the city of Huayin by means of yet another canal, and undertook irrigation work in the far northwest. The only major exceptions to his concentration on the infrastructure serving the capital region were irrigation canals developed in the Huai River valley.[4]

In A.D. 25, after a period of unrest, the restored Eastern Han dynasty (A.D. 23–220) established its new capital at Luoyang on the central plain. Frequent resettlement of surrendered barbarians in the Guanzhong region, combined with the central government's inability to defend against uprisings there, led to the "barbarization" of the Qin heartland. Chang'an's prestige declined, while the irrigation and transport canals around it fell into disrepair and gradually ceased to function. Around Luoyang, the dikes of the Yellow River were kept in good condition and small-scale irrigation works further east were organized by local officials. The Eastern Han abandoned the policy of provisioning the capital through long-range transport across the Yellow River basin and reverted to the older pattern in which the material needs of the capital, like those of other cities, were extracted from the immediate hinterland.[5]

This practice of regional provision continued after the fall of the Han, when for four centuries China was divided into a number of short-lived dynasties in the north and south. The northern states (including the Three Kingdoms state of Wei, the Jin, the Sixteen Kingdoms, the Northern Wei, Northern Qi, Northern Zhou, and Sui) routinely resettled large numbers of Chinese peasant farmers and nomadic herdsmen in the vicinity of their capitals to help provide for the needs of city-dwellers and the court. After the Jin court fled south to the lower Yangzi in 317, it also provisioned its new capital city, Jiankang (modern Nanjing), mostly from nearby agriculture, as did the military commands in the middle Yangzi region. Labor in the south was provided by large numbers of refugees from the north, along with kidnapped or coerced indigenous people.[6]

After the Sui reunification of China in 589, the dynasty's founder chose to situate his new capital, Daxingcheng, near the ruins of Han Chang'an, mainly because he and his closest allies were members of the semibarbarized elite of the northwest.[7] However, establishing a capital in Guanzhong was difficult, since the economic center of China had by this time moved decidedly to the east and south. Some grain could reach the city by traveling down the Yellow River and through reconstructed canals alongside the Wei. But the bulk of it would have to come through a series of reconstructed waterways linking the Yellow River and its tributaries with the south. This ambitious engineering project, which connected the capital with every productive region of the empire except Sichuan, would become known as the Grand Canal.

Like their Sui predecessors, the Tang founders descended from a northwestern military family, and they too made Daxingcheng in the old Guanzhong region their capital, renaming it after the ancient city Chang'an. Within a few decades of the dynasty's founding, however, the growth of the imperial bureaucracy and its supporting population required the government to move temporarily to Luoyang, where food supplies and other necessities were more accessible. Under Empress Wu, whose domination of the court in the second half of the seventh century put her in a constant state of tension with Guanzhong's elite, Luoyang was declared the empire's secondary capital and its Sacred Capital. After Empress Wu's fall from power, Emperor Xuanzong appointed Pei Yaoqing as commissioner to restore the Grand Canal and its associated granaries; the completion of this work allowed the Tang court to return to Chang'an in 736.

Due to its proximity and ease of transport to the capital, the fertile Fen River valley and its tributaries were the focus of some thirty-five irrigation projects during the Tang, the third most numerous for any region. But the difficulties of provisioning a court "inside the passes" continued to mount, as the interlinked problems of deforestation, erosion, gullies, water shortages, and silting of waterways took their toll.[8] The forests of north China had been disappearing for centuries, due to their overexploitation for building materials and heating. The requirements of wood for palaces, temples, government buildings, and residences for a capital were particularly onerous. The elevated population due to the capital's presence also resulted in increased burning of wood. A canal built by the government to ship firewood to the capital further hastened the decline of the forest cover. Finally, the government's attempt to raise horses in the northwest, to replace grasslands lost to Tibet, led to the destruction of marginal grasslands and the erosion of slopes as herdsmen cut down trees for shelter and heat.

Evidence from pollen counts has shown that trees steadily receded from the river valleys and up the sides of hills, and completely vanished in the northern half of the capital region. The erosion following deforestation further silted up the canals that carried grain supplies to the capital. Thus, the location of a capital in Chang'an, with its associated money and population, had the perverse consequence of degrading the environment and impoverishing the economy. A poem written around the beginning of the ninth century by the essayist and poet Liu Zongyuan described a common scene:

> The official guardians' axes have spread through a thousand hills,
> At the Works Department's order hacking rafter-beams and billets.
> Of ten trunks cut in the woodlands' depths, only one gets hauled
>   away.
> Ox-teams strain at their traces—till the paired yoke-shafts break.
> Great-girthed trees of towering height lie blocking the forest tracks,
> A tumbled confusion of lumber, as flames on the hillside crackle.
> Not even the last remaining shrubs are safeguarded from
>   destruction;
> Where once the mountain torrents leapt—nothing but rutted
>   gullies.
> Timbers, not yet seasoned or used, left immature to rot;
> Proud summits and deep-sunk gorges—now brief hummocks of
>   naked rock.[9]

In what was clearly a political poem, the felling of trees symbolized the fate of talented men at the hands of a corrupt court. But the fact that the destruction of forests came readily to mind as a metaphor suggests just how common a sight the denuding of hills was during the Tang dynasty.

In long stretches of the Yellow River east of the Hangu Pass, where the water slowed down, spread out, and consequently lost its carrying capacity for silt, continuous soil deposition along the bottom of the river caused the water level to rise and breach the dikes. As erosion increased, the rate of deposition rose, and breaches became more frequent, even as the dikes were built higher and higher. Changes in the rate of recorded breaches from one dynasty to the next suggest the rate at which erosion occurred in the northwest.[10] During the last decades of the Western Han, when efforts to produce crops in Guanzhong were at their peak, the frequency of breaches downriver accelerated. During the Eastern Han, when parts of the northwest were abandoned, the rate declined gradually and dropped off rapidly following the dynasty's collapse. But after the Northern Wei reunified north China in the early fifth century, the rate of dike failures again started to rise. Around the middle of the Tang dynasty, the breach rate (once every ten years) was slightly below the Western Han peak of once every nine years, but in the next couple of centuries it soared to once every three to four years. These figures show not only the loss of fertile soil in the northwest but the increasing frequency of devastating floods in the northeast, which were the cause of much suffering.

At the Tang's founding, the northeast had become more productive than the central plain, due to its relative stability under the Northern Wei empire and during the subsequent civil war that divided it into eastern and western halves. Consequently, in its first century, the Tang established two granaries there to store agricultural surplus for shipment to the capital. The Yongji Canal—built by the Sui as a northeastern extension of the Grand Canal—served primarily to transport grain from the northeast back to Chang'an. The Tang added several tributary canals to the Yongji to improve irrigation, move grain from producers to the main canal, and raise its water level. In addition to these improvements, agriculture was extended as far north as the Yan Mountains, and mixed agriculture and animal husbandry advanced even further.[11] While eventually this cultivation of marginal lands would lead to erosion and desertification, during the Tang dynasty these territories remained productive.

In the wake of the An Lushan rebellion, the Tang court lost control of much of the northeast and was no longer able to extract taxes or grain from the region. Also, the large professional armies in the northeast were now consuming so much of the local surplus that even provinces loyal to the court could no longer transfer any significant portion of their harvest to Chang'an. The prosperous south became the sole source of food and revenue to maintain the central government. As Du Mu (fl. 830–852) wrote, "The Huai and Yangzi rivers are now the lifeline of the dynasty."[12]

A new geopolitical axis from the northwest to the southeast defined the Tang empire's structure after the middle of the eighth century. In the far

northwest, key military provinces controlled by the court blocked the ongoing threat of the Tibetans and Uighurs. Immediately to their southeast
lay Guanzhong and the capital. In the far southeast lay the fertile lower
Yangzi, which produced most of the foodstuffs and disposable income
for the court and the northwest. Grain and other tax wealth, probably in
the form of silk cloth, moved north and northwest up the Grand Canal to
the court. This geopolitical structure, in which a wealthy but relatively
demilitarized south materially and fiscally sustained a capital located for
strategic reasons in the north, set the pattern for later imperial China.
The only difference was that subsequent courts were located in the northeast rather than the northwest.

The Northeast, the Central Plain, and Sichuan

After the fall of the Western Jin dynasty in 316 and the migration of the
Jin court to the south, many families who remained in northeast China
took refuge in forts located on hillsides and in wastelands. The Northern
Wei's unification of north China, completed in 439, led to greater peace
and security, but many families of Han descent continued to shelter in
forts, where women as well as men became expert riders and archers. In
contrast with the axiom of the Han dynasty that "Guanzhong produces
generals, while Guandong produces ministers," under the Northern Wei
the ratio of military officers from the east to those from the west was five
to one. When the Northern Wei dynasty broke into western and eastern
states in 534, the Eastern Wei dynasty and the Northern Qi that succeeded it continued to recruit military officers from northeastern families.
Armed forts remained a major base of power in the region, most notably
during the civil war at the end of the Sui.[13]

The militarized character of the northeast was also linked to the settlement there of numerous non-Han peoples after the southern migration of
the Jin court in the fourth century. In camps and forts, Han Chinese from
military families mingled freely with non-Han soldiers, including Khitan,
Xi, and other tribes. During the civil war that led to the Tang's founding,
the single greatest rival of the Guanzhong-based Tang house was the
scion of a wealthy northeastern family of Xianbei descent, Dou Jiande. A
former village head, Dou modeled his actions on the traditional gangsters' and bravoes' (*xia*) code of private justice and mutual devotion unto
death that many bandit groups in the northeast had adopted. When
Dou's forces were decisively defeated in 621, the military men of the

northeast—reassembled under the titular leadership of his former cavalry commander, Liu Heita—continued to resist Tang expansion for more than a year. Consequently, the Tang founder "wanted to completely kill [Dou's] faction, to leave the area east of the mountains totally empty."[14] The rise of independent military governors after the An Lushan rebellion made the northeast a permanent center of resistance to the Tang court.

The middle reaches of the Yellow River (modern southern Shanxi and northern Henan), around the eastern capital of Luoyang, experienced problems similar to those of Guanzhong: deforestation, erosion, silting up of rivers, and the carving up of agricultural land by gullies. The area south of the river was highly productive in places, but it was also the site of several major cities that absorbed much of the region's agricultural production. Because this region had less exportable grain, the Tang state largely ignored its irrigation, focusing on maintaining canals for shipping grain from the southeast to the capital. This tension between irrigation and shipping in the central zone of the Yellow River intensified after the An Lushan rebellion, when military governors in the region became important political actors. Needing to feed and pay their armies, the governors withheld grain and taxes from the court and diverted ever-greater quantities of water to irrigation. This sometimes left water levels in the canals so low that nothing could be shipped on them. And because irrigation works were not well maintained, much water was lost through breaks in the system, reducing further the total quantity available. Battles between the court and the military governors over this crucial scarce resource became a key feature of ninth-century politics.[15]

While the central plain was politically and economically secondary for the court, it continued to enjoy tremendous cultural prestige in the Tang dynasty. As the ancient capital of the Eastern Zhou state (771–256 B.C.) and the Eastern Han, Luoyang retained its aura as the great nonmilitary capital of the empire—the natural hub of a Chinese literary culture in the east that stood in opposition to the old Qin military stronghold in Guanzhong. For centuries, scholars and poets had celebrated Luoyang as the true center of China and the world. The term "central plain" (zhong yuan) in a narrow sense referred to the region around Luoyang, but it could also stand for the whole of China, representing all that was "central" to its culture. Luoyang, as the spiritual capital, claimed a status that Chang'an could not rival.

These claims figured in a ninth-century dispute over whether the true Chinese empire during the four centuries of division had been in the north or the south: "Historians of today all take Eastern Jin [the southern state] as illegitimate, which is a great error. To those who maintain that the Tuoba [Northern Wei] held the 'central states,' I reply that rites and propriety are what constitute the 'central states' and that the lack of these is what constitutes the barbarians. How could it depend solely on geography?"[16] While challenging their position, this writer accepted that most scholars in his day defined the legitimacy of a Chinese dynasty by its possession of the central plain around Luoyang.

Sichuan, an isolated, mountain-ringed region in the southwest, was not as economically critical to the Tang as the lower Yangzi valley to the southeast, but beginning with the rise of Tibet and Nanzhao in the second half of the seventh century it emerged as a major military center. Sichuan routinely provided the base for the southern prong of a pincher movement against Tibet's armies in what is now Xinjiang, in combination with armies from the Ordos Plateau. During the An Lushan rebellion, Sichuan provided a safe haven for the fugitive Emperor Xuanzong, and in the second half of the dynasty for emperors Dezong and Xizong (Fig. 1).

But travel into and out of Sichuan was difficult. Like earlier dynasties, the Tang maintained a network of roads radiating out from Chang'an and Luoyang to facilitate the movement of officials and documents around the empire. These tree-lined roads were made of packed earth and were bowed in the center to drain rainwater off to the side. About two-thirds of them ran from the capitals toward frontiers in the north. However, the Tang vastly expanded the network in the south, where Sichuan became a linchpin. Roads running through the region linked modern Yunnan and Guizhou in the southwest to the rest of the empire and reached to the southeastern coast as well. Due to the trade along these roads and the Yangzi River, Sichuan became a wealthy commercial center in its own right, as the poet Du Fu noted:

> The travelers from Shu [Sichuan] accumulate great wealth,
> Men from the frontier, they easily gain noble rank.

Sichuan was particularly noted for the beautiful clothing it provided for women of the court, along with precious musical instruments, paper, and printed matter.[17]

In addition to expanding the network of overland transportation and trade, the Tang established a rapid-relay postal system, with 1,297 way

Fig. 1   Copy of a painting depicting the flight of Emperor Xuanzong to Sichuan. Palace Museum, Taipei.

stations placed at intervals of approximately ten miles along the roads. Teams of horses were kept ready for quick changes, and if horses were scarce, trained runners were used. It took between eight and fourteen days for a message to travel from Chang'an to the most distant points in the empire, so even once-isolated Sichuan was brought into regular contact with other regions. Rapid delivery was so important that delay was punished with eighty blows from a heavy rod for the first day past the deadline, and the punishment increased to two years of penal servitude if a message was late by six days. Tardiness in delivering messages of military importance could result in capital punishment, especially if the delay led to deaths.[18]

The Dujiangyan irrigation project at Chengdu, constructed during the Qin dynasty, allowed Sichuan to produce large quantities of grain to feed a substantial population. As in other parts of the empire, housing and heating for these people led to substantial deforestation. By Tang times, the original forest cover in Sichuan's central basin and on the surrounding hills had been completely cleared, so that farmers had to grow their own firewood by planting alders and other fast-growing trees. This practice was noted by the celebrated poet Du Fu, who lived in Chengdu in the 760s:

> West of the moat, round my thatched hall, there was missing a
> grove of trees,
> And who was there, other than you, aware of my deep-hidden
> feelings?
> I'm happy to hear that alder saplings can reach a good height in
> three years
> And will make me an acre or so of shade, along the creek bank.

In a poem written a few years later he wrote:

> My grove of alders blocks off the sun. The breeze sighs through the
> brush.
> The huge bamboos blend with the mists, their tips bedewed with
> droplets.[19]

The deforestation of even the tallest hills in Sichuan forced soldiers responsible for maintaining the region's perishable wooden bridges and cliffside roads to go ever-greater distances to find suitable timber. Like farmers, they were encouraged to actively cultivate the trees they needed for this purpose.[20]

Deforestation had even occurred in the verdant southeast. A memorial written by a southern official in the fifth century noted that vegetation on the hills around Jiankang—the lower Yangzi capital of the Eastern Jin—

was being systematically burned off to make room for fruit orchards and bamboo groves, despite a penalty in place since 366 that threatened perpetrators with public beheading.

The South

One of the most significant developments in the Tang dynasty was the steady emergence of the south as the economic and demographic center of China. The rising importance of this region was tied to its distinctive geography and climate. During the Tang, "the south" consisted of the river basins of the Yangzi and its four major tributaries (in modern Hubei, Hunan, Jiangxi, Shaanxi south of the Qinling range, southern Anhui, southern Jiangsu, northern Zhejiang). Although the region was hilly, rainfall was regular and lakes, rivers, and streams were abundant. The south also had a considerably longer growing season than the colder north, allowing for more extensive multiple cropping. Given these superior natural conditions, land in the south produced far higher yields than areas of comparable size in the north, once the most advanced agricultural technologies and drainage practices had been introduced.

Apart from Sichuan, population and agriculture along the Yangzi was concentrated in the central and lower reaches of the river during the Tang. The central Yangzi was defined by two great lakes, Dongting and Poyang, along with many lesser lakes and marshes that collected the runoff from excess rain. These lakes were fed by three of the Yangzi's great tributaries: the Han, the Xiang, and the Gan rivers. After it passed the Gan River, the Yangzi slowed down and became so wide that the opposite bank could not be seen. The sediment that it dropped as it approached the sea built up the great delta that continues to advance into the East China Sea at a rate of one mile every seventy years.[21] This alluvial soil, once it was properly drained, proved to be extremely fertile. During the Tang dynasty, agriculture in the Yangzi basin was possible only in the river valleys and delta of the lower river and in the marshy land around the great lakes of the central lowlands, not on hillsides.

Like the Yangzi basin, the far southeast coast (roughly equivalent to modern Fujian province) was hilly but its river valleys were fertile. It first came under Chinese influence due to migrations following the collapse of the Han dynasty, but it remained lightly settled until well into the Tang. It was not represented at the imperial court until the eighth century. Like Sichuan, this region was a world apart, separated from the rest of the empire by mountains, and at the end of the dynasty it split off to form the independent state of Min.[22] With its abundance of natural harbors, the southeastern coast relied more on fishing and international trade than did any other part of China. Ultimately developing strong ties with Taiwan, Japan, and Southeast Asia, this region came to play a key role in China's trade with the outer world. This trade became particularly important near the end of the Tang and in the following centuries.

The southwest, embracing the modern provinces of Yunnan and Guizhou, was settled by the Chinese only in the course of the eighteenth and nineteenth centuries. In the Tang period the region was gradually united under the emerging state of Nanzhao, which became a significant actor in the enduring diplomatic and military conflicts between the Tang empire and Tibet.[23] This area was mountainous, and its lowlands were covered with jungle. In Tang times it was occupied by dozens of different tribal peoples, many of which still exist as "minority peoples" in China today.

In Chinese literature down into the Tang period, "the south" was portrayed as a dangerous and exotic land of jungles, swamps, diseases, poisonous plants, and savage beasts—and a place of exile from which many disgraced officials did not return. While these images remained constant throughout the Tang, the region to which "the south" applied moved steadily toward the equator. In the Han the term applied largely to the Yangzi basin, while by the end of the Tang it applied to what is now Fujian, Guangdong, and Guangxi. This shift reflected the ongoing southward push of the Chinese people over these centuries, and the alterations in the landscape that they brought about.[24]

The chief environmental problem throughout the south was not drought or flood but the excessive wetness of its mosquito-infested lowlands, which were often too swampy for farming. As more Chinese migrated into the region, they engaged in large- and small-scale drainage projects that over the course of centuries turned huge expanses of wetland into productive fields. The state left responsibility for draining marshes and irrigating fields in the hands of the region's great landlords, although the government sometimes provided advice on water control and remitted taxes for those who settled in marshy areas—a subsidy that helped to underwrite the activities of families who were influential at court. Consequently, landlords in the south played a bigger role in introducing technologies for opening new land and improving yields, built up larger, more productive estates, and dominated local society to a higher degree than their counterparts in the north—a regional difference that continued through the late imperial period.

The greater importance of landlords in the south reflected the different kind of water control required throughout the region. In north China, flooding was controlled through the use of large dikes built and maintained by the state, while the region's irrigation systems drew water from tributaries and wells dug by farmers. The Huai and Si river basins in central China and the lower and middle reaches of the Yangzi had very different local ecologies and therefore very different systems for water control. In central China, slow-moving rivers were generally dammed to form reservoirs from which water was released through sluices into smaller canals and then allowed to flow into fields through the force of gravity. In the Yangzi valley, by contrast, the primary technology was to drain off excess water into artificial pools or tanks from which it could then be drawn when necessary. Dikes were used both for flood control and for land reclamation in low-lying areas. Such projects were easily built by groups ranging from a few dozen people to a few thousand, under the management of large-scale private organizations run by the great families of the region.

The steady opening up of the south by influential local families and their followers left little trace in Tang writings, which focus on activities at the highest level of society, but some evidence survives. Tang population figures largely reflected the census of urban areas and were limited by the degree of state control in a given region. But even under these circumstances, the fact that the registered population of the lower Yangzi increased several fold in the first half of the Tang certainly indicates a significant expansion of the rural population. This would have been possible only through the opening of more land to agricultural exploitation. The Tang histories also list dozens of water control projects distributed throughout the lower Yangzi; their frequency increases considerably across the first half of the dynasty, and even more in the second half. While the larger of these projects were organized by the state, many of them were relatively small-scale works that were almost certainly locally sponsored. The growing reliance of the court on grain from the southeast is another indication of the rising productivity of the region, which was able to feed its own population while sending ever-larger quantities of grain to the north.[25]

The clearest evidence for the pivotal role of local families in the agricultural development of the south comes from the period after the An Lushan rebellion. At a time when the court was weaker and more impoverished than previously, the construction of irrigation works accelerated in the south, especially in the area around Lake Tai, which because of its abundant marshes and rivers was well-suited for the multiple smaller-scale projects typically pursued by landlords. And in the lower Yangzi and Huai river valleys, which were crossed by the Grand Canal, constant struggles arose between government officials, who sought to concentrate all available water in the canal to facilitate grain transport to the north, and local agriculturalists, who sought to divert as much water as possible to irrigate their fields. Again, this conflict of interest indicates that while the government attended to the needs of the water transport system, maintenance of the region's irrigation system was largely the work of locally powerful families.[26]

With growing numbers of people living in south China during the Tang dynasty, rice became the central food crop of the empire. Although dryland varieties were cultivated in the north, rice grew best in the wet paddy fields of the south, where the special features of its cultivation affected the social order in at least two ways. First, since water was the major carrier of nutrients to growing plants, successful cultivation depended less on the quality of the soil than on control of the quantity and quality of the water and the timing of its application. Consequently, even in the water-rich south, elaborate irrigation and water control systems had to be constructed, operated, and maintained. This necessity encouraged considerable initiative, experimentation, and leadership among elites at the local level. Second, wet-rice cultivation was extremely labor-intensive, and yields were highly dependent on the industry and skill of individual farmers. Keeping the water's depth uniform, preparing the soil, and maintaining banks required constant labor. Most demanding was transplanting the seedlings, which required precision in timing and spacing. Consequently, experienced, productive peasants were valuable assets in the agricultural economy of south China during the Tang dynasty.[27]

Water Transportation

Water transport was the only means of moving grain and other bulk goods any considerable distance at an affordable cost during the Tang. In north China, major river systems were few in number and needed constant dredging to remove silt. But even with dredging, the rivers were often so twisting and shallow that transport canals were dug to replace the natural channels. Rainfall in the north was also unreliable, and as more water was diverted through irrigation canals to grow crops, less water flowed into rivers to carry heavily loaded barges. As a result, water transport in north China remained limited through the first half of the Tang.

One consequence of this limitation was to constrict the movement of large armies. While bandit gangs at the beginning and end of the Tang could swarm from region to region, plundering everything in sight and then moving on, armies serving a state could not operate in this way. To provision a force of several tens of thousands of soldiers—perhaps even a hundred thousand—required regular shipments of grain from granaries or other storage facilities. The larger the army, the greater the limits on its mobility imposed by the need to stay within reach of a substantial water channel.[28]

But the major consequence of limited water transport was that each city and region had to rely on the agricultural production of its own locale, which restricted economic specialization. For most of China's history before the middle of the Tang, empires were primarily regional constructs, with each locale providing its own material needs. The only goods that moved across large distances were precious items of tribute from distant lands or luxury items for elite use. With the rise of long-distance bulk trade, however, a region could devote itself to the production of a few highly profitable goods that other regions could not produce, and could then use its profits to purchase basic supplies such as grain or clothing. The introduction of water transport was an essential precondition for the surge in economic production that is sometimes called the medieval economic revolution.[29]

To improve water transport in the north and provision its court at Daxingcheng (Chang'an), the Sui emperors expended considerable energy and wealth to construct the Grand Canal, as well as granaries at key points along the waterway to allow for storage and seasonal transshipment when water and labor were available. In 584 the first Sui emperor restored the old Han canal paralleling the Wei River, which was prone to silting and seasonally shallow, so that bulk commodities could be shipped from the fertile floodplain of the Yellow River to the overpopulated capital (Map 3). A second leg of the canal linked Luoyang with the Huai River along the Tongji Canal and then, via the old Han Conduit, to the Yangzi near Jiangdu (modern Yangzhou). This was begun in 605 by the second Sui ruler, Emperor Yang, as part of his effort to restore Luoyang. A third leg—again largely following older canal routes—went from the Yangzi near Jingkou (modern Zhenjiang) along the Jiangnan Canal to the head of Hangzhou Bay at the town of Yuhang.

The final leg, the Yongji Canal, led from the confluence of the Luo and Yellow rivers near Luoyang to the vicinity of modern Beijing in the northeast. Begun in 608, this section—the only part of the Grand Canal that

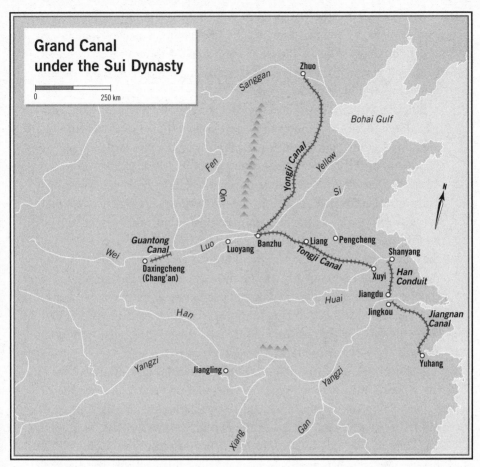

MAP 3

entailed significant new digging—linked the northeast to the central plain and thereby to the south.[30] Because it passed through drier regions of the northeast, maintaining a sufficient water level was difficult. Digging new channels to bring in additional water created more soil erosion during summer runoff and more silting. Over the centuries, reservoirs and special feeder channels were built to keep the canal from clogging, but the unpredictable flow of water continued to wreak havoc with the ecology of the northern floodplain.[31]

The Grand Canal thus linked almost every region of China, as described by the seventh-century official Cui Rong: "Boats gather on every stream in the empire. To one side they reach into Sichuan and the Han River valley. They point the way to Fujian and Guangdong. Through the

Seven Marshes and the Ten Swamps, the Three Rivers and the Five Lakes, they draw in the Yellow River and the Luo, embracing also Huai'an and Haizhou. Great ships in thousands and tens of thousands carry goods back and forth. If they lay unused for a single moment, ten thousand merchants would be bankrupted."[32]

Emperor Xuanzong of the Tang ordered a massive refurbishing, completed in 736, of the Grand Canal, and in the following two decades the additional grain that Chang'an required was shipped largely from the floodplain of the Yellow River—a pattern of provisioning similar to that of the Western Han. After the An Lushan rebellion, however, when most of the northeast was controlled by independent or semi-independent military governors who withheld grain from the capital, and the central plain was under the command of loyal governors whose armies consumed all the local grain, the only source of additional grain—primarily rice—was the southeast. Consequently, the Grand Canal, which had been a useful supplement for the Tang state before the uprising, suddenly became an indispensable lifeline. After 763, all imperial Chinese capitals, with the sole exception of the Southern Song, would be provisioned with grain shipped along this network of inland waterways.

The rise of long-distance bulk trade produced a new lifestyle, that of the itinerant merchant who lived on his boat and traveled along the canals of China wherever commercial opportunities might lead. This mode of life became a poetic theme in the period, indeed a cliché. Many major poets of the late Tang wrote satiric poems with titles such as "The Pleasures of the Wandering Merchant," like this example by Zhang Ji (d. 780):

> On the west bank opposite Jinling are many traveling merchants
> Living out their lives on shipboard, enjoying their existence amid
>   wind and waves.
> About to set sail, they move their ships near to the entrance to the
>   Yangzi
> And on the ships' prows pray to the spirits and libate them with
>   wine . . .
> On the autumn river, the new moon and the chattering of apes;
> The lonely sail sets out by night from the banks of the Xiao and the
>   Xiang.
> The sailors ply their sweeps to pull against the dark currents
> Straight past the mountainous cliffs after the boat ahead.

Year after year, in search of profit he goes west and east again,
His name and surname are not found on any district's registers.

Similar poems with the same title were composed by Yuan Zhen and
Liu Yuxi, but the most celebrated example was Bo Juyi's ballad entitled
"The Salt Merchant's Wife," written around 808:

The salt merchant's wife has gold and silver in plenty,
Yet she does not work in the fields or tend silkworms.
Wherever she goes, north, south, east or west, she never leaves her
    home.
Wind and waves are her village, her ship her mansion.

These poems strike a common theme—the contrast between the merchant's water-borne adventures, traversing the empire in pursuit of profit,
and the peasant's life of toil, rooted in place as he barely ekes out a living
from the land.[33]

In addition to producing new social niches with distinctive ways of life,
the rise of long-distance water transport enriched many cities, which
were physically reorganized to add new docks and other facilities for the
movement of thousands of large craft. Exemplary in this regard was
Jiangdu (Yangzhou) on the lower Yangzi. Previously a mid-sized city,
it became a major junction point on the Grand Canal and the economic center of China, as recognized in the late Tang saying, "Jiangdu is
number one, Yizhou [in Sichuan] number two." Boats passed through
Jiangdu from every part of the empire, including Sichuan, Guangdong,
Fujian, and what is now Vietnam. Even travelers from Chang'an to
Sichuan often passed through Jiangdu on their way up the Yangzi.
Ocean-going vessels reached the city, linking the Tang's great internal water network to the outer world.[34]

The "Inner" and "Outer" Realms

Since the Qin unification of China in 221 B.C., the area ruled by the state
had been essentially defined by the drainage systems of its two great
rivers. Within this "inner" area, people led sedentary lives based on either agriculture or urban trades. Outside this area, the tribes to the north
and far west (present-day Inner Mongolia, Gansu, and former Soviet
Central Asia) relied on pastoral nomadism, the city-states of Xinjiang

combined trade with oasis agriculture, and the tribes of the northeast combined pastoralism with agriculture and the exploitation of forests. The economic structure of the Chinese empire, in which a network of cities extracted income from taxation on crops and cloth, meant that these "outer" areas could never be securely incorporated. The Chinese state could not extract enough income from these nonagricultural areas to support the costs of garrisons and administration.

This division between China proper and the outer realms enjoyed an ancient literary pedigree. The inner zone of direct rule corresponded to the world described in the canonical *Tribute of Yu* (*Yu gong*), probably written during the Warring States period in the fourth century B.C. This text divided the area of the two river valleys into nine regions defined by their distinctive products; the term "nine provinces" eventually identified the whole of China. The *Tribute of Yu* ended with a model of a broader world centered on the civilized ruler and ringed by concentric zones that grew wilder and more barbaric the farther they were from the capital.

This concentric model was challenged during the later Warring States period and the Western Han by an enlarged vision of the world in which the nine provinces were just one corner of a vaster continent. Ambitious rulers such as the First Emperor embraced this expanded worldview, which justified their expansion beyond the regions known to earlier states. However, during the Han, when the court fixed the Confucian canon as state orthodoxy, with the *Tribute of Yu* as part of the canon, literati and courtiers grew increasingly suspicious of military expansion. Consequently, the model of the nine regions—with its civilized center directly administered by the empire and ringed by semicivilized peoples, beyond whom were the true barbarians—became the generally accepted model.[35]

In the centuries following the Han, China's relation to the outer realms in the northeast, north, and northwest changed significantly. Every dynasty that ruled either all or part of the Yellow River valley after the early fourth century A.D. was of non-Chinese origin. The northern world outside China proper had become inextricably enmeshed with the inner political order, above all as a provider of armies and rulers. Beginning in the late Han and continuing well into the Tang, the internal migration of non-Chinese peoples also transformed the ethnic makeup of the population. Some modern scholars estimate that at the beginning of the Tang, non-Han immigrants made up as much as 7 percent of the empire's population, and 12 to 14 percent of the population in the north. Estimates for later years of the Tang range from 10 to 19 percent.[36]

Nevertheless, the old model of a world divided into an inner China and an outer realm of barbarians continued to be influential. Most Tang writers associated alien peoples and cultures with the outer regions and identified China with a set of cultural norms centered on the lands described by the *Tribute of Yu*. For many literate Chinese, this division was built into the order of the cosmos, as expressed by the chief minister Di Renjie in the late seventh century:

I have heard that when Heaven gave birth to the barbarians [*yi*], they were all outside the enfeoffed territories of the former sage-kings [the realm of the *Tribute of Yu*]. Therefore, to the east they were separated by the deep blue sea, to the west they were separated by the flowing sands, to the north they were sundered by the great desert, and to the south they were blocked by the Five Peaks. These were the means by which Heaven delimited the barbarians and separated inner from outer.[37]

Since this neat division of inner and outer clearly did not describe the actual state of affairs in the Tang, when large numbers of foreigners lived not only in frontier zones but in China's major cities, Tang writers developed an elaborate vocabulary to distinguish those lands that were merely controlled by the empire from those of China proper. The areas that are now Inner Mongolia, Xinjiang, and even parts of western Sichuan belonged to the former, leading Bo Juyi and other writers to argue that the loss of such alien territories should not matter to Tang people.

The contrast between land that was truly Chinese and alien land temporarily occupied by the Tang was most clearly articulated by Chu Suiliang in 642, during the court debate over the disposition of the recently conquered Gaochang (near Turfan, in Xinjiang):

I have heard that in antiquity when wise monarchs ascended the throne and enlightened kings established their enterprise, they inevitably placed the Han [*huaxia*] first and the barbarians [*yidi*] second. They extended to all the transforming power of their virtue, but they did not deal with the remote wilderness. Therefore when King Xuan of the Zhou dispatched an expedition, it reached the bor-

ders and then returned. However, when the First Emperor of Qin
went far beyond the frontier barriers, the Middle Kingdom was rent
asunder. Your majesty [addressing Emperor Taizong] has destroyed
Gaochang and extended your authority to the Western Regions.
Now you wish to take in this leviathan and turn it into prefectures
and counties . . . Hexi [western Gansu] can be compared to our own
heart and bladder, but Gaochang is like the hands and feet of another person.[38]

In this elaboration of the classic model, the division between China
proper and the outer world was set by the sages, and the villainous First
Emperor's crime was to confuse this fundamental distinction through territorial expansion.

Most Tang literati endorsed this ideal worldview, and many alien peoples who remained suspicious of China agreed with them. Nevertheless,
some leading Tang political actors, notably Emperor Taizong, advocated
an inclusive vision in which all peoples could ultimately be drawn into
China. Along with some of his successors, he attempted to incorporate
the Turks and others into the state. But even proponents of inclusion accepted that a fundamental difference between Han Chinese and alien
peoples would remain, despite the fact that both were living within the
confines of the Tang empire. This view led Taizong to declare himself
both Heavenly Emperor and Heavenly Qaghan. The message was clear:
the moral and political system that culminated in the position of Chinese
emperor did not include the Turks, whom he would rule in a different capacity. While the two could be part of a single empire, they would converge only in the person of the ruler, who was exalted precisely because of
his ability to transcend regional divisions between China and the outside
world.[39]

The clearest institutional expression of this vision was found in the
"loose-rein prefectures." Like the "dependent states" founded by the
Han, these were relatively autonomous districts in which tribal peoples
dwelling inside the Tang frontier were administered by their own chieftains, upon whom the Tang had bestowed titles and seals of office. Although they owed obligations to the empire and sometimes provided military forces to assist the regular armies, they were usually not subject to
the same forms of administration as the registered Chinese population,
nor to the same taxes and labor service. Loose-rein prefectures were
largely buffer states between the Tang and the truly alien "barbarians."

Established on an ad hoc basis and often lacking clear or fixed boundaries, they appeared and disappeared, sometimes shifting location, as
Tang power waxed and waned. They were particularly dense in the frontier zones marking the transition from sedentary agriculture to pastoral
nomadism.

The existence of two parallel administrative systems for two types of
peoples was articulated by an eighth-century Tang geographer as a structuring principle of the world: "For the Central Kingdom we take the
Tribute of Yu as the beginning, while for the outer barbarians [*yi*] the
Book of the Han (Han shu) is the source. The former records the increase
and decrease in commanderies and counties, while the latter narrates the
fall and rise of barbarian [*fan*] tribes."[40] Rather than focus on the crime
of the First Emperor, this writer cited two separate literary sources for the
parallel social and administrative forms of the Chinese people and the
aliens with whom they intermingled. In this way, he drew the lands
of northern and Central Asia into the Chinese world without blurring
the clear distinction between inner and outer realms around which that
world was structured.

2

FROM FOUNDATION
TO REBELLION

LOOKING back from the ninth century on the fall of the Sui, the poet Wen Tingyun wrote of the last Sui emperor's decision to abandon the north and sail down the rivers and canals to the south, where he was ultimately assassinated:

> The second ruler of the house of Yang, safe within his nine-fold
>   gates,
> No longer drives his bright carriages, tired of his dragon steeds.
> Instead a hundred brocade sails, filled with the wind's power,
> Spread to the edges of the sky, like golden lotuses.
> Pearls and kingfisher feathers match the stars, their brightness now
>   put out.
> Dragon-head boats split the waves, lamenting fifes resound . . .
> In one moment of intoxication, the whole world was lost.
> The four directions overturned, raising smoke and dust.
> But he was still in the fragrance of his dreaming soul,
> In the Last Lord's weed-grown palace, the morning orioles
> Come flying, cut off only by West River's water.[1]

The drainage basin of the Yangzi River was already the basis of the Tang economy by the time Wen Tingyun was writing, but in this poem he presented south China as a fragrant, exotic trap that had swallowed up a series of failed emperors. Just as the decision of the man who overthrew the Qin, Xiang Yu, to return to his home in the south had doomed him to defeat at the hands of the Han founder who occupied Guanzhong, so the decision of the Sui Emperor Yang to sail south and leave Guanzhong to his rivals assured their triumph.

While Wen's vision of the dangerous south tells us more about the poetic conventions of the ninth century than its political realities, the fact remains that in the late Sui and early Tang the strategic stronghold of Guanzhong offered a more secure and defensible base than the verdant south, with all its riches.[2] The founding of the Tang in the northwest and the dynasty's gradual consolidation of the realm marked the last time in Chinese history that Guanzhong would serve as the basis of an empire.

Consolidating the Tang Empire

When rebellion broke out against the Sui in 613, the future Tang founder, Li Yuan, was a garrison commander in Taiyuan (Map 4). His family, of frontier origins and almost certainly of mixed blood, had provided military service since the time of his great-grandfather, and Li Yuan had served as a general for a decade.[3] After biding his time for several years in the shelter of the Taihang Mountains, Li marched on the Sui capital, Daxingcheng, in 617. The following year he accepted the emperor's abdication and founded the Tang dynasty.

At the beginning, Li Yuan's new dynasty controlled only Guanzhong. The northeast, the central plain, and the south were still occupied by major rivals who commanded hundreds of thousands of troops.[4] It took five years of campaigning, much of it led by the imperial princes Li Jiancheng and Li Shimin, before the last contender was defeated. While armed resistance did not abate until 628, the situation was sufficiently secure in 624 that Li Yuan was able to disband large numbers of his troops and reorganize the remaining soldiers into an army with 633 units of 800 to 1,200 men. Most of these units were garrisoned around Guanzhong. The Li family and their followers pursued the classic dynasty-founding activities of seeking out supernatural portents and performing imperial rites. They enjoyed the active support of major Daoists who embraced the ancient belief that the surname of Laozi, the religion's founder, had been Li and that a messianic ruler with that surname would bring about the Daoist millennium.[5]

Despite the end of open hostilities in 628, much of the Chinese realm was not completely pacified. The local elite of north China, who had survived the political turmoil of the preceding centuries by gathering their followers into forts, still clung to these armed camps. In the early de-

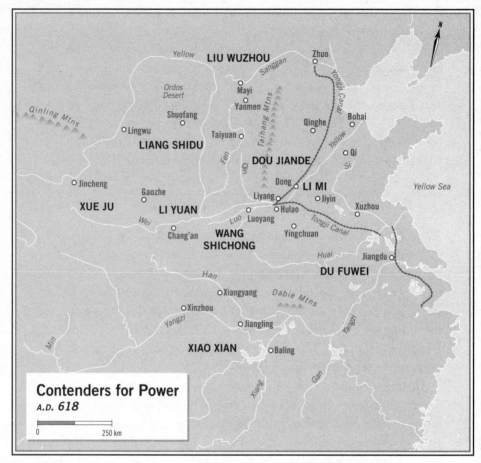

Yellow   **LIU WUZHOU**   Zhuo

Ordos
Desert   Mayi
              Yanmen
Shuofang   Qinghe   Bohai
Lingwu   Taiyuan
LIANG SHIDU   Qi
              Fen   **DOU JIANDE**   Si
Jincheng   Dong   **LI MI**
Gaozhe   Liyang Jiyin
XUE JU   **LI YUAN**   Hulao   Xuzhou
Wei   Luo Luoyang
Chang'an   **WANG**   Yingchuan
           SHICHONG
                              Huai   Jiangdu
Han   **DU FUWEI**

Qinling Mtns

Taihang Mtns

Sanggan

Yongji Canal

Tongji Canal

Yellow Sea

Xiangyang   Dabie Mtns
Xinzhou
Yangzi   Jiangling
Min
XIAO XIAN   Baling

Xiang   Gan   Yangzi

Contenders for Power
A.D. *618*

0   250 km

MAP 4

cades, the Tang government set up forty-three regional military commands (*zong guan fu*) across China in an attempt to impose order beyond Guanzhong, but their distribution reveals large empty spaces where the Tang apparently had no military presence at all. In many cases, local forces had nominally submitted to the regional commands, but when the emperor briefly considered enfeoffing members of the imperial family, the sites where these princes were to be placed did not include the regional commands. This suggests that these areas were not truly under the Tang's bureaucratic control.[6]

In addition to restoring security throughout the empire, the early Tang state needed to reestablish fiscal solvency. Facing a treasury emptied by war, the state reinstituted the equal-field system of state-granted land in order to ensure a steady flow of tax income. Its proper functioning required an active local administration, which the Tang achieved by establishing a system of prefectures and districts. In 621 the government also began to mint copper coins as a way to stabilize the currency, which had collapsed through debasement and forgery in the late Sui. By 755, just before the An Lushan rebellion, the government had eleven mints with ninety-nine furnaces producing copper coins. Despite these efforts, currency shortages continued to bedevil the state throughout the dynasty, and in many cases cloth rather than coins became the medium of exchange and tax payment.[7]

Another problem confronting the new dynasty was the power of the Turkish empire to China's north and west. The Turks had dominated the steppes and grasslands of north China since the sixth century, making them the focus of Sui foreign policy. During the civil war that caused the Sui's collapse, the Turks had played off the various warring parties against one another, in the hope of keeping the Chinese empire weak and divided. When the Tang's internal opposition started to wane in 623, the Turks launched large-scale invasions against the dynasty over the next three years. The Tang founder attempted to relieve the pressure with payments to the Turks, but these failed to stop the invasions.[8]

The situation at the northern frontier began to change when Li Shimin, a younger son of the founder, who had displayed considerable military skill in the conquest of the northeast and central plain, killed his brothers and imprisoned his father in a coup d'état in 626. Li Shimin (best known by his posthumous title Emperor Taizong) at first continued his father's policy of payments to avert a Turkish invasion. But in 627 a fortunate combination of a division of the Turks into two empires, rebellions against the Turkish qaghan, and a heavy snowfall that killed the Turks' flocks gave him the opportunity to destroy the eastern Turkish empire and place his own Turkish allies in control at the frontier. In 630 they granted him the title of Heavenly Qaghan, implicitly recognizing his right to settle disputes beyond the Chinese border. Taizong promptly resettled the surrendered eastern Turks on the Ordos Plateau and launched a policy of encouraging rebellions and civil wars within the western Turkish empire, which controlled most of the area from China's Jade Gate (modern Yumen in Gansu) to Sassanid Persia in the west. With the formal submission of the western qaghan in 642, the Tang claimed unchallenged mastery in Central Asia.

Taizong's triumph over the Turks was the great achievement of his reign, but in China he has been celebrated for reasons that have less to do with his own performance than with subsequent Tang history. The next reign, that of Emperor Gaozong, was dominated by Empress Wu, who has been reviled by Chinese historians as the only woman in Chinese history who sought to rule in her own right. In 690 she replaced the Tang with her own Zhou dynasty before being overthrown in 705. Emperor Zhongzong was restored to the throne, but his ineffectual five-year reign was dominated by his wife, Empress Wei, who was accused by historians, without evidence, of poisoning her husband. Emperor Xuanzong took control in 712, and his long reign marked the Tang's apogee. However, his negligence led to the An Lushan rebellion in 756, from which the dynasty never fully recovered. Consequently, Taizong's era has been traditionally singled out as the one truly successful reign in what has been conventionally regarded as the most powerful dynasty in China.

Chinese historians have celebrated Taizong for his conspicuous display of Confucian virtues—a policy he adopted to compensate for the bloody, unfilial origins of his reign. In the early years he devoted himself to the tasks of government with great industry and frugality, gathering a remarkable collection of civil and military officials and making a point of publicly seeking their opinions and following their advice. The name of his reign period, *Zhenguan* (627–649), became synonymous in later Chinese history with good government. By the 630s, however, as Taizong began to feel secure in his authority, his cultivation of morality, frugality, and other virtues ceased. The last two decades of his reign were marked by constant quarrels with his officials, and even his foreign policy, where he had seen his greatest triumphs, soured after several disastrous campaigns against the Korean state of Koguryŏ. Taizong's timely death in 649 saved him from reenacting the fate of the last Chinese emperor who invaded the Korean peninsula, Emperor Yang of the Sui.[9]

At the end of Taizong's reign, much of the north China plain was still effectively controlled by local powers. Regional commands and military units were still concentrated in Guanzhong and other regions that the Tang had controlled from the dynasty's earliest days. Taizong was unable to perform the *feng* and *shan* sacrifices at Mount Tai in the floodplain, despite twice making plans to do so, because security in the region was lacking. Furthermore, despite major efforts to regularize local administration and register the population, surviving records suggest that at the end of his reign the population under the dynasty's control was scarcely a third that of the Sui and only marginally greater than it had been under his father. Large areas of China remained beyond Tang control.[10]

The reign of Emperor Gaozong (r. 649–683) was marked by the rise to power of Wu Zetian (Wu Zhao), a concubine who became his second empress. While Gaozong largely adhered to the policies of his father, Taizong, his reign witnessed a couple of significant departures. He sponsored revisions of the Tang legal code and issued an empire-wide genealogical text based on new principles of kinship. In foreign affairs, while continuing to dominate the Turks at considerable expense, he finally managed to conquer Koguryŏ in 668. This was achieved by taking advantage of the death of that state's ruler, forming an alliance with the state of Silla, and abandoning the previous land-based invasions in favor of a route across the sea and through the state of Paekche (Map 5). These foreign achievements, however, proved to be fleeting.[11]

Empress Wu had begun to dominate the court by the mid-650s, and

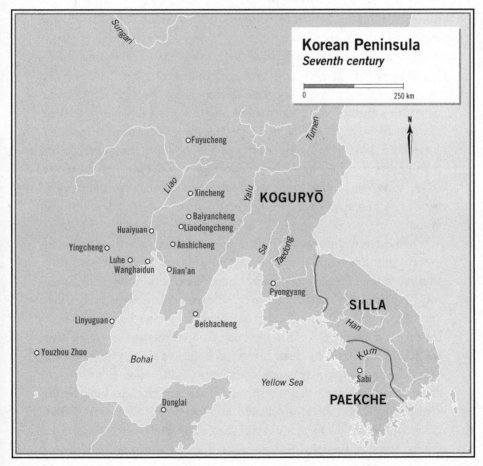

MAP 5

from the time of her husband's death in 683 until her deposition in 705 she reigned as the empress dowager and empress of her own dynasty. Despite the length and importance of this period, we have little reliable or useful documentation about her activities, apart from a few inscriptions and a handful of Buddhist texts. This deficiency stems from the fact that Wu Zhao was a woman. All the records of the period were composed and edited by men who were not only her political enemies but who regarded her entire career as a perversion of nature. Even modern historians, fully aware of the unreliability of the documentary record, still cannot escape this polemical web of enmity. The venerable *Cambridge History of China,* after pointing out the bias of the record, accepts unchallenged Wu's supposed murder of her own child in a plot to supplant a rival, her mutilation of the people she supposedly executed (already a cliché about female rulers in her own day), her sexual liaisons with leading supporters (another hoary cliché), her superstitious nature and manipulation by necromantic frauds (a tendency conventionally attributed to all women), and many other such slanders.

While it cannot be demonstrated that some of these events did not happen (how could one prove a negative?), historians have no evidence that should lead them to trust any of these accounts in the slightest. Unfortunately, this means that six decades of events at the Tang court are virtually a blank slate.[12] The one thing the records do demonstrate is the extraordinary level of animosity aimed at Empress Wu. That she held the reins of power as long as she did speaks highly of her intelligence and resolve, and suggests that whatever savage acts she may have committed were likely necessary to survive in a world of enemies who would stop at nothing.

While affairs of the court during this period remain opaque, public events can still be usefully examined. One of the most significant was the shifting of the capital to Luoyang. Under Taizong the court had temporarily moved to the eastern capital on at least three occasions, when food and other supplies became scarce in Chang'an. In 657 Luoyang was declared the permanent eastern capital, and in Emperor Gaozong's reign the court moved there at least seven times. In 684 the empress dowager Wu, now in control of her son's court, established seven temples to her ancestors, a privilege hitherto reserved for the imperial line. In an associated Act of Grace she also declared Luoyang to be the Sacred Capital (*Shen du*). When she formally established a new dynasty in 690 after deposing her son, Emperor Ruizong, she moved the capital to Luoyang, where it remained until she was overthrown by Li family supporters in 705.

There were at least two reasons for the shift to Luoyang. First, it removed the court from the heartland of the Tang ruling house and from the Li family's closest supporters. Second, Luoyang's location was superior to Chang'an's with respect to communication and commerce throughout the realm. Located on the Grand Canal, it had easy access to trade routes leading south and communication lines leading northeast. By contrast, the only connection Chang'an had to the rest of China was by river and canal links that frequently silted or dried up. Even after Chang'an was re-established as the official capital following the restoration of the Tang, later emperors still frequently had to move the court to Luoyang.[13] With the Tang's collapse, Chang'an (modern Xian) declined to the rank of a provincial city of little political importance.

In addition to the premonitory shifting of the capital away from Chang'an, Empress Wu's reign was also marked by a changing relation between ruler and bureaucracy. Several historians have argued that she recruited officials through the recently established examination system, relying on it to weaken the old families and the northwestern elite and to fill the court with men of humbler origin who were dependent on her good will. A large number of top officials who emerged in her reign did indeed come from the east or northeast and rose through the examination system.[14] However, the examinations were an exceptional path to office throughout the Tang, and Empress Wu used it less frequently than those who came immediately before or after her. She had other techniques to weaken the power of the bureaucracy and establish a more autocratic regime.

First, like the Tang founder Li Yuan, she created numerous new posts that she filled with her own allies, while using her imperial prerogative to regularly dismiss her chief ministers. Originally, the title of chief minister referred to heads of the three central ministries, but in time it was granted to holders of other posts, sometimes as many as fifteen. In Taizong's early reign, these officials developed a high degree of solidarity that allowed them to challenge the emperor's actions, and Taizong seems to have permitted or even encouraged such behavior. Empress Wu, on the other hand, removed 80 percent of her chief ministers by the end of her reign, sending many of them to exile or death. She also developed an elaborate system of special rewards for cooperation.

Outside the official bureaucracy, Empress Wu developed a think tank of nonofficial advisers called the Scholars of the Northern Gate, who prepared decrees, composed numerous literary works issued under the empress's name, and designed policy. In cases where the official bureaucracy proved recalcitrant, the Northern Gate scholars took over the tasks of deliberation and drafting that were necessary to conceive and carry out imperial edicts. Depending on their attitudes toward the empress, modern scholars have described this group variously as a "sinister" and "secret" secretariat or as an anticipation of the Hanlin Academy, a group of scholars without administrative posts who participated in government activities. In the histories, the rise of the Hanlin Academy is celebrated as a move toward efficient government.[15] A more accurate formulation of the empress's advisers might be as an "inner court" on the model of the Han and subsequent dynasties. While Empress Wu's policies were in part a replay of the power shift toward the center that had been a recurrent feature of imperial Chinese history up to that moment and were in part a result of her present need to assert her own authority against a defiant bureaucracy, they also anticipated the long-term development of the Chinese empire in the direction of ever-greater autocracy.

The period of Empress Wu's domination at court was notable for its foreign policy struggles, particularly the conquest of Koguryŏ that had eluded Chinese rulers for a century. It was also in this period that the Chinese first encountered the expanding power of Tibet, which began to encroach in Central Asia and, from 670, into the western edges of the Chinese realm. Between 670 and 680 the Chinese lost several key strategic citadels around the Tarim Basin (Map 6) and in northwestern Sichuan, and in 695 the Tibetans inflicted a disastrous defeat on a large Chinese army to the west of Chang'an. In the same year a major rebellion by the previously allied Khitan people in the northeast and incursions by the revived eastern Turks created a multi-front crisis. Empress Wu and her government managed to foment dissension among the Tibetans and, after two years of mass mobilization, to drive back the Khitan forces. After this struggle, she established permanent military commands in the north and the northeast, the single greatest innovation of her reign in defense policy but one that would have calamitous long-term consequences for the Tang dynasty.[16]

The overthrow of Empress Wu and restoration of her son Zhongzong (r. 705–710) did not immediately put the Li house back in power. For the next seven years the court continued to be dominated by a series of strong-willed women and their allies. These included the wife of Zhong-

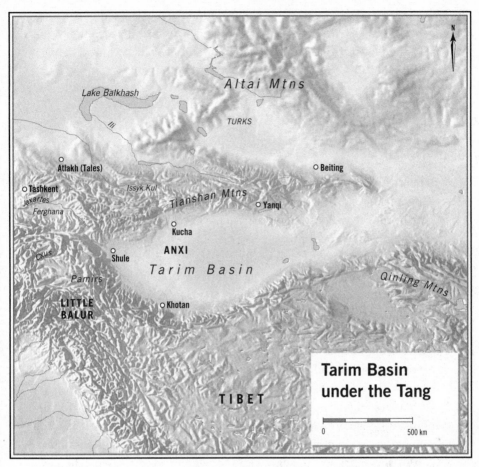

Tarim Basin under the Tang

MAP 6

zong, Empress Wei, and Empress Wei's daughter, the Anluo Princess. But above all, Empress Wu's daughter, the Taiping Princess, remained a power at court throughout the period, sometimes in association with her cousin Wu Sansi, sometimes together with a group of female associates including Shangguan Wan'er, and sometimes in isolation.

In 710, after Zhongzong died, perhaps by poisoning, Empress Wu's previously deposed son Emperor Ruizong returned to the throne. Depressed by his lack of power and by the inauspicious omen of a comet, however, he decided to retire two years later and pass the succession to one of his sons favored by Empress Wei. Unable to dissuade Ruizong from retiring and afraid that the balance of power was turning against her, the Taiping Princess attempted first to poison the new Emperor

Xuanzong and then to overthrow him and put a younger son of Ruizong in power. When these assaults failed, she was forced to commit suicide, thereby bringing to an end this unprecedented period of female domination.[17]

Emperor Xuanzong's Reign and An Lushan's Rebellion

Chinese historians conventionally treat the early decades of Xuanzong's reign as a high point of the Tang dynasty, a new golden age comparable to that of Taizong. They describe an industrious ruler working together with outstanding ministers to restore effective government after sixty years of rule by women. This was also the age when the greatest poets in Chinese history produced their works. But in his later years, the story goes, the aging emperor fell under the spell of yet another ambitious woman. Leaving the affairs of state to the care of a single unreliable minister, he surrendered himself to the bliss of a late-blossoming passion. The mismanaged government stumbled into a catastrophic military rebellion that led to the death of the beloved concubine, the deposition of the ruler, and the near-collapse of the dynasty.

Not only is this traditional account based on misogynistic moral judgments and the self-flattery of the literati, but a two-part division of Xuanzong's reign is not the most analytically useful. A more appropriate framework would divide the reign into three segments. The first period, from his accession in 712 until roughly 720, saw considerable continuity both in personnel and policies with the reign of Empress Wu. The next period, between 720 and 736, was marked by the resurgence at court of the great families of Guanzhong and the first appearance of specialist commissioners with extra-bureaucratic appointments and staff. In the final period, between 736 and the outbreak of the An Lushan rebellion in 756—apart from the conventionally cited withdrawal of the emperor into private life, the control of the court by two successive ministers, and the rise of factionalism—the army became fully professionalized, military governors obtained high official appointments, and the Tang dynasty increasingly shifted into a defensive foreign policy.[18]

During the first of these three periods, all the chief ministers and leading advisers to Emperor Xuanzong originated in eastern and northeastern China and had risen through the examination system under Empress Wu. By the time Emperor Xuanzong came to the throne, increasing reliance on the examinations as a form of "fast-track" career path leading to the highest positions had furthered the tendency of Tang officialdom to split into those with appointments in the capital and those with positions in the provinces, which, despite high ranks and ample salaries, were viewed as a form of exile. Most ambitious officials in this era declined service in the provinces, regardless of edicts and pressure from the emperor and chief ministers. Moreover, the various empresses had filled the court with supernumerary officials as a means of weakening bureaucratic resistance and, in some cases, of supplementing government income through the sale of offices. While leaders in the early reign of Xuanzong recognized these problems, they found no way to resolve them.

One significant shift during the first phase of Xuanzong's reign was to reverse Empress Wu's policy of keeping chief ministers in office for short periods only. Xuanzong appointed just two or three chief ministers at a time, one of whom was always clearly the leader, and allowed them to remain in office for many years. The emperor's respect for his high officials and willingness to give them a genuine role in decision-making are probably the greatest reasons why Xuanzong's early reign is generally celebrated. Whether this practice made for better government is not clear. The major problems that had confronted the realm—natural disasters, debased currency, under-registration of the population with its consequent loss of tax revenue, and the increasing inadequacy of the old military system to meet the growing threats at the frontiers—all remained unresolved.

The middle years of Xuanzong's reign, from 720 to about 736, were marked by the revival of the leading families of Guanzhong as a force in the court and by the emergence of special commissioners in several fields outside the regular bureaucracy. The revived influence of the Guanzhong elite was relatively short-lived and may not have contributed much to developments outside the court. If Empress Wu's elevation of men from the east and northeast was intended to counterbalance the Li family's traditional reliance on their fellows from the northwest, then Xuanzong's reign may have simply marked a restoration of the earlier state of affairs. On the other hand, some evidence in imperially-sponsored comprehensive genealogies suggests a partial resurgence of claims on the part of the old northwestern families to a uniquely exalted status. The most reliable evidence we have comes from court appointments, where, in post after post, officials whom Xuanzong had inherited from the court of Empress Wu were replaced by men drawn from the northwest, until in 729 every leading position at court was filled with a Guanzhong man.[19]

More important for the later history of the dynasty was the new practice of appointing special commissioners outside the normal bureaucratic hierarchy and giving them great powers in matters of key importance. The clearest early example was the appointment of Yuwen Rong as commissioner charged with the task of finding and registering households that had escaped the government's records. His success led to the registration of 800,000 households and their land in the early 720s, a feat that helped to bring fiscal stability to the empire. A commissioner of land and water transport, Pei Yaoqing, was charged with improving the infrastructure for shipping grain on the Grand Canal, thereby making possible the court's permanent return to the old capital. He was succeeded in the 740s by Wei Jian, as part of a new wave of aristocratic financial experts who came to dominate fiscal policy in the court. These financial commissions contributed to the power of Xuanzong's chief ministers during the last decades of his rule.[20]

Groups of scholars, such as the Hanlin Academy, also acted as de facto commissions outside the normal bureaucracy and were sometimes used by rulers to supplant it. The military governors (*jie du shi*) who came to dominate the frontier and ultimately much of Tang politics were also types of special commissioners, as were the heads of the salt monopoly in south China during the ninth century. The holders of such offices were instrumental in leading the Tang state to its period of greatest fiscal and military strength, but they also nearly destroyed the dynasty when they began to act independently.

In the final period of his reign, starting with the establishment of the chief ministry of Li Linfu in 736, Xuanzong gave himself over to religion, art, and infatuation with his favorite young courtesan, Yang Guifei. Consequently, all power at court came to reside in the hands of a single chief minister. Li Linfu was at first paired with another minister, his devoted follower Niu Xianke, who was the first chief minister to reach his post by serving in one of the new frontier commands. After Niu Xianke's death in 742, Li Linfu conducted savage purges of real or potential adversaries to assure his continued power at court. By 747 he was a de facto dictator, and the court had been emptied of all real talent, including leading military figures and any financial administrators who had fallen afoul of the chief minister. This concentration of all power in a single man, the emptying out of all other talent, the crushing of initiative, and the consequent separation of the court from the world at large created dangerous conditions for confronting the crisis that broke out in the next decade.

The concentration of dictatorial powers at court was paralleled by the rise of military governors in the northern provinces. During the mid-730s Niu Xianke and Li Linfu had served as *in absentia* military governors of areas to the north and northwest of the capital. However, Li Linfu soon reversed himself and adopted the policy of employing only non-Chinese as military governors. By entrusting his armies to men without ties to the court, he hoped to prevent any potential rivals from gaining political power on the basis of military success. But this policy meant that the men who truly held power outside were becoming steadily more alienated from the central government. The rebellion of one such general in the northeast, An Lushan, would end the High Tang and deliver a damaging blow to the dynasty.[21]

Xuanzong himself played a part in the events leading up to the rebellion. As the aging emperor grew increasingly obsessed with Yang Guifei, he elevated to lofty positions several of her kin, most notably Yang Zhao (renamed Guozhong by the emperor). As Yang Guozhong rose rapidly in the court, he began to challenge Li Linfu's power, first covertly and then openly. He also cultivated a local base in Sichuan, where he had first entered government service and where he became the only military governor of Han Chinese descent. At the same time, An Lushan, the most powerful non-Chinese general and commander of the empire's largest single concentration of forces, which was in the northeast, remained a client of Li Linfu. When Li Linfu died in 752, Yang Guozhong assumed control of the court and set out to eliminate An Lushan, who still enjoyed the protection of Emperor Xuanzong and Yang Guifei, An Lushan's adoptive mother. As Yang Guozhong's hostility grew, An Lushan began to prepare his forces for rebellion, and reports of these preparations in turn encouraged further denunciations from Yang Guozhong.[22]

In the eleventh month of 755 An Lushan set out from his base in Hebei, and before the year's end he occupied Luoyang. His armies were blocked from proceeding west into Guanzhong by defenses at the Tong Pass (just to the west of the Hangu Pass), where the Tang had transferred their large northwestern frontier armies. Tang loyalists blocked his attempted moves south and threatened his supply lines through areas he had not fully subdued during his rapid march to the eastern capital. Several large rebel armies were defeated, and by the sixth month it seemed that the rebellion was about to collapse.

At this point Yang Guozhong made a fatal strategic error. Believing that his power was being challenged by the general in command of the northwestern armies, he persuaded Emperor Xuanzong to order an eastward assault through the Tong Pass. Trapped in a narrow defile, the Tang forces were destroyed. When news of the disaster reached the capital, Yang Guozhong persuaded the emperor to flee to Yang's secure base in Sichuan, and their small party departed in the night with a military escort; An Lushan soon entered the capital in triumph. A couple of weeks after the emperor left Chang'an, however, his escort mutinied and forced him to execute both Yang Guozhong and Yang Guifei. Xuanzong was then allowed to proceed to Sichuan, but he was soon stripped of his position by his heir, Emperor Suzong (r. 756–762), who took charge of the resistance in Guanzhong and began the task of restoration.[23]

The Tang Military System

Although the Li family claimed to be the true successors to the vanished Han, the Tang dynasty incorporated many adaptations from the so-called barbarian or semi-barbarian dynasties that had ruled north China in the fifth and sixth centuries—the Northern Wei, Northern Zhou, Northern Qi, and Sui. The early Tang state was in many ways a summation of the institutional history of these two centuries. This pattern can be seen in its military institutions, semi-hereditary aristocracy, legal code, and linked systems of land ownership and taxation. All of these institutions shared a vision of a society divided into hereditary groups that varied in their status and function.[24]

The distinctive feature of the military system that the early Tang inherited from previous centuries was its reliance on a military population, consisting of military households and non-Chinese troops, that was separate from the peasantry. The best-known element of the early Tang system was the "regimental army" (fu bing), but it also included a hereditary Northern Army in the capital, the princely guards recruited from the sons of elite families, and non-Chinese nomadic mercenaries. The regimental army was composed of members of elite families in the northwest. It had been introduced under the northern dynasties by a coalition of non-Chinese and "barbarized" Chinese elites in Guanzhong who actively cultivated their military traditions. When the Tang formally refounded this army in 636, it was composed of about 600 regimental headquarters, each of which controlled between 800 and 1,200 men. These units were spread over the countryside but were concentrated around the capitals, with about two-thirds within 170 miles of Chang'an or Luoyang.

Initially, these men were chosen from large, well-to-do landed families who could afford to allow one adult male to devote himself exclusively to military training. In the early days of the dynasty, regimental members were listed on special military registers and were largely exempt from taxation and labor service. Each soldier was given an allotment of land that he or his family and serfs could work. He was expected to supply his own basic arms and some provisions, with armor and more elaborate weapons provided by the state. In this way the troops attained near professional quality without draining the state's budget. Regimental units provided manpower for the local police force, and selected elements of each unit served for periods of time at the capital or in expeditionary armies. Armies at the frontier were also drawn from regimental soldiers, who served alongside non-Chinese mercenaries.

In addition to the regimental army, the core of the Tang military was the central army located in the capital. These forces consisted of princely guards selected almost exclusively from sons of elite families in the area and of the Northern Army, a force composed of descendants of Li Yuan's original army. Expeditionary armies were composed of selected soldiers from the regimental army, the central army, and non-Chinese allies, primarily Turks. These armies, composed of well-trained soldiers brought together for a single campaign, were designed to deliver rapid, smashing victories like those for which Emperor Taizong was famous, while reducing costs and preventing frontier armies from developing personal ties to their commanders through protracted time together in the field.[25]

Thus, in the first century of the Tang, the military forces of the dynasty were composed of hereditary military households of high social status and of foreign allies or mercenaries. The ruling elites of both the Sui and the Tang, including the Tang ruling house itself, and the so-called Guanzhong aristocracy that dominated the Tang court under the first two emperors, came from families with a military tradition. Moreover, these forces, which were concentrated in Guanzhong, reproduced the dynasty's political structure; the rest of the empire was controlled largely through accommodation with local powers in the east and south, which the court did not trust. However, with the growing threat of Tibet in the west, Nanzhao in the southwest, the Khitan and Bohai in the east, and a renewed Turkish empire to the north, the Tang regimental and central armies became obsolete. During military crises in the early 690s, Empress Wu was forced to keep large forces at the frontier for indefinite periods, a task for which the early Tang army was unsuited.[26] Members of well-to-do landed families began to avoid military service, forcing the regimental army to meet its quotas by recruiting men from poor and peasant families. As the prestige of military service declined, the elite central army in the capital and the foreign mercenary forces at the frontiers gradually supplanted the regimental army. By 749 regimental soldiers were no longer called up to serve at the capital or frontier.[27]

With the regimental army in decline, the great frontier armies emerged as the major Tang military force. When the rotation of soldiers proved inefficient for manning garrisons on the borders, the Tang state in 717 resorted to offering payments for voluntary extensions of tours of duty, and it also recruited peasants who had been displaced from the land by the formation of large estates among wealthy families and the Buddhist order. These permanent recruits were called "sturdy lads," a term originally used for elite elements of the earlier regimental army. In 737 the shift was formalized in a decree that called on each frontier command to determine the number of long-term recruits it required. The state would reward the men with salaries, permanent exemption from taxes and corvée, and land at the frontier for any dependents who accompanied them. Within a year the quotas were filled and recruitment was halted. In addition to these now-permanent military professionals, the frontier commands also routinely incorporated non-Chinese cavalry forces. A decade prior to the An Lushan rebellion the Tang frontier forces numbered about half a million men.

The regional military commands also developed a new style of officer corps. The leadership of earlier armies had been drawn from members of the local elite who commanded forces from their own communities. Empress Wu's attempts to recruit professional officers through military examination had been unsuccessful, and by the mid-eighth century officers in the army were largely promoted from within the ranks. As the old military families began to avoid service, the officer corps—like the men they commanded—came largely from poor Han Chinese families or from non-Han soldiers.[28] By the late Tang, a military career was a well-traveled avenue for upward social mobility, doing as much or more than the examination system to bring new men to power.

In 742, the Tang military forces were reorganized to provide a comprehensive defense against mobile enemies who were often more interested in pillaging than in occupying Chinese territory. The Tang distributed their armies among ten frontier commands: seven stretching in an arc from Fanyang in the east to Jiannan in the west (Map 7) and three in the far west (modern Xinjiang and Gansu). In most of these commands, one

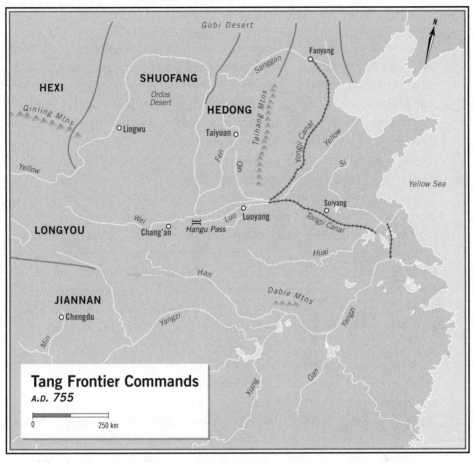

Map 7

large army was located at the commander's headquarters and under his
direct control. This army usually contained just under half of the total
forces, including most of the cavalry. The rest of the forces, largely infan-
try, were distributed in fortified positions that formed a static defense.
The static forces defended the borders against low-level incursions, while
the armies at the headquarters formed a strategic reserve that could meet
larger groups of invaders or serve as mobile strike forces to carry war beyond the frontier.[29]

The command of these frontier armies was entrusted to military governors. These men were another version of the extraordinary imperial commissioners who had assumed such responsibilities as provisioning the
capital and registering "vagrant households." The position of military

governor was created in the eighth century as an improvised response to the necessity of coordinating and commanding the operations of numerous garrisons and armies within a region. Over decades, some governors were granted extensive economic powers and the concurrent office of investigating commissioner. This gave them considerable authority over the region's civil administration. By the middle of the eighth century these men had become de facto provincial governors at the frontier, with concentrations of regional power that threatened the empire's central authority. However, the state's requirements for frontier defense took priority over any concern about internal rebellion.[30]

In addition to gradually concentrating power in the hands of military governors, the Tang court changed the nature of the office. Into the 740s most military governors held concurrent posts as civilian officials of high rank and regarded their time in the military as a means of obtaining a higher post in the central government. All military governors of the northeast prior to An Lushan served as chief ministers in the capital at least once in their careers, and as military governors for a relatively brief period, typically no more than four years. They usually did not develop strong personal ties to their officers and men. The sole exception was in the far west, in the commands of Central Asia and the Tibetan border.

But in 747 Li Linfu made the mistake of decreeing that all military governorships should be filled with non-Chinese professional soldiers.[31] While this change, made on the pretext that professional soldiers were more effective commanders, helped to prevent the emergence at court of rivals to Li Linfu, its primary beneficiaries were Geshu Han, who commanded armies in the northwest, and above all An Lushan, in Hebei. Remaining permanently with his army at the northeastern frontier and with broad civil powers over the region, he was in an excellent position to challenge the Tang as soon as the death of his old patron, Li Linfu, ruptured his ties to the imperial court.

China's Medieval "Aristocracy"

As early as the ninth century, Chinese historians noted that a small group of leading families had developed in the late Han and risen to a powerful social and political position in the centuries after that dynasty's collapse.[32] A relatively small number of surnames and lineages came to hold, by hereditary privilege, the right to automatic entry-level posts in the bureaucracy. Although no family remained at the pinnacle of power for more than two or three generations, the status of this hereditary group enabled them to enjoy both local and empire-wide prestige for centuries—greater than that of many dynastic families who appeared and disappeared in China between the Han and the Tang.

As was first suggested by Shen Gua (1031–1095) in the Song dynasty, the Tang elite consisted of two distinct strata.[33] At the top level were a tiny number of lineages who were famous throughout the empire and enjoyed high titles and immense privilege at court. The most prestigious were the four great families of what was then called Hebei (primarily modern Shandong), who claimed to be representatives of the purest Chinese cultural traditions and would marry only among themselves. These families looked down on the imperial Li family, whom they regarded as parvenus with a heavy taint of barbarian blood and culture.

Almost as proud, and perhaps even more powerful, were the great families of Guanzhong, of which the Li family was one. These families had risen to eminence under the nomad-based conquest dynasties in the fifth and sixth centuries and had regularly intermarried with non-Chinese ruling families and nobility. They dominated the highest offices at court until Empress Wu took charge. Under Emperor Xuanzong they steadily regained their former power, and during the dictatorship of Li Linfu they held a monopoly at court. Less powerful were the great families of Shanxi and the aristocratic families who had dominated the southern dynasties in the Yangzi valley. They were generally excluded from the highest offices during the first century of the Tang.

Below these great families were several thousand lineages that enjoyed prestige in their own commanderies and provinces but did not have access to high offices at court, which were reserved for those who had noble titles or whose fathers had held those offices. Families of these local elites did not figure prominently in Tang histories, but the names of many of them have been preserved in fragments of genealogies recovered at Dunhuang. These families were the primary beneficiaries of the examination system and other alternative modes of gaining office under Empress Wu. But more important than positions obtained through the examination system were the extra-bureaucratic careers that opened up for them in the service of the new special commissioners and military commanders, and later in the salt and iron monopolies.

While the Tang dynasty did not formally recognize the existence of an aristocracy, it gave de facto recognition to an imperial elite by reserving the highest offices at court for certain families and granting them special

legal privileges. As early as 638, Emperor Taizong approved a comprehensive genealogical record for the entire empire that listed 293 surnames
and 1,651 lineages in the order of their social standing. This list went
well beyond the tiny imperial elite to include many of the locally eminent
families. And since it was based on previously existing genealogies, it
amounted to an imperial ratification of the generally recognized social hierarchy (with some modifications, for Taizong insisted on ranking the imperial Li family first and demoting one of the four great Hebei families
that had claimed the highest rank).

A similar listing including even more lineages was compiled in 659,
but, perhaps reflecting Empress Wu's attempt to reduce the power of the
great families, this list was based entirely on court rankings and prestige
under the Tang. She also issued edicts prohibiting intermarriage among
the greatest families and restricting the size of dowries to amounts corre-
lated with official rank. But in the first decades of the eighth century, after
her overthrow, a veritable fever of genealogical activity, both private and
court-sponsored, reasserted the rankings based on family prestige rather
than on offices held under the Tang.[34]

After the An Lushan rebellion this genealogical passion rapidly cooled.
The major listings of surnames in the ninth century no longer offered
comprehensive rankings but only long, unranked lists of famous families
organized by rhyme groups, which would have been the equivalent of al-
phabetical order.[35] By the time of the Five Dynasties period that succeeded the Tang, the great medieval Chinese aristocracy had vanished.

The Tang Legal Code

Chinese dynasties had promulgated legal codes since the Warring States
period, but until the discovery of much of the Qin code in a tomb in the
early 1970s the Tang code was the earliest that had been preserved intact.
Earlier ones were known only through fragments in historical texts or on
bamboo strips.[36] In imperial China the legal code was viewed as the written expression of the will of the emperors, and part of the founding of
any dynasty was the act of promulgating a new code, which formed a key
element of its institutional framework. These codes focused primarily
on penal and administrative law and tended to slight commercial or
contractual law.[37] Many of the short-lived dynasties after the Han simply
adopted the code of their predecessors, while others attempted a more
general reworking. While the Tang code carried forward many features

of the earlier Han code as transmitted through intervening dynasties, it also made significant modifications. The structure of the Tang legal code reveals the ruling house's vision of the social order, although not necessarily the reality.

When he established the Tang dynasty, Li Yuan rejected the legal code of the last Sui emperor, whose putative crimes had justified his own accession to power, and announced a radically simplified legal code modeled on the three laws of the Han founder.[38] But like the Han founder, Li Yuan rapidly discovered the need for a more detailed legal framework, which he announced in 624. It consisted of the first Sui emperor's code but with fifty-three added clauses, along with new administrative statutes and ordinances. The statutes were the general rules for the central government, while the ordinances were lesser rules concerned with limited areas of the law. These administrative statutes and ordinances were supplemented at an even lower level by regulations to allow modified applications of laws under different circumstances.

In 637 Taizong proclaimed the first systematic reworking of the Tang legal code, including limitations on the use of torture, abolition of the amputation of feet (the last mutilating punishment still in use), and reduction of the number of crimes punishable by death.[39] In 651 Emperor Gaozong revised the code, and in 653 for the first time a commentary was added to the code to educate legal officials in the proper conduct of trials. Each subsequent emperor or empress proclaimed a new code, although apparently making only minor modifications. In 725 Xuanzong promulgated the fullest expression of the Tang legal code, which remained in force in China until the fourteenth century.[40]

Many of the basic principles of this code were similar to those that underlay Han penal law. The Tang code still embraced the notion that the human and natural worlds were intimately linked and that the natural world was unsettled by criminal actions. Punishment served not only to intimidate the disobedient but also to restore the cosmic balance between *yin* and *yang*. To maintain this balance, anyone shown to have falsely accused another person received precisely the punishment that would have befallen the falsely accused. If it was proved that a person had been wrongly exiled, the state made reparation to him by remitting taxes for the number of years he had wrongly suffered. There was no reparation for unjust beatings, which were apparently considered a trivial matter, or for executions. Since the emperor had to personally approve all capital punishment and since imperial error was not recognized by the legal code, there could never be an unjust execution in the eyes of the law. As part of the theory of balance, repeated natural calamities could lead to general reductions in sentences, and in order to compensate for unknown injustices it was the practice to grant general amnesties on the occasion of a new emperor's accession, sometimes on the emperor's birthday, or on other auspicious occasions. There were 174 empire-wide amnesties in the course of less than three hundred years of Tang history. Frequent amnesties had also been given in the Han, and this practice set early imperial China apart from the post-Song period.[41]

Like the Han code, the Tang laws repeatedly invoked the number five or its multiples: five kinds of punishment (beating with a light stick, beating with a heavy stick, penal servitude, exile, and execution by strangling or decapitation), five degrees of relation used in determining the seriousness of crimes within a family, five kinds of life exile, ten abominations (the most serious crimes), five hundred articles in the code (actually 502), and so on. Also like the Han, the Tang code treated with special severity any crimes against the emperor or imperial family. For plotting rebellion or sedition the code invoked the full range of collective punishments: execution of the father and sons of the criminal as well as the enslavement of female relatives, all children under fifteen, and male relatives for three generations in either direction. Any criticism of the emperor or resistance to his officers was punishable by law, and even an improperly filled prescription for the emperor or the breakdown of one of his boats or chariots was treated as an act of rebellion. The punishment for robberies of ordinary people varied according to the value of what was stolen, but any theft from the emperor or his family, however trivial, was punished with severity. Like the rest of the ten abominations, these crimes could not be pardoned nor redeemed through the surrender of cash or rank, and the accused could be tortured.[42]

Three features of the Tang code set it apart from its Han predecessor: the legal recognition of status groups, both aristocratic and servile; rigorous gradations of punishment based on relative status in the family or bureaucracy; and detailed legal concern over the organization of offices. Men of high hereditary rank in both the imperial aristocracy and much of the so-called provincial aristocracy were automatically granted entry to officialdom at the fifth rank, along with sons of officials of the third rank and higher. Among the privileges enjoyed by these men were immunity from torture, the need to have three witnesses to obtain any conviction in a legal case, the right to redeem punishments by surrendering rank or cash payments, and, for officials of the third rank and above, the right to have all punishments automatically reduced and to follow special procedures for any crime that could involve the death penalty.

At the other end of the social spectrum, a variety of so-called "base people" were legally defined as being below free commoners. These servile classes were divided into those who belonged to the state and those who belonged to individuals, and they included hereditary service households, musicians, personal retainers, bondsmen, and slaves. A crime against a base person by a commoner was punished less severely than a similar crime against a fellow commoner, while the crimes of base people against commoners were punished more severely. Within the class of base people, other distinctions pertained. For example, bondsmen who committed crimes against commoners were punished less severely than slaves who committed similar crimes, and crimes by anyone against slaves were punished less severely than those against bondsmen.

In other words, the Tang code meted out differential punishments based on the status of the victim and the status of the criminal, with slaves at the bottom of the hierarchy, bondsmen one step higher up, and free commoners higher still. Particularly severe were punishments for bondsmen or slaves who harmed their masters. Plotting to kill a master was punished by decapitation, whether or not the plot was successful, and even a plot against one of the master's relatives merited strangulation. On the other hand, if a master killed a slave for some offense without first obtaining the government's permission, the master was merely beaten. The totally unprovoked killing of a slave by his master resulted in one year of penal servitude.[43]

In addition to marking out these broad legal status groups, the Tang code used differential punishments to enforce rankings within the bureaucracy and the family. Offenses against a bureaucratic superior were treated more severely, those against an inferior less so. Within families, the closer the degree of relationship as defined by specified mourning obligations, the heavier the punishment for a junior offender and the lighter the punishment for a senior. Men of the same generation were ranked by age. A father who beat his son was not guilty of any crime at all, nor was a husband who beat his wife. But the reverse situations were deemed serious crimes involving penal servitude. Crimes against senior relatives were among the ten abominations.[44]

Children were legally obliged to support their parents and paternal grandparents and were subject to penal servitude if they failed to do so.

Failure to perform proper mourning for ancestors was punished by exile. In deference to ancient Confucian precedent, members of families as well as their slaves and personal retainers were allowed to conceal one another's crimes, except for crimes against the state. In all, roughly one fifth of the articles dealing with commoners pertained to relations within the family, including six of the ten abominations.[45] Because a person's liability and the severity of his punishment depended heavily on his bureaucratic status, the code had to spell out in considerable detail how the bureaucracy was to be organized and what ranking each of the different offices possessed. The greater divisions between full officials and the secretarial staff, or between the pure offices (those above the fifth rank devoted to high policy) and the impure (devoted to carrying out assigned tasks), as well as all the minute gradations within each rank, were consequently written into Tang statutes.[46]

Land Ownership and Taxation

In the first century of the Tang dynasty, particularly in the northern part of China, landholding, taxation, and labor service formed an integrated complex centered on the adult male head of household. The basis of this complex was the equal-field system, which had developed in north China during the fifth century. The southward migration of the Chinese peasantry beginning in the late Han dynasty, coupled with the pressures of constant invasion and civil war, had led to the abandonment of large tracts of land on the north China plain. Various dynasties claimed this land and moved in peasants to cultivate it. In 486 Emperor Xiaowen of the Northern Wei instituted a modified version of the earlier Jin dynasty's policy, in which extensive state-owned lands were divided into family-sized plots and given to peasants in exchange for taxes and labor service on imperial construction projects. With modifications, this policy was continued by subsequent dynasties and carried forward into the Tang.[47]

The principle of this system was that each married couple was entitled to a specified grant of land from the state for the duration of their working, or rather taxpaying, lives. If there was more than one adult male in a household, the size of the grant was, in theory, doubled. Households that had slaves received a small additional allotment of land for each adult male slave. In the northwest, land was also allotted for the keeping of herds of cattle, but this was not practiced elsewhere. Each land grant remained the property of the state and was returnable when the couple reached the age at which they were no longer obliged to pay taxes or provide labor service.

Because mulberry trees, which were essential to silk production, needed continuous cultivation over decades before they became productive, a separate category of "hereditary land" was also created. In theory, this land was passed from generation to generation within the same family, subject to legal limits on the size of total holdings. But documents from Dunhuang and Turfan, where land was scarce, indicate that in practice families were not always allowed to inherit all the land to which they were legally entitled. In regions where hemp rather than silk was the primary product, the land permanently set aside for mulberry trees was replaced by land permanently set aside for hemp. But since hemp was an annual crop just like food grains, this exception for hemp undercut the original rationale of the system and ultimately allowed wealthy families in some regions to accumulate larger and larger plots of land under the name of "hemp fields." There were other local variations in the way the system worked, such as a distinction in Turfan between double-cropped land and single-cropped land.[48]

In places for which documentary evidence has survived, the actual amount of land received was well below the amounts provided by law. Nevertheless, because the basic purpose of this system was to bring as much abandoned land as possible under cultivation, the original grants had been quite large, about seven times as large as the average farm in nineteenth- or twentieth-century China. The law was also intended to limit the accumulation of large estates by officials and leading families, but this worked no better than similar attempts under the Han and intervening dynasties.

In exchange for these land grants, households were obliged to pay taxes and perform labor service. The basic unit of taxation was the same as the unit for granting land: the individual adult male, generally the head of a household. Thus, taxes took the form of a fixed capitation tax and associated labor service, with no consideration of actual wealth or income. Like the equal-field system, the tax structure was inherited from dynasties that ruled north China in the fifth and sixth centuries. It was established in 619, the first year of the Tang dynasty, and was preserved largely unchanged in later editions of the statutes. Commonly called *zu yong diao*, where *zu* refers to a tax paid in grain, *yong* to labor services, and *diao* to a tax paid in cloth, this system actually imposed four obligations on most peasant families: a tax paid in grain, a tax paid in cloth, and two types of labor service—the regular annual corvée, which amounted to twenty days per year, and so-called miscellaneous labor services, which were owed to the local authorities. These liabilities were fixed and did not take account of the actual circumstances of the household, since in theory all landholdings were directly proportional to the size of the household and therefore should be proportionately taxed.[49]

In practice there were many variations on this seemingly rigid tax system, just as there were variations in the equal-field system of landholding. First, in many border regions the taxes were levied in commodities distinctive to that area: rice in the south, special types of silk in Annam (modern Vietnam), salt in areas that produced it, even cash in economically advanced cities such as Jiangdu. In addition, many distant areas converted their grain tax into a cloth equivalent, because cloth was cheaper to transport in bulk. Similarly, the annual corvée was almost invariably converted into a tax payment, which was in theory used to hire labor. This presumably freed peasants to spend more time cultivating the land. In the seventh century, households were rated on a scale of nine categories from richest to poorest, and in places where hemp cloth was paid in lieu of grain the tax rate was progressive, in accordance with household wealth. In the seventh and eighth centuries the government introduced two minor supplementary taxes that were to a degree dependent on wealth, the household tax and the land tax.[50] However, these modifications had only a minor impact; the core of the system was still based on the idea that all adult males owned equal land and thus owed equal taxes.

The great exceptions to this principle were based not on wealth but on membership in privileged status groups. Anyone even distantly related to the imperial family, all families with noble titles, all officials and many people working for the government, all holders of official rank, and all members of the Buddhist and Daoist clergy were exempt from taxation and labor service. Exemption could also be granted as a special privilege for morally exemplary individuals or for regions that had suffered major catastrophes. In short, the taxation system, like the legal code and the military, was structured on the principle of segmenting the population into legally distinct status groups.

One final type of people who escaped taxation were the unregistered "runaway households." Families who left their registered place of residence escaped the exactions of the government, and if they could find shelter as tenants on one of the large estates around the capital or, more often, in the south, they could permanently avoid the tax and labor owed to the state, although they would have to pay it in other forms to their landlord. Great estates belonging to the Buddhist monastic order also served as refuges for peasants.[51] Despite repeated attempts by the government to register these missing households, a substantial number remained off the tax rolls, a problem that reached crisis proportions after the An Lushan rebellion.

3

WARLORDS AND MONOPOLISTS

A RECURRENT theme in Chinese history is the tension between the centralization of authority and the forces of regional autonomy. The An Lushan rebellion between 756 and 763 both resulted from and led to the breakdown of the institutional framework of the early Tang empire—the equal-field system, the regimental army, the *zu yong diao* tax—and ushered in an era of regional powers dominated by warlords and administrators of monopolies. These changes in turn brought an end to the aristocratic social order and marked the beginning of an economic revolution that created the world of late imperial China.

An Lushan's power reached its peak with the capture of Chang'an in 756. Despite several attempts, his armies could not advance west beyond the immediate region of the capital, and efforts to move southward toward the Yangzi were also blocked by loyalist resistance in key cities. Early in 757, perhaps frustrated by the lack of progress, a group of An Lushan's immediate followers assassinated him and installed his son in his place. But this change alienated An Lushan's other followers, most notably Shi Siming who had taken the lead in occupying Hebei in the northeast. This internal dissension undermined the rebels' power, so that the Tang court led by Emperor Suzong (r. 756–762) was able to resume the offensive in the autumn of 757.

The reassertion of imperial power at this point was based on two new policies that had long-term repercussions for the Tang dynasty. First, the Tang established an alliance with the Uighurs, a Turkic tribe who had replaced the Eastern Turks as the dominant power on the Mongolian steppes during the 740s. This alliance was negotiated by Pugu Huaien, a

Tang general who was descended from a related tribe.[1] The Uighurs contributed more than 4,000 cavalrymen to the Tang army, which, under the
command of the veteran General Guo Ziyi, routed the rebel armies and
reoccupied Chang'an in autumn of 757. However, this temporary success
had long-term negative consequences. The Uighurs demanded an additional payment to assist with the recapture of Luoyang. After the eastern
capital was taken two weeks later, the Uighur armies departed, leaving
the Tang forces to fight on with no real cavalry. During the last great
campaign of the rebellion in 762, when the rebels had managed to reoccupy Luoyang, the Uighurs intervened again but only on the condition
that they be allowed to sack the city. Immediately prior to taking the city,
they whipped to death several leading Tang courtiers who had offended
their commander. In the pillaging that followed, in which the Uighurs
were joined by Tang troops, tens of thousands of Tang subjects were massacred, and the eastern capital was burned to the ground.

Meanwhile, Tibetan forces had occupied bases ever closer to Chang'an
and had taken over the best Tang pasturelands in the northwest, which
prevented the government from raising horses for its cavalry. In 763 the
Tibetans attacked and occupied the western capital. Although they soon
abandoned the city, Tibetan invasions became an annual event for the
next thirteen years, with the Chinese armies unable to match the
mounted Tibetan forces. In subsequent decades the Uighurs exploited
the Tang's loss of grasslands to Tibet by selling them inferior, sickly
horses for inflated sums. They also established what amounted to extra-
territorial rights for Uighurs and Sogdian merchants who resided in the
capital and other major cities. The enduring abuse of these privileges, and
the domination of urban money-lending by Sogdians, caused deep-seated
resentments that exploded in anti-foreign riots in the ninth century.[2]

In addition to an alliance with the Uighurs, the second great innovation that allowed the Tang court to push back and ultimately destroy the
northeastern rebels, but again with major negative consequences, was the
decision to set up military governors like those of the established frontier
commands throughout areas of the interior under Tang control. The
army that reconquered the two capitals consisted of forces from nine
military governors, of which only three held commands that had existed prior to the rebellion. Each governor also maintained control of his
own forces, coordinating with the others on a purely voluntary basis.
Moreover, neither of the two leading commanders—Guo Ziyi and Li
Guangbi—was willing to be subordinate to the other. By this time the

court was so suspicious of its generals that, rather than try to establish a supreme commander, Emperor Suzong dispatched a favorite eunuch to try to synchronize the actions of the disparate forces, to no avail.

When Shi Siming confronted the Tang armies in 759 on the central plain, a sudden dust storm led the armies on both sides to withdraw from the field, and each of the nine military governors retreated to his own base. This left Shi Siming free to eliminate An Lushan's son and reoccupy Luoyang. As a result, the rebellion dragged on for another four years. When it finally ended in 763, approximately forty military commands were distributed throughout north China, with each general holding a concurrent office as civil governor of the region under his control.[3]

Regional versus Central Power

At Suzong's death in 762, he was succeeded by Emperor Daizong (r. 762–779), who immediately made the decision to allow Uighur forces to sack Luoyang. This was not the only fateful decision Daizong would make. After rebel generals presented him with the head of Shi Siming's son, who had killed his father in 761, Daizong appointed the former insurgents as military governors across what is now Hebei and northern Henan. This action gave institutional permanence to the rebellion of the northeast and set the stage for a rivalry between the court and the military governors that would last for the rest of the Tang dynasty.[4]

The reigns of Suzong and especially Daizong were also marked by the rise of the eunuchs' power at the Tang court to unprecedented heights. Eunuchs had been forbidden to hold high office in the first century of the dynasty's rule, although Emperor Xuanzong had given high rank and power to the eunuch who had assisted his ascent to the emperorship, Gao Lishi. However, in the wake of the An Lushan rebellion, eunuchs became regular power-holders at court. Individual eunuchs such as Li Fuguo (d. 762), who controlled access to Emperor Suzong, came to participate in court decisions, make provincial appointments, and even engage in armed interventions in the imperial succession. This development took on permanent, institutional form during the Tibetan attack on Chang'an in 763, when a eunuch for the first time emerged as commander of the central army. After fleeing from the capital, Emperor Daizong was rescued by the Divine Strategy Army commanded by the eunuch Yu Chaoen. Upon his return to the city, Daizong incorporated this force into the palace guard, where it became the major component of the central army. Regularly commanded by eunuchs in the following decades, the Divine Strategy Army formed an enduring base for eunuch domination of the court.[5]

It was also under Suzong and Daizong that specialist commissioners began to play a prominent role in the financial administration of the state. In 758, a new commissioner for salt and iron was appointed to set up monopolies in the sale of these products that would produce revenue for the central court. The salt commission provided income after much of the north was lost and eventually became the chief fiscal agency of the late Tang state in the south, taking on administrative roles that made it virtually a shadow government in the lower Yangzi valley.[6]

After Emperor Daizong's death in 779, his successor, Emperor Dezong (r. 779–805), continued this effort to re-establish the fiscal foundations of the state through major reforms introduced in 780. The new system is conventionally called the two-tax system, referring to the collection of taxes twice a year according to the agricultural cycle, but it went far beyond a change in schedule. Most significant was the abandonment of an imaginary typical male adult as the unit for calculating taxes. Instead, assessments were calculated on the basis of property and cultivated land. The equal-field system, which had ceased to function as the basis for tax collection during the An Lushan rebellion, was formally abandoned, along with the jumble of surtaxes that had been tacked onto the old system to produce more revenue. For the first time in Chinese history, the government attempted to base tax revenue on actual measurements of individuals' wealth and property. A second feature of the new system was to allocate different tax quotas to different provinces. This policy, for the first time, officially recognized the existence of provinces as an intermediate level of administration between the state and the prefectures and acknowledged that economic productivity varied in the different regions of the empire.[7]

Although the new tax system, together with the salt monopoly, began to enrich the Tang state and provide the foundation for restoring central power, Dezong's first attempt to bring the governors to heel ended in failure. In the two decades following the formal end of the An Lushan rebellion, the surrendered rebel governors of Hebei in the northeast and the governors of the provinces of Pinglu in Shandong, Xiangyang in the Han River valley, and Huaixi on the upper Huai River had all become de facto rulers of their respective territories. Apart from sending tribute and taxes to the central court, they were free to administer these areas as they saw fit. They even claimed the right to name their own successors, which in practice meant that they had become hereditary rulers. The governors were not formally allied with one another and occasionally fought over land. But their common interest in preserving their regional power against the central authority of the court elicited informal cooperation whenever the court tried to interfere in their affairs, above all their rights of succession.

The first military struggle broke out in 781, when Emperor Dezong refused to recognize the heir of the recently deceased governor of Chengde in the northeast. Governors loyal to the court initially defeated the rebels, but the court's failure to sufficiently reward them and its attempt to destroy the power base of the defeated rebels caused these once-loyal governors to rebel in their turn. One of them, the governor of Huaixi, cut the canals that carried the capital's grain supply from the southeast. Dezong tried to send out the capital army under the brother of one rebel governor, but the meagre rations provided for this force led the troops to mutiny and their commander to declare a new dynasty. Dezong was forced to flee Chang'an—the third Tang emperor to do so in the span of twenty-five years—and take refuge in the northwest, accompanied by only a handful of courtiers and a small force commanded by eunuchs.

At the advice of one of these officials—the young scholar Lu Zhi (754–805), who became his chief adviser for the rest of his reign—Dezong offered amnesties to the rebel governors so that he could concentrate on defeating the mutineers in the capital. Like the An Lushan rebellion of which it was a continuation, this conflict ended in a compromise in 786 that recognized the de facto independence of the northeast and several other major provinces.[8]

Apart from beginning the fiscal revival of the Tang and failing to reverse the rise of regional powers, Dezong furthered the development of the "inner court." After his appointment of two eunuchs to command the Divine Strategy Army, the Tang army remained permanently under the command of eunuchs. Not only did eunuchs become the masters of the late Tang's central army, but they also served as the primary source of the army supervisors who were appointed to the staffs of loyal provincial governors. Indeed, most of these governors themselves were recruited from the Divine Strategy Army. Anyone who wished to attain one of these posts had to ingratiate himself with the eunuchs, often through the payment of bribes.[9]

Dezong also increasingly relied on both Hanlin Academy scholars and eunuchs to help him make decisions and then carry them out, without any interference from the official bureaucracy. While the social backgrounds and values of the academicians and eunuchs were radically opposed, these two groups shared the common attribute of being solely answerable to the emperor, who at this time was suspicious of the formal bureaucracy. His hostility toward regular bureaucrats was dramatically demonstrated in the career of Lu Zhi, who as an academician had been a close companion and leading behind-the-scenes adviser to Dezong. But once Lu Zhi was promoted to chief minister and all his remonstrances and admonitions became public, he completely alienated the emperor. By this point the emperor took advice only from people outside the bureaucracy.[10]

To ensure that decisions and actions of the inner court would not be blocked for lack of funds, Dezong sought out illegal or semi-legal contributions paid directly into his private treasury. The primary source was so-called tribute payments from governors. At the beginning of his reign, he had rejected these payments or had conspicuously transferred them to the public treasury. But in the wake of his military defeat by the governors, he switched to openly encouraging what were effectively bribes. Because tribute contributions came at the expense of regular tax quotas, they transferred wealth away from the formal bureaucracy and into the emperor's own hands. This practice, which became ever more frequent in the final century of Tang rule, entailed an implicit commonality of interest between Dezong and the rebel military governors: both sides benefited from the weakening of the formal bureaucracy and the tax structures that fed the state treasury.[11] However, this shared interest proved to be only temporary, for the funds Dezong accumulated allowed his successor to use military means to partially restore the authority of the court over the provinces.

Dezong's reign was also marked by developments in foreign relations. In the west, Dezong negotiated a treaty in 783 that recognized Tibet's conquests and thereby sought a temporary end to the annual Tibetan invasions and allowed an exchange of prisoners. However, when the Tibetans decided the next year to back the rebel military governors, this treaty became a dead letter. Dezong next attempted to deal with the Tibetans by reviving the Tang alliance with the Uighurs, to whose ruler he gave one of his daughters as a wife, as well as a lavish gift of silk. However, in 790 the

Tibetans defeated the combined Tang and Uighur forces. The Tibetan occupation of two key regional garrisons ended Chinese administration in eastern Turkestan for almost a millennium.

China's decline in the west was halted by a revived alliance with Nanzhao, an ethnically Tibeto-Burman state in what is now Yunnan. This government was originally modeled on the Tang, to whom it paid tribute, but it had gradually become a Tibetan client. In 794 Wei Gao, the Chinese governor of what is now western Sichuan, persuaded Nanzhao to switch allegiance from Tibet back to the Tang. In 795 he won a battle near modern Kunming and in 801 led an invasion of Tibet. This victory, following shortly on the death of the Tibetan king and his chief minister, brought an end to five decades of war in the west.[12]

The successful invasion of Tibet set the stage for Emperor Xianzong's (r. 805–820) attempt to restore court authority in the east and parts of the south. Emperor Dezong's death in 805 brought Xianzong to the throne, and the death in 806 of Wei Gao in Sichuan afforded him an early opportunity to reimpose the emperor's right to name the governor's successor, a decision that was ratified with a surprisingly easy military victory. The next year the Divine Strategy Army performed well in enforcing imperial commands on the governor of Zhexi in the Yangzi delta. A first attempt to intervene in the northeast led to an indecisive campaign against the province of Chengde in 809. But after a military pause of several years, Xianzong received an unexpected gift when the new governor in the northeastern province of Weibo voluntarily submitted to the court.

Between 814 and 819 the emperor fought a series of campaigns against rebel governors. His most notable victory was the defeat and incorporation of Huaixi province in the Huai River valley. This campaign lasted from 814 to 817, exhausted the imperial treasury, and by its last year became a target of universal censure at court. Only the resolve of Emperor Xianzong, the decision of the chief minister Pei Du to personally take charge of integrating the disparate armies, and General Li Su's bold strike directly at the provincial capital extracted a decisive victory from seeming disaster. Huaixi was eliminated as a province, Chengde voluntarily submitted, and a final expedition against Pinglu led that province's armies to mutiny and submit. With Pinglu now divided into three small provinces, Xianzong had successfully restored almost the whole of China, at least formally, to direct rule.[13]

Xianzong also initiated new tax policies and patterns of military administration in order to weaken the power of the provinces. When the two-tax system was initiated in 780, taxes were assessed in cash (strings of coins) to standardize amounts, but, because cash was scarce, they were often paid in goods, usually grain or cloth. The tax rates set in 780 reflected a period of high inflation that had followed in the wake of the An Lushan rebellion. But during subsequent decades of stability, abundant harvests and greater cloth production had reduced the prices of these goods. This deflation meant that peasant households had to give over larger and larger quantities of goods to the state in order to meet the cash-denominated rates fixed in 780. Since the provinces were responsible for tax collection, with the court simply setting quotas, they manipulated the conversion rate of goods to cash to maximize provincial income while paying only a fixed amount, if any, to the court. With his new tax regulations, Emperor Xianzong hoped to place limits on provincial revenue.

A second and related decree in 809 modified the distribution of tax income. Whereas previously tax income had been divided among the court, the province, and the prefecture, under the new policy provinces could receive tax income only from the prefecture of the provincial capital, which was, in turn, free from any obligations to the court. All other prefectures divided their tax income between themselves and the imperial court, with no payments to the province. This policy sought to restore a system like that of the early Tang, when the central government had dealt directly with the prefectures, and to eliminate the province as an intermediate level of administration.[14]

Xianzong's new military policy introduced after his victories in 819 followed a similar pattern. Provincial governors would command only the troops of their own prefecture, which contained their central army, and any non-Chinese troops. Lesser garrisons and forts in other prefectures of the province were to remain under the command of their prefects. This was the first time that prefects had enjoyed military powers since the Northern and Southern Dynasties. This strengthening of the prefects, as well as the abolition of the governors' power to appoint district magistrates, weakened the ability of military governors to mobilize their provinces.[15]

A correlate of Xianzong's reassertion of imperial authority and his weakening of the provinces was the continued growth of eunuch power, as the autocratic emperor increasingly relied on eunuchs to carry out his policy and impose his will on both the court and local officials. Eunuchs commanded the Divine Strategy Army, which was crucial to the revival of imperial power, and also served as army supervisors employed by the emperor to watch over his generals. The Divine Strategy Army became a standard path for official recruitment at the prefectural and provincial levels, so that those who put Xianzong's regional policies into effect were largely selected by eunuchs. The eunuchs' power was further institutionalized in the office of commissioner of privy affairs, a post established in 810 and occupied by eunuchs for the rest of the century. These commissioners constituted an informal palace council that coordinated communications between the emperor and the bureaucracy. Later in the century the commissioners came to dominate even chief ministers, although under Xianzong they were still tightly controlled.[16]

After the death of Xianzong in 820, reportedly poisoned by a eunuch but more likely a victim of Daoist alchemy gone wrong, the resurgence of imperial power ended. Xianzong's military campaigns had emptied the treasury. In 821, when three northeastern provinces rebelled, the new court decided, after a brief and unsuccessful military campaign, to do nothing. The government effectively wrote off this region. For the remainder of the dynasty these three provinces were only ceremonially attached to the empire. Hereditary succession became so conventional that it was described as "the Hebei custom," although mutiny and usurpation were also frequent modes of attaining governorships. The governors of the northeast still recognized the nominal suzerainty of the court, and the emperor's refusal to recognize a succession often provided a pretext for mutiny or rebellion. Nevertheless, imperial decrees were ignored. Thus, as the Japanese pilgrim Ennin noted, the suppression of Buddhism proclaimed by Emperor Wuzong was not carried out in the northeast.[17]

Factionalism

Three weak rulers followed Emperor Xianzong over the next two decades, all placed on the throne by eunuchs, who played a major role in every transfer of imperial power after the death of Xianzong. These three emperors were unable or unwilling to impose their policies on the court, and consequently the political history of these decades, and indeed most of the ninth century, is conventionally dominated by the theme of factionalism.

Since pre-imperial times, the term "faction" (*dang*) had been a mark of opprobrium. Officials were supposed to be single-mindedly devoted to the public good embodied in the ruler, so any alliance among them indicated selfish goals that caused moral decay in the court and the realm. While officials always formed loose coalitions to push forward their goals and purposes, a powerful ruler would punish such actions if they became too public. Thus, while loose factions or parties were a constant feature of the court, they entered into the record and became part of history only when the absence of a firm guiding hand made it safe to openly pursue, and openly discuss, alliances for political advancement. The last century of Tang rule was such a time.[18]

The most celebrated factional struggle, between the cliques of Niu Sengru (d. 847) and Li Deyu (787–850), originated in the *jinshi* examination of 821, just after the death of Xianzong. A large proportion of the successful examination candidates in that year were "sons and younger brothers" of leading figures at court. A protest by several officials, including Li Deyu, necessitated a new examination, which all but one of the successful candidates failed. The original examiners were disgraced. However, this exam was not more corrupt or subject to outside influences than other Tang examinations, which were not yet conducted according to the later Song dynasty's ideal of selection based purely on writing talent. Typically, Tang candidates provided their examiners with a list of five metropolitan officials who vouched for their character and background. They next established social relations with their examiners, paying calls on their houses, noting old links between their families, and offering them samples (often substantial) of their writings. Examiners were thus expected to have a sense of the candidates prior to the writing of papers, and even to allow this sense to predispose their later decisions. Since virtue and good conduct were supposedly more important than talent, some argued that knowledge of a candidate's background and character encouraged the selection of worthy individuals, whereas choosing solely on the basis of anonymous writing rewarded only glibness. Indeed, several leading protestors in 821 left written traces of soliciting examiners on behalf of their own candidates.[19]

Whatever the merits of the original dispute between the cliques of Niu Sengru and Li Deyu in the 820s, struggles between these two factions structured the court for the next four decades. It seems that factionalism was restricted to the top levels of the bureaucracy and was driven almost entirely by the desire to find allies who could help an official obtain a higher post and avoid exile.[20] However, court factionalism was also linked to major ceremonies associated with the examinations. In the "ceremony of gratitude," all those who passed the examination assembled at the residence of the chief examiner, where they announced their names and family backgrounds, thanked the examiner with effusive expressions of appreciation (often weeping), and received a robe and bowl. This last practice assimilated the ritual to the transmission of teaching from a Buddhist master to his leading disciple, an analogy that was reinforced by calling the examiner "abbot" (*zuozhu*) and the candidates "disciple" (*mensheng*). Such ceremonies—with their emphasis on emotional ties, personal gratitude, and lifelong debt—formed patron-client relationships among officials that were criticized by many people as leading to factions. The practice was banned temporarily when Li Deyu became chief minister under Emperor Wuzong, but it was restored as soon as Wuzong's death led to Li Deyu's dismissal, and it persisted as a standard practice until the end of the dynasty.[21]

In addition to its ties to the examination system, factionalism was closely linked to the rise of eunuch power. As eunuchs became more influential in the imperial administration, they ceased to form a single bloc but rather divided into several groups with conflicting interests: the commanders of the Divine Strategy Army, the heads of the privy purse, the commissioners of privy affairs. As the permanence of eunuch power became clear, more and more members of the regular bureaucracy accommodated themselves to this fact. Routine contacts between eunuchs and officials multiplied, and the pursuit of power generated alliances across the boundaries between the inner and outer courts.

The apogee of the intertwined problems of eunuch power and factionalism came with the Sweet Dew Incident in 835. Emperor Wenzong had been put on the throne in 827 at the age of seventeen by eunuchs who had murdered his predecessor, Emperor Jingzong. Although indebted to the eunuchs, he was troubled by their domination, and in 830 he began to discuss ways of restraining them. Growing weary of quarrels between the Niu and Li factions, between whom he alternated his support, he increasingly supported his physician and a Hanlin academician who together plotted to assassinate the leading eunuchs. The assassins were discovered, however, and the Divine Strategy Army forcibly seized control of the court. A subsequent purge based on evidence extracted by torture led to the execution of the leading conspirators and their families, along with large numbers of innocent officials. The eunuchs did not assert public control, probably out of fear of military intervention by provincial governors, but for the next five years Emperor Wenzong was, as he himself was said to have observed, the slave of his household slaves.[22]

The next two decades witnessed a modest resurgence of imperial power under two active emperors, Wuzong (r. 840–846) and Xuanzong(2) (r. 846–859; the 2 is to distinguish him from the earlier Xuanzong, whose title used a different character with the same romanization). Wuzong brought a respite to the factional disputes by appointing Li Deyu as chief minister and leaving him in place, in contrast with his indecisive predecessor, who had switched from faction to faction every few years. Li Deyu temporarily ended the Tang practice of dividing power between at least two chief ministers and was responsible for several significant achievements.

He began by restoring the management of government business to the Secretariat rather than the Hanlin scholars. He also increased his power to interfere with the composition of court histories, thereby asserting the prerogative to declare certain information "classified" so that he could act without interference. With the emperor's support and the death of the most powerful eunuch, Li Deyu gradually reduced the eunuchs' influence. In foreign policy, he availed himself of a Kirghiz victory over the Uighurs to finally eliminate their intrusions in China and to suppress the Manichean faith of which they were the patrons. He also forcibly reimposed the court's control of Zhaoyi province, home of the merchants who controlled trade between the northeast and the rest of China. And finally Li Deyu supported Wuzong's suppression of Buddhism in 845–846, a policy that benefited the court and the economy through the confiscation of huge amounts of copper and precious metals in the form of statues, along with large quantities of land, grain, and slaves. The suppression also indirectly struck at the eunuchs, who were avid Buddhist patrons.[23]

Emperor Xuanzong(2) was the uncle of the three preceding emperors. Like the Roman Emperor Claudius, he had survived to adulthood by passing as a harmless eccentric with no interest in politics. Once in power, however, he proved to be an active and intelligent ruler who was particularly devoted to the patronage of literature and who sponsored several major government compilations on administration, law, and history. Especially attentive to men who had risen through the literary exams, he was celebrated for his careful preparation before attending court and for savagely interrogating his officials. In foreign policy, his reign witnessed the final break-up of the Tibetan state, which had been the greatest adversary of the Tang since the late seventh century, and the consequent reintegration of parts of the northwest.

After the death of Xuanzong(2) in 859, the Tang empire went into its final decline. The reigns of the last three genuine emperors saw the court's power steadily shrink in the face of rising local militarism and banditry. Up until this point the post–An Lushan structure of the Tang had been defined by tension between the central court and local military governors, who tried to extend their power to act independently and control the succession in their provinces. Nevertheless, the governors remained committed to the existence of the Tang and even supported the dynasty against the increasing threat of eunuch usurpation. However, in the final half century of Tang rule the burden of supporting the court's expenses, which had fallen largely on the regions of the Yangzi River basin, led to massive impoverishment which in turn exacerbated banditry, salt smuggling, and other forms of local criminality and resistance. After 856 the Tang also suffered numerous garrison mutinies provoked by lack of pay, especially in the south, which had previously served as the foundation of late Tang power.

But banditry and mutinies were only the background conditions of the Tang's fall. A chain of southern rebellions beginning in 858 introduced the crucial social elements that finally destroyed the dynasty. In the southern province of Xuanzhou, a rebellion in 858 nominally led by the bandit Kang Quanti was in fact instigated by members of the local elite in league with local authorities. These rebels included both merchants and landowners who had purchased military staff positions. Some had also organized militia groups that they mobilized to resist the government. It was the emergence of such armed, local powers linked to local administration that undermined the foundations of the Tang. Moreover, the rebellion led to the appointment of the first military governor in the south, setting off the same trend toward local independence that had long marked the north. During a rebellion that broke out in 859 in the area south of Hangzhou Bay, rebels for the first time linked together large numbers of bandit gangs into a unified military force. To suppress it, the government mobilized local militias on a large scale. Thus, in the course of these rebellions both the state and its opponents furthered the trend of massive regional militarization.[24]

The subsequent wave of insurrections included garrison troops in the far south under Pang Xun in 868, bandits under Wang Xianzhi crisscrossing China from 874 to 878, and finally the bandit armies of Huang Chao. Between 878 and 884, Huang Chao occupied Luoyang (rebuilt after the Uighurs sacked it in 762), destroyed Chang'an through repeated pillaging, and effectively toppled the dynasty.[25] While these armies were filled with dispossessed peasants, local bandits, and mutinous garrisons, their leaders were from a counter-elite that emerged in the general social breakdown of the late Tang. This new elite combined militarized landlords, merchants who doubled as salt smugglers, and powerful local strongmen who were sometimes just bandit chiefs or armed local thugs. What they all shared was some degree of expertise in military affairs and a commitment to the virtues of "bravoes" (*xia*), an ethic of mutual loyalty, devotion to the death, and self-protection. They ranged from little more than gangsters to people like the "knights-errant" of later popular fiction for whom they provided the model. In a world of generalized violence, where the state no longer offered protection, the task fell to leaders like these. They gathered gangs or militias of a few dozen to a hundred men, to whom they often granted their own surnames, and then threw in their lot with whatever military man promised either security or wealth.[26]

While ever larger armies of bandits moved across the late Tang landscape, combining and recombining in a complicated pattern as one or the other met with success, the court's response was marked by a pattern of recurrent failure. Factionalism continued to divide the court, so that no strategy could be effectively pursued. Any commander who won a victory immediately became an object of suspicion and fear as a potential rival, so that successful commanders were never rewarded. Consequently, leading generals ceased to act as agents of the court, instead treating their armies as a personal resource with which they hoped to establish themselves as local rulers like the earlier military governors. Thus, while the court army won several victories, they did not translate into any permanent civil order. As the years passed, fewer commanders and local officials were willing to risk their lives and positions to secure a court that seemed certain to betray them. As the position of the court and the capital grew more precarious, even the eunuchs most closely tied to it devoted themselves to building up local bases in Sichuan or other safe havens. This often entailed adopting sons who acted as their local agents.[27]

With the court incapable of a sustained or coordinated defense, the burden fell upon local governments, which became mirror images of the forces against whom they fought. By the end of the Tang the entire empire was divided into armed local self-defense groups, militarized provinces, and, at the highest level, regional armies who fought one another for the privilege of founding the next dynasty. The only political actor without armed forces was the Tang ruling house itself. When his capital was burned to the ground by Huang Chao's forces in 880 and its last ruins finished off in 883, Emperor Xizong was taken by his eunuchs to Sichuan. He returned to the capital's ruins in 885, but he, along with his two successors over the next two decades, were mere puppets passed from the hands of one ambitious warlord to another. In 907 the most powerful of these warlords, Zhu Wen, was in a position to stage the abdication of a teenage ruler specially placed on the throne a few years earlier to serve this very purpose. With this act, the Tang empire formally ended.[28]

Varieties of Regional Power

The basic principle of administration in the early Tang, as in the Han, was to make administrative units so small that no locality could threaten the tranquillity of the realm. The most important level of administration was the prefecture (*zhou*), with an average size of 25,650 households or 146,800 people. Below the prefecture was the district (*xian*), with an average population of about 30,000. The officials of these units were directly answerable to the imperial government and had no armed forces at their disposal. Taxes were sent to the central government, which returned as much money as it thought necessary to meet local needs. Local officials were barred from serving in their native prefectures, where family ties and personal connections could divide their loyalty to the court. They were also periodically transferred to prevent the formation of bonds within their new locality. The same restrictions applied to the local officials' immediate subordinates. Their ultimate loyalty was to the dynasty, and securing a post in the central government remained their primary objective. Through most of the Tang, posts outside the capital, even important ones, were treated as a form of exile.

Continuity within the local administration depended not on these ambitious officials but on petty subordinate officers who never rose above their own localities. Although very low in rank, these men handled most daily government business and were indispensable repositories of local knowledge, usage, and administrative precedent. Their importance in this respect cannot be exaggerated, for variations in law and customary usage were considerable in Tang times. In many regions the magistrate could not even understand the speech of the people he ruled, so he was totally dependent on his petty officers.[29] As indispensable as clerks were to their local administration, it is unlikely that they represented the genuine interests of their locality. These posts tended to be hereditary, owing to the required literary skills and knowledge of precedent, and their holders often became a small, distinct social group. Dependent on the magistrate for prestige and power, they did not participate in any local ambitions toward autonomy.

Where a more local focus could be found was outside the walls of the prefectural or district towns, among the powerful landowning families of the countryside. Unlike subordinate officers, these families formed an integral part of the structure of rural society. Their social networks included not only other powerful clans but also small farmers, tenants, and tradesmen. Since the typical prefect had a staff of only 57 men to administer 140,000 people, he relied on the influence of these great families to arbitrate disputes and preserve order in the countryside. These families represented a more distinctively local interest, but they were generally not hostile to centralized power as such. The court's officers protected their possessions and passed much of the tax burden on to their poorer neighbors. Moreover, the threat of imperial punishment was usually enough to keep such local magnates in line.[30]

In short, the entire structure of Tang regional administration was designed to prevent the formation of any authorities representing distinctive local interests. As long as the Tang government remained firmly in control, this system worked as designed. But in the years leading up to and following the An Lushan rebellion, changes in military organization allowed regional powers to grow up along the frontier that challenged the authority of the central government (Map 8). To suppress the uprising, the government set up regional commands not only in border provinces but throughout the drainage basin of the Yellow River.[31] The empire was split up into approximately forty provinces (*dao*), and their governors were given wide powers over subordinate prefectures and districts (Map 9). The province became an intermediate level of administration between the weakened central government and the prefectural and district authorities. By the end of the Tang, when the court was stripped of all military power, real authority lay in the hands of some fifty provinces.[32]

The most independent military governors in the post–An Lushan period were four rebel generals in Hebei who, in return for surrender, were allowed to remain in command of their armies and to govern large tracts of land. In 775 one of these commands absorbed another, leaving the "three garrisons of Hebei" (Youzhou, Chengde, and Weibo). Though

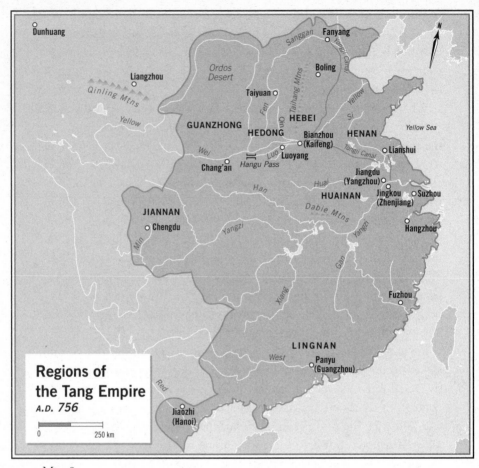

MAP 8

these former rebel leaders accepted Tang titles and owed nominal allegiance to the imperial government in Chang'an, they governed their own
territories as independent fiefdoms. They appointed their own officials,
raised armies, collected taxes, and tried to establish family dynasties
through systematic intermarriage.

Several of the leading military governors in Hebei—heirs of Li Linfu's
ethnic policy to keep rivals out of military office—were non-Chinese. The
Tang court sometimes intervened when a governor died or was driven out
by one of the frequent mutinies. However, the most it achieved was to secure a promise of a larger share of tax revenue in exchange for ratifying
the successor's position, and in practice the Tang court was never able to
extract significant revenue from the northeast. For a short time after the

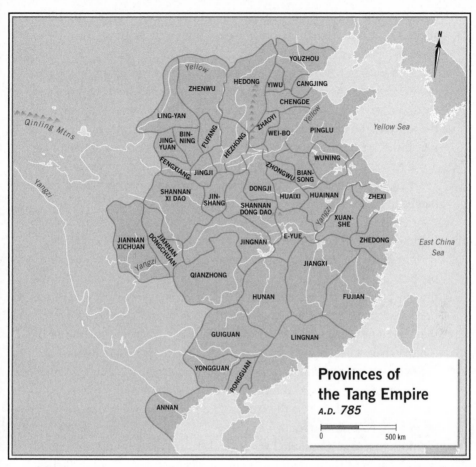

MAP 9

Yuanhe reign period (806–820), when Xianzong had crushed the independent military governors of Henan, the Hebei armies accepted court
appointees, but these were soon driven out by mutinies. The situation reverted to what it had been, and remained unchanged until the end of the
dynasty.[33]

The semi-independence of Hebei was not simply a matter of a few top
generals, for if it had been it would not have lasted very long. It was
based on a strongly held and broadly based separatist sentiment in the
Hebei armies, and perhaps in the provincial elite at large. This sentiment
probably dated back to the 690s, when the province was occupied by the
Khitans and subjected to devastating pillage for several years. Some Tang
officials argued that the Khitans' success had been due in part to local

collaboration and that the province should be left to its fate. Accounts suggest that bitter local resentment over this perceived betrayal by the court lingered for decades.

As An Lushan rose to power in Hebei, his court formed a natural magnet for those disaffected with Tang rule. Rebel forces held the province for seven years before nominally surrendering to the Tang. Settlement of the Khitans and related peoples in the region, which had already been significantly "barbarized" in the sixth century, further reduced any sense of loyalty to the Tang. Nonpayment or reduced payment of taxes to the court lightened the burden on peasants, who consequently would have had little inclination to support any Tang restoration.[34]

After the Tibetan victory of 790, the border provinces of Guanzhong became the northwest frontier of China and remained heavily garrisoned with troops from one or another of the palace armies. The governorships of these small provinces were regularly filled by military men, and although proximity to the capital, declining productivity, and small size prevented them from becoming autonomous in the manner of Hebei, they developed their own variety of local independence. During the ninth century their officer corps became a largely hereditary group. By this time deforestation, erosion, and desertification had already begun to significantly reduce the amount of arable land in the regions to the north and west of the capital, so that the armies, like the capital itself, depended on grain shipped from the south.

Another region dominated for several decades by military governors was Henan and the Shandong peninsula. The latter was controlled by the powerful Pinglu military governorship, and although this region was successfully divided into three smaller units by the Tang court in the 820s, it remained under the domination of military regionalists. Henan was largely controlled by pacified rebels who ruled as semi-autonomous governors for several decades after the rebellion. Because Hebei and Shandong enjoyed de facto independence, Henan became a key frontier zone situated between the court and the governor-generals in the northeast. It was crucial because it had no natural, easily defensible borders and was of strategic importance because of the presence of the Grand Canal, on which the capital depended for survival. Thus, the Tang court struggled to keep the Henan military governors under control by stationing large garrisons in the area, but these soldiers mutinied repeatedly in the last decades of the eighth century. Only after a series of campaigns in the second decade of the ninth century did Emperor Xianzong restore effective administration to the region. But what had once been a productive area was now depopulated, and both the local population and garrisons relied on southern grain.[35]

While Hebei, Shandong, Henan, and Guanzhong were dominated by military governors in the last century of Tang rule (Hedong remaining less militarized), as were the border provinces of Sichuan (Jiannan) to the southwest (bordering on Tibet and Nanzhao), the provinces of the Yangzi drainage basin had a very different kind of local administration. Most appointments there were not military governors but civil ones, and the military forces at their disposal were little more than token units. The men who filled these offices were largely career bureaucrats who had temporarily fallen out of favor but still hoped to return to service in the capital. In many ways they were like the prefects of the early Tang, but with one important difference. They now ruled over millions of people and, at least in the lower Yangzi (Huainan and neighbors), disposed of immense revenues. Though officials bemoaned such posts in the conventional tropes of exile poetry, they presented an opportunity to accumulate a vast personal fortune. Early in the ninth century a governor returning from the south was able to buy up whole wards of Chang'an.[36]

Even if scrupulously honest, such officials wielded great financial power, and the court was totally dependent upon them to provide both its income and sustenance. The southern governors became financial magnates able to exert tremendous economic pressure on the capital, just as the northern generals exerted military pressure. However, unlike their northern military counterparts, southern governors remained dependent on the court for appointments and hoped for an eventual return to the capital. For all their regional power, they remained agents of the court. Moreover, there is no evidence in this period that any southern region enjoyed the deep-rooted and pervasive local loyalties, the established sense of regional identity, the strong feeling of local patriotism, and the close-knit, local ruling elite that characterized Hebei, Shandong, and Guanzhong.

Military Regionalism and New Political Roles

Much of the secondary literature on the military governors focuses on the balance of power between them and the Tang court, but this consisted largely of disputes over the distribution of tax revenue and the right to appoint local officials. Revenues collected by the prefectures were first used to pay local expenses, and what was left was passed up to the province. The governor extracted his own expenses—primarily what was needed to clothe and feed his soldiers—and then sent whatever remained, if anything, to the court. The campaigns of Dezong and Xianzong to restore central authority aimed at little more than the right to place officials at the provincial level to guarantee that an adequate share of revenues reached the court. Indeed, in theory prefects were directly subordinate to the court, with the governor existing in a separate and parallel administrative track, but in practice military governors in the independent provinces asserted control over prefects. Yet even loyal provinces in the north often paid few taxes to the court, because everything was swallowed up by the extraordinary costs of paying their armies.[37]

The greatest impact of military governorships lay not in this struggle for control of revenue but in the new patterns of local power and recruitment created by military men. In the last half of the Tang, through the Five Dynasties (907–960), and into the beginning of the Song dynasty, the single most important development was that a military career became the primary avenue of advancement into local administration. Thus, the power previously wielded by established landlord families in their localities fell into the hands of military officers. The armies also gradually formed self-conscious political and social groups that asserted themselves against the conventional values of the literati. This development was furthered by the transformation of professional soldiers into a hereditary group. In the decades leading up to the An Lushan rebellion, military governors had filled their armies with long-term recruits who soon became full-time professionals. At least in Hebei and Shandong these military positions became hereditary, with son following father into the army.

This shift to lifelong and hereditary military professionals was made possible by three factors. First, the civil wars had driven hundreds of thousands of peasants from their land, and they provided a pool of ready recruits for the armies. Second, the improved productivity of agriculture based on the now almost universal practice of raising three crops in two years on the north China plain allowed for a lower ratio of peasants to soldiers. And finally, the ancient ideal of the peasant soldier that had traditionally been advocated primarily by literary men and civil officials was rejected by both peasants, who dreaded the duty, and soldiers, who admired military professionalism and had no interest in farming.[38]

Now a distinct professional group, these new soldiers espoused values

radically at odds with the civilian ideals of the old imperial elite. The sol-
diery was far more hostile to incorporation within the empire than were
the military governors, as is shown by the frequent mutinies that occurred when revenues sent to the capital threatened the soldiers' livelihood or when a military governor secured appointments for his family at
court. The 150 years between the An Lushan rebellion and the fall of the
Tang saw more than 200 recorded cases of mutinies against commanders
or military governors, and usually succession to an autonomous governorship depended on the support of the army. Thus, beneath the tension
between the court and the governors lay a new social fact, the existence
of professional armies. The interests and ambitions of these men infused
the political struggles of the period with a deeper social significance. Even
the Tang court increasingly relied on the Divine Strategy Army, which
was filled with professional soldiers and commanded by eunuch officers,
and consequently evinced values and behavior little different from those
of the military governors' forces.[39]

Serving directly under the military governors were "inner" armies
composed of elite units of the finest soldiers. Such armies became the basis of political power in the Five Dynasties that ruled north China immediately following the Tang collapse. Consequently, men from their ranks,
who lived largely outside the bounds of conventional society, emerged as
the rulers of many of the states of this period, and included the founder of
the Song dynasty. Moreover, professional soldiers in the middle ranks
served as a primary source of government officials in the Five Dynasties
and the early Song dynasty. This new source for recruitment played a major role in the disappearance from the political stage of the leading families that had dominated the Tang court.[40]

A final important development within the new armies was the use of
fictive kin ties to secure relations between a commander and his immediate followers. All the military governors and commanders of this period
had small personal armies that acted as body guards, and it was common
for the general to adopt these men as his sons, to lend authority and permanence to their social ties. Fictive kinship between commanders and
their troops had deep cultural roots that developed over the course of the
Tang. Adoption of subordinates was standard practice in Central Asian
states, and from there it was imported into the northern dynasties during
the period of division. It became even more prominent under the Tang,
whose ruling house was linked by culture and kinship to nomadic peoples. Eunuchs at court developed a similar reliance on adoptive sons to

secure their power. Fictive kinship was even more widespread and influential at the end of the Tang and in the Five Dynasties, as part of a general
social movement toward reliance on kin ties—by marriage and adoption
as well as by bloodline—to create local power bases.[41]

Militarized power in the late Tang was not limited to professional armies under the command of military governors. After the An Lushan rebellion, many governors employed peasants in village militias for local
police action and bandit control. After the first establishment by local
governments of a militia in 859 and the extension of the pattern by the
court in 876, regional militias sprang up all across China, from Sichuan,
through modern Guizhou, to many sites along the Yangzi River. These
militia units usually consisted of the personal following of members of
the local elite, often a large landowner who mobilized his tenants and
poorer neighbors. Larger defense forces emerged in some market towns,
and even larger regional forces appeared in the garrison towns. They
were often absorbed into the command structure of the provincial governor, so that the garrison town became a low-level administrative center
and its commander both an officer in the provincial army and the local
administrator. These militias, the product of local forces, were one of the
principal mechanisms whereby emerging military powers became rooted
in local society and ambitious men rose into state service.[42]

Fiscal Regionalism and New Political Roles

The final aspect of late Tang institutional reform significantly affected by
regionalism was the transformation of financial administration. The An
Lushan rebellion resulted in the flight or death of substantial numbers of
peasants in north China, the loss of extensive household and tax records
from the regions affected by the armies, and the disappearance of state
control across much of north China. This precipitated a financial crisis of
unprecedented proportions. The state resorted to stopgap measures such
as the sale of Buddhist ordinations, but in the decades that followed the
rebellion an assortment of new taxes, expanded versions of old ones, and
state monopolies were patched together to provide a revenue stream that
funded the last 150 years of the Tang dynasty. In its basic outlines it
lasted up to the Ming dynasty's founding in 1368.

The key institution in the new fiscal reforms was the two-tax system
promulgated in 780 by Emperor Dezong to replace the old equal-field
system of taxation. This new tax was in fact a fusion of the old house-

hold tax—based on a nine-degree ranking of households according to wealth—and the grain tax levied on the standard output of plots of land graded into three levels. These two taxes were merged into one cash payment, based on the wealth of the household and the size and quality of its landholdings rather than the number of adult males. It was called a two-tax system because it was paid in two installments, one in the summer after the harvesting of winter wheat and the other in the fall after the harvesting of millet.[43]

Thus, just as the amount paid was intended to correspond to the actual wealth of households and to reflect the government's recognition of unequal divisions of land and wealth, so the pattern of payment was intended to correspond to the new agricultural calendar, with its multiple harvests spread through the year. With this reform the Tang government abandoned the centuries-old ideal of peasant homogeneity and the direct administration of all households by the state. It reduced its role to that of a simple collector of revenue based on wealth. This withdrawal of the state from any attempt to directly control the day-to-day activities of the population marked one of the great changes between early imperial China and the late imperial period.

Through the household tax, which was levied without regard for the nature or origins of the wealth being taxed, the government for the first time began to regularly collect taxes on merchant wealth, an increasingly significant source of revenue. This tax also established the principle of progressive taxation—that those who had more wealth should pay not just a proportionate tax but a larger proportion of their wealth in taxes. Other taxes levied on merchants included transit taxes and taxes on certain goods, notably tea.[44]

Moreover, shortly after the An Lushan rebellion the government established a Salt and Iron Commission to administer its monopoly on these essential goods, and it later attempted to impose a monopoly on alcohol, although this failed because of the relative ease of bootlegging. Because salt production was limited to a few clearly demarcated areas, a monopoly was not difficult to enforce, except for salt pits in what is now Hebei, Sichuan, and Shaanxi that remained under the control of military governors. From the 770s on, this monopoly became one of the primary sources of revenue for the court. Indeed, income from the south—primarily derived from the salt monopoly—sustained the Tang state after it lost much of its ability to extract taxes from north China following the rebellion.[45]

This new fiscal regime became a major factor in the development of regionalism in China. In general, revenue in the north was derived largely from the two-tax system administered by the Public Revenue Department, while revenue from the south came from the salt monopoly administered by the Salt and Iron Commission. Throughout the late eighth and early ninth centuries the administrators of these two authorities battled for fiscal domination of the empire and used their tax offices as bases of local power and imperial influence. In time the salt monopoly extended its control into the minting of money, mining, the taxation of tea and other goods, and the imposition of transit taxes. In 810 an edict recognized the financial division of the empire between these two authorities when it made agents of the Salt and Iron Commission responsible for revenue from the two-tax system in the Yangzi valley.[46]

The Salt and Iron Commission not only controlled the fiscal administration of the south but also threatened to assume control of the civil administration. This new organization was independent from the old Board of Finance and indeed from almost any form of court control. It was in fact an independent bureau controlling the state's finances in central and south China. From the 780s onward, the commissioners—already the most powerful financial officers in the empire—began to receive concurrent territorial jurisdiction over the rich and productive provinces of the Yangzi delta. This combination of immense financial resources with territorial control of a vital productive region that accounted for a large part of the state's revenue was perhaps a graver threat to the dynasty than the activities of the military governors of the north, who remained loyal except for the payment of taxes.

The possibility of a regional government in the lower Yangzi valley with effective control over the bulk of the empire's revenue took concrete form in 786–787 when Han Huang, governor of a province that comprised the whole Yangzi delta, was given the concurrent post of commissioner of salt and iron. Fortunately for the dynasty, he died within three months, whereupon his province was divided into several smaller units. However, in the 790s the practice of appointing civil governors concurrently as salt commissioners was revived, and in 805 one of them led a provincial rebellion in Zhexi. He badly bungled the attempted insurgency, and after that the government was careful to separate fiscal posts from civil administration.[47]

Apart from giving rise to a distinctive southeastern pattern of regional autonomy, the new financial administration had a significant impact on several aspects of political power. Just as the new armies encouraged professionalization in the military, so the new fiscal services led to professionalization in finance. All the statesmen who controlled the Salt and Iron Commission and the Public Revenue Department rose to their positions through the experience they had gained in financial posts, and it became the pattern to select administrators from the protégés of earlier commissioners. Thus, expertise in the administration of fiscal matters, rather than in conventional bureaucracy or in the literary skills tested on examinations, became an avenue by which new men ascended to power and influence. In time these patterns of patronage and professional training were reinforced by intermarriage to create the fiscal aristocracy that would dominate Song government in the eleventh century.[48]

This tendency toward professionalization was even more pronounced at the provincial level. In addition to professional military officers, governors put fiscal specialists on their staffs who were their personal adherents. The Salt Commission and the Public Revenue Department also established local offices where experts in finance took charge of revenue from more generalist local officials.[49] Many of these new professionals were originally recruited from among merchants who in their work had developed expertise in handling accounts and using cash. Thus, although different forms of regional government emerged in the north and the south, both recruited new men from local society and thereby began the large-scale opening up of government service that would culminate in the meritocracy of the Song dynasty.

One last aspect of late Tang regionalism that involved the rise of new men was the pattern of recruiting eunuchs. As noted by several writers in the period, most of the eunuchs at court were children of families in the southern frontier regions of modern Fujian and Guangdong. Many of them, including the famous Gao Lishi, were said to be descended from non-Han peoples. This tendency was even more marked in the early decades of the ninth century, when southern aboriginal origins were imputed to large numbers of eunuchs. Thus, an 808 examination essay attacking eunuch domination said, "As for these remnants of barbarian ancestors and cripples, this rabble from remote and isolated regions with their menial posts, how can they be entrusted with the ruler's very life and the control of the armies, on the inside taking charge of the closest adviser, and on the outside serving as his eyes and ears?"[50]

Military governors, fiscal agencies, provincial governments, and even the eunuch staff offered avenues of advancement to men who could not gain office at court through the traditional hereditary means. It was these new career options, rather than the examination system, that truly spelled the end of aristocratic dominance at court. The highly diversified elites who arose during the Five Dynasties and the first century of the Song exemplified a new spirit of professionalism with roots in the late Tang. They also pioneered the practice of creating local power bases through marriage alliances, fictive kin ties, and the building up of large estates. This spirit and these practices were the means by which the nascent gentry of Song China established themselves, particularly in the twelfth century. Thus, in the career patterns and social strategies of the rising men of late Tang China we see in embryonic form the processes that would create the great gentry families of the late imperial period.

4

URBAN LIFE

THE MAJOR features of Tang cities were inherited from preceding centuries. These included the separation of political, residential, and business quarters; ritual structures to distinguish the imperial capital from other cities; and semi-public spaces provided by temples and gardens. But Tang cities also underwent major changes, most notably in the way that business and trade transformed their physical structure and their links to larger networks.

In the late sixth century the Sui dynasty began building its new capital, Daxingcheng, near the old Han city of Chang'an, which in the intervening centuries had been repeatedly sacked, burned, and rebuilt. By the time Yang Jian established the Sui, Chang'an was cramped, run-down, and suffering from a scarce and brackish water supply. The edict of 582 called for Daxingcheng's construction on a new site nearby that would allow the capital to be canonically correct according to the program articulated in *Records for the Scrutiny of Crafts* (*Kao gong ji*), the late Warring States text that described the ideal imperial capital. The Sui founder's commitment to this classicist program, which had been slighted in the planning of the Han capital, overrode the concerns of the builder, Yuwen Kai, who wanted to lay out the city in accord with proto-*fengshui* principles that he had derived from the *Canon of Change* (*Yi jing*).[1] The sole significant modification in the canonical program was the placement of the Imperial Palace, where the ruler and his family lived, along the northern wall. This had become standard since the Eastern Han, when it was introduced into the building of Luoyang, the first capital patterned on the *Scrutiny of Crafts*. The principle that the ruler should stand in the north and face south took precedence over the idea that he should be at the center.

The self-conscious classicism of Daxingcheng (whose name reverted to Chang'an under the Tang) was controversial. Placing the Sui court in Chang'an was highly problematic for an empire seeking to unite the Yellow River and Yangzi drainage basins. Already in the Han the Guanzhong region could not provision a capital and had difficult access by water transportation to the demographic, economic, and cultural centers of the empire. The increasing importance of the Yangzi region exacerbated these problems. In part, the Sui chose Guanzhong because the dynasty was a successor of the Northern Zhou state, whose elite had been based in that region. Equally important, the restoration of the capital to Chang'an marked a clear break with the intervening centuries of division and a return to the ideal of a unitary Chinese state for which the great precedent was the Western Han. The Sui's insistence on the canonical character of the new capital was also part of its program of denying recent history by appealing to an ancient model that embodied imperial China's greatest achievements.[2]

The programmatic archaism of the capital was articulated in the first of a set of ten poems on Chang'an written by the second Tang emperor, Taizong. After a preface declaring the ideal of "restoring antiquity," the emperor wrote:

> In the streams of Qin, a powerful emperor's residence,
> In Han pass, a mighty royal dwelling.

This assimilation of the Tang capital to that of the Qin or Han, which would become conventional in Tang poetry, showed the desire to see the Tang as a rebirth of the united empires. The poem itself is a tissue of clichés drawn from earlier rhapsodies on the Han capitals, mixed with unfortunate echoes of a poem on Jiankang, the ill-fated capital of the southern dynasties. Just as Taizong tried to reject the palace poetry that he had inherited from the southern dynasties but could not find another way of writing, so he wanted to reclaim the Han capital but could not escape the inheritance of the intervening centuries.[3]

The Layout of Chang'an and Luoyang

The city inherited by the Tang was aligned with the compass and ringed by an outer wall that was slightly rectangular, with east-west sides of

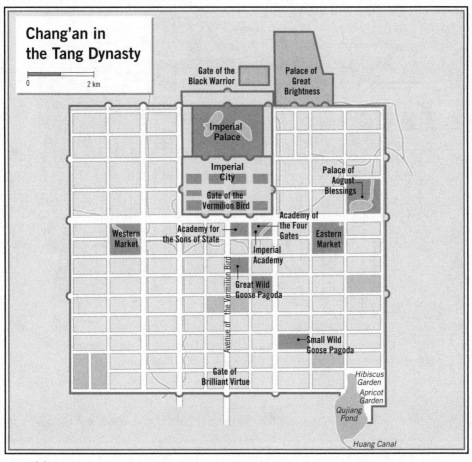

Chang'an in
the Tang Dynasty

0   2 km

Gate of the
Black Warrior

Palace of
Great
Brightness

Imperial
Palace

Imperial
City

Palace of
August
Blessings

Gate of the
Vermilion Bird

Academy of
the Four
Gates

Western
Market

Academy for
the Sons of State

Imperial
Academy

Eastern
Market

Avenue of the Vermilion Bird

Great Wild
Goose Pagoda

Small Wild
Goose Pagoda

Gate of
Brilliant Virtue

Hibiscus
Garden

Apricot
Garden

Qujiang
Pond

Huang Canal

MAP 10

5.92 miles and north-south ones of 5.27 (Map 10). The wall itself was of
packed earth, and only the timber framing of the gates and the adjacent
wall were lined with brick. Twelve gates opened into the outer city, three
into the Imperial City at the center of the northern wall (as well as two on
each side), and two between the northeastern sector of the city, filled with
the mansions of the elite, and the Palace of Great Brightness that lay just
outside the city walls. Given the brevity of the Sui reign, much of the area
inside the newly built capital walls remained empty when the dynasty fell
in 618, and many unsettled spaces remained within the Tang city walls.
In the middle of the eighth century the eight southernmost wards lining
the main north-south street still had no real housing and continued to be
farmed. Other wards were partially given over to gardens that grew me-

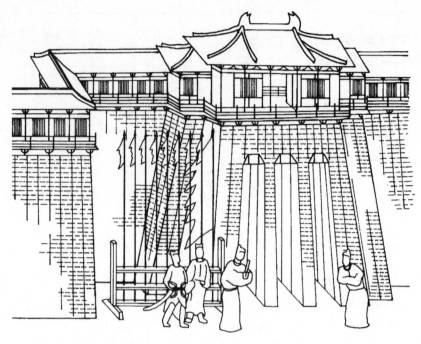

Fig. 2   Drawing of a city gate with a tower and roof covering the entrance, as
suggested by a mid-Tang painting from Cave 172 at Dunhuang.

dicinal herbs and vegetables for the palace; half of one ward was used as
a cemetery.[4]

The city itself consisted of four elements: the Imperial Palace and later
two additional palace districts, the Imperial City where the offices of the
government were located, two markets (Eastern and Western), and the
residential city, which consisted of a grid of walled wards. The Imperial
City lay immediately south of the Imperial Palace, separated from it by a
large open square where the emperor performed certain rituals. The Imperial City contained not only the offices of civil and military officials but
also the headquarters of the palace guard, the residence and offices of the
crown prince, the ancestral temple, and the altars of state.[5] The Imperial
Palace and City were separated from commoners by walls more than 33
feet high, with even higher gates (Fig. 2). No one was allowed into the
Imperial City without permission. Even climbing to a high place in order
to look into these districts was punishable by one year's imprisonment.[6]

The commoners' city was laid out in a full-blown grid pattern that, in
less perfect form, had characterized major Chinese cities for centuries.

Fig. 3   Drawing of a wall painting in Cave 85 at Dunhuang, which depicts a Buddhist paradise laid out in a grid of wards, suggestive of the layout of the Tang capital Chang'an.

The eighth-century poet Du Fu began a poem lamenting the sorry state of the capital after the An Lushan rebellion by saying, "Indeed Chang'an looks like a chess-board." This grid was formed by fourteen east-west and eleven north-south roads that divided the city into wards. The six largest roads, which led to city gates, were collectively known as the Six Avenues. The greatest of them, the Avenue of the Vermilion Bird, was over 150 meters wide and divided the city into eastern and western halves. Like the dynasty's network of intercity roads, these avenues were made of packed earth that was raised in the center and lined by substantial ditches for water runoff. These ditches provided not only drainage but irrigation for the shade trees planted alongside the streets (Fig. 3).[7]

The wards varied in size depending on their location. The largest, to either side of the Imperial City, were about 3,280 by 2,620 feet, while the smallest along the Avenue of the Vermilion Bird were only 1,940 by 1,650 feet. Each ward was surrounded by walls of rammed earth, nine or ten feet high, designed to keep the populace under control, particularly at night. Each of the four walls was pierced by a gate, and their roads converged at the ward's center, dividing it into four quadrants. A headman of each ward was entrusted with keys to the gates, which he locked at night. The penalty for climbing the wall was ninety blows with a thick rod.[8]

Beginning in 636, the opening and closing of the wards was signaled by prolonged drumming along each of the major thoroughfares, which gave people sufficient time to return to their homes at dusk or prepare to set out in the morning. The way these hundreds of drumbeats fixed the daily rhythms of people's lives, and of the cosmos itself, is dramatized in a poem "Drums in the Streets of the Officials" by Li He (791–817):

> Drums at dawn rumbling like thunder, hastening the sun,
> Drums at dusk rumbling like thunder, calling out the moon.

Only commissioners bearing official documents, wedding processions with special permission, people seeking a doctor, and those announcing a death were permitted to travel on the main roads at night. Anyone else sighted by the patrols would be given a warning twang of the bow, followed by a warning arrow, and then would be shot down. The exception was the Lantern Festival on the fourteenth, fifteenth, and sixteenth days of the first lunar month, when people were permitted to freely stroll from temple to temple at night to view the lanterns.[9]

After being subdivided by the crossing of two main roads, most residential wards had no further grid pattern; winding alleys filled in the rest of the space. Within their home ward, commoners were free to move about as they pleased at all hours. Wards were divided into smaller units called *li* for the purpose of tax collection and mutual surveillance, under the supervision of a headman. Ward gates were a choice location for shops, which benefited from the channeling of traffic past their doors. In the celebrated literary tale "Ms. Ren," the hero spends the night with a fox spirit and arrives at his ward gate shortly before dawn. Because the gate is still closed, he avails himself of a shop by the gate selling Turkish pastries.[10]

Buddhist and Daoist temples, as well as the dwellings of officials above the third rank, were permitted to have their own gates opening directly onto the main streets, indicating that these buildings were not subject to curfew. Most aristocrats and high-ranking officials lived in the northeastern wards, in the triangle formed by the Imperial Palace and Imperial City on the west, the Palace of Great Brightness to the north, and the Palace of August Blessings to the east. Elite residences could also be found just to the south of this triangle, in the area around the Eastern Market.

Fig. 4   Pottery sculpture of a garden landscape.

One ward along the northeast wall was particularly desirable, because an eminent fortuneteller of the Sui had detected an aura of nobility there. The southernmost wards along the Avenue of the Vermilion Bird and those to the far southwest were lightly populated and still contained arable land. Wards in the far southeast clustered around the Qujiang (Curved River) Pond, also sparsely populated, were devoted to gardens— the most celebrated being the Apricot and Hibiscus gardens—and other scenic venues (Fig. 4). Commoners lived primarily in the western wards. The areas around the Western Market and the northwestern gates were heavily populated by non-Chinese.[11]

The wards immediately to the west of the Eastern Market contained the city's major educational establishments, which served to prepare future officials for posts and, later, students for examinations. These schools also played an important role in Tang foreign relations. Their students included the offspring of Tang subjects of non-Han ancestry, who were to be assimilated into Chinese culture through study of the classics and literature. Also numerous were sons of foreign royalty or nobility who were sent to Chang'an as hostages. After years or decades studying Chinese literary culture in the schools and later in offices at court, these young men would be sent back to their homelands where they could put in place government institutions modeled on the Tang and disseminate the Chinese writing system and its classics. Many foreign students, notably from Korea and Japan, also came voluntarily to absorb High Tang culture. In addition to the imperial academies, major Buddhist temples provided education that attracted thousands of foreign believers. After long periods in the Tang capital, these students carried religious doctrines and other elements of Chinese and Buddhist culture back to their homelands.[12]

The city also contained many destitute people and beggars who had drifted in from the countryside. No evidence indicates the numbers of such people, but some of those who became involved with the elite turned up in the anecdotal literature. One story tells of an old man and his daughter who sang in the streets to eke out a living. A general, entranced by the beauty of the woman's voice, took her into his home as a private entertainer and concubine. The hero of "The Tale of Li Wa" (*Li Wa zhuan*) finds a position as a professional mourner and lives in the funeral hall when he is left destitute; later, he becomes a beggar. The scale of the capital's homeless problem was large enough to catch the attention of Emperor Xuanzong, who banned beggars from the streets in 734, entrusting them to special wards for the sick managed by the Buddhist order. Food relief came from nearby fields farmed by newly settled peasants. However, this welfare program ended with the outbreak of the An Lushan rebellion.[13]

In addition to official buildings, residences, academies, agricultural fields, and scenic gardens, Tang Chang'an also contained many religious institutions (Map 11). A handful of these served the spiritual needs of resident foreigners—such as temples for Zoroastrianism, Manicheism, and Nestorianism—but most were dedicated to Daoism and, above all, Buddhism. Daoism was the most exalted religion in Tang China, owing to the imperial family's claim to be descendants of Laozi, who had become a central Daoist deity. The vast majority of Daoist temples were imperial foundations established to celebrate auspicious events, commemorate the

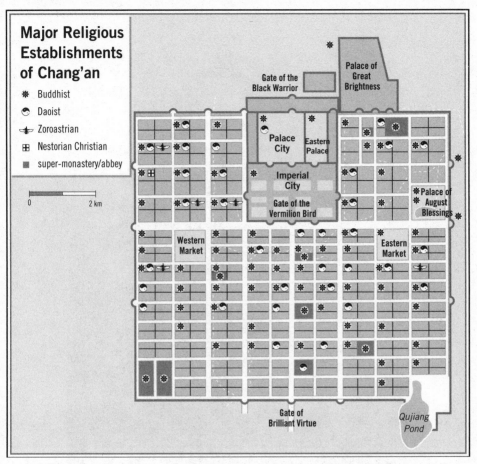

Major Religious Establishments of Chang'an

✳ Buddhist
☯ Daoist
⚜ Zoroastrian
⊞ Nestorian Christian
▦ super-monastery/abbey

0   2 km

Gate of the Black Warrior

Palace of Great Brightness

Palace City
Eastern Palace

Imperial City

Gate of the Vermilion Bird

Palace of August Blessings

Western Market

Eastern Market

Gate of Brilliant Virtue

Qujiang Pond

MAP 11

death of an imperial relative, and accommodate favorite religious masters or ordained members of the imperial family. Several were founded by imperial princesses who became nuns and abbesses of their own foundations.

Despite the official pre-eminence of Daoism, Buddhist foundations were three to five times more numerous (depending on the source consulted) and much wider in their patronage. Most wards had at least one Buddhist temple, and the Japanese pilgrim Ennin said there were three hundred in the city.[14] While this is probably an exaggeration, and nothing like the more than 1,300 temples in Luoyang under the Northern Wei state, temples were a major feature of the cityscape, and their pagodas were the tallest structures in the city. The Great and Small Goose Pagodas

Fig. 5   The Great Goose Pagoda in Chang'an.

are the only structures of the Tang capital that have survived to the present day (Figs. 5 and 6). The visual impression made by the former was described in a poem by Cen Shen (715–770):

> In shape the pagoda seems to bubble up
> High and alone, jutting to Heaven's palaces.
> I climb for the view and bypass the world's bounds

Fig. 6   The Small Goose Pagoda in Chang'an.

On a stairway of stone that winds through the void.
Up-thrusting, it weighs down the holy domain,
Towering as though of demon's work.
Its four corner eaves blot out the bright sun,
Its seventh story rubs the blue sky's vault.[15]

Other religious structures that played a crucial role in Chang'an were
the major ritual centers of the government, both inside the wall and in
the city's immediate suburbs (Map 12). The imperial capital was distinguished from other cities by its role as the site for the great rituals that
embodied the cosmic role of the ruler as Son of Heaven and of the impe-

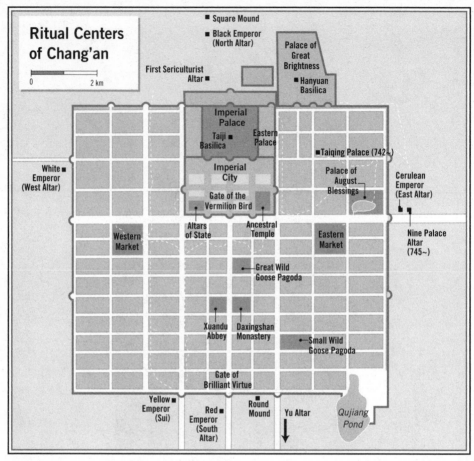

Ritual Centers of Chang'an

MAP 12

rial house as holder of the Mandate. The chief codification of Tang imperial ritual, the *Rituals of the Great Tang in the Kaiyuan Reign Period (Da
Tang kaiyuan li)* of the mid-eighth century, lists some dozen major ritual
sites in and around the capital, including the Ancestral Temple, Altars of
State, Altars to the First Agriculturist and Sericulturalist, Bright Hall,
suburban altars in each of the four directions, and the southern Round
Mound for the cult of Heaven.[16]

Chang'an had two major official markets, symmetrically placed to the
east and west of the Avenue of the Vermilion Bird. These walled areas
were administered by an official staff who guaranteed that goods on sale
met legal standards and that all measures and currency were proper.
Records of transactions were filed with these officials, who were also

charged with preventing collusion or price-fixing. The opening of the market at midday and its closing at dusk were signaled with three hundred beats of the drum. As in earlier dynasties, the market was also the site for public executions and the display of the heads and corpses of criminals.[17]

Each market was about twice the size of one of the smaller residential wards and was surrounded by wider-than-usual roads to accommodate crowds and prevent congestion. Market walls were pierced by two gates on each side, and roads running from gate to gate divided the market into a grid of nine squares. These squares were in turn subdivided into lanes (*hang*), with each category of trade grouped in its own lane, as in the earlier Qin and Han markets. The different trades were marked with legally stipulated signage. The surviving literature records the presence of butchers, apothecaries, axe makers, saddlers, goldsmiths, silversmiths, fishmongers, and makers of clothing, among others. Depending on their status, the shops were built facing the main streets or the internal lanes. Some shops, especially businesses that made secured loans, were owned by Buddhist monasteries. Warehouses and wholesale outlets lined the outer walls of the markets, and similar facilities were provided in many larger inns nearby.[18]

While the Eastern and Western Markets were the major sites for commerce in Tang Chang'an, they were not the only ones. Smaller markets, called the Southern Market and the Middle Market, were opened for certain periods in the seventh and eighth centuries, and there was also a Northern Market in the suburbs. Thus, four markets operated in Chang'an at certain times.[19] More significant, however, was the commerce conducted outside the markets, within the residential wards (Maps 13 and 14). Inns that also functioned as warehouses were located there, as were a variety of hostels and lodging places for travelers. Even more common were wine shops and restaurants, as well as street vendors offering food. Small shops within the wards selling breads or pastries operated in the hours when the markets were closed. The emerging custom of tea drinking led to the appearance of teahouses both in the major markets and in some residential wards. Shopkeepers specializing in funerary wares, along with brewers, musical instrument makers, ironmongers, copyists of Buddhist scriptures, and other craft enterprises, were scattered throughout the residential wards.[20]

Chang'an was the primary capital and the best documented both textually and archaeologically. However, the eastern capital, Luoyang, was

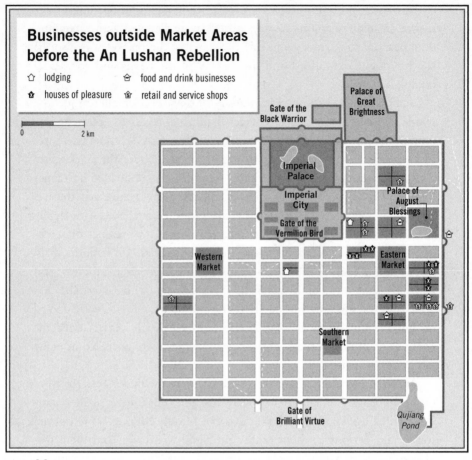

Businesses outside Market Areas before the An Lushan Rebellion

⌂ lodging   🏠 food and drink businesses

🏠 houses of pleasure   🏠 retail and service shops

0   2 km

Palace of Great Brightness

Gate of the Black Warrior

Imperial Palace

Imperial City

Palace of August Blessings

Gate of the Vermilion Bird

Western Market

Eastern Market

Southern Market

Gate of Brilliant Virtue

Qujiang Pond

MAP 13

also a thriving metropolis, especially during the reign of Empress Wu. Its revival as a capital was closely linked with the figure of the Sui Emperor Yang, whose extravagance was blamed for the fall of that dynasty. Luoyang had been burned to the ground in the mid-sixth century during the civil war that destroyed the Northern Wei. In rebuilding the capital, Emperor Yang filled it with extravagant palaces and gardens, according to hostile reports:

> Every month the Emperor conscripted two million laborers. In order to fill the new capital he moved in the people from the suburban areas of Luozhou [around the city] and several ten thousand families of rich merchants and great traders from all the prefectures of the

MAP 14

empire . . . Unbroken processions [of laborers] extended one after another for a thousand *li*. Among the laborers drafted for the eastern capital, four or five out of every ten fell prostrate and died on account of being under such great pressure. Every month in carrying the dead bodies east to Chengkao and north to Heyang [along the Yellow River] the carts were always in view of each other on the road.[21]

As this critical account indicates, Luoyang was closely associated with the mercantile wealth of the south, to which it was tied by the Grand Canal. This was part of a more general suspicion that the city was too closely tied to southern culture, which during the Tang combined images

of refinement with a sense of corruption and decadence. However, the
secondary capital also enjoyed ties to the venerable Zhou state of the central plain, the spiritual center of Chinese civilization since ancient times,
and for this reason many people considered Luoyang to be culturally superior to Chang'an.

Luoyang shared many structural features with the primary capital: a
roughly square outer wall, an Imperial Palace and Imperial City walled
off from the commoners' city, a grid of wards, several regulated markets,
and numerous Buddhist and Daoist temples (Map 15). As in Chang'an,
the main gardens and scenic preserves were in the southeastern corner of
the city. The Imperial Palace and Imperial City were even more clearly
separated from the larger city than in Chang'an because they were imme-

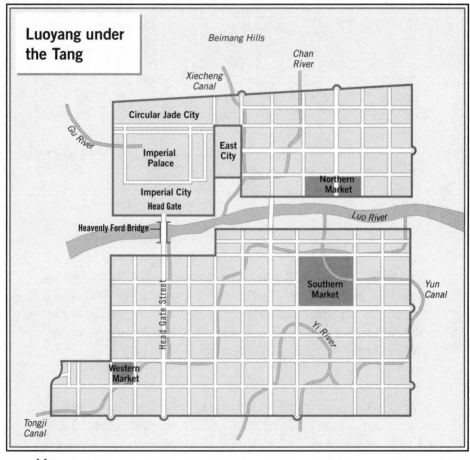

MAP 15

diately north of the Luo River. And to connect with the imperial park, they were placed in the northwestern corner. The residential wards of Luoyang were smaller, allowing for tighter control of the population, and the streets narrower.

The main difference from Chang'an was the relation of the eastern capital and its markets to the water network upon which interregional trade relied. Luoyang had three official markets, all situated for access to water transport. The Northern Market was immediately north of the Luo River, the Southern Market was two wards to the south but connected to the river by a canal, and (after 610) the Western Market in the southwest of the city was placed directly on the Tongji Canal, the section of the Grand Canal that connected the Yellow River to the Huai River.[22] Thus, Luoyang's markets and government offices were located for practical convenience rather than considerations of symmetry. Not only was the eastern capital in a more productive region of China and better situated for shipments from the south, but the city itself was shaped to a much greater degree by the needs of commerce and transportation. In this way it was a hybrid of a classical capital and the new trade-based city that emerged in connection with large-scale water transport in the Tang.

The Pleasure Quarters of Chang'an

Specialized pleasure quarters as the center of a large trade in alcohol and sex were not an innovation in the Sui and Tang, but earlier dynasties have left us little information other than the names of these districts.[23] Fortunately, at the end of the Tang a man named Sun Qi wrote a detailed account of life in the ward that housed the highest levels of the sex trade in Chang'an. According to this *Record of the Northern Hamlet* (*Bei li zhi*), the women working there were government-registered courtesans who served officials, wealthy merchants, nobles, and above all candidates for the civil service examinations. These women were trained in the composition of verse and the performance of music and thus were cultural ancestresses of the celebrated literary courtesans of the Ming dynasty as well as Japanese geishas. Lower on the social scale were common prostitutes, entertainers, and bar maids, who worked in brothels and bars throughout the city, though we have only scattered references to them in verse and anecdote.[24]

The "Northern Hamlet" (a literary term referring to areas dedicated to the sex trade, dating back to the Han) was located in the northeast quadrant of a ward between the Imperial City and the Eastern Market (see Map 14). The Directorate for the Education of the Sons of State, where examination candidates studied, and the examination halls themselves (located inside the Imperial City) were both close to this ward, so candidates often rented lodgings nearby. The district itself consisted of three parallel east-west lanes where the courtesans lodged with madams. The houses that were successful in business were spacious, with multiple salons for receiving guests and smaller rooms for the private entertainment of those willing to pay. If business did not go well, as in the case of one house described by Sun Qi, the women supplemented their income by selling herbs and fruit.

References to the economic structure of the sex trade are scattered throughout Sun's work. The courtesans were sold as children to their madams, who were called "mothers" of their "daughter" prostitutes. Consequently, the courtesans themselves were often described as elder or younger "sisters." Some were sold by poor families, others were recruited from beggars, and some were daughters of good families who had betrothed them for a bride price to a man who then resold them for profit to the madam. Should a woman desire to leave the profession, she had to pay back her purchase price, often with accumulated interest. Even to leave the house for a day—usually to visit a nearby Buddhist temple—she had to make a substantial payment to her "mother."

The standard fee for a banquet at a brothel was 1,600 cash, and double that for any first-time guest. Musicians who lived near the district were usually brought in, and they had to be paid by the client as well. Each round of drinks cost another 1,200 cash, and the price doubled after the first set of candles burned out. Thus, a single evening's entertainment could cost a huge sum, and Sun Qi noted cases where madams seized the carriages and even the clothing of customers who outspent their means. Even worse fates befell some unlucky visitors to the pleasure district. Sun Qi tells of men who were murdered by another guest—in a case of mistaken identity—or by a prostitute and her madam. Men who desired to establish a more lasting relationship with a favored prostitute sometimes entered into mock marriages; the men were often described as "brides" in a carnivalesque inversion of conventional practice.

Most inhabitants of the pleasure district aspired to ultimately escape, often by finding enamored patrons who would take them as concubines or, in some cases, legally marry them. The husband-to-be redeemed his new bride by paying off her purchase price. Later, if the noble patron

grew bored with his new concubine or she engaged in an illicit liaison
with another man, he paid her off with a lump sum or arranged a marriage with someone lower in the social hierarchy. He could in theory take
her to court for adultery, but the embarrassment involved usually prevented such action. Some women, having spent their settlements or having become dissatisfied with the humble life of their second household,
returned to their former work in the pleasure district.

Other literary sources show that not all government-licensed courtesans resided in the Northern Hamlet. One woman—celebrated for her
matchless talents as a singer, dancer, and hostess at banquets—lived in a
ward along the southeast wall of the capital. The sons of the nobility and
officials reportedly squandered vast fortunes in seeking out her company.
The southeast quadrant became a secondary unofficial district for prostitution, perhaps due to its public gardens and scenic preserves. The celebrated poetess Yu Xuanji was apparently not a licensed prostitute, but as
a paid singer and dancer she entertained the same clientele that patron-
ized the Northern Hamlet. After a brief period as a concubine, she returned to the capital to become a Daoist nun. But Yu Xuanji continued to
entertain officials and men of talent, including the celebrated poet Wen
Tingyun, for whom she wrote the following verse, in which she addressed
Wen as the famous third-century poet and essayist Xi Kang:

> By the stones of the stairs, the crowded crickets chirp,
> On the trees in the courtyard, the misty dew is clear.
> Under the moonlight, nearby music is heard,
> From my room, distant mountains are bright.
> A chill breeze settles on the pearly mat,
> A message of regret rises from the jade zither.
> If you, my Xi Kang, are too lazy to drop me a note,
> What else will assuage my autumn feelings?[25]

The *Record of the Northern Hamlet* also offers a window onto an important aspect of life in the Tang capital: the link between the sex trade
and the new examination culture. Special examinations at court had been
employed by the Chinese government since Han times, and occasional
exams in regional cities had been a means of recruiting talent. However,
in the Sui and Tang dynasties examinations became a regular (although
not the most common) means of recruiting officials. From the period
when Empress Wu dominated the court, examinations became a presti-

gious "fast track" to the highest offices. But there were no local examinations or public education to prepare candidates in the provinces, as there would be under the Song dynasty. The only schools to prepare for the exams were in the capital. Moreover, candidates went through a lengthy process of introducing themselves and presenting samples of their best writing to the examiners. Consequently, examination candidates in their late teens or early twenties had to spend protracted periods in the capital city, separated from families who often provided them with substantial sums of money. For young men in these circumstances, the pleasures offered by licensed courtesans in the Northern Hamlet—social, cultural, and carnal—were almost impossible to resist.

A celebrated story that serves as a parable on this intertwining of examinations, prostitution, and the hazardous transition to adulthood is "The Tale of Li Wa."[26] A young scholar is sent to the city by a father who dreams that the son's examination success will make his family's fortune. A chance encounter with the prostitute Li Wa, with whom he enters into a mock marriage, leads him to take up a life among entertainers and courtesans that soon exhausts his wealth. Tricked and abandoned by his new "family," he falls desperately ill until rescued by workers in a funeral parlor, where he eventually becomes employed as a professional mourner. At a competition between the leading funeral parlors, he wins the prize as the most moving singer of mourning songs, a parody of the examination success to which he originally aspired. An old servant recognizes the young scholar and identifies him to the father, who had failed to recognize his own son. Outraged, the father takes his son to the Apricot Garden (where examination candidates consorted with prostitutes and eventually celebrated their success) and beats him, leaving him for dead. Li Wa discovers her "husband" near death and, repenting her treachery, pays to redeem herself from her madam. Playing the role of a true mother, she nurses the scholar back to health and prepares him for the examinations. His academic triumph leads to reconciliation with his father and eventually a fairy-tale marriage to Li Wa.

This story dramatizes several aspects of Tang urban life beyond the temptations facing young examination candidates from the countryside. One of the most notable is the manner in which money defines all social ties. The scholar's relation to his father is a mirror image of Li Wa's relation to her "mother," each child being the means by which the parent hopes to become rich. Similarly, the first "marriage" to Li Wa, as a purely financial transaction, parodies arranged marriages among the elite. The tricking and abandonment of the scholar hinges on the rapid hiring and relinquishing of rental quarters, a feature of city life in which the seeming solidity of land and buildings masks an impermanent, floating population. At the funeral parlor, the duty to mourn one's dead kin—the most important of human obligations in Chinese society—devolves into yet another cash transaction in which mourning is provided by hired professionals.

An anecdote in the *Record of the Northern Hamlet* further illustrates the commercialization of love and friendship in the Tang capital. The courtesan Yan Lingbin was a skilled poet who collected verses from examination candidates. When she fell ill and was soon to die, she held a banquet at which she requested that all the men present write funeral dirges for her. Since it was conventional for someone in her position to request money to help pay for her funeral, members of her professional household were outraged by her willingness to accept poetry in place of cash. Her "mother" threw away all the dirges sent by her clients, but a hunchback musician romantically linked to Lingbin collected the discarded poems, set them to music, and arranged for their performance in her funeral procession. The songs spread throughout Chang'an and were performed by many professional mourners for years to come. This story demonstrates the confusion of love, poetry, and cash in the economy of the pleasure quarters, the prevalence of verses being set to music, and, again, the role of professional mourners in Tang ritual.[27]

But the Northern Hamlet was first and foremost a place where young men could meet *one another*, form friendships, show off their poetic talents, and make social connections. Gatherings there were both a preliminary and an adjunct to the examinations, which in addition to providing access to the highest positions at court also served to form lifelong ties with fellow candidates and the examiners. Elaborate banquets bringing together candidates and courtesans were organized by both successful and unsuccessful candidates (as celebration or consolation) and cemented alliances that might endure through long political careers. These banquets followed the same pattern as those staged by prostitutes in the pleasure district, so that some of the same anecdotes figure both in Wang Dingbao's record of rituals related to examinations and in Sun Qi's account of the Northern Hamlet.[28]

This linkage of the exams to the pleasure quarters is articulated most clearly in a poem written in response to the sight of a verse inscribed by Cui Chuixiu on a prostitute's thigh:

> Below the pagodas of Mercy Temple, close by, a plastered wall;
> Smooth and supple, gleaming white, quite surpassing jade.
> But why should this Mister Cui, fortieth of his rank in Boling
> [home of the Cuis],
> Engage in Ouyang's brushwork on this golden-hillock thigh?[29]

It was customary for successful examination candidates to inscribe their names on the wall of the pagoda at Mercy Temple, so here the concubine's thigh figures as the wall on which examination triumphs are inscribed. This anecdote dramatizes the courtesan's body as a site of masculine competition, and the examinations as a locus of carnal desire.

Another aspect of capital life dramatized in "The Tale of Li Wa" was the connection between examination success and marriage. After punctuating years of study with relaxation among the courtesans and then celebrating examination success with banquets in the pleasure district, young men replaced the temporary liaisons or pseudo-marriages of their student days with actual weddings to respectable women. Exam degrees became the leading criterion in the Tang for selecting sons-in-law, and between half and two-thirds of each year's graduates used their academic success to confirm conditional betrothals to the daughters of eminent families. These engagements were celebrated in a large equestrian parade of future sons-in-law that was integrated into the formal round of examination ceremonies. Indeed, pursuit of an exalted marriage may have motivated exam participation as much as pursuit of a government office.[30]

The culmination of examination success in marriage forms the dramatic climax of a song lyric by Wei Zhuang:

> Drums move through the street, the Forbidden City opens,
> Visitors return from Heaven.
> Phoenixes holding golden tablets emerge from the clouds;
> Suddenly a single clap of thunder.
> The warblers are banished, the dragons transformed.
> All night, chariots and horses fill the city,
> Crowds of exquisite beauties on the towers of every family
> Vying to watch the "Cranes Soar to the Skies."[31]

The phoenixes, dragons, and cranes in this verse all refer to successful examination candidates, who have just received their "golden tablets" from the emperor. Their triumph culminates with crowds of daughters from wealthy families struggling to catch a glimpse of these hugely desirable new heroes.

A final aspect of Tang capital life, and of elite life in general, that figures in the tales of scholar-courtesan liaisons was the sexualization of poetic and musical performance. After the fall of the Han dynasty, lyric verse had emerged as a leading form of social exchange and refined conversation between friends. From at least the sixth century, this exchange increasingly took the form of remarks on erotic themes and flirtation between the sexes. The translation of social conversation into sexual banter is the single greatest theme of the *Record of the Northern Hamlet.* Certain prostitutes were celebrated for their skill in presiding over the banquets of the pleasure quarters, guiding the conversations, introducing and participating in games of verse composition, and chastising those whose language or conduct offended the literati ideals of the company. According to Sun Qi, prostitutes who were not physically attractive often won devoted admirers or lovers through their skill in conversation and poetic composition. These stories celebrated not just the charms and talents of the courtesans but the cultural sensitivity of their admirers, who valued linguistic skill over mere fleshly beauty. The courtesan quarters thus provided a self-image of literati society, where appreciation of true character and skill in verse formed a counter-society to that of mere power or wealth.[32]

The pairing of courtesan and scholar, marked in their shared exchange of lyric verse or song, was the central theme of one of the most celebrated Tang poems, Bo (Bai) Juyi's "Ballad of the Pipa." The poet describes his encounter with a woman who was once a celebrated courtesan in the capital but has now become the wife of a traveling merchant. In her playing of the pipa (a form of lute; Fig. 7) and the heart-breaking narration of her experiences, the poet recognizes the tale of his own life. In another lyric contrasting a youthful prostitute with her hoary client, Bo Juyi sees in the plight of a courtesan his own melancholy fate as an aging poet:

> Dark beauty, young miss Xie,
> White-haired old Gentleman Cui.
> He brags he loves the snow of her breasts,
> But what of the frost on his head?[33]

Links between courtesans and poet-officials remained a feature of Chinese society throughout the late imperial period.

Fig. 7   Pottery figurine of woman
pipa (lute) player.

Government-licensed courtesans in the Northern Hamlet were not the
only professional female performers in the Tang. Official documents
tell of women who sang, played musical instruments, or danced in the
Pear Garden or other government facilities as "court entertainers." These
women were apparently not prostitutes. The state also employed women
as "official entertainers" and "camp entertainers" to provide music,
company, and sex for officials and military men. Many acrobats—notably tightrope walkers and people who performed tumbling tricks while
balanced on suspended poles—were also women. Most performers of
"transformation texts," mixed verse and prose stories accompanied by
illustrations, seem to have been women. Moreover, wealthy men pos-

sessed female "family entertainers," some of whom are described in the poetry of their owners.[34]

In private bars and brothels outside the pleasure district, women worked for money as owners, barmaids, entertainers, and prostitutes, although the lines among these occupations were often not clear. Many such women were mentioned in passing or described in detail by Tang poets, most notably Li Bo (Bai) and Du Mu. One anecdote portrays the interplay of verse, song, and sex in the public bars. Three celebrated poets—Wang Changling, Gao Shi, and Wang Zhihuan—were drinking in a tavern when a group of instrumentalists and four lovely singing girls entered the room. The women began to sing some of the most celebrated quatrains of the age, while the poets, laughing and exclaiming, kept count of which poet's verses the girls performed. Finally, the musicians inquired about the source of the amusement, and, upon discovering who the men were, the instrumentalists and singers joined them for drinking and socializing.[35]

As music became more important in the life of the capital and other Tang cities, individual star performers emerged in the literary record. The names of dancers and comical storytellers also appeared, but the most celebrated performers were musicians (Fig. 8). When a leading player of the transverse flute gained the attention of Emperor Xuanzong, the manner by which they met became the subject of poems and stories, and these ultimately were incorporated into the celebrated Qing dynasty drama *The Hall of Eternal Life* (*Chang sheng dian*). According to another anecdote, a lute competition was staged as part of an imperial ceremony to secure rain, and the winners received an audience with the emperor.

The poet Liu Yuxi described a particularly celebrated lute player thus:

> The big strings sound mournful, the little ones clear,
> So one thinks of snow swirling in the wind.
> Whoever has once heard Cao Gang play the piece *Bomei*
> Will for the rest of his life never be willing to leave the capital.[36]

The poet depicts the performances of this star as a life-changing experience of a kind that only China's greatest city could offer (Fig. 9).

A Passion for Flowers

Art and eroticism in Chang'an's pleasure district were often fused with a passion for flowering plants. Courtesans and singing girls were routinely

Fig. 8   Pottery figurines of female musicians and dancers.

associated with the fragrance and beauty of flowers as both a metaphor for their appearance and a tool of their trade. The first great anthology of the courtesan-linked song lyric was entitled *Among the Flowers* (*Hua jian ji*), and most of the poems it contains refer to flowers of both kinds.[37] But the significance of flowers in Tang cities went far beyond bars and brothels.

Flowers were generally not a major element in Chinese gardens, which were devoted to the skillful arrangement of rocks, water, and greenery. Instead, flowering plants were used to decorate houses, temples, public parks, and ponds. Of all the flowers used to decorate such sites, the most important was the tree peony (*mudan*), as Liu Yuxi's "Praise of the Peony" explains:

> The milk-peony in front of the courtyard is entrancing but without
>   style,
> The lotus on the pond is pure, but lacking in feelings.
> Only the tree peony is the most beautiful in the land,
> When it opens its blossoms, the whole capital stirs into motion.[38]

Fig. 9   Drawing of a female
musician playing the panpipes.

China's tree peony craze started with the Sui and Tang emperors and
spread throughout metropolitan society. It was not an emblem of spiritu-
ality, like the lotus (associated with Buddhism), but of riches and honor,
as indicated by its nickname "flower of wealth and honor" (*fugui hua*).
The poem's reference to the whole capital being stirred into motion al-
ludes to the fact that every year in the middle of the third month the population of Chang'an mounted horses and wagons to visit places celebrated for the beauty and abundance of their tree peonies. Particularly

famous was the Buddhist Temple of Mercy and Compassion, noted for its luxuriant blossoms which, in one courtyard, opened two weeks earlier than elsewhere and, in another, two weeks later. Particularly remarkable blossoms became the topic of "records of the strange," receiving treatment comparable to the appearance of a deity. A few private dwellings were also known for the splendor of their flowers, and their owners invited chosen guests from the pinnacle of Chang'an society to enjoy the colors and compose poems in their honor.

The best known of these flower-loving aristocrats was General Hun Zhen, whose peonies were feted in verses by the leading poets of the day. Bo Juyi described them as possessing the finest fragrance and color in the capital.

> Mournful, the red peonies in front of the steps,
> In the evening, only two branches still in bloom.
> When early in the morning the wind resumes, they will all be blown
>   away.
> So at night, grieving for the vanishing red, I grasp a lamp to observe
>   them one last time.

Not only was the rating of peonies in poetry a social convention, but Emperor Wenzong once also rated what he considered to be the finest poems composed about the flower.[39]

The passion for flowers led to jealousy and sometimes to crime in the Tang capital. In one anecdote, a monk showed a group of young people a tree peony that produced blossoms in a unique shade of red. They were so entranced that they arranged for friends to lure the monk out to view blossoms elsewhere, so that they could steal his plant. They left gold and tea to "redeem" their theft (through payment of a fine), but the tree was never recovered. The passion for flowers also led to the growth of businesses devoted to their cultivation. One text mentions the payment of 5,000 cash for a magnolia tree. Competitions were held to see who could produce the finest plants, and leading families paid considerable prices for those judged to be best.[40]

Although most of the evidence regarding the passion for blossoming plants and the associated businesses refers to Chang'an, during Empress Wu's reign her Sacred Capital, Luoyang, became a center of tree peony cultivation. And at least one anecdote indicates that the peony craze spread to the south. The famous official-philosopher Han Yu once renounced his nephew as a lost cause but decided to give him another chance when he discovered that the young man had developed the art of producing peonies in an extraordinary range of colors by feeding dyes into their roots. Since the nephew had grown up in the south, this anecdote suggests that the Tang obsession with peonies had permeated that region as well. It is likely that crowds were viewing flowers and paying high prices for the best specimens in the southern markets of Jiangdu, Hangzhou, and Suzhou.[41]

Gardens also flourished in the cities. The imperial court possessed gardens operated by specially trained officials for the production of fruits, vegetables, and medicinal herbs. Leading political figures and writers built private gardens, and anecdotes show that their creation and cultivation had become a business. Professional gardeners were held in high esteem, as this statement from Liu Zongyuan demonstrates: "Camel [Guo] planted trees for a living. All the great families and wealthy people in Chang'an, whether interested in landscape gardening or fruit cultivation, vied with each other to invite him to their houses to live."[42]

The cultivation of flowers and gardens was, then as now, primarily associated with the urban middle classes. Inhabitants of Tang cities, and above all those given to reading and writing, longed for an absent "nature" but only in its most artificial form. For elites dwelling in cities, "nature" was always something other than a truly natural environment. While privileged rulers, nobles, and great religious establishments expressed this yearning by designing large landscaped parks, urban families who were prosperous without being truly wealthy had to content themselves with smaller enclosed courtyards adorned with compact shrubs and potted flowers.[43] In response to these spatial constraints, cultivators concentrated on plants whose individual blossoms were exquisite, and they worked hard to produce varieties of flowers with extreme shapes, colors, and fragrances. In this respect, the Tang passion for peonies resembled the seventeenth-century Dutch mania for tulips.

The Commercialization of Tang Cities

The early imperial restriction of trade to official markets—apart from the sale of food, drink, and entertainment—had been part of a larger strategy to control the assembly of crowds and people's movements, especially at night.[44] The gates of walled wards were closed at curfew, and only high officials and monasteries had private entrances onto streets outside the wards. In the mid-eighth century, one of the first signs that this system was breaking down was the appearance of complaints that people had pierced the outer walls of their wards to gain direct access to major thoroughfares. By 831 the police commissioners noted that everybody was now violating the curfew. The casual renting out of officials' residences allowed people without qualification of office to gain uncontrolled access to the streets. Many people, notably soldiers, were setting up shops and stalls on boulevards, extending the early Tang practice of allowing food vendors to ply their trade freely along avenues. Regular night markets also sprang up in the capital, as well as in Jiangdu, Panyu, and other provincial cities. The wards between the Eastern Market and the Imperial City became the busiest area in the city, with shops and commercial enterprises open day and night, so that lamps were kept continuously lit.[45]

In addition to opening up the walls and expanding night-time commerce, residents of the late Tang capital also began to "encroach on the street," building structures out into the spaces between ward walls and the circulation of traffic on the avenue. This was possible because the narrowest of the main boulevards were some 80 feet wide, while those along the city wall were more than 300 feet wide, not counting ten-foot wide drainage ditches on either side. A complaint by a police inspector in 849 that a military commander had built a nine-bay structure into the street is the last record of any attempt to control these encroachments.[46]

At the same time, specialized commercial districts began to spring up throughout the city. One ward near the Western Market gradually turned into a precinct of jewelers and goldsmiths, who later became proto-bankers. A ward next to the Northern Hamlet emerged as a major center for musical instrument makers. Other streets in the same area came to specialize in fabric shops, as well as more conventional food stalls. In an attempt to block uncontrolled commercialization, an imperial decree issued in 851 called for the restoration of the old official markets and outlawed any marketplaces in districts that had not previously had them. This attempt was a complete failure, and it was revoked only two years later.[47] By the time the interlinked system of walled wards and official markets completely disappeared in the eleventh century, urban trade was largely carried out along large streets whose buildings served as both merchant residence and shop.

More important than commercial changes within the capitals was the emergence of new urban centers that thrived on bulk trade in commodities along the Grand Canal (Fig. 10). Underlying this was a shift in long-distance trade from supplying luxury items to providing basic necessities. The emergence of substantial interregional trade in staples such as rice and timber, as well as an empire-wide market for the specialized products of particular regions, changed the character of Chinese society. The Chinese peasantry, following the lead of the owners of large estates, became a class of adaptable, profit-oriented, petty entrepreneurs. In the hills, they grew and processed timber for the booming boat-building industry and the construction of houses in expanding cities. On farmland, they produced fresh vegetables and fruits for urban consumption. All sorts of oils were pressed for cooking, lighting, and waterproofing; sugar was refined and crystallized; hemp, ramie, and silk textiles were produced for sale in countless villages. With the introduction of printing, paper production soared to meet the demand for books and government documents, as well as lampshades, toilet paper, and even clothing. In the more trade-oriented south, people specialized in commercial crops and relied on a vast interregional market to supply their daily foodstuffs. Even raw mate-

Fig. 10   Dunhuang mural of a carriage crossing a bridge, with a boat passing under it.

rials for rural production such as fish roe for fish ponds and mulberry leaves for silkworms were imported, processed, and then re-exported as finished products.

All of this trade passed through rising urban centers. The most significant trade-based city of the Tang dynasty was Jiangdu, located at the intersection of the Yangzi River and the Han Conduit. All goods from the south intended for the capital passed through Jiangdu. As the court came to depend almost entirely on the southeast for its most basic needs, this great trade emporium became the economic linchpin of the empire. It was the main trans-shipment center for salt, tea, wood, gems, medicinal herbs, and manufactured products ranging from copper wares, silks, and brocades to ships. It grew even wealthier when the salt monopoly was established there after the An Lushan rebellion. The city's population rose from around 40,000 at the turn of the seventh century to just under 500,000 in the middle of the eighth century.[48]

This southern city, even more than the northern capitals, could not be confined by rules and regulations. Not only were buildings extended into the major boulevards, as in Chang'an and Luoyang, but the urban area sprawled beyond the city walls. A new outer wall was built to contain a population that had spread out across the plain to the south of the old city along the banks of the Official Canal. Inscriptions on tombstones unearthed in recent years show many wards located outside the gates, particularly to the east, and Tang writings testify to numerous Buddhist temples in the same areas. The abundant business conducted in these extramural neighborhoods was described by the Japanese pilgrim Ennin, who visited the city in 838.

Not only did the local markets continue after dark, but much of the river traffic along the canal was still moving in the middle of the night. Descriptions of Jiangdu's night markets and its night-time illumination by lanterns appear in several poems and essays by Tang writers. A line in a poem by Zhang Hu (792–852) indicates that the great east-west thoroughfare linked market after market, right through the city and out into the suburbs. The great north-south streets were also major business venues. Two of them ran along canals, showing the importance of water transport in structuring the city. Archaeological excavations indicate that these canals were lined with buildings. In 826 the shallowness of the canals led the Salt and Iron Commissioner to build a ring canal around the city, so that deep-draft boats carrying salt could proceed more expeditiously to the north. The urban canals were then entirely turned over to business, lined with sidewalks and stalls, and filled with little boats selling produce.[49]

South of the Yangzi, many other cities grew large and wealthy on a network of trade routes. Across the Yangzi from Jiangdu, Jingkou was described by Li Deyu as ringed by "more than six hundred miles of watery land, and more than ten thousand masted boats." The "watery land" was the area around Lake Tai, which in the second half of the Tang was the most productive agricultural region in the empire and a major source of Jingkou's wealth. In the middle of the eighth century the writer Wei Jian noted that merchant craft from Jingkou arriving in the capital were second in number only to those from Jiangdu. To the southeast of Jingkou were Suzhou and Hangzhou. Bo Juyi noted that Suzhou was even more populous than Jiangdu, and its wards were more active than Chang'an's. The poet Du Xunhe celebrated the night markets of Suzhou and Hangzhou as follows:

> By the bridges, lights from night markets gleam,
> Outside the temples, boats rest in the spring wind.

Another author described how at Hangzhou the masts of more than thirty thousand ships stretched along the canals for almost nine miles.[50]

Bianzhou, along the Grand Canal just south of the Yellow River, became a trading center, but did not develop in the explosive manner of the southern cities because of the military struggles that plagued the region and the burden of supporting large armies. But in the half-century of the Five Dynasties, it became the capital of two states and (under a new name, Kaifeng), it emerged as the capital of the Northern Song. Chengdu in Sichuan was reputed to be second in wealth only to Jiangdu, largely because of its crafts production. It was celebrated for its high-quality paper and its tea, but above all it was famous as a center for weaving cloth. Damask City south of Chengdu was celebrated throughout the empire, as in the poetry of Wei Zhuang:

> In Damask City, in the silkworm markets,
> Hairpins of pearl and emerald fill the street.
> A hundred thousand rouged faces, jade cicadas and gold peacocks
> In priceless coiffed hair, earrings of tinkling flower bouquets

And embroidered gowns.

The sun tilts. They go home.

It's hard to see them, for the blue houses [brothels] are distant.

The city also prospered by importing exotic commodities from Nanzhao (Yunnan). However, trade to the north had to cross difficult mountain passes, while shipments down the Yangzi went through dangerous rocky gorges. As a result, bulk trade could not develop as it did in the southeast.[51]

Taxes and Currency

In addition to transforming life in the cities and the countryside, the expansion of trade in the Tang dynasty facilitated the state's development of an internal customs network for the collection of taxes on commerce. By the later eighth century officers in the major provincial cities inspected the goods of merchants and levied taxes of twenty cash per thousand. In the ninth century, military men who held power in the provinces turned the government's control stations along roads and waterways into customs houses. In the unofficial markets that developed in the countryside, an influential local landowner or merchant usually contracted to collect taxes for the government and became the head of the market. Some of the larger rural markets were eventually placed under government supervision for tax purposes. These taxes provided the fiscal foundations of military men whose local administrations developed into the numerous states into which the Tang empire divided after its collapse.[52]

With the rise in interregional trade came the need for financial transactions that spanned the empire. Consequently, the period between the late Tang and the Song witnessed a revolution in paper money, promissory notes, and other forms of paper credit to supplement the bulky, heavy strings of copper coins known as cash. Bills for the transfer and exchange of cash and commodities across distances had already developed in the early Tang. At the same time, paper money was used to transfer wealth to the dead, along with other goods made out of paper that were sent to the world of the afterlife by burning.[53]

The most important early form of paper money for the living was "food tickets" that allowed members of the regimental army to use bills purchased with grain in their home regions to buy food in the areas where they served. In the eighth century the Tang government developed "flying cash," whereby merchants purchased a certificate from the government at the capital which, when presented at any provincial treasury, entitled them to draw an equivalent sum of cash. Both the state and the merchants thereby avoided the hazard of transporting large amounts of copper cash. During the late Tang the private sector also produced a number of paper credit instruments. Deposit shops stored cash, gold, and silver for a fee and would honor checks drawn against these funds by a depositor. These moneychangers, along with goldsmiths and silversmiths, issued promissory notes that gradually came to be used much like money.

In the tenth century, after China fractured into many independent states, regional economic specialization forced these rivals to continue to cooperate in what had become an "international" trade in essential goods. Because of a scarcity of copper, several states minted lead, iron, and even pottery coins for use as legal tender. To avoid a drain on their valuable copper supply, other states followed suit and banned the export of copper. This world of nations, at once trading and fighting with one another, produced policies much like the mercantilism or bullionism of seventeenth- and eighteenth-century Europe, in which rulers attempted to hoard large reserves of precious metals and copper for strategic purposes and prevent any net outflow from their domains.

The lead, iron, and ceramic currencies that replaced copper can be regarded as primitive fiduciary currencies, meaning that they were based on convention and trust rather than the inherent value of the metal of which the coin was made. In other words, they functioned much like paper money, except that they were made of base metals and clay. Thus, it is not surprising that paper money proper was introduced by the Song government, in Sichuan in 1024. Although copper remained the primary form of currency, paper money and bills of credit came to play a major role in the economic history of late imperial China.[54]

Another important change in Chinese society brought about by large-scale trade was the increased complexity of business transactions and the consequent appearance of new business roles. Shipping brokers, who arranged suitable vessels to carry diverse commodities, became crucial figures along the major waterways. Ship captains and crews were hired by merchants or groups of investors to carry their goods, and the boatmen along the Grand Canal gradually became a large and distinct community who developed their own religious cults. As the storage of commodities being shipped became an independent trade, warehouse managers with permanent staffs of watchmen served as overseers for private warehouses and also for the huge state granaries established along the canals to store primarily rice during seasons when the water level was too low to move it.

State-licensed brokers—previously restricted to mediating, recording, and taxing deals in real estate, livestock, or human beings—became key agents in every market center, where they coordinated the activities of traveling merchants and retailers. Many wealthy businessmen hired permanent managers, who sometimes lived in a relationship almost like that of serfs to their employers, to handle their wide-ranging financial concerns. As the demand for business managers grew, they sometimes were able to accumulate considerable wealth of their own. While most of these commercial innovations developed fully only under the Song, they first appeared in the late Tang.[55]

5

RURAL SOCIETY

BETWEEN the eighth and the twelfth centuries, Chinese society was transformed by what is sometimes described as a medieval economic revolution. Although this culminated during the Song dynasty, its core modifications began in the Tang and had already profoundly altered the lives of Chinese men and women by the Five Dynasties. While many of these economic advances were most evident among city-dwellers and tradesmen along the Grand Canal, Tang rural society also witnessed a number of transformative innovations during this period. These included changes in landholding patterns, advances in farming technology, the commercialization of agriculture, the growth of regional market towns, and the production of crops for long-distance trade.

New Patterns of Landholding

The early Tang state attempted to impose the equal-field system that it inherited from the Northern Zhou and Sui dynasties, distributing state-owned land to peasants for the duration of their working lives. The Tang policy, which carried forward the Han ideal of a small-scale yeomanry providing taxes and service for the state, was the last in a series of attempts by Chinese governments to convert large amounts of abandoned property into state-owned land worked by refugees or by those forcibly resettled through imperial decree. But the equal-field system was limited from the beginning.

First, it could be carried out only in certain regions. During the period of disunion, the earlier Northern Zhou and Sui states could impose the system only where they ruled, in Guanzhong and the northwest. The Tang tried to extend the practice to the northeast, but tenuous control of that region meant that the system was never fully carried out there. The An Lushan rebellion put an end to it throughout the north. The equal-field system was also probably never carried out in the Yangzi region, as shown by the fact that after the An Lushan rebellion, state income there derived largely from the proceeds of the salt monopoly and business taxes, not from taxes on peasant households. Since the An Lushan rebellion did not disrupt the south, there was no reason that an existing equal-field system should have vanished.

A second major limitation of the equal-field system was that legal exceptions made a mockery of its underlying claim of equality. Legal reforms at the beginning of the Tang drastically reduced the amount of land to which individual peasant households were entitled, principally by not taking women, slaves, or herds into account when determining the size of the grant. At the same time, other categories of the population received ample tracts for reasons having nothing to do with the number of adult males in the household. Buddhist and Daoist temples owned large quantities of land, government officials received land to be held in perpetuity in proportion to their rank, and income from designated state land was used to pay salaries. Given the size of the Tang bureaucracy, particularly after the reign of Empress Wu, the amount of land lost to officials and their salaries was substantial. In addition, the state regularly rewarded both religious institutions and officials with gifts of land.

Another group of people receiving land were the families of soldiers in the regimental army. Most of these families were located in the Guanzhong region, as were families of officials. As a result, a huge portion of the land that could have been awarded to peasant households was taken out of circulation in the one region where the government had the power to impose a truly "equal" system. Finally, the state reserved large tracts of well-irrigated and productive agricultural land to provision and pay military garrisons and provide income for local governments. Grasslands used to raise horses for the army were also removed from circulation.[1]

A third major limitation on the equal-field system was the government's acceptance of large landed estates that had been built up during the Northern and Southern Dynasties, the Sui, and the early Tang. These belonged to leading families at court, local landlords, rich merchants, major Buddhist monasteries, and, to a lesser extent, Daoist temples. While the scale and number of landed estates in the early years of the dynasty cannot be measured, frequent references in the histories suggest that a considerable portion of land, particularly around the capital, was tied up in landed estates during the period when the equal-field system was being imposed.

The problem grew worse as individuals bought and sold land ostensibly owned by the state. Repeated imperial decrees forbidding the concentration of landholdings were issued, but their effectiveness is doubtful, as this document written a decade before the An Lushan rebellion makes clear:

> The nobles, officials, and powerful local families set up their estates one next to the other, swallowing up the peasants' land as they please without fear of the regulations. Those who use "opening new land" as an excuse snatch away mature fields, while those who herd livestock occupy hills and valleys without limit. They illegally buy the peasants' equal-field land, in some cases altering the population registers, in others describing it as "borrowing against the land." They thus leave the peasants with no place to live.[2]

While the rhetoric here is hyperbolic and conventional, it gives a sense of actual conditions in the countryside.

As large estates developed, peasant households disappeared from state records, along with their taxes and service. As the passage just quoted indicates, landlords who were expanding their holdings would sometimes remove tenants from local records to mask the illegal transfer of land. These "missing" peasant households were motivated to sell their fields both by pressure from landlords and by their desire to escape tax and service burdens imposed by the state. As in the Han dynasty, peasants in the Tang may have been better off as anonymous tenants of a rich landlord than as recognized subjects of the empire. Other small-time farmers disappeared from rural areas in the north, driven off by landlords whose investment in new tools and draft animals allowed them to work larger fields with fewer people. Some of these peasants made their way to cities as destitute beggars, but many migrated south to open up new land in what was still, in the early Tang, a developing region.

The problem of the missing peasant households became so severe that special commissioners were charged with the task of locating such farmers and granting them land, sometimes offering temporary tax relief in order to restore them to the population rolls. In 723 the best known of these commissioners, Yuwen Rong, together with a large staff, restored over 800,000 peasants to the official registers—a number that indicates the scale of the problem. Further measures to find missing households continued right up to the time of the An Lushan rebellion.[3]

Thus, from the beginning of the dynasty, the equal-field system of state-owned land existed together with extensive privately-held land, and the latter probably exceeded the former. Over time, the state's practice of granting land to officials and monasteries, the purchase of large tracts by families that were augmenting their wealth through trade and commercial farming, and the opening of new land in the south steadily increased private holdings at the expense of state-owned land, though the opening of new lands worked by previously "missing" households in the first decades of the eighth century masked this growing privatization somewhat. As the regimental army declined and military governors became responsible for provisioning their troops, several key roles formerly played by state-owned land declined in importance. The equal-field system completely collapsed in the wake of the An Lushan rebellion, due to the destruction of registers, the control of the northeast by semi-independent governors, and the loss of income from the middle reaches of the Yellow River because loyal governors took all the income of their provinces to pay for troops.

The breakdown of the equal-field system and the concentration of private land were not altogether detrimental to the interests of the empire. The development of large estates facilitated the rise of new families who used the accumulation of wealth to establish local power and influence as an ultimate springboard to political power. The histories and anecdotal literature tell how men of humble background had "fertile estates south of the capital, with several dozen of them linked up one after the other," or how a parvenu in the vicinity of Luoyang had "millions in capital and numerous estates."[4] These new families were crucial to the power of Empress Wu and many subsequent rulers.

More important, there was a clear link between the emergence of estates and the rise of new agricultural technologies and long-distance trade—two developments that raised both the standard of living for many people and taxable wealth for the state. One of the most important technologies that required greater wealth was the milling of flour. The Tang period witnessed a growing consumption of milled products, particularly from wheat in the north and sago in the south, along with the

southern grass whose white seeds are called Job's tears, as described by
Wei Zhuang:

> Grains are shamed, lacking Job's tears;
> Flours rejoice, having sago palm.

Particularly in the capital and other northern cities, Turkish cakes and
pastries sold by street vendors and small shops became very popular, but
the taste for flour-based foods spread throughout the empire.[5]

As a demand for these products rose, wealthier landholders could devote considerable agricultural land to the production of wheat for sale in
urban markets without risking the livelihood of their family in the event
of crop failure. Those with substantial capital were able to build and
operate their own water-powered mills to produce flour for this market. New milling technologies had benefited Buddhist monasteries and
a few lay landlords during the Northern and Southern Dynasties, but in
the Tang a large number of princes, nobles, high officials, monasteries,
Daoist temples, and businessmen began to operate or lease mills for
profit. The Taiping Princess, who dominated the court between the abdication of Empress Wu and the rise of Emperor Xuanzong, engaged in extended struggles with Buddhist monasteries for control of water-powered
mills.[6]

The diversion of water to power the mills reduced the amount available for irrigation, and in 777 a petition was organized by peasants demanding that the chief official of the capital district destroy all mills in
the vicinity, including those belonging to imperial princesses and to General Guo Ziyi, whose forces had played a major role in defeating An
Lushan. Sometimes the state issued orders to dismantle mills, but these
actions had little lasting impact. The decline in supply of flour simply
pushed up the price, making the building and operation of new mills all
the more profitable. Also, the state itself earned income from a mill tax
and was not willing to shut down these enterprises for extended periods.
In the long run, the pursuit of profit by the powerful and wealthy took
precedence over the subsistence claims of the peasantry.[7]

The large landholdings of wealthy families and monasteries in the
Tang were organized into a new style of estate that had emerged primarily during the southern dynasties and spread north. The prototype
can be seen in the estate of Kong Lingfu in the early fifth century: "In

Yongxing [near Jiangxi] he set up an estate. It was nine miles in circumference and about three hundred and seventy acres of water and land. It included two mountains and had nine fruit orchards."[8] While in some ways similar to the estates of the great families in the Han dynasty, Kong Lingfu's estate was different in a few key respects. One was the presence of abundant water, as more and more estates were located in the wetter south. Another was the prominence of mountains, whose aesthetic qualities become much appreciated in the southern dynasties. Third was the abundance and variety of fruit trees. While orchards were a long-established feature of Han estates, during the period of division prior to the Tang fruiting trees gained in popularity over fields producing staple grains, due to the greater profits available from the sale of fruit.

The estates of the Tang dynasty (*zhuang yuan*) had many features in common with those of earlier centuries, but particularly after the An Lushan rebellion they also differed in major ways. The early estates generally consisted of a single, unitary block of land and its contents. Even after several generations had divided the family property into multiple holdings, these smaller estates were still adjacent and this contiguity facilitated joint action by kin. The Tang *zhuang yuan*, by contrast, were usually dispersed holdings, with some plots of land thirty or forty miles from the owner's house. In extreme cases the holdings of a family were scattered across much of a region. The literature from the period contains references to rich individuals possessing "several dozen" or "numerous" estates. Ambitious land developers, and even middling landlords, acquired fields and orchards wherever opportunities presented themselves. Only the relatively small holdings of lesser landlords would have been a single unit.

The farmer Lu Guimeng, a modest landlord, is a case in point. He owned a small farm of just under sixty acres about fourteen miles east of Suzhou in the south. But he also had a mountainside that he used for timber, located seven miles west of the city, and a tea plantation a hundred miles away.[9] Each of Lu's three holdings was put to a different economic use. The tea and timber were doubtless sold commercially, with the profits from this trade going toward the purchase of whatever goods and food were lacking at each of his different holdings. His physically divided estate was united only in his financial accounts. The tendency toward scattered estates both resulted from and facilitated the increasing commercialization of agriculture. Rather than producing all the diverse requirements of a farming enterprise at a single self-sustaining site, the landlords of the Tang produced diverse products for sale at several scattered locations, all of which were necessarily tied into the market for agricultural commodities. Whereas Lu held only three units of land, each for a different product, truly rich landlords like those in the capital region could have dozens.

Monastic land was also divided into several holdings. A stone inscription on a monastery in what is now Shaanxi lists its ownership of "seven estates [*zhuang*], both large and small," as well as a stand of timber and some unexploited hillside land. In the diary of his travels, the Japanese monk Ennin described how he stopped for tea at the fruit gardens of the Liquan monastery in Shandong. The monastery itself, about two-thirds of a mile away, was "dilapidated, and there is not much vegetarian eating. The holy sites are gradually going to ruin, and there is no one to repair them. Some of the monastery's fifteen estates remain today. There were originally about a hundred monks, but they have now scattered in accord with their destinies, and now only about thirty live there." Even in its state of serious decline, the monastery still owned a handful of separate properties.[10]

Over time, each parcel of land in a *zhuang yuan* came to be known as an estate in its own right. An anecdote about the former minister Cui Qun shows that each "estate" was assumed to be a distinct unit of business: "When he retired, his wife, Madam Li, took advantage of any occasion to urge him to set up estates to provide for his descendants. He laughingly replied, 'I have thirty excellent estates, whose fine fields cover the empire, what need is there for you to worry?' His wife replied, 'I had not heard of this property of yours.' Qun said, 'Last year I planted thirty men in the list of successful examination candidates. How could these not be excellent fields?'"[11]

An important difference between the late Tang *zhuang yuan* and earlier estates was the legal status of tenants. The Tang legal code divided the population into three groups: free people at the top of the hierarchy (including both official families and commoners), slaves on the bottom, and bondsmen (*buqu*) in the middle. *Buqu* was a term used from the late Han for soldiers, and later for soldiers in private armies. By the early Tang dynasty, *buqu* or "bondsman" was a legal category of "base people" who were hereditarily bound to powerful families as dependent tenants. Sometime in the late Tang the term *buqu* disappeared, replaced by a variety of categories of tenants. In the subsequent Song dynasty, some peasants remained legally bound to wealthy estates, although in a few cases they could also have property of their own and even their own tenants. While the relations of peasants to landlords were highly variable throughout the Tang and beyond, the disappearance of a clearly demarcated legal category of base people represents some form of significant improvement in the status of peasants.[12]

The Tang estate, like its predecessors in earlier centuries, became not just a source of wealth but also an object of aesthetic contemplation and literature. Rhapsodies written by Xie Lingyun and other poets on the estates of the Northern and Southern Dynasties had followed the pattern of earlier rhapsodies on the imperial hunting parks in treating the estates as integrated spatial units. The poetics of the new Tang estates, however, imitated the fragmentation of the estates themselves. The classic example, written in the first half of the eighth century, was the "Wang Stream Collection," a set of twenty quatrains (verses of four lines, each with five characters) written by Wang Wei together with his friend Pei Di. In a completely new poetic form, the two men composed verses evoked by twenty named sites at his Wang Stream estate:

JIN BAMBOO RIDGE
Lissome stalks shine in deserted bends
And wave, green and sapphire, in the ripples.
Enter unseen on the Shang Mountain road,
And even the woodsmen do not know.

PAVILION OVERLOOKING THE LAKE
A light scull greets my worthy guest
Who comes from afar across the lake.
We will sit facing wine by the balcony
With lotuses blooming on every side.

GOLD DUST SPRING
You drink each day from Gold Dust Spring,
With a little you'll live a thousand years.
A blue phoenix coach soars with striped dragons,
Feathered ensigns go to the Jade Emperor's court.

This set of verses—closely linked to a celebrated early landscape scroll by Wang Wei on the same theme—took the reader on a programmatic journey through the landscape, pointing out each new object of interest. It was such an artistic success that by the second half of the eighth century it had inspired many subsequent quatrain series on related themes.[13] This practice of breaking down an estate or a garden into a designated itinerary of named sites set to verse became a standard mode of landscape appreciation in late imperial China.

Agricultural Technology

The Tang dynasty witnessed several major innovations in agricultural technology, particularly in the lower Yangzi, that increased yields and reduced bad harvests. The first advance was in the preparation of seeds and soil. During the Han dynasty the Chinese had pioneered the practice of preparing seeds by soaking them in boiled-down mineral-rich solutions and sowing them in specially prepared beds to preserve moisture. By the time the *Essential Methods of the Common People* (*Qi min yao shu*) was written in the sixth century, such seed preparation had become an elaborate process. Additional substances were added to the soaking seeds to protect the young plants from insects and disease. For example, salt was added to melon seed and arsenic to wheat seed to act as insecticides. By the late Tang, farmers in southern China prepared rice grains by steeping them in a solution made from boiled animal bones, sometimes mixed with silkworm droppings or sheep dung, and then sowed the grains in special seedbeds that had been prepared by repeated deep plowing to break up the soil. Next, the beds were covered with wood ash and turned over several times with the plow at the beginning of spring before being fertilized with animal or human manure and rotted hemp stalks. By preparing fields in this way for the same staple crops year after year, Chinese farmers actually improved the fertility of their soil over time, while decreasing the threat of insects and disease.[14]

In addition to using new methods of seed preparation, Tang farmers used new materials as fertilizers. During the late Tang and into the Northern Song, organic animal manure became the primary fertilizer in the south, and farmers began to build brick-lined manure houses near their dwellings for storing this precious commodity. The availability of animal fertilizer was closely linked to the increased use of draft animals in plowing. The farmer Lu Guimeng, in a blessing for an ox pen, described how large numbers of oxen were raised together in pens, from which fertilizer could be extracted easily. At a rate of twenty-five cubic yards of manure per ox per year, Lu Guimeng, who owned about a dozen oxen, could have met most of his need for fertilizer from his own animals. Farmers who exceeded their own needs sold the excess as a commercial product.[15]

The sale of human manure (nightsoil) became an important business in this period, as entrepreneurs began to specialize in collecting human excrement in cities for sale in the countryside. While the use of nightsoil as fertilizer may have dated from ancient times (a question that is difficult to resolve because the terminology does not distinguish human waste from animal), the first clear records of this practice date from the late Tang. Nutrient-rich mud scooped from the bottoms of rivers—which were numerous in the south—became another important fertilizer during the Tang, as did lime in certain areas. Farmers of the Northern and Southern Dynasties had introduced green manures—fertilizers made from plants grown solely for the purpose of being plowed back into the soil to improve its fertility and make it easier to work—most notably nitrogen-fixing beans. This practice continued into the Tang, with an increase in the variety of plants that were used. Silkworm droppings, the water in which rice had been washed or cooked, and other organic liquids were also used as fertilizers, although primarily for soaking seeds prior to planting.[16]

Another major innovation was the widespread use of a more effective plow and harness to prepare fields for planting. By at least the second century A.D., Chinese had developed a plow pulled by three or four oxen that was capable of turning over the dry sod of north China to form a deep furrow. While the technology was known in the southern dynasties, ox-drawn plows remained rare in the Yangzi region until the Tang. The reasons had to do with the limited space that had been opened, the technological conservatism or parsimony of the northern families who settled in the south, the frequency of war, and the difficulty of the hilly terrain. It was only with the introduction of a new style of plow in the eighth and ninth centuries that ox-drawn plows become commonplace in the south, as noted by Lu Guimeng and several Buddhist writers. This advance allowed the region to become the food-producing center and the economic mainstay of the empire.[17]

A key feature of the new plow was its ability to work a variety of soils, owing to a device that allowed the plowman to alter the depth of the furrow as desired. The plow's ability to dig deep made it useful for cutting the roots of bushes and wild grasses that had to be removed before new land could be put under cultivation. This was especially important in the middle and lower Yangzi, where unexploited terrain was still available. The adjustable depth also made it efficient both in the muddy, heavy soils of newly drained areas or rice fields and the sandy soils of coastal regions and riverbanks. Plowing mud in the south required less pulling power than did hardened dry soil, so only one ox or water-buffalo was needed, rather than the three or four customary in the north. Nevertheless, the most common pattern in the south was to use two oxen. This type of plow remained the dominant form throughout the history of late imperial China.[18]

To be pulled effectively, the new plow required major innovations in the methods of harnessing. The long, straight beam that had previously attached the plow to the oxen's yoke had to be replaced by one that was shorter, although not yet as short as in later centuries. This beam was linked not at the yoke but at a pivoted crossbar (known as a whipple-tree) behind the ox. Two cords that ran to either side of the animal joined the bar to the yoke. The yoke itself was significantly curved, individually fitted to each animal, and secured in place by a throat band. The resulting ensemble had several substantial advantages. First, it could be used to harness almost any number of animals, depending on the soil type and terrain. Second, because the harness did not slip, chafe, or catch at the ox's throat, an animal could pull harder without difficulty. Third, the shorter beam not only significantly reduced the weight but gave the ox and plow a much tighter turning radius, which allowed the plowman to switch directions or maneuver easily in any shape or size of field. This new maneuverability was especially important in small, irregularly shaped rice fields and on sloping fields, where one ox could pull a plow up and down steep inclines. Agriculture was thus no longer restricted to flat plains or terraces of friable soil, as in the north, but could be expanded across the hilly terrain that characterizes most of southern China. Although hillsides would not be fully exploited for agriculture until the introduction of American food crops in the sixteenth century, the new plowing ensemble brought some hills into systematic cultivation for the first time.

The most important contribution of the new plow was to greatly improve the preparation of rice paddies in the south, where the goal was to produce a layer of puddled mud at the surface of the field and a compacted hardpan below it to prevent water from soaking into the ground. This required the farmer to guide his ox (or, more commonly, buffalo) back and forth across the field, which was usually cut in an irregular shape to fit the lay of the land. The animal's hooves packed down the hardpan, making it more impermeable, while the plow progressively pulverized the upper layer of soil. Next, a roller created a smooth finish to the mud that made rice planting easier. In contrast with dry land, each year of plowing a southern paddy field improved its productivity.[19]

After a dry field was plowed, an ox-drawn harrow prepared it for planting by breaking up the remaining clods of earth and smoothing the ground. In the ninth century, farmers in the Yangzi delta developed a new deep-toothed harrow that was much more effective at this task than earlier models. Stone rollers were also used on dry fields, as were wooden rollers with and without spikes. In north China, the old-style Han plow was combined with a new model of seed drill to increase the efficiency of planting. By Song times this device had been widened to cut and sow four furrows simultaneously. It was attached to a container that automatically fertilized the seeds with sieved manure or silkworm dung as it planted them. In this way, the north, too, expanded its production, although not to the degree achieved in the south.[20] The relative scarcity of human labor in the Yangzi region during the Tang dynasty created ideal conditions for the widespread use of draft animals in the many tasks associated with cultivation. But once the population in the region became extremely dense and the cost of human labor plummeted, the economic advantages of draft animals vanished. During the Ming and Qing dynasties, the use of oxen in southern agriculture steadily declined.[21]

In addition to new seed preparation, new fertilizers, and new ox-drawn equipment, another major innovation in the Tang was the introduction of new varieties of plants that allowed for the possibility of multiple cropping. While more than one crop in a single year remained unusual until the Song, three crops within two years were common by the middle Tang in much of China. In the north this was achieved by alternating summer millet, winter wheat, and then again summer millet. In the south, it consisted of three crops of rice. In addition, vegetables and beans were interplanted with the major grains, both to provide variety in the kitchen and to enrich the soil.

In the later Tang and the Song there was also an increase in the range of rice seeds with more desirable properties that facilitated multiple cropping. The most famous of these was Champa rice from central Vietnam, which was first introduced into China in the tenth century and widely adopted at the order of the Song Emperor Zhenzong in the eleventh. He obtained a variety from what is now Fujian in the far southeast in 1012 A.D. and disseminated it throughout the lower Yangzi. This rice, with its low gluten content, was unusually drought resistant, ripened faster than the old Chinese varieties, and could be grown on poorer soils than high-gluten rice. Its defects were that it produced lower yields per plant, was tough to eat, and was more prone to spoilage. Tang farmers probably initially planted it as a form of insurance against droughts. At this time farmers in the lower Yangzi already divided their rice into early- and late-ripening varieties, but the truly early-ripening varieties provided by Champa rice were not in regular use during the Tang.

However, through selective breeding over the decades, farmers produced numerous new strains of rice that combined and improved on the virtues of the older ones. By the twelfth century, dozens of varieties of rice—most of them derived from Champa rice—were available, and all the strains in use before the middle Tang had disappeared. South China was gradually covered with a complex, variegated pattern of cropping that was carefully adjusted to the different soils, climatic conditions, and economic circumstances of each locality. Combining early-ripening and late-ripening rice allowed agricultural work to be spread more evenly over the year, reducing the problem of seasonal unemployment and the risks from bad weather; if one crop was lost, the next might still be saved.[22]

Farmers of the lower Yangzi further expanded their productivity by bringing northern crops such as wheat, millet, and barley into drier areas of the south. The southward migration of wheat started during the period of disunion but became significant only under the Tang. By the Song it had transformed the southern economy. Writing in the late tenth century, Yang Yi described how in one area of the Yangzi drainage basin people survived the failure of the rice crop because good spring rains allowed a bountiful harvest of wheat and millet. In some areas of the south, Song landlords based their rent on just the rice yield, leaving the wheat crop entirely to tenants for their subsistence. However, alternating wet rice with wheat on the same field was extremely labor-intensive, because rice paddies had to be thoroughly drained before wheat could be planted. Many landlords tried to block the alternation of these crops, believing that it reduced the productivity of the fields as well as that of the peasants who worked them.[23]

While improvements in agriculture—ranging from better seed preparation to multiple cropping—were essential for the productivity gains that underlay China's medieval economic revolution, the Tang's greatest achievement was better water control for irrigation, flood prevention, and land drainage. In the north, canals that followed the contour of the land carried water from tributaries of the Yellow River to agricultural land further downstream. In the extensive areas where irrigation canals did not reach, water had to be drawn from deep wells. The Yellow River itself often ran low during the early summer, when water was needed for agriculture, while substantial dikes were needed to contain potential floods during the irregular downpours of late July and August. Both the dikes of the Yellow River and the irrigation channels of its tributaries were built and maintained by the state.

In the south, by contrast, water control was primarily the responsibility of wealthy landowners. The challenge was to drain swampy lowlands for agricultural use and manage the water from mountain streams through the use of dams and dikes. In general, in the drainage basin of the Huai and Si Rivers in central China, large reservoirs were formed by damming rivers, whose water was released through sluices into channels that directed its flow into fields. In the Yangzi drainage basin, on the other hand, the land tended to be either flat and swampy or very hilly. In both cases, water was collected—either by diversion in the hills or drainage in the lowlands—into artificial pools or tanks that were built by wealthy individual families or by small groups of a few dozen households. Such tanks were already in use in the Han dynasty, but they became widespread in the Tang.[24]

The single greatest area of agricultural expansion during the Tang dynasty was the marshy land around Lake Tai and Lake Dongting. The key technology for reclaiming this land was the "polder" field (though "encircled fields" and "counter fields" used a similar approach). Dikes were built in a large ring to hold back the water at a higher level than the field they surrounded, and sluice gates in the embankment walls controlled the amount of water that was allowed to flow in to irrigate the field. Polder fields probably existed even in pre-imperial times, but they seem to have been widely used only in the Tang. The acreage recovered from lakes and river basins through the use of embankments like these increased enormously in the ninth and tenth centuries, and by the twelfth century the whole Yangzi delta was covered with polder fields. These represented a substantial advance in technology, with large numbers of sluice gates that were capable of draining off the exact amount of water needed at precisely the time that it was required. Some were sponsored by the government and reached twenty-eight miles in circumference, but most were smaller and belonged to private estates.

If the soil was too swampy to be drained, farmers constructed "frame fields," which were floating wooden frames covered with mud and aquatic plants (usually zizania). Seeds were planted in the soil on top of the frame, which rose and fell with the water level, so that the frame field was supposedly never plagued by flooding. Guo Pu described such fields in a poem written in the early fourth century:

> Covered with an emerald screen,
> They drift buoyed up by floating zizania.
> Artlessly the seeds of canopied cereals are scattered,
> And fine rice plants thrust up of their own accord.

Several Tang poems mention what seem to be irrigated terraced fields, although clear references to terracing do not appear until the Song dynasty.[25]

In more mountainous regions, farmers built tanks to store runoff and diverted streams laterally to water their fields. Stone dams to collect water were introduced into the mountain gorges of Fujian province during the Tang, and they ultimately dotted the hillsides throughout the south. In addition to all these adaptations of dikes and irrigation methods to every type of land, water control in the Tang also included protective embankments along the shores of major lakes and the seaside. As a result, the Tang had the fewest problems with flooding in the lower Yangzi of any dynasty in Chinese history.[26]

The consequence of these new techniques and the wider extension of older ones was a massive increase in the amount of land being worked throughout southern China and in its productivity. The areas around Lakes Tai and Dongting were brought completely under cultivation, and major inroads were made into regions further south and west. The area around Suzhou, which in the southern dynasties had remained largely unexploited, became a center of agricultural productivity. The mountain valleys of what is now Fujian were also developed. Not only were the number and distribution of these irrigation works far greater than in the preceding period, but the scale of the individual projects was also much larger.[27]

Both drainage and irrigation benefited from the introduction of several devices for moving water. The simplest of these was the counterbalanced bucket or well-sweep. The noria was a wheel with bamboo tubes that filled with water at the bottom of the rotation and then emptied it into an aqueduct at the top. It was useful only in hillier country where streams moved with sufficient velocity to turn the wheel. Elsewhere, farmers relied on the more mobile and adaptable treadle-pallet pump, which required human (or sometimes animal) labor to turn a wheel that carried tubes or pallets from the stream or pond to the aqueduct. All of these devices developed under the Tang, though they were not widely used in agriculture until the tenth century.[28]

The development of woodblock printing in the Tang also made a major contribution to agricultural innovations, as printed manuals helped to disseminate new farming techniques among literate landowners. The Tang government produced the first printed manual on agriculture, and the Song government sponsored editions of the *Essential Methods of the Common People* and the *Key Points for the Four Seasons* (*Si shi zuan yao*), the two greatest agricultural manuals produced to that date. Newer instructional manuals were also composed, and in the Song they were accompanied by illustrations. Local officials distributed briefer printed manuals, often illustrated, to farmers in their vicinity in order to propagate the latest agricultural techniques.[29]

These manuals primarily benefited the literate, well-to-do owners of the numerous large estates that developed after the An Lushan rebellion. The scale of agriculture practiced on these estates encouraged experimentation and also allowed for the accumulation of capital to introduce new techniques. Thus, although Chinese historians tend to portray the concentration of landholding during the Tang as a negative development, in all likelihood it was precisely this concentration that made possible the great changes in agriculture that began in the late Tang and culminated during the Song.

Long-Distance Trade and Commercialization

From the ninth century forward, expanding markets for agricultural produce led farmers to abandon any idea of self-sufficiency, aiming instead to maximize output by concentrating on crops that grew best in their own particular area. The search for greater yields also led to substantial increases in labor and capital. This was particularly true for the emergent estates, which—with sufficient capital and widely scattered holdings in

different kinds of terrain—were better suited for commercial production
than were individual peasant households, which had to worry about simple survival.[30]

Specialization for the market reached its highest development in the
south, where the production of such nongrain crops as fruits, tea, and
sugar became substantial economic activities in the second half of the
Tang. Nowhere was specialization more extreme than in Fujian, which
grew numerous products for sale in other Chinese provinces but also devoted considerable acreage to the production of lychees and oranges for
foreign export. Other areas concentrated on the production of high-
gluten rice (used in rice wine), sugar cane, farm-raised fish, timber, paper,
and lacquer.

Regional specialization was sustained by a counterbalancing flow of
food grains from other parts of the empire. By the twelfth century,
Fujian's coastal prefectures and the orange-growing areas around Lake
Tai all relied on rice imports from the Yangzi delta.[31] The bulk transport
of grain in turn depended on a dramatic increase in the carrying capacity
of China's water transportation network, although roads allowing land
transport of goods and government communications were also vital links
in the chain. Both the Tang and Song governments strived to maintain
and improve the major land routes of the empire, roads of packed earth
that suffered serious damage from increased commercial traffic. In the
eighth century, major repairs to the road across the pass that linked
Guangdong to Jiangxi allowed it to carry heavier commercial traffic. The
Tang government also expended great effort in maintaining the wooden
bridges and cliffside galleries that moved traffic in and out of Sichuan, a
task made increasingly difficult by deforestation. Under the late Tang, the
network of major roads was expanded into southern China, making
Fujian, Hunan, and Jiangxi all easily accessible by land. By the Song dynasty, once-isolated frontier towns had become major centers of communication.[32]

The official road system served to relay information on weather conditions, droughts, and relative prices from all parts of the empire. It thus
furthered the commercialization of Chinese agriculture and the rise of interregional specialization. One late eighth-century official who used the
official courier system to gather commercial information was described
as follows: "He regularly spent large sums of money to hire good runners, and set up relay stations in contact with one another, with the task

of observing and reporting the prices of commodities everywhere. It took only a few days for all the news from distant places to reach the authorities. The power to control the prices of goods lay entirely in his hands."

After the An Lushan rebellion the semi-independent military governors of the northeast and the great civil governors of the south began to keep Offices for Forwarding Memorials at the capital. These allowed two-way transmission of information, orders, and requests. The officials in charge of these offices privately copied out important government documents relating both to the area concerned and to the empire as a whole and sent them to their masters in the provinces. This practice gradually developed into an official gazette issued by the Song government, the world's first "national" newspaper. The same communication routes facilitated the movement of paper currency.[33]

But it was large-scale, water-based commercial shipping that truly transformed China in the Tang and subsequent dynasties. Huge fleets, often numbering more than three thousand vessels, moved along the Grand Canal and provisioned not only the capitals but the northwestern frontier. At the end of the seventh century, one observer claimed that commercial boats could be found on every navigable stream from one end of the empire to the other. A century and a half later, Li Chao wrote that no county in the southeast lacked water transport and that trade within the empire completely depended on boats. He also described how at dangerous places such as the Yangzi gorges local boatmen had developed techniques for avoiding shoals and rocks. In the tenth and eleventh centuries this development was furthered by the invention of new types of canal locks that allowed boats to skirt dangerous passages altogether, without the special assistance of local laborers. This ability to navigate previously impassible stretches turned China's separate waterways into an integrated system that allowed the emergence of an empire-wide market between the late Tang and the Song.

Depending on the nature of the waterways, inland vessels used sails, poles, hauling ropes, oars, sculls, or sweeps. Paddle-wheel boats were used as tugs in harbors. Most shipping was in the hands of boating families, like the traveling merchants whose homes were their boats, as described in verse. Little boats became the dependents of larger vessels and engaged in regular joint operations. Partnerships to sponsor individual expeditions appeared in the late Tang, and by the Song these had developed into complex forms of investment in which numerous persons of modest means pooled resources to hire a manager and sponsor individual ships or even whole fleets. A new category of specialist emerged to organize such fleets. At the same time, merchant brokers set up warehouses in the great river and canal towns, where they bought and stored the goods brought in by boat. They also negotiated with captains and vessels to carry the goods of merchants, who paid them a fee for their expert knowledge of shippers and shipping.[34]

The ultimate foundation of interregional trade in the Tang was a network of local market towns that allowed farmers to bring their produce into the trade circuit and perhaps buy necessary goods. Under early Tang regulations, markets were banned outside administrative centers (the lowest level of which was the district town) because there were no officials in smaller towns to collect taxes, guarantee the accuracy of weights and measures, verify the quality of goods, and regulate prices. However, district capitals were widely spaced, so it was impossible for most peasants to reach the nearest official market with any regularity.

Consequently, from early in the Tang, there were periodic rural markets, called "straw markets" in the north and "empty markets" in the south, whose essential feature was their impermanence. These transient local assemblies, arising out of the needs of rural society, were independent of government control. People gathered at convenient sites, set up their straw huts, traded with other producers, and then dispersed, leaving the site empty—hence their names. Song dynasty texts show that markets followed a fixed schedule, and this was probably also true in the Tang. In all likelihood, local merchants began to travel according to this schedule, so that they could move with their goods from one temporary market to the next. They also offered opportunities for recreation and entertainment that would have enlivened the otherwise dreary lives of peasant farmers.[35]

These periodic markets gradually developed into more permanent settlements. Many of them sprang up at road junctions, bridges, and fords. Others were held around temples or shrines, or near a major estate, sometimes in association with periodic fairs. Still others emerged around inns or roadside stores that provided services to traveling merchants. In addition to food and lodging, these settlements provided safe storage for goods, shelter for animals, and sometimes horses or mules for hire. Some also sold goods on commission for merchants who stayed there on a regular basis in the course of their travels. Found along all major transportation routes, these sites attracted both traveling merchants and nearby peasants, who could exchange their respective goods.[36]

The commerce in rural markets can be deduced only by tentatively projecting Song evidence back into the Tang. Local farmers presumably brought in grain, vegetables, and livestock, which they traded for fish, firewood, or charcoal supplied by other local producers, or items that could not be produced locally and were brought in by merchants, such as salt, tea, preserves, some tools, or material for handicraft production that could be pursued as a secondary occupation. If the merchants moved along a fixed circuit, then they not only linked the various local markets to one another but also tied them to higher-level commercial centers, which sometimes developed periodic markets just outside their walls. Thus, this late Tang trading network represented the embryonic form of the great nested hierarchical network of towns, small cities, and metropolises that articulated the geography of late imperial China.[37]

In some areas, special market gatherings that corresponded roughly to the Western fair were held at longer intervals. These often took place at a local temple or shrine at the time of a major religious festival and hence were called "temple markets." They marked another manner in which temples or monasteries provided new public spaces in China and also altered the structure of time through the introduction of new festivals in the ritual calendar. With their links to festivals, these temple markets served as a focal point for local entertainers: jugglers, storytellers, singers, acrobats, and the like. In addition to religious fairs, there were also a few annual fairs devoted to specialized commodities, notably in Sichuan. Horse fairs, for example, were organized by the government in order to purchase mounts for the army, but there were also medicine fairs and a silkworm fair, which consisted of a succession of local fairs held in a circuit of fifteen towns in Sichuan.[38]

In many provinces, especially in the north, local military governors encouraged the growth of new market towns, which, unlike the established district and prefectural cities, lay outside the administrative network of the imperial court and could thus be easily co-opted. In the late Tang, Five Dynasties, and early Song periods, many of these towns, often labeled "garrisons," became important market centers where taxes could be collected on trade.[39] Market towns, consequently, not only contributed to a general increase in commercial activity in rural society but also to the government's fiscal shift away from farming and toward commerce as a source of revenue.

Tea and Sugar

While the single most important commercial crop in the Tang remained rice, the dynasty was notable for the emergence of nongrain "recreational" foods. These did not contribute to peasant subsistence but were sold in the market to meet increasing consumer demand, primarily in cities. They arose together with new fashions or styles of consumption by which people defined who they were and to what social groups they belonged. The most important were tea and sugar.

Tea is the only food crop that originated in China to become part of worldwide cuisine. There is now widespread agreement that the tea plant first appeared in China, and universal agreement that the Chinese were the first to process and steep tea leaves to make a drink. Beyond that, the early history of tea drinking is difficult to trace because of shifting nomenclature; the original character used for the plant also named types of bitter vegetables, and the term for medicinal tea varied as well. As the Qing scholar Gu Yanwu originally demonstrated through studying stone inscriptions, the modern character (*cha*) did not become standard until the ninth century. However, the available data suggest that tea was being cultivated and processed as a drink in Sichuan by the Warring States period (481–221 B.C.). There is also a Han reference to buying tea in one city for shipment to another. By the end of the Han dynasty in A.D. 220, the cultivation and consumption of tea had spread to the lower Yangzi, and during the Northern and Southern Dynasties tea drinking became associated with the south, in contrast with the yoghurt drinks that marked the north. Accounts in herbals from the period show that tea was also used medicinally, often boiled together with other plants such as scallions or ginger.[40]

But it was only in the Tang that tea became an empire-wide drink linked to a range of cultural activities. The spread of tea drinking in the north was closely connected, for many reasons, with its use in Buddhist monasteries. Monks were not supposed to eat solids after noon, so they relied on liquids, and tea was especially good for helping them stay awake and attentive during sustained periods of meditation. The serving of tea also became a standard means of welcoming travelers, who frequently stayed in Buddhist monasteries, as attested in Ennin's diary, and its use as an expression of hospitality gradually spread among lay Buddhists as well. Because the best tea was grown on hillsides, where many monasteries were located, Buddhist monks began to produce tea themselves, as one of their many economic activities.

Tea drinking soon spread from Buddhists to the rest of Chinese society. Given the prestige of Buddhism in the northern dynasties, it seems likely that at least knowledge of the monastic habit of tea drinking was transmitted to the courts, where tea was sometimes used in ceremonies but not as a drink for pleasure. More important, tea figured prominently in the social interactions of monks and literati, as this ode to tea makes clear:

> Tea
> Fragrant leaves
> Tender shoots
> Admired by poets
> Loved by monks . . .

Yuan Zhen composed this verse on the principle of beginning with a line of a single character, then a couplet of two characters, then a tercet of three characters, and so on. Poems on the theme were so numerous that some people even referred to "tea poetry" as a literary genre.[41]

The first great work on tea, and the basis for most of our knowledge concerning its cultivation and preparation, is Lu Yu's *Tea Classic* (*Cha jing*), which was published in the 760s. Orphaned at an early age, Lu Yu was raised in a monastery and buried next to the reliquary stupa of his original Buddhist master. According to a contemporary, his book created a craze for tea sets and other paraphernalia, and by the end of the Tang dynasty he was worshipped as a god in many of the tea houses that sprang up as new venues for urban entertainment. The book included discussions of the names and qualities of teas, their picking and processing, the associated utensils, the art of boiling, the art of drinking, historical references, and the finest teas of each region.[42]

Indeed, the regional character of tea was crucial to its development as a commercial product. More than forty prefectures scattered throughout the south had substantial tea production, and there was constant dispute over which produced the finest teas. This competition took the form of each region sending its first crops to the emperor at court, where they were consumed during the imperial banquet for the Pure Brightness (*Qingming*) festival in the spring. Tea from areas on the border between Jiangsu and Zhejiang became particularly celebrated in the Tang. Late Tang emperors even gave officials promotions for sending them particularly choice teas. Tea drinking games developed at the court, and tea also became the drink of choice for candidates during examinations. Tea production helped reshape the regional economy in what is now Hubei, Hunan, Jiangxi, Anhui, Zhejiang, and Fujian provinces, where it was a valuable crop.[43]

The preferred method for processing tea was to make it into cakes. These were produced by steaming the leaves in special implements, pounding them in a mortar and pestle, pressing them into an iron mould, and then drying them in an oven. The cakes were then hung together on a cord for storage and shipping. The purchaser roasted the cake, allowed it to cool, ground off a portion as a powder that was passed through a sieve, and then poured hot water onto the tea in a special tea bottle. Froth on the tea was considered its essence, as it still is in Japanese tea ceremonies. More rarely, tea could be prepared by steeping loose leaves in a pot. Prior to sale, loose tea was stir-fried, as indicated in a poem by Liu Yuxi (772–842):

> I lean on the luscious bushes to pluck the eagle's beak,
> The leaves are stir-fried; the room is filled with the scent of tea.[44]

As a commercial crop, sugarcane was not as important for the Tang economy as tea, and would come into its own only during the Song.[45] It was introduced into south China from eastern India or Southeast Asia probably no earlier than the third century B.C., but prior to the Tang it remained an exclusively southern plant, being described as such in the sixth-century *Essential Methods of the Common People*. The production of its juice and amorphous sugar (boiled into a mass with no clear crystalline structure) became a major enterprise in Indian Buddhist monasteries, where the juice was used as an afternoon drink. Sugar products also played a major role in the preparation of medicines and in several Buddhist rituals. When diverse forms of sugar came to the attention of the Tang court through Buddhist pilgrims, Emperor Taizong sent envoys to India in 647 to learn the art of making them. The emperor then established a sugar production facility in what is now Zhejiang. Amorphous sugar from this site was sent to the court, and from there its use spread to other members of the elite.

By the late Tang, nine prefectures in the empire, including several monasteries, were sending sugarcane or sugar products to the court. Cane sugar manufacturing developed as far north as Dunhuang, where the only record of Tang sugar-producing technology was discovered, but this seems to have been for local use only. Outside the monasteries and the court, the primary urban demand for sugar products seems to have been among the Arab and Persian communities in Chang'an, Luoyang, Jiangdu, and Panyu, who put sugar products into sauces, drinks, and pastry confections. To the extent that urban Chinese consumed sugar, it seems to have been largely in the context of enjoying exotic foreign cuisines. Even in the late eighth century, Emperor Daizong bestowed twenty stalks of sugarcane as a "rare and wonderful gift."[46] Only in the Song dynasty would cane sugar become a familiar item to urban consumers. In the Tang dynasty it remained an exotic product, but as such it could stand as an emblem for the pivotal role in this dynasty of the exotic and the foreign.

6

THE OUTER WORLD

IN CHINA'S relations with the outer world, the Han dynasty was a time of discovery, exploration, and military expansion, while the Northern and Southern Dynasties was a period of reversal, when alien groups moved into northern China in large numbers and elements of foreign culture, above all Buddhism, transformed the lives of the Chinese. The Sui and Tang dynasties combined both these patterns, expanding outward while simultaneously drawing in large numbers of foreign peoples and their cultures. It was the most open, cosmopolitan period of Chinese history.

During the sixth and seventh centuries both the Sui and Tang dynasties, hoping to be heirs of the Han, devoted large amounts of time and resources to recovering lost Han territories. Expansion into northern Vietnam, wars against the Turks, the occupation of the oasis kingdoms of Central Asia, and expeditions to restore former Han colonies in southern Manchuria and Korea were the result. Emperor Yang's vision of matching the Han led to the abortive invasions of the Korean peninsula that destroyed the Sui dynasty, and Emperor Taizong of the Tang almost suffered the same fate. But just as the Tang dynasty could not avoid incorporating numerous institutional features that had evolved during the period of disunion, so the Tang emperors' dream of restoring the Han world had to adapt to a new international order.

Under the Han, China had been bordered to the north by tribal peoples whose cultures, socio-political structures, and lifestyles were totally different from their own—and, in the Chinese view, distinctly inferior. The Xiongnu tribal coalition had invaded and occupied parts of China, but they remained politically unstable, were incapable of administering a settled agrarian population, and had never challenged the feeling of cultural superiority among the Han. Defining the Chinese through systematic contrasts with nomads at their borders had become a key feature of the Han notion of civilization. In the centuries after the Han, however, when nomad-derived ruling houses controlled north China, the distinction between Chinese and foreign was blurred. Under the Sui and Tang dynasties, the situation changed again, creating an eastern Eurasian world of multiple states in which China was at the center but no longer the ruler.

The Tang dynastic house and its closest followers had strong cultural ties to the peoples of the steppes to the north and west, who in this period were dominated by Turks. This cultural familiarity allowed the formation of a Sino-Altaic (Turkic) system based on shared diplomacy, warfare, patrimonial political networks, and ideologies of heavenly-sanctioned rule. Within this system, the Tang rulers were able to manipulate fissures in the Turkic empire to their own advantage, draw the Turks and lesser tribes into a broader imperial system through patrimonial patron-client ties and diplomatic rituals, and draw Turkish allies into their armies. This large-scale reliance on foreign troops helped achieve security in the seventh century, but ultimately led to the An Lushan rebellion.

To the east, south, and southwest, Tang China, unlike previous dynasties, confronted alien peoples in new states that were organized along the same lines as China itself, albeit on a smaller scale. Their rulers embraced similar ideologies, patterned major elements of their government on China, and in the cases of Korea, Japan, Vietnam, and Nanzhao (in what is now Yunnan province in southwest China) conducted their government business in the Chinese written language, according to Chinese legal procedures. Although they paid tribute to the Tang, they were independent of Chinese control, and the Chinese treated them as respected, if not totally equal, neighbors. Even Tibet to the west, which became the great military rival of China from the late seventh century until the middle of the ninth century, was a sedentary (not nomadic) state that borrowed major political features from China. Combined with the extraordinary influence of Buddhism and the consequent prestige of India and the Central Asian states from which Buddhism came, these changes at China's borders set the scene for a new pattern of foreign relations that culminated in a concept of "China among equals" during the Song dynasty.

It was also during the Tang dynasty that China "lost" Central Asia to Islamic civilization, abandoning for nine centuries attempts to politically control this region. The project of Chinese dominance over the Western Regions (modern Xinjiang) had begun under the Han, largely lapsed during the northern dynasties, and resumed in the first century of Tang rule. The rise of Tibet initiated a diplomatic and military struggle involving all the powers that ringed Xinjiang, and in the context of this struggle Islamic armies first entered Central Asia. Their defeat of Tang forces, followed by the weakening of the Chinese state during the An Lushan rebellion, meant that even after the collapse of Tibet in the middle of the ninth century the Tang never successfully reasserted authority in Xinjiang. Not until the Manchu Qing dynasty in the eighteenth century would any Chinese empire move back into the region.

The simultaneous sinicization of East Asia and the Islamization of Central Asia caused a permanent rebalancing of China's relations with the outer world. The Tang's abandonment of Central Asia and its silk roads, along with growing Chinese settlement in the south and closer contacts with Chinese-oriented states in what are now Korea and Japan, stimulated a major extension of sea-based trade that came to dominate international exchange during the Tang. Largely in the hands of foreigners until the Song dynasty, China's commerce with neighboring states developed into a massive ocean-based trade in silk and porcelain that made China an integral element of a larger global system connected through water transport.

And as both a cause and consequence of this, the character and scale of the foreign presence in China changed dramatically during the Tang dynasty. Under the Han dynasty, the only foreigners in China were resettled nomads concentrated along the frontier, but by the Tang, the growing importance of international trade and Buddhism resulted in the presence of large numbers of merchants, students, and pilgrims. This new-style foreign population was largely concentrated in major cities, where foreigners came to play a dominant role in money-lending and the interlinked trade in wine, entertainment, and prostitutes. Although the cosmopolitan character of the empire declined in the ninth century, for at least two centuries the Tang dynasty's embrace of foreign peoples and cultures was a defining element of Chinese civilization.

The Tang Ruler as Heavenly Qaghan

The first clear distinction between the Tang international order and its classic Han predecessor was that the Tang ruling house and its closest followers, who made up the elite of the Guanzhong region, had over the preceding centuries intermarried with non-Chinese peoples and adopted many elements of nomadic culture, particularly military skills. While the distant origins of the founding Li family remain unclear, by the sixth century the family consisted of a line of prominent military men who were members of the mixed Chinese-Xianbei-Turkish aristocracy that had dominated northwest China under the Northern Zhou state and the subsequent Sui dynasty.[1] While Tang supporters tried to mask these origins, positing descent from an influential Han family, the Tang empire's new foreign policy toward the Turkish empire that had reunited the steppes was heavily based on the ruling house's cultural ties with non-Chinese nomads to the north and west.

This new policy emerged in the reign of the second emperor, Taizong, when the Tang empire abandoned the founder's policy of appeasing the Turks and set out instead to conquer them. Through a combination of conquest, diplomacy, and the dissemination of Tang culture, Emperor Taizong attempted to extend Chinese power in every direction. However, his only success in foreign policy was to temporarily incorporate the Turks into the Tang through conquest and diplomacy, a policy made possible by his and his advisers' familiarity with Turkish political and military structures.[2] After briefly avoiding foreign adventures in the name of stabilizing Tang rule, Taizong gradually conceived of a great dual empire that combined mastery of China, embodied in the traditional title of Son of Heaven, with lordship over the Turks, indicated by the new title of Heavenly Qaghan.

The Turks had established their empire in the middle of the sixth century by defeating their former lords, the Rouran. In a rapid series of conquests the founder, Tumen, established a nomadic confederacy stretching from the Caspian Sea to Manchuria. As in most nomadic states, however, the constituent tribes remained under their own rulers, linked to the supreme lord by patron-client ties. Moreover, the Turkish realm was divided into eastern and western wings, held together only by the kinship ties of their respective leaders. Succession passed laterally from brother to brother, and there was no system for excluding potential heirs or regulating the succession when it passed from one generation to the next. Thus, each transition from one qaghan to the next was marked by great tension and potential for violence, and generational shifts regularly led to civil war.[3]

When the Turks first arose, however, it was the Chinese who were divided. During the sixth century, Sino-Turkic relations formed a complicated diplomatic game in which each side sought to exacerbate and exploit divisions within the other side. Thus, under the Qaghan Mugan (r. 553–572), the rival Northern Zhou and Northern Qi courts sent lavish annual gifts of silk to the Turkish court in hopes of securing its support. This silk was, in turn, distributed to subordinate chiefs or traded to Iran and Byzantium. Around 581, just as the Sui was becoming established in north China, the Turkish empire split into eastern and western qaghanates, and a series of rival cousins subdivided the eastern section even further. Internecine struggles in the east allowed the western qaghan to assert his supremacy in 601, but his eastern campaign only gave discontented allies an opportunity to rebel against him.

When the Sui dynasty collapsed in 618, the newly divided Chinese once again became prey to manipulation by the Turks. The leading Chinese rebels sent ambassadors and gifts to the court of the eastern qaghan, who in turn granted them titles and small numbers of horses. Refugees from the Sui court, to which the qaghan was related by marriage, also sought protection with the Turks. The Tang founder himself, Li Yuan, wrote a personal letter to the qaghan requesting that the Turks join forces with him against the other Chinese rebels, or that the Turks at least sign a treaty of peace and receive his gifts. This letter was signed with a term by which Li Yuan, who may have been only one of several aspiring dynasts who sought Turkish aid, acknowledged inferior status. The qaghan replied that he would assist in quelling the rebels only if Li Yuan declared himself emperor. The Turks thus played off the Chinese contenders against one another to secure their own position, collect gifts, weaken China, and guarantee that whoever took power in China would be in their debt. When Li Shimin (Emperor Taizong) staged his coup d'état in 626, he secured his position by paying for protection from the eastern Turks who had invaded the capital region.[4]

In the very next year, however, the pendulum of unity and division swung back. The Turkish qaghan had begun to employ Sogdians to collect taxes, which provoked considerable discontent among subject peoples. When disastrous weather killed flocks and produced famines, the continued collection of taxes induced an open revolt led by yet another rival qaghan. With Tang support, the Xueyantuo, a Turkic people who had been subjects of the qaghan, now broke with the Turkish state. In 629 Tang armies joined the Xueyantuo and other peoples known as Tielo Turks to launch a surprise attack when the eastern qaghan was suing for peace, destroyed the Turkish forces, and brought an end to the eastern qaghanate.[5] Supposedly at the request of the newly conquered peoples, Taizong took for himself the title of Heavenly Qaghan and thereby claimed suzerainty over both China and the Turks.

Taizong's success at this juncture was due in part to his personal immersion in aspects of steppe culture. The model of combat by which he had risen to eminence as a prince was directly patterned on nomadic practices (Fig. 11). Skilled with horse, bow, and sword, Li Shimin had personally led his troops into combat, often placing himself at the front of a decisive charge. In contrast with the heavily armored cavalry employed by the northern dynasties and the Sui, the more mobile and flexible cavalry commanded by Li Shimin and subsequent Tang generals was usually described as "light cavalry," meaning that the horsemen wore armor but the horses did not. This seems to have been adopted from Turkish practices in order to confront the mobile nomad forces at the frontier. Li Shimin's cavalry tactics were patterned on those of the Turks as well.[6]

Even as a prince, Li Shimin had sworn personal oaths of blood brotherhood with Turkish associates, and his coup d'état was ratified with a horse sacrifice drawn directly from Turkish ritual practice. These religious and ritual borrowings from the Turks, and the use of adoptive kinship to secure ties, were part of a broader pattern of appeals to nomad culture with its emphasis on a charismatic leader who distinguished himself from other contenders through his cunning and heroism in battle. Even Li Shimin's rise to power through fratricide had more in common with the succession practices of the steppe than with those of Chinese tradition.[7] Taizong's skill in both fomenting dissatisfaction with the Turkish ruler and then manipulating that dissatisfaction to secure his own triumph seems to have grown directly out of his familiarity with steppe culture.

While the new title of Heavenly Qaghan was largely symbolic, it was not insignificant. Moreover, it testified to Taizong's vision of the empire as encompassing both Chinese and nomads, a vision that he regarded as his own particular contribution. Thus, he stated that the barbarians and Chinese shared a common nature and that a ruler's beneficent protection must extend to both of them. He also said, "The emperors since ancient times have all appreciated the Chinese and depreciated the barbarians. Only I view them as equal. That is why they look upon me as their parent."[8] This idea of equality was translated into practice in Taizong's policies of employing non-Chinese officers, granting them military titles, and even bestowing the imperial Li surname on many of them. Reliance on

Fig. 11   A battle scene depicted on a mural at Dunhuang, showing Tang armor and weapons.

non-Chinese commanders and troops came to dominate Tang military practice by the late seventh and eighth centuries.

The title of Heavenly Qaghan presumably appealed to the newly conquered Turks and other subject peoples, who also espoused a doctrine that the supreme ruler was chosen by Heaven. Their willingness to fight for the Tang may have been related to their recognition that their own political traditions were one important aspect of the empire. In the eighth

century, the crucial support that the Tang received from oasis states and
the Uighurs to the northwest in combating a revived Turkish empire and
in quelling the An Lushan rebellion also stemmed in part from the special
relationship marked by Taizong's new title.[9]

The Tang policy of incorporating nomads as functioning elements of
the army and of local administration was manifested in the institution of
subordinated commands and prefectures (*ji mi fu zhou,* literally "loose-
rein commands and prefectures"). Surrendered barbarians were grouped
into progressively larger units of districts, commanderies, prefectures,
and—in strategic areas—military commands. Rather than being directly
under the central government, these were under "protectorates" patterned on the Han institution that had administered the Western Regions.
Local chieftains or rulers were largely left in place to supervise their own
people. The offices they held were given Chinese titles, but they were hereditary. By the early eighth century a line of protectorates ran along
China's frontiers: Anxi (over the Western Turks, the Western Regions,
and Tibetans), Beiting (the Türgish people), Chanyu (ruling the Eastern
Turks), Anbei (over the Uighurs and other Tiele nomads), Andong (over
the Koreans, Khitan, Xi, and Mohe), and Annam (over non-Chinese in
what is now Vietnam). Together with the Tang frontier armies, which
were heavily barbarian and commanded by non-Chinese military governors, these protectorates formed the basis of Tang border defense and administration.[10]

The policy of incorporating the Turks into the Tang state bore fruit in
victories over other non-Chinese peoples. An expeditionary army consisting largely of surrendered Turks and the Xueyantuo occupied Gaochang
in 639, thus enabling the first Tang prefecture and protectorate in Central
Asia to be established. Availing himself of a succession struggle, Taizong
crushed the Xueyantuo, his former allies, in 646 and the following year
established them in a protectorate at the frontier. Over the next decade
the nomad allies of the Tang pushed further into the Western Regions, defeating the Western Turks and occupying first Kucha in 648 and then
Karashahr. In 649, after Taizong's death, the Western Turks again rebelled, but they were finally decisively beaten in 659. In the next few
years the Tang established more than one hundred commands and prefectures in the region, pushing their boundaries as far as Persia. This was the
farthest that any Chinese dynasty would ever press into the west.[11]

However, in contrast with many other peoples conquered by the Tang
in this period, the Turks placed under Chinese administration or resettled

inside China did not adopt Chinese institutions or its writing system. Moreover, the death of Taizong and the accession of his sickly successor Gaozong weakened the link between the Tang and the Turks. The rise of a government dominated by court favorites and examination-selected bureaucrats blocked the access of non-Chinese to government posts and reduced the status of military service.[12] In the 660s, when Chinese forces were preoccupied with campaigns in Korea, the rising Tibetan state conquered the Tuyuhun people in what is now Qinghai. In 670 they occupied Kucha, thus driving the Tang largely out of the area south of the Tianshan Mountains. A Tang counter-offensive was crushed at Kokonor, and in 678 another Tang expeditionary force was routed. These defeats allowed the Turks to form a new empire that militarily threatened China for several decades.[13] The Turks remained major actors on the Chinese political stage even after their empire fell apart in 745, and when the Tang itself fell in the early tenth century much of north China was occupied by Turkish rulers.

The Emergence of East Asia

In addition to new policies toward the nomadic peoples of the north and northwest, Tang China's foreign relations were also shaped by the emergence of sedentary states to the east, south, and southwest that adopted major elements of Chinese civilization. The most important of these were Korea, Japan, and Nanzhao (Yunnan), although there were also important exchanges with the region that would become Vietnam.

The emergence of these states is a classic example of secondary-state formation, that is, the development of polities in part through the intrusion of an existing state that serves both as provocation and model. States around China were often founded through an investiture process in which chosen local chieftains sent gifts to the Chinese court, for which they received titles as kings or dukes and the appropriate seals of office. While Chinese emperors claimed the status of universal rulers and recognized neighboring states only as vassals, it is significant that in many cases these neighbors actively sought recognition as elements of the Chinese world order.

In the northern part of what would become Korea, the early state of Koguryǒ sent tribute to the Han in A.D. 32, and then its rulers adopted the title of king. A later state in the south of the Korean peninsula, Paekche, established relations with the Jin court in 372, and by 386 its ruler had received titles from the Chinese court as a general and deputy king. In the third century, Himiko, a priestess-chieftain in the Japanese islands, sought titles from the Wei court, and in the fifth century more than a dozen tribute missions were sent from the aspiring Japanese court in hopes of receiving titles and support from the dynasts of south China. These titles distinguished ambitious local chieftains from their rivals, bestowing prestige and influence on them from the reflected splendor of the Chinese empire.[14] While the submission of these foreign rulers was purely formal and those who received titles would often actively combat Chinese influence and armies, the language and practices of statecraft in East Asia derived from the Chinese model.

At the beginning of the Tang, the Korean peninsula was divided into the kingdoms of Koguryŏ, Silla, and Paekche (see Map 5). The expense of unsuccessful campaigns against the first of these had led to the fall of the Sui dynasty, but at the installation of the Tang all three states sent tribute to the new court. With the return of all Chinese prisoners in 622, Gaozu agreed to recognize the independence of the Korean states as nominal Chinese vassals. In 640 princes of the Korean states, along with those from Gaochang (in modern Xinjiang), Japan, and Tibet, all studied at the imperial academy in Chang'an.

However, in 642 a Koguryŏ minister overthrew the prince who had studied at Chang'an, mutilated his corpse, and set up his younger brother on the throne. In response, Taizong led expeditions against Koguryŏ in 645, 647, and 648, but like the earlier Sui offensives these bogged down in the muddy roads of Liaoning and achieved nothing. Under the next emperor, Gaozong, the Tang allied with Silla, which had adopted the Chinese writing system and government institutions, occupied Paekche, and used their new base in Korea to launch an expedition against Koguryŏ. The death of Koguryŏ's ruler in 666 led to internal dissension, and in 668 the Chinese finally occupied the state and carried off more than 200,000 prisoners to Chang'an. In the 670s the newly sinicized Silla succeeded in uniting most of Korea, and the Tang, focused on the rising menace of Tibet, could no longer pursue the conquest of the peninsula. Korea remained a nominal Tang vassal institutionally modeled on the Chinese state.[15]

In 630 the Japanese sent their first delegation to the Tang, and, although Japan was too distant to interest the Tang court, the reform element in the Japanese leadership eagerly accepted China as a cultural and political model. In 649 the Japanese court launched a series of major political reforms that recreated Japan as a centralized monarchy with a legal code, military system, landholding patterns, and taxation all modeled on the Tang. The Japanese government also adopted the Chinese writing system for all official and literary activities, although modifications were required to adapt Chinese writing to the unrelated Japanese language. Other elements of Chinese elite culture, such as clothing, poetry, and music, also became models at the Japanese Heian court. With Buddhism emerging as a dominant intellectual and religious force in Japan, Tang China also became the destination of tens of thousands of Japanese pilgrims, who studied at monasteries and acquired statues and copies of scriptures to take back to Japan. These pilgrims and Japanese tribute missions became familiar sights in many Chinese cities.[16]

In 264 the large southeast region that had been known as Lingnan under the Han was permanently split into two regions, Guangzhou and Jiaozhou, which roughly corresponded to what would become Guangdong and north Vietnam. During the period of division, Jiaozhou, centered on the Red River valley, split off as a largely autonomous region and formally declared its independence in 541. It was retaken by the Sui but became independent again when that dynasty fell. The Tang reconquered most of modern Vietnam and in 679 established a southern protectorate-general that ruled the area until the end of the ninth century. Through most of the Tang, Jiaozhou remained an orderly region of the empire, but its capital, Jiaozhi (Hanoi), steadily lost its role in international trade to the rising entrepôt of Panyu (modern Guangzhou). When the Tang empire collapsed at the beginning of the tenth century, Jiaozhou became the scene of a bloody struggle for power that ended in 938 when a man named Ngo Quyen established an independent state that eventually became Vietnam. However, this state continued to employ Tang script, weights, measures, and coinage. Confucian culture patterned on that of China also flourished there.[17]

The southwest area that would later become Yunnan province was gradually forged into a unitary state known as Nanzhao. This kingdom, which emerged in the middle of the seventh century, played off Tang China against Tibet, leading each state to think that it was an ally, then supporting Tibet in the middle of the eighth century, only to reverse again and ally with Tang China as the century drew to a close. Its early kings received seals and titles from the Tang court, and its bureaucracy and examination system were largely patterned on the Tang, although the state also incorporated elements of Tibetan political practice, such as sumptuary regulations on the wearing of tiger skins.[18]

While these states were primarily linked through their shared imitation of Tang political and legal institutions, they also shared a common adherence to Buddhism (although Nanzhao formally converted only in the late ninth century) and a common nonalphabetic script. Buddhism had come to China along with Buddhist merchants from India and Central Asia. From China it spread to Korea, Japan, and the Vietnam region, so that the whole of the emerging East Asian cultural sphere shared a common Mahayana Buddhist faith. This common religion encouraged considerable movement of people in search of education and sacred objects.[19] The East Asian cultural sphere was also defined by its use of Chinese writing. A nonalphabetic script had helped the first Chinese empires unite peoples who spoke mutually unintelligible languages, and in the same way Chinese script became the *lingua franca* in which Chinese, Japanese, and Korean people could read and understand the same text, even though they pronounced it in radically different ways. More importantly, since Chinese graphs carried a fixed semantic element, the introduction of the writing system brought with it a specific vocabulary with an associated ideology. The shared script thus encouraged the spread of certain root concepts or values throughout the East Asian sphere.[20]

The Chinese empire had always defined itself through an artificial, court-based culture that transcended regional variation to draw together elites from what had been independent states. This translocal culture, as defined through a literary language and its texts, in turn provided a model of civilized life whose values were disseminated throughout East Asia under the Tang dynasty. The belief in ritual as a model for social behavior, the centrality of the family, the emphasis on hierarchy, the clear separation of genders, and the importance of text-based learning were among the ideas carried to Korea, Japan, and other new states of East Asia, along with the Chinese political and legal system and script.[21] To the extent that there is any content to contemporary propaganda about "[East] Asian values," it stems from ideas disseminated in this period.

The Reconfiguration of International Trade

Even as the Tang model spread east and south, developments began that would lead to China's abandonment of Central Asia and the rupture of the trade routes that had served as the primary avenue for importing Buddhism from India to China. This shifting balance started before the outbreak of the An Lushan rebellion in 756. Silla's unification of Korea ended Tang attempts to annex the peninsula, and the rise of the Khitans in the northeast revived a northern threat that seemed to have vanished with the Turks. Soon the Turks themselves would form their second empire and once again raid China's frontiers.[22]

However, the greatest changes occurred in the west. The rising power of Tibet, which offered nominal allegiance to the Tang in the 630s, continued to expand to the north and the west. After destroying the Tuyuhun, they began to threaten Tang positions in the southwest, where the rising Nanzhao kingdom allied with the Tibetans, and in the northwest, where the Tibetans expanded into the Chinese western protectorate-general in the Tarim Basin (see Map 6). To counter the Tibetan threat, the Tang court not only pressed militarily into the Western Regions and destroyed the Western Turks but also engaged in a frenzy of diplomatic activity with Kashmir, the Ganges valley, and parts of what is now Afghanistan. Following the route pioneered by the famous pilgrim Xuanzang (ca. 596–664), more than fifty diplomatic missions between 637 and 753 went to northern India in search of both trade and allies against Tibet.[23]

The An Lushan rebellion marked the pivotal moment when the balance between the Tang and the outside world reversed. As foreign mercenary servants of the Tang state claimed dominance, many other foreigners similarly asserted themselves. When Emperor Xuanzong fled into temporary exile in Sichuan, the Uighurs, formerly vassals of the Eastern Turks, played a key role in rescuing the Tang dynasty. But when the Tang's reward did not meet the Uighur leader's expectations, he withdrew his support. Taking advantage of Tang weakness, the Tibetans in 763 occupied modern Qinghai and Gansu, pushed into Shaanxi, and pillaged Chang'an. Under Guo Ziyi, the Tang army recaptured the capital, only to face a combined Uighur and Tibetan army that once again captured the Tang capital, in 765. Only the death of the Uighur commander and the subsequent rupture between the Uighurs and Tibet allowed the Tang to seize the initiative, form an alliance with the Uighurs, and regain Chang'an.

For more than half a century the Tang depended on the support of the Uighurs to defend against regular Tibetan incursions, and this dependence led Uighur soldiers and merchants living in China to disregard imperial authority in the late eighth and early ninth centuries.[24] Only an internal split in the Uighur leadership allowed another Turkic people, the Kirghiz, to attack them from the northwest. Eager to escape foreign domination, the Tang allied with the Kirghiz to defeat the Uighurs, who settled into a quiescent existence in what is now Xinjiang. Emboldened by their success, the Tang imposed a ban on all private dealings with "the darker races" that ended the Uighur dominance of money-lending in northwest China.[25]

In spite of its on-again, off-again alliance with the Uighurs, the Tang dynasty was unable to reassert its authority in Central Asia. The Tibetans continued to control most of modern Qinghai and Gansu provinces and destroyed the western protectorate-general. However, in the southwest, the Tibetans' inability to maintain their alliance with Nanzhao prevented them from occupying the province of Sichuan despite a massive invasion in 779. A major Tang victory in 802 brought an end to serious Tibetan incursions, but in 821 the Chinese signed a treaty with the Tibetans that recognized the current boundaries. In doing so, the Tang, whose military and political energies were totally concentrated on restoring the central court's power over the military governors in the northeast, formally renounced all claims to its former position in Central Asia.[26]

After checking Tibetan ambitions in the southwest, the Nanzhao kingdom invaded Sichuan in 829 and reached the outskirts of the capital, Chengdu. Despite formally amicable relations with Tang China to the north, in 859 the kingdom turned its attention to the east, overran Guizhou, and attacked the Annam protectorate-general. After repeated attacks, the capital, modern Hanoi, fell in 863, and more than 150,000 Tang subjects were taken prisoner. When the Tang recovered Annam in 863, Nanzhao once again invaded Sichuan and reached the capital but failed to take it.[27]

Even after the Tibetan kingdom had collapsed by 850 and Nanzhao had gone into permanent decline in the last decades of the ninth century, the Tang empire still did not regain its position in Central Asia. This region fell under the sway of the expanding Arab power that was spreading Islam across Asia. Having destroyed the Persian Sassanian empire in the seventh century and swallowed up a number of smaller city-kingdoms, in 751 Arab troops clashed with Chinese forces for the first time, crushing them at the battle of the Talas River. The outbreak of the An Lushan rebellion and conquests in northwest China by Tibet left the Arabs free to push into Central Asia. The success of this invasion meant the loss of Chinese control west of the city of Dunhuang until the Manchu conquest in the eighteenth century. It also meant the permanent loss of Central Asia as a part of the Buddhist world and the Chinese cultural zone.[28]

The old oasis cities of the Tarim and Dzumgarian basins, abandoned by the Tibetans, were occupied by the Uighurs, who had been driven from their steppe homeland by the Kirghiz. The rich and complex cultures of the area, an amalgam of Indo-European, Iranian, Indian, and Chinese influences, were destroyed under the successive onslaughts of Turks, Chinese, Tibetans, Arabs, and Uighurs. During the succeeding centuries the whole region up to the border of Gansu became a frontier zone of the Islamic world rather than an outpost of Chinese cultural and political influence. The disappearance of Buddhism in Central Asia and its simultaneous decline in India meant that after the suppression of Buddhism in the 840s in China, itself an expression of growing anti-foreignism, Chinese Buddhism could no longer look to its old Indian wellsprings for inspiration. Instead, dominated by indigenous intellectual traditions such as Chan and Pure Land, Buddhism emerged as a truly Chinese religion, permeating society in both the annual ritual calendar and several life-cycle rituals. The spread of Buddhism across Korea and Japan made China the center of a newly structured East Asian Buddhist world.[29]

In addition to the old silk roads, a few other land routes were significant to international trade under the Tang (Map 16). The products of Manchuria and Korea came through the forests and plains of Liaoyang and down the coast of the Gulf of Bohai through a narrow passage between mountains and sea that became the east end of the Ming Great Wall. Another overland route, very old but little used before the Tang, passed south from Sichuan through Nanzhao (Yunnan), split into two roads through the chasms of the Irrawaddy in modern-day Burma, and led from there into Bengal. China's efforts to develop this route were frustrated by the rise of Nanzhao in the eighth century, which was friendlier to the Tibetans than to the Tang. Buddhist pilgrims sometimes took the difficult route from China through Tibet to India, descending by way of Nepal, but this mountain path was too hazardous and slow to be useful for trade.[30]

The Tang's shift in orientation away from Central Asia and toward the east changed both China's relations to Buddhism and its trade ties to the outer world. As Chinese culture and political influence declined in Central Asia and broke its ties to India, it made deeper inroads in the east. Buddhism, particularly its Mahayana form, increasingly became an East Asian religion with China as its center. Only Tibet, more a part of Central than of East Asia, turned to India as its source for Buddhism in the Tantric form that marked the final flourishing of Indian Buddhism in the Pala state (750?–1155) of what is now Bengal. Consequently, over

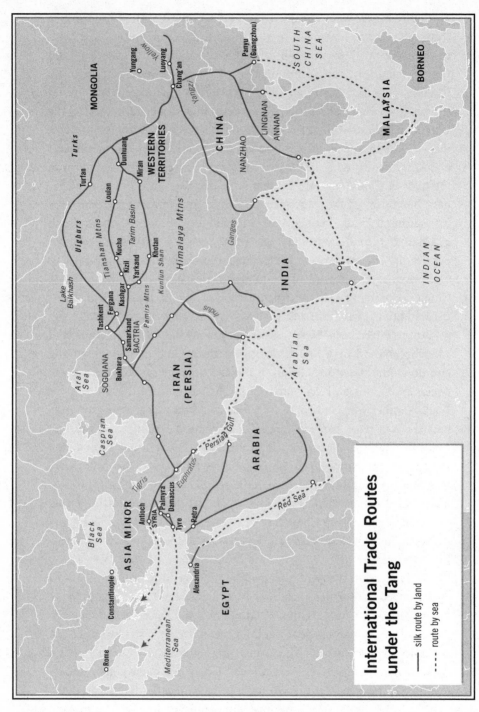

International Trade Routes under the Tang

——— silk route by land

----- route by sea

MAP 16

the course of time commerce between India and China increasingly became the sphere of non-Buddhist traders, maritime routes became more important than the silk roads, and international trade focused on nonreligious luxury and bulk products. Even explicitly Buddhist objects and substances that had earlier been purchased from India, including esoteric ritual paraphernalia and lapis lazuli, would be eventually produced in China.[31] But during the Tang dynasty, Buddhism remained a significant influence on foreign trade and on the relations of China with India and western Central Asia.

As overland routes into China—dominated by Sogdians, Parthians, and Indians and often trading precious goods used in Buddhist rituals—went into a slow decline from the middle of the Tang dynasty, new sea-based routes dominated by Muslim traders rose to prominence.[32] From the establishment of the Sassanid state in A.D. 225, Persian traders had begun to dominate maritime trade between China, India, the Persian Gulf, and the Red Sea. Consequently, Persian became the *lingua franca* among maritime traders between the Red Sea and southeast China. The idea that all Persians were wealthy merchants was such an established stereotype in Tang China that the phrase "poor Persian" was considered an oxymoron. When Arab forces conquered Persia in the seventh century, many of the Persian traders converted to Islam and were joined by Arab merchants, although it was only in the Song dynasty that Arabs would became the leading non-Chinese merchants in East Asia.

Tang merchants themselves relied on foreign vessels. Tombs on the west coast of India and copper-plate edicts from the east show the spread of Arab merchant communities across India in association with the trade. An Arab writer indicated that thousands of Arab traders were massacred in Panyu (Guangzhou) when rebel forces under Huang Chao occupied the city in 879. By the late tenth century, Muslim merchants were transporting Chinese silk and porcelain through or around southern India to the Persian Gulf and shipping aromatics and spices back in the other direction.[33]

From the middle of the eighth century, these maritime routes across the Arabian Sea, the Bay of Bengal, and the South China Sea became more popular than the increasingly dangerous overland routes. This trade was governed by the periodic shifts of the monsoon. Ships outbound from Panyu sailed in late autumn or winter, before the northeast monsoon, while fleets from the Persian Gulf, thousands of miles to the west, relied on that same winter monsoon to carry them across the Indian Ocean. In

June they caught the stormy southwest monsoon to carry them north-ward from Malaya across the South China Sea to their destinations in south China. The rule, when going both east and west, was southward in winter, northward in summer.

From the seventh to the ninth century, the Indian Ocean was a safe and rich sea protected by the Abassid caliphate, particularly after its capital was moved from Damascus to Baghdad, which was much closer to the head of the Persian Gulf. The Persian and Arab merchants headed out from the gulf, stopped at Muscat in Oman, and then either risked the pirate-infested ports of the Sind or proceeded directly to Malabar and then Sri Lanka, where they purchased precious gems. Then they sailed on to the Malay Peninsula, through the straits of Malacca and, riding the summer monsoon, north to Jiaozhi (Hanoi) or Panyu.[34]

This growth of maritime trade was stimulated by developments in technology. As early as the eighth century, Chinese writers describe large sea-going vessels that could carry a thousand men along with a full cargo. The hulls of these so-called Kunlun ships (a general term for the dark-skinned people who came to China from the south and for the lands that produced them) were made from wooden planks tied together with cords made from the bark of coconut trees. Also known as "sewn" vessels, these ships were employed by both Arab merchants and those from South or Southeast Asia. During the Tang there is no evidence that Chinese merchants engaged in sea trade, and only in the Song dynasty do we find records of a maritime trade dominated by Chinese vessels that had bulk-heads and nailed hulls, and navigated with the aid of the magnetic com-pass and accurate charts.[35]

Because large ships can carry bulk cargos across great distances at rea-sonable expense, the rise of maritime trade changed the nature of the commodities China sold to the outer world. In previous dynasties, it had primarily exported silk to India along land routes, often in exchange for precious goods used in Buddhist rituals or for Buddhist ritual para-phernalia. Chinese silk declined as an export commodity after the tenth century, when Muslim Turks introduced sericulture and silk cloth pro-duction to India and the Middle East. Thereafter, porcelain became the major Chinese commodity trans-shipped through India. The Indians ap-parently did not use the porcelain themselves but made large profits by re-exporting it to the Persian Gulf and Red Sea, while local rulers filled their coffers with taxes from the sale of these goods.[36] Long-distance trade in such a heavy, fragile commodity, which sold at a relatively low price, was possible only with the advent of sea trade. The production and sale of porcelain would become a major world industry under subsequent Chinese dynasties.

The shift of Chinese trade toward the southern seas changed the pattern of Tang imports. In place of precious metals, semiprecious stones, coral, and similar luxury goods, the new maritime trade allowed China to import greater quantities and varieties of spices and medicines and several types of timber from southeast Asia. By the tenth and eleventh centuries, other imported staples included horses, sulphur, ivory, and cinnabar. The great supply of such goods was made possible by integrated interregional trading networks that delivered these products to any city in China and guaranteed a good return on the costs of purchase and shipping.[37]

Maritime trade and large-scale exchange of bulk commodities constituted the first steps toward a genuine world economy, an integrated economic structure that transcended all defined political units. Unlike mere contact or low-level exchange between states or civilizations, a world economic system exists only when the social and economic order within each of its constituent elements is significantly altered by participation in the whole. By the late Song dynasty, world trade consisted of three large circuits: Western Europe, the Middle East, and East Asia. In each of these areas the scale of foreign trade was sufficiently large to alter the social and economic order, so that a common division of labor bound all the areas together. This system, in contrast with the modern one, had no single center, but China was the greatest exporter and consequently the end point to which precious metals increasingly flowed. While this three-part global structure did not yet exist in the Tang, the East Asian maritime trade circuit through which China joined the world economy came into existence at this time. Thus, the pre-modern world economy, with China as its single greatest participant, was built on a foundation of maritime trade to the Tang empire pioneered by Muslim merchants in the eighth and ninth centuries.[38]

Foreigners in Tang China

Two keys to the vitality of the Tang were eclecticism (its ability to draw on all the cultural strands that constituted the history of the preceding centuries) and cosmopolitanism (its openness to foreigners and their diverse ways of life). Foreigners and foreign cultures were a prominent element throughout the Tang empire, particularly in the cities, and did much to define its culture. Among the most important kinds of foreigners were envoys, merchants, performers, soldiers, and clerics, representing the great interests of politics, commerce, entertainment, the military, and religion.[39]

Envoys entered Tang China in a steady stream, as more and more peoples sought to establish diplomatic ties with East Asia's greatest empire. This practice began when relations were established with eastern Central Asia during the Han dynasty, and continued as Japan, Korea, and other states sent emissaries and tribute in exchange for recognition during the Northern and Southern Dynasties. By the time of the Tang dynasty, an elaborate protocol specified the frequency of visits, the relative priority of visitors from each state, and the conduct of their audiences with the emperor. Any state that desired the favor or patronage of the Tang offered nominal submission in exchange for Chinese titles and insignias. Emissaries were then expected to periodically visit the Tang capital, where they received special insignia (half of a wooden fish) that the ambassador presented upon his arrival at court. Since these delegations were officially bearers of tribute, they would appear at court in their native costumes and carry precious objects characteristic of their state. The presence of such exotic visitors in the capital was a tangible sign that the powers of the Tang ruling house were world-encompassing.

In the seventh and early eighth centuries, foreign tribute bearers were a popular subject for court painters, who portrayed these wild foreigners with a certain condescending curiosity. Painters such as Yan Liben and Yan Lide rose to prominence at court primarily through their ability to paint the strange visages and outlandish costumes of tribute bearers (Fig. 12). Although only a few copies of such works survive, we know from pottery figurines and wall paintings in tombs that it was usual to emphasize the visitors' pointy noses, full beards, curly hair, and native costumes (Fig. 13).[40]

Tribute bearers would have been a visible presence to ordinary Chinese people only along the roads to the capital. By far the most common and influential foreigners in Tang China, and those most frequently depicted in the art and literature of the period, were merchants. These men brought slaves, dwarves, entertainers, wild animals, furs, feathers, rare plants, tropical wood, exotic foods, perfumes, drugs, textiles, dyes, jewels, metals, and diverse *objets d'art* both secular and sacred, as well as books and maps that told of foreign places. Tang people living in cities

Fig. 12 Depiction of foreign tribute bearers from a Tang scroll.

Fig. 13 Detail showing the clothing and features of foreign tribute bearers, as depicted on a Tang scroll.

Fig. 14   Pottery figure of a foreigner riding a camel.

would have known and appreciated such foreign wares and would have viewed as a bumpkin anyone who knew only about things Chinese. Thus, at least in the cities, the Tang international order led to an internationalized Tang.[41]

Like the clothing of tribute bearers, the distinctive costumes and physical appearance of foreign merchants became a colorful element of Tang civilization (Fig. 14). Perhaps because men from the Western Regions

Fig. 15   Pottery figure of a foreigner mounted on a horse.

were the most important foreign traders, they provided the stereotypical physical markers of a foreigner. The high nose and deep-set eyes were formulaic in accounts of alien physiognomy (Figs. 15 and 16). Thus, a monumental history of Chinese institutions, the *Comprehensive Institutions* (*Tong dian*) compiled by Du You (735–812), stated, "The inhabitants of the country to the west of Gaochang mainly have deep eyes and high noses. Only in Khotan do the people resemble not so much Hu [Central Asian] as Han." The same image was also reworked into hyperbolic

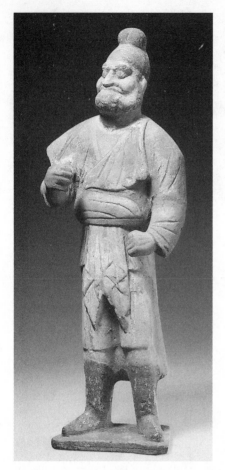

Fig. 16 Pottery figure of a foreign groom.

verse, as in a poem of praise presented to the daughter of a non-Han acquaintance:

> Eyes deeper than the Xiang and Yangzi rivers,
> A nose higher than the Hua and Yue mountains.[42]

During the Tang, in sharp contrast with the Han, the foreign presence in Chinese cities was large and permanent, and the distribution of foreign merchants followed the patterns of trade. To the northeast, navigation lay largely in the hands of Koreans, with the Japanese playing a limited role. These sailors usually followed the coast around the north edge of the Yellow Sea to reach port in Shandong. After Silla conquered Koguryŏ and Paekche in the 660s and blocked Japanese ships, traders from Nagasaki attempted to skirt the Korean monopoly by crossing directly to the mouth of the Yangzi or Hangzhou bay. However, this was a risky venture, and consequently most Japanese pilgrims, merchants, and emissaries traveled on Korean vessels or on those of the Manchurian state of Pohai. Consequently, Korean traders formed a significant foreign group in the towns along the canals connecting the Yangzi to the Yellow River, above all in Jiangdu (Yangzhou) and Lianshui. As with all communities of foreigners in Tang China, they lived in special wards under government supervision but enjoyed a variety of extra-territorial legal privileges and were directly administered by chiefs from their own states.[43]

In southern China, the great center for foreign merchants was the port of Panyu, then a frontier town on the edge of a tropical wilderness populated by savages and wild beasts. A large part of the 200,000 inhabitants consisted of foreigners: Indians, Persians, Arabs, Javanese, and Malays. A foreign quarter south of the river was set aside by imperial sanction for these people. Gradually this settlement became a permanent sprawling foreign community that was much larger than the walled Chinese settlement. As elsewhere in Tang China, the foreign quarter of Panyu was headed by a designated elder, who in the ninth century was an Arab. The port flourished until 758, when a fleet of Arab and Persian pirates looted the warehouses and then burned the city to the ground. For the next half century it was eclipsed by Jiaozhi, only recovering in the early ninth century. The primary form of trade in this city was the exchange of gems, tropical wood, and medicines for Chinese silk, porcelains, and slaves frequently kidnapped from among the aboriginal inhabitants of the far southeast.[44]

Smaller communities of Arabs and Persians developed in towns along the routes from Panyu north to Jiangdu, at the intersection of the Yangzi River and the Grand Canal. As the hub not only for trans-shipment along the canal but also for empire-wide trade in tea and salt, this city became the commercial and banking center of the empire. The head of the salt monopoly, who was based there, was the most powerful figure after the emperor in the late eighth-century Tang government, and salt merchants were the wealthiest businessmen in the realm. Thousands of non-Chinese traders established shops in Jiangdu, and in 760 a rebel army, in an early outburst of anti-foreignism, massacred several tens of thousands of the city's foreign merchants. Nevertheless, Jiangdu remained a major center of East Asian trade into the late eighth century.[45]

In the north, the greatest concentrations of foreign merchants were in the two capitals, especially Chang'an, which was the endpoint of the silk roads and the Grand Canal. Consequently, its international population differed from that of the southern ports, consisting primarily of Turks, Uighurs, and Sogdians, in contrast with the Chams, Khmers, Javanese, and Sinhalese who thronged Jiaozhi, Panyu, and Fuzhou. But like the southeastern cities, Chang'an also hosted many Arab, Persian, and Indian traders, concentrated around the capital's Western Market. The Iranian population was so large that the Tang government established a special office in the city to look after their interests. As one proceeded westward from Chang'an, the cities all had large foreign communities, and in towns in the Gansu corridor, such as Dunhuang and Liangzhou, foreigners far outnumbered Chinese.

By the ninth century, the Uighurs' domination of the money-lending profession in Chang'an had become notorious, and these foreigners were universally despised for their arrogance and their contempt for Chinese law. In the early decades of the ninth century, as prices steadily rose, many Chinese businessmen and officials fell into debt to the Uighurs and were forced to pledge land, furniture, slaves, and even sacred relics or family heirlooms to their Turkic creditors. When a Uighur murdered a Chinese merchant in broad daylight, he was helped to escape by his chief while the Chinese government stood by helpless. The situation grew so bad that in 836 all private intercourse with "various dark peoples" was banned.[46]

In addition to money-lending, foreigners in Tang China dominated several other trades that were important to the urban populace. Wine shops were most commonly run by Sogdians or speakers of Tocharian, and there was a strong non-Chinese flavor to both the entertainment and the prostitution on offer. The foreign-owned wine shop with its Central Asian serving girl or female entertainers was a standard theme in Tang poetry and art, as was the foreign wine vendor (Fig. 17). Central Asian music was popular throughout the cities, and in the capital it spread from bars and official pleasure quarters to every site where entertainment and sex could be bought. By the eighth century, Chinese popular music was scarcely distinguishable from that of the oasis states of Central Asia. This was true even at the court, where the favorite song of Emperor Xuanzong and his beloved consort, Yang Guifei, was an adapted Central Asian melody. The music of the state of Kucha, sometimes as modified in the frontier province of Liang, was particularly popular, and even emperors stud-

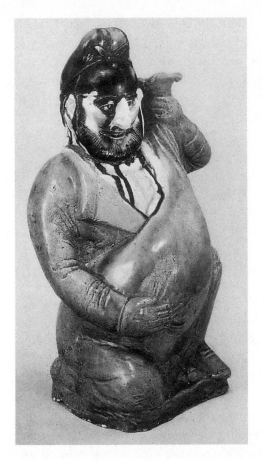

Fig. 17   Pottery figurine of a
foreign wine merchant with a
wine bag.

ied its performance. Exotic tunes from the states of Southeast Asia and
Korea also became popular.

Dancers from foreign lands were major figures in Tang culture, whose
poetry is full of references to young boys and women performing exotic dances in their distinctive native costumes. In the Western Prancing
Dance, boys from Tashkent wore high-peaked hats, tight-sleeved shirts,
and long belts whose ends floated freely as they whirled and leaped. In
the Dance of Chāch, named after its place of origin near Tashkent, young
women danced in colorful gauze caftans, silver girdles, high-peaked caps
with bells, and red brocade shoes. At the conclusion of this erotic dance,
the women pulled down their blouses to expose naked shoulders. Perhaps most striking were accounts of the Sogdian dance of the Western
Whirling Girls. Women clad in crimson robes with brocade sleeves, green

damask pantaloons, and red deerskin boots twirled on top of rolling balls. Emperor Xuanzong and Yang Guifei loved this dance, and in the poetry of the period its erotic and foreign nature was treated as both a sign of imperial corruption and an omen of the impending rebellion:

> Whirling girl, whirling girl,
> Heart answers strings,
> Hand answers drum,
> When strings and drum resound together,
> Both of her sleeves lift high,
> And she drifts in twirls like circling snow,
> Dancing the spinning tumbleweed.
>
> . . .
>
> When An Lushan did the Whirl,
> He bewildered the ruler's eyes.
> Even when troops crossed the Yellow River,
> It was doubted he had rebelled.
> When Yang Guifei did the Whirl,
> She befuddled the ruler's heart;
> When she was dead at Mawei Station,
> He yearned for her ever more.[47]

As this poem indicates, a final foreign presence that hung menacingly just inside the borders of Tang China was the large mercenary armies, recruited primarily from foreigners, that defended China from the Tibetans, the Khitans, and the Turks. The size of these armies grew steadily, especially after chief minister Li Linfu, seeking to prevent his adversaries at court from gaining military power, placed frontier armies under the command of foreign military governors. One such army, commanded by a Sogdian named Rokushan (represented in Chinese characters as An Lushan), launched the rebellion that almost destroyed the Tang and marked a sharp turning point in the history of China.

Buddhists as Foreigners

In addition to envoys, merchants, entertainers, and soldiers, another sizeable foreign element in Tang society was Buddhist teachers and pilgrims. India and the oasis towns of Central Asia had provided China with learned monks and scholars who introduced Tantric and other doctrines into China, although these were no longer as influential as in the past. More important, large numbers of Buddhists from Korea and Japan flocked to visit famous Chinese sites and to study at the great monasteries. Their wanderings carried a visible foreign presence into the countryside and the distant hilly regions where many monasteries were located. Zoroastrians, Manicheans, worshippers of Mazda, Nestorian Christians, and Jews also entered Tang China as merchants and missionaries, but Buddhism was the great foreign faith.[48]

One important question is the degree to which Tang Buddhism remained a "foreign" religion. Over the centuries Buddhism had become an inextricable element of Chinese culture, and in China's relations with the outer world it had facilitated the emergence of a new sinocentric East Asian cultural sphere. Moreover, during the Tang dynasty, forms of Buddhism developed in China itself came to dominate the religion, and most of the population participated in Buddhist festivals and Buddhist forms of the cult of the dead. Nevertheless, in certain ways Buddhism remained an alien faith for many Chinese, in contrast to the indigenous traditions of Daoism and Confucian teachings.[49] The foreign nature of Buddhism was marked in its origins, and some art depicted the Buddha and his followers as foreigners (Fig. 18). Anti-Buddhist polemics likewise insisted that Buddha was a barbarian. The most extreme expression of this position consisted of memorials calling for the suppression of Buddhism that the Daoist priest Fu Yi presented in the 620s:

[Before Buddhism] there were no barbarian [yi] deities within the emerald seas . . . Everyone revered the teachings of Confucius and Laozi because there was no barbarian [hu] Buddha . . . From that time [the introduction of Buddhism] forward, the evil barbarians multiplied and flourished, and the majority of them mixed with the Han [hua] . . . The dissolute language of the evil barbarians was even used in the study of Confucius. It is warped like the singing of frogs, and in listening to it the root of Confucianism was lost . . . Corvée laborers and skilled craftsmen do nothing but set up mud barbarians [statues of Buddha]. They strike Chinese bells and gather together the false crowds of barbarian monks to dazzle the eyes and ears of innocent folk . . . In the Western Regions barbarians are born from mud. Therefore they naturally worship pagodas and statues made from mud and tiles . . . If we were to transmit the teachings of Confucius to the Western Regions, the barbarians would certainly be un-

Fig. 18   Detail from a wall mural of the death of the Buddha, showing disciples who are depicted as foreigners.

willing to practice them . . . The Buddha is a household ghost of one particular clan and cannot simultaneously act as a ghost for other lineages. How can a living Han be urged to give offerings to a dead barbarian?[50]

Diatribes such as this were met with hostility from the Buddhist establishment, contempt from most court officials, and rejection by the emperor. But since the imperial family claimed descent from Laozi and endorsed Daoist claims to primacy, a weakened version of Fu Yi's rant became accepted court doctrine.

This memorial is an early example of the idea of a world divided between China, in which Confucianism was the dominant doctrine, and the outer realms of Central Asia, where Buddhism was embraced and the Chinese sage had no place. Drawing on the basic categories of Chinese religion, Fu Yi also insisted that the Buddha was not a "god" who could receive offerings from believers at large but was merely a ghost or ancestor who could receive legitimate offerings only from his own kin. This argument distinguished cults proper to the Chinese from those proper to barbarians, arguing that while Buddhism was a legitimate cult for people of Indian genealogy, it was unacceptable for those of Chinese descent.

Some Confucian scholars also attacked Buddhism as a barbarian importation. The best-known example is Han Yu's *Memorial on the Bone of the Buddha* (*Lun Fogu biao*):

> Buddhism is merely one of the religions of the barbarians. It entered the Central Kingdom beginning in the Eastern Han, but it never existed in high antiquity . . . Now, the Buddha was originally a barbarian man. He did not comprehend the language of the Central Kingdom, and his clothes were of a different cut. His mouth did not speak the model words of the former kings . . . If he were still alive today and, having been commanded by the state, came to an audience in the capital, Your Majesty would tolerate and receive him. However, it would be limited to a single meeting at the Xuanzhang Palace, one feast appropriate for a guest, and one suit of clothing as a gift. He would then be sent to the border under guard so as not to allow him to delude the masses.[51]

In this memorial, Han Yu explicitly linked the Buddha to the foreign tribute bearers who filled the capital, and called for the Buddha's forcible expulsion, a treatment applied to foreign delegations that stayed too long living comfortably in the Tang capital at the expense of the court. While Han Yu's tone was more restrained than that of Fu Yi, and he replaced the rhetoric of implacable ethnic hostility with the image of the controlled entry and departure of foreign peoples actually practiced by the court, the identification of Buddhism as a foreign creed remained central to his argument.

While some polemics stressed Buddhism's foreign origins, others emphasized its alien doctrines and practices. The most visible, and most frequently denounced, was the monks' practice of shaving their heads. This violated a primary Confucian teaching that the son should keep intact the body he received from his parents. Head-shaving also linked Buddhism with some foreign peoples, notably Turks, who shaved all or part of their heads (a practice that would later be imposed on the Chinese by the Manchu Qing dynasty). Similarly, the passionate mutilation of the body by burning or chopping off fingers and limbs that figured in the public worship of Buddhist relics echoed the use of self-mutilation to demonstrate grief in non-Han mourning rituals.[52]

Even Buddhist practitioners themselves often embraced the religion's foreign character. Some placed India at the center of the world, reducing China to a position at the margins. Others described Buddhism and Confucianism/Daoism as parallel creeds, each expressing comparable truths within different cultures. While both these models rated Buddhism as either superior or equal to Chinese teachings, they accepted the idea that Buddhism was foreign. Major pilgrims, notably Xuanzang and Yijing, also thought of Buddhism as foreign. These monks made long and dangerous journeys to India, spending decades abroad, because they believed that the ultimate truths of Buddhism were to be found there (Fig. 19). To the extent that accounts of their travels found an audience in Tang China, such as the warm reception offered to Xuanzang by Emperor Taizong, it was because they provided information about the outside world rather than information about Buddhism. The links between searching for Buddhist scriptures, establishing ties with foreign peoples, and conducting China's foreign policy reaffirmed Buddhism's alien character.

However, the most visible testimony to the alien nature of the Buddhist religion was the presence of foreign monks. Non-Han monks became prominent in Chinese literature, providing early examples of what would become major themes in late imperial literature. One of the most common portrayals was of foreign monks as sexual predators, active in kidnapping and selling women or engineering their seduction. Another stereotype, that monks had magical powers, mixed suspicion of foreigners with the belief found in many cultures that people from distant lands possessed unique abilities. Some tales emphasized the deceptive nature of monks' magic, which was exposed or thwarted by righteous Confucian officials. The Buddhist hagiographic literature, on the other hand, treated some forms of magic as demonstrations of enlightenment. A few Tantric

Fig. 19   Dunhuang painting depicting a pilgrim carrying
scrolls of scriptures back from India, accompanied by a tiger.

Buddhists who had recently arrived from India, including Amoghavajra
and Vajrabodhi, gained great influence at court by performing magic on
behalf of the ruler or state. Other tales portrayed foreign monks as the
kind of nonhuman creatures with which foreigners were often identified.
The idea that they were fox spirits was facilitated by the fact that the
words "foreign" and "fox" were both pronounced *hu*. In a tale set in
813, an Inner Asian monk turned out to be a camel.[53]
    Such written polemics were relevant only to literate members of the

elite. For most people, the foreign nature of monks was revealed in their strange features and attire, as seen in major cities and towns along Buddhist pilgrimage routes. With the emergence of a fully Chinese Buddhism and of China as the center of the East Asian Buddhist world, increasing numbers of foreign monks were drawn as students and pilgrims to the Tang empire as a sacred destination. Ironically, it was the increasingly Chinese character of Buddhism that resulted in an ever-greater visual display to the population at large of Buddhism's foreignness.

7

KINSHIP

THE TANG dynasty is often depicted as a golden age for Chinese women, a period of relative autonomy and power prior to their subjugation under the Neo-Confucianism of the Song dynasty, with its emphasis on widow chastity, widow suicide, strengthening of the patriline, and the new fashion of foot-binding.[1] This generalization is true only in part, because the Tang was also the period when the commercial market in women became a prominent part of city life and when that market was transferred to the household in the form of concubines. Both of these developments were part of a process that would reduce the status of Chinese women.

In other areas of Tang kinship relations, the rise of a more distinctively Chinese Buddhism led to the incorporation of Buddhist rituals and festivals into ancestral cults and the broader relations between the living and the dead. In this period we also have the first clear evidence for a practice that became important in the later empire: the arranging of marriages between a living person and a ghost, or between two ghosts, to appease unhappy spirits.

But the most significant development in kin relations during the Tang was the eventual disappearance of the empire-wide "super-elite" of prominent families who, through cultivated genealogy, selective intermarriage, and persistent success in securing offices, had maintained their social eminence for centuries. This disappearance is generally regarded as the single most important factor marking the transition from the Tang to the Song as a shift from a "medieval" culture to an early modern or late imperial one.

Women in Tang Families

The image of the Tang as an age of unprecedented female prominence arises in large part from the domination that Empress Wu, her daughter the Taiping Princess, and Empress Wei exerted over the empire for more than half a century. But this high point of female political power in imperial China was merely the culmination of a long process that began with the fall of the Han. The nomad warriors who occupied north China after the Han brought with them the greater equality of men and women that characterized nomadic societies. As described in the sixth century by Yan Zhitui, women in northern cities handled legal disputes, associated with the politically powerful, and entered government offices to submit petitions and complaints on behalf of their male kin. Although the Northern Wei imposed rules to limit the power of dowager empresses at court, these directives could not stop such women from controlling the court for decades in the late fifth and early sixth centuries.

Emperors' wives often acted as political advisers to their husbands, and this pattern continued after the Sui dynasty reunified China in 589. The Sui founder's wife was his inseparable companion and his most trusted political adviser. The couple were described as the "two sages," and the emperor continued to follow his wife's judgment in political matters despite a falling out after the empress had one of his favorite concubines murdered. It was the empress, not the emperor, who ultimately determined that the succession would pass to her favorite son, Yang Guang.[2] Like his father, Emperor Yang looked to his wife as his primary confidante throughout his life. She played a major role in introducing him to southern culture and shaping, for better or worse, the southward orientation of his policies.[3] The Tang founder was politically assisted not only by his wife but also by a daughter, the Pingyang Princess, who fought in the campaigns of conquest. Emperor Taizong likewise managed state affairs with the help of the Empress Zhangsun.[4] Thus, the power of Tang empresses from the second half of the seventh century simply continued a northern tradition in which women actively participated in the affairs of the realm.

In addition to powerful empresses, the Tang was noted for the prominence of its many princesses who participated in politics. In addition to the Pingyang Princess who assisted the founder, the Taiping Princess supported and then carried on the work of her mother, Empress Wu. The

Anle Princess performed a similar service for Empress Wei, who dominated the court after 705. Indeed, the history of the court in the first decade of the eighth century is largely a battle between the Taiping Princess
and her two major enemies, the Empress Wei and the Anle Princess. In
710 this struggle ended in a bloody coup in which Li Longji (the future
Emperor Xuanzong) led an armed force that invaded the palace and
killed the Empress Wei and her daughter. The Taiping Princess personally
dragged the puppet boy emperor from the throne and established her
brother in his place. "Whatever she wished, the emperor granted. From
the chief ministers down, appointment and dismissal hung on one word
from her . . . The most powerful people in the land flocked to her door-
way as if it was the marketplace." Only because the Taiping Princess
carelessly allowed Li Longji to use his new-found prestige to gather Tang
loyalists around him did her power begin to wane. After several years of
back-and-forth struggle, her attempted coup in 713 failed, and her forced
suicide brought an end to the period of female domination of the Tang.[5]

Princesses were also useful in sealing political alliances with foreign
rulers. The practice of giving a princess in marriage to a foreign leader
dated back to the "harmonious kinship" policies used by the Han dynasty to appease the Xiongnu. The story of Wang Zhaojun's forced marriage to a barbarian chieftain became a major theme in literature.[6] Many
women sent out under the Han had been princesses in name only, however, whereas the Tang dispatched actual princesses, although in at least
one case the daughter of a surrendered tribal chieftain was named a Tang
princess just in time to be sent out to a ruler in Turkestan. The frequency
of political marriages was much greater in the Tang than in previous dynasties, and the earlier ones in particular, such as the marriage of the
Wencheng Princess to the Tibetan king under Emperor Taizong, allowed
the princesses to play a significant political role in securing alliances.

As the power of the Tang declined, so did the influence of princesses
living at foreign courts. Although there is no evidence of actual abuse,
they were often left without the necessities of a proper Chinese lifestyle,
such as texts to read. The most disastrous case was the Taihe Princess,
who was sent out as the wife of the Uighur qaghan in 821, only to be kidnapped in 842 by a rebel ruler who forced her to petition the Tang court
for recognition and support. Emperor Wuzong chided her in a letter for
failing to secure peace and leading barbarians to the Tang frontiers, and
when she finally returned home, the other princesses at court refused to

welcome her. Although Wuzong punished the princesses for their conduct, the story shows the difficulties to which a princess might be subjected, and their freedom of action at court.[7]

While many Tang princesses had no influence on domestic or international politics, they became notorious in the histories for their insistence
on personal freedom and for the sexual license that orthodox Chinese
historians attributed to any autonomous or powerful woman. Princesses
were sometimes ordained as Daoist priestesses, thereby obtaining high-
status positions in the capital that left them free to pursue their own interests. But even the princess-priestesses were accused of lascivious behavior, which once again was a conventional code to designate an autonomous woman. Sexual fantasies about Daoist priestesses in China were
not unlike those about the supposed shared carnality of priests and nuns
in Europe.

Many princesses treated their husbands with contempt and openly hu-
miliated or cuckolded them, leading to an unprecedented number of di-
vorces and remarriages. Consequently, leading officials sought to avoid
marriage with the imperial family, as in the case of Zheng Hao, who bore
an enduring grudge against the man who recommended him for marriage
to a princess under Xuanzong(2). This only aggravated the emperors' resentment of the generous betrothal gifts that high officials gave to the
most prominent old families in exchange for the opportunity to marry
one of their daughters. In this exchange, daughters of the social elite often became tokens in a political marriage market, paralleling the situation of imperial princesses.[8]

The great families of the Northern and Southern Dynasties had increasingly married among themselves to preserve their pedigree, but
sometimes more humble families, through substantial payments, were allowed to marry the daughter of a leading family. As Yan Zhitui described
the practice: "In the present age, when marriages are arranged, some people sell their daughters for the betrothal gift or buy a wife by making a
payment of silk. They compare the ancestry [of the two parties], calculate
down to the smallest sum, demand much and offer little, exactly like bar-
gaining in a market place."[9] This practice became so conventional in the
late fifth and sixth centuries that the Northern Qi court unsuccessfully
decreed that the size of betrothal gifts should be determined by the political rank of the bride's father rather than the prestige of her patriline.

The emphasis on genealogy over rank continued into the Sui, when
even the most powerful official at court had to pay "extremely generous"

betrothal gifts so that his son could marry into the prestigious Cui patriline. Throughout the first half of the Tang, one emperor after another complained that the leading families, above all the four great families of the northeast, demanded large betrothal gifts and that leading officials would pay whatever they asked. The marital exclusivity of eminent families allowed them to demand especially high prices from *arrivistes* who hoped to secure new political or economic power by allying with wielders of enduring social prestige.[10]

While critics spoke of families "selling their daughters," it seems that the practice of setting a high bride price had more to do with the great reluctance on the part of these families to marry outside their exclusive circle, a reluctance sometimes overcome by the fact that an illustrious lineage was no longer economically prosperous. Under those circumstances, a marriageable daughter may have been the family's greatest economic asset. The writer Bo Juyi noted that the rise of the concubine Yang Guifei to political power led parents to "no longer value the birth of a son but value the birth of daughters." However, for many of the most prominent families in China this had been the case for centuries, in large part because of betrothal gifts.[11]

Following the collapse of the Tang and the end of the great families' eminence, the flow of wealth associated with marriage reversed direction. During the Song dynasty, instead of husbands' families giving lavish gifts to elite families in exchange for their daughters, families with daughters started providing dowries that their daughters took into the marriage. The reasons for this change are not entirely clear, though it was probably related to the increasing monetization of the economy as well as to new strategies for strengthening a lineage.[12] Whatever its cause, this shift in marriage finance meant that Song women were no longer valued in a way that could command generous payments, and this entailed a decline in their role in forming interlineage networks. Moreover, marrying out a daughter now led to a significant reduction in the family's property. In the long run this contributed to the decline in the status of women among elites.

Beyond their political activities and value as brides, another source for the notion that the Tang was a great age for women was the visual representation of elite women and court entertainers preserved in tomb art. Some of these images depict women riding horseback, playing polo, and shooting a bow (Fig. 20); others show them dressed in low-cut gowns or even in the attire of foreign males. In still others, women wander at ease

Fig. 20   Pottery figurine of a woman shooting a bow (which has rotted away).

in gardens, perform on musical instruments, enjoy board games such as *wei qi* (Japanese Go), donate to religious establishments, and play with children. Processions of important court women and their attendants appear in many tombs, notably that of the Taiping Princess herself. Even more abundant, although perhaps less indicative of female freedom or influence, are representations of female dancers and musicians who provided entertainment at court (Fig. 21).[13] This extravagant display of women's freedom in Tang tomb art declined in later dynasties.

The relative autonomy of Tang women is also demonstrated in an unlikely source, manuals of female conduct. This tradition of writing, initiated by the Han woman writer Ban Zhao (45–114), insisted on women's complete submissiveness to their husbands. Its recurring themes were

Fig. 21   Painting of a female dancer on the wall of a tomb.

that the husband was a woman's "Heaven," requiring adoration and obedience, while the woman herself should remain silent and invisible. Several writers continued this tradition in the Tang, in the *Canon of Women's Filial Piety* (*Nü xiaojing*) and the *Analects for Women* (*Nü lunyu*). While these books followed Ban Zhao's model, the *Analects* was distinctive in providing detailed prescriptions for everyday conduct in the household and describing women who should *not* be imitated: "Don't

imitate those who jump at disgusting opportunities, screaming and shout-
ing at venerable old folks. They complain about hardships and difficulties, don't come when called, and don't give a whit about other people's
hunger and cold."[14] In the same way that imperial edicts reveal what people actually did by attempting to ban those activities, these descriptions
of conduct that women should eschew—scolding in-laws, sewing slop-
pily, laughing loudly, gossiping, nibbling on food intended for dinner, and
getting drunk at banquets—indicated how many women in the Tang actually behaved.

While the Tang was a time of relative freedom and power for elite
women, others became economic commodities who were literally bought
and sold in the urban marketplace. Thus, beneath the courtesans' surface
equality with clients in poetic conversation at banquets and in the rituals
of romance, the brute economic reality was that the client-lover possessed the money upon which the courtesan was completely dependent.[15]
The best a courtesan could realistically hope for in life was to be purchased as a concubine—the form in which women as commodities were
imported in increasing numbers into the Tang household.

Concubines were members of a household who served as secondary
sexual partners of the master, providing him with sensual pleasure and, if
necessary, heirs. These women, below the wife in legal status, had existed
in China since ancient times but only in the noblest or wealthiest households. During the Song dynasty, the possession of concubines would
spread among those who were merely well-off, becoming conventional in
well-to-do families in all subsequent dynasties.[16] While the practice was
not as common in the Tang as it would later become, there is evidence
that it was sufficiently widespread to affect relations between spouses
and the structure of power within the household. Anecdotes in literary
sources indicate the existence of concubines, including some owned by
businessmen, and several texts take it for granted that any household
with property would have many concubines. The *Transformation Text
on Mulian* (*Mulian bianwen*) refers hyperbolically to having "wives and
concubines enough to fill the mountains and rivers."[17] Funerary inscriptions mention concubines, and a considerable number of inscriptions at-
tach lists of children other than those of the primary wife, without men-
tioning the mother by name. This cumulative evidence indicates that the
possession of concubines was already conventional among the literate
elite.[18]

The Tang legal code devotes considerable attention to the relation of concubines to their masters, the difference between a concubine and a legal wife, and the status of a concubine's children. All of these matters were discussed in the ritual classics but were elaborated and given the full force of law in the Tang legal code.[19] It, in turn, was largely transcribed into the subsequent laws of the Song dynasty. While concubines shared some features with wives—for example, they could not be of the master's surname, and sex with any other man was punishable as adultery—most ritual and legal strictures focused on clearly separating the status of the wife from that of the concubines.

In a legal code where punishments varied according to status differentials between the perpetrator and the victim, concubines were placed between wives and maids. A husband or his kin were punished less severely for killing a maid than a concubine, while a concubine was punished more severely than a wife for harming the master's kin. Wives were formally betrothed through a process that included rituals and the exchange of gifts, whereas concubines were simply purchased outright in the same way as maids. A wife's relatives became kin of the husband's family, but the relatives of a concubine did not. The law allowed a man to have only one wife at a time, but he was permitted to purchase as many concubines as he could afford. Concubines served the wife in the same manner as did the maids. Sons of concubines had the same rights of inheritance as sons of the wife, but all sons had to treat the wife as their legal mother. The wife could claim and rear any of the concubine's offspring, and if the master died she was their legal guardian. A widowed wife had claims on the household and its property, but a concubine could simply be expelled.[20]

Distinguishing wives from concubines was important both to the institution of marriage and to a broader sense of social hierarchy in the Tang. Confusing a wife with the concubines was tantamount to confusing the master with his servants. Among the elite, wives came from good households, while concubines, like maids, derived from the lower classes. Thus, in many anecdotes men were appalled to find that the wife or daughter of an official had been reduced to the position of a concubine, and they raised money so that she could be formally married.[21] It is thus not surprising that by the Qing dynasty in the seventeenth century, when women's status was in eclipse, the legal and social divisions between wives and concubines became less strict.

While Tang administrators and literati strove to maintain a clear legal separation between wives and concubines, as owners of concubines they could not acknowledge that the institution in any way threatened the position of the wife or her conjugal bond with her husband. Ritual codes described marriage as the means of reproducing the family while maintaining the social hierarchy; emotional and physical ties between spouses did not figure. In the typical elite family, the wife was expected to produce heirs and manage the household, while the husband was permitted to seek intimacy and sexual pleasure with courtesans or concubines. Concubines were also offered as a morally proper recourse to produce an heir if the wife proved to be infertile. While such an arrangement might work on paper, it required the wife to accept the enduring existence of deep emotional and physical bonds between her husband and other women, and it required the husband not to allow his protracted social and physical intimacy with those women to influence his conduct. The difficulty of the latter is indicated by the careers of the two most famous Tang women, Empress Wu and Yang Guifei, both of whom used their position as the emperor's concubine to supplant official wives and influence the course of the empire through their power over its ruler.[22]

Injunctions to wives to tolerate their husbands' need for concubines ring hollow in light of the many cases where concubines came to dominate the affections and conduct of their masters. The self-serving hypocrisy of these directives, not to mention the near impossibility of living peacefully in the same household with a rival, did not silence Tang writers on the subject of "jealous" wives. The dynasty witnessed an efflorescence of stories about "shrews" who used any means to try to prevent their husbands from taking concubines. The wife of the Sui founder was repeatedly described as being "irrationally" jealous of her husband's concubines and was reported to have killed his favorite.[23] Similar tales of jealous women appeared in pre-imperial China and flourished in the Northern and Southern Dynasties, but in the Tang they emerged as an independent genre, with whole collections devoted to the theme.[24]

One extreme example is as follows: "Yan, wife of the Guiyang magistrate Ruan Song, was extremely jealous. While Song was entertaining guests with several female singers, Yan, her hair all tossed up, baring her arms and feet, rushed in to the banquet with a knife in her hand and scattered the frightened guests. Song himself hid under the bed, and, shaken up, the entertainers escaped." The power of female jealousy was even read into the landscape in the legend of the Jealous Wife's Ferry. When one man praised the mythic beauty of the Goddess of the Luo River, his jealous wife supposedly drowned herself in order to haunt the river and demand the lives of women prettier than herself. Unexplained accidents and loss of life near the river were attributed to the malevolent force of disembodied female jealousy feeding on itself.[25] Such stories suggest the intensity of the passions and collective anxieties built into the emerging polygamy of the Tang family. Like the stereotyped accusation that all powerful women were lascivious, the theme of the jealous shrew became a cliché of later Chinese historiography and literature, but one that thinly papered over a contradiction built into the structure of Chinese elite households.

Changes in the Ancestral Cult

Kinship patterns in Tang China were also affected by changes in the manner of burying the dead and worshipping ancestors. Prior to the Tang, there is no evidence of collective worship of ancestors outside the residential family. Children made offerings at the graves of parents or grandparents, but the common descendants of more distant ancestors did not gather for the kind of collective ancestor worship that would establish them as a meaningful social group. However, at the end of the seventh century or in the early decades of the eighth, kin related through male descent began to meet at the Qingming Festival (also known as the Cold Food Festival), held 105 days after the winter solstice, to clean the tombs of ancestors as distant as four or five generations and to make offerings to them.

The earliest story linking the Qingming Festival with graveside offerings appears in a text dating from the 660s. By 732 the practice had become widespread, as indicated by a decree of that year noting that while the classics did not mention visiting graves at the Cold Food Festival, it had become customary and should be encouraged: "For gentlemen and commoners who do not get together to make offerings in family altars, how else can they exhibit their filial sentiments? They should be allowed to visit the graves and together perform the rituals of bowing and sweeping at the tombs." Liu Zongyuan (773–819), who was in exile, lamented that while around him even the ancestors of horse doctors and field laborers received offerings at their graves, he alone could not visit the tombs of his ancestors. Etiquette books from the period even included models for letters to be sent on the occasion of visiting graves for the festival.[26]

The ritual recognition of more distant ancestors during the Cold Food

Festival raised the number of descendants who could identify themselves as kin. This increased the possibility of larger kin groups who could gather for common action or to provide mutual assistance. However, we have no evidence that these graveside gatherings in the Tang ever consisted of huge numbers of remote kin, and a few poetic references and essays suggest that the routine care of ancestral graves remained primarily the responsibility of individual households.[27]

Another important development in Tang death cults was the annual Ghost Festival, which employed Buddhist rituals to secure better rebirths for unhappy spirits. The festival ultimately derived from fifth-century scriptural accounts of how the Buddha's disciple Mulian rescued his mother from hell and a bad rebirth as a hungry ghost by invoking the power of the Buddhist monastic order. Their collective merit was sufficient not only to rescue his mother but also "seven generations of relatives and six kinds of relatives," the same formula that appears on many votive inscriptions. This event became the prototype for an annual festival in which lay people, on the fifteenth day of the seventh month, donated part of their harvest to the monastic community in exchange for ensuring the well-being of dead kin and any aggrieved spirits. By the middle of the sixth century this festival was celebrated throughout south China, where it entailed decorating temples and collectively making music. By the Tang it had become one of the major events of the annual ritual calendar, described in many historical and poetic accounts.[28]

The story of the Ghost Festival's origins is notable because it highlights the devotion of Mulian to his mother rather than his father. The emphasis on Mulian's mother was already a feature of canonical accounts, but it came to the fore in the Tang in a dramatic version of the story told in a "transformation text" (*bian wen*) from around 800.[29] This new genre combined prose and poetry as a way to entertain popular audiences with stories performed by professional entertainers, often women singers. The oral accounts were accompanied by pictures to which the performers pointed while reciting the poetic passages. This combination of poetry, prose, and pictures was called a "transformation text" because it dealt with the different manifestations of Buddhas, gods, and heroes, thus combining edification with entertainment.[30]

Barely touching on the fate of his father, Mulian's story focused instead on his powerful sentimental ties to his mother, his insistence on the infinite debt that he owed her, his horror at her sufferings in hell, and his desire to substitute himself for her. Over the centuries, the story became the best-known Chinese account of mother-son ties, and one of the most popular themes for ritual plays performed in association with funerals.[31] It gave formal expression to a strong and enduring bond in Chinese households that previously had been left in public silence.

The Ghost Festival and the myth of its founding dramatized what was implicit in earlier Buddhist inscriptions and images: for believers, Buddhism had become an essential mechanism for assuring the well-being of ancestors and hence for constituting a family, protecting its members, and advancing its interests. Traditional ancestor worship had been reserved for kin, and only the state could make offerings to nonkin. In the new order defined by the Ghost Festival and related practices, offerings to ancestors had to pass through Buddhist monks to be effective. This made the Buddhist establishment an indispensable element of kin structure. This change is demonstrated in passages from the Mulian transformation text, where people suffering in hell lament the inefficacy of traditional ancestor worship:

> Once the gates of Hades slam shut, they never open again.
> Though there be a thousand kinds of food placed on our grave-
> mounds,
> How can they alleviate the hunger in our stomachs?
> All our wailing and weeping, in the end, will be to no avail.
> In vain do they trouble themselves to make folded paper money.
> Take a message to the sons and daughters in our homes telling them:
> "We entreat you to save us from infernal suffering by performing
> good deeds."[32]

In another passage, people in hell ask Mulian to tell the living that elaborate coffins and expensive funerals with music and song cannot mitigate the suffering of the dead, which can only be alleviated through charity to the Buddhist order. When Mulian finally meets his mother in hell, she tells him that one of her crimes was to engage in ancestor worship—to "slaughter pigs and goats on a grand scale to sacrifice to ghosts and spirits." While such arguments never led to widespread abandonment of the traditional ancestral cult, they did encourage permanent modifications in the rituals for securing the safe transition of the dead to a new state of existence.[33] While many of the ideas underlying these cosmological and ritual systems derived from Buddhism, by the late Tang and the Song they began to merge into a Chinese religion that flourished outside institutional Buddhism, Daoism, and Confucianism.

One of the clearest examples of Buddhism's influence was the elaboration between the seventh and tenth centuries of a punitive underworld bureaucracy and a set of rituals to cope with it. Like the invention of purgatory in the West, this development offered an entirely new means by which people could assist their deceased kin. This new purgatory, best described in the tenth-century *The Scripture on the Ten Kings,* consisted of a series of ten courts through which the deceased must pass. In each court (depicted on the model of Tang courts of law) the ruling king acted as a judge who examined records of the person's life and, if necessary, imposed tortures to force an exhaustive confession of sins (Fig. 22). After leaving the courts, the deceased would be assigned to his or her state of rebirth in the next life, with good deeds leading to a higher rebirth and bad ones to a lower (Fig. 23).[34]

In association with the Ten Kings purgatorial system were rituals by which the living could assist the passage of the self or of kin through the realms of torture and judgment. Elements of these rituals had appeared in texts from the Northern and Southern Dynasties, which established

Fig. 22   Scene of a king of hell judging the dead, as depicted on a modern Japanese collotype reproduction of a Dunhuang scroll. From Teiser, *"The Scripture on the Ten Kings" and the Making of Purgatory in Medieval Chinese Buddhism* (University of Hawai'i Press, 1994).

Fig. 23   The dead being assigned to their appropriate rebirth, as depicted on
a modern Japanese collotype reproduction of a Dunhuang scroll. From Teiser,
"The Scripture on the Ten Kings" and the Making of Purgatory in Medieval Chinese Buddhism (University of Hawai'i Press, 1994).

the idea that the purgatorial rituals should be performed at seven-day intervals, up to forty-nine days, to coincide with the deceased's passage through the courts. *The Scripture on the Ten Kings,* however, contains far more elaborate descriptions of the sufferings that await the deceased if their surviving kin fail to act on their behalf:

> At one hundred days dead people are subjected to more troubles;
> Their bodies are canqued and shackled and they are wounded by
>   whips.
> If sons and daughters exert themselves in cultivating merit,
> Then [the dead] will be spared from dropping into the underground
>   prisons,
> Those places of eternal suffering.

It also differs from the earlier texts in that its rituals were performed by the family itself or by a religious specialist not necessarily affiliated with an institutional faith. If the family neglected to perform offerings to the Ten Kings, their deceased relative would suffer an inferior rebirth, but if they made substantial payments of paper money and goods, they could guarantee a happy outcome. These payments became popular in part because they were much less expensive than the offerings to Buddhist monks in the earlier rituals. Both the Buddhist and Daoist clergy developed elaborate rituals of their own similar to those in *The Scripture on the Ten Kings,* but it was the latter that spread rapidly throughout all classes of Chinese society and in subsequent centuries into Korea and Japan.[35]

The triumph of the Ten Kings model of purgatory beginning in the tenth century suggests two important features about the development of religion in late imperial China. First, it highlights the fact that some central ideas of Buddhism became so widespread that they detached from their explicitly Buddhist background to become part of a pan-Chinese religion observed even by those who did not consider themselves Buddhist. The correlate of this was the emergence of a distinctively "Chinese" Buddhism in the Tang. Second, the rituals of the Ten Kings were part of a broader shift toward a new set of religious attitudes that were distinctly commercial in tone. Paper money was used in funerals by the seventh century, and by the twelfth century paper currency had become the standard offering to the officials of purgatory. In the religious economy of late imperial China, it was widely believed that a person incurred a spirit-monetary debt at birth that had to be repaid in full at or before death. The Ten Kings of purgatory became the chief officers of this spirit bank.[36]

A final new religious aspect of kin ties under the Tang is spirit marriage. Early Chinese religion taught that "the living and the dead had separate paths." Consequently, sexual union between a living man and a female ghost (the reverse pattern was rare) was a dangerous affair that routinely resulted in the death of the man. In such stories, women who died unmarried and hence could not receive offerings from descendants became powerful, dangerous spirits whose unsated desires dragged men to their doom. Liaisons with goddesses, while less consistently negative than liaisons with ghosts, could also threaten life, although, unlike ghosts, goddesses could usually be warded off with appropriate spells. Sometimes such matings were actively sought.[37]

After the Han, these ideas began to change, as people arranged marriages between two dead people or between the living and the dead. Deceased minors (especially women) were given in marriage to living men in order to provide the spirits with a means to receive sacrifice and relieve their unspent desires. While the origins of these marriages are unclear, they were practiced by the Tang. However, in the anecdotes that have survived, the marriage of the living man to the dead woman results in the death of the former, so these spirit marriages appear as formally sanctioned cases of the fatal, illicit liaisons between the living and the dead. Spirit marriage thus was not yet entirely separate from spirit vampirism.[38] Nevertheless, references to families joining spirits in marriage show that this was becoming an accepted social practice, if not a canonically sanctioned one.

Tang stories about marriages with ghosts also demonstrate the growing commercialization of relations with the spirit world. Several such anecdotes overlap thematically with stories in which a mortal who provides a vital service to divine beings is rewarded with great wealth or with marriage to a divine woman that leads to wealth or immortality. In one of these stories, wealth is obtained from a gift of some rolls of silk, together with advice on how these can be sold for a large sum of money. An identical method of enriching a mortal lover, involving a horse rather than silk, is used by the fox demon Ms. Ren in the story that bears her name.[39] Fabulous, often illicit, wealth gained through sexual liaisons with nonhuman beings became a major theme in late imperial China.

The Great Families of the Tang

The most important shift in kinship patterns during the Tang was the disappearance of the great families who at the beginning of the dynasty had formed an empire-wide super-elite defined by social status. The recognition of a relatively small number of families as uniquely prestigious had developed during the Northern and Southern Dynasties, and their exalted position in the Tang was reinforced through marriages restricted to their peers or to those who offered substantial bridal gifts. The idea that such a group existed but was already declining emerged in the Tang itself. Thus, Su Mian, whose administrative encyclopedia *Collected Essentials of the Tang* (*Tang hui yao*) was completed in 803, observed that all those who founded the dynasty and became high ministers in the early decades came from "noble lineages" (*gui zu*). He observed that nothing like this group had existed in earlier Chinese history, but its position was already waning in his own day.

The Song scholar Shen Gua (1031–1095) likewise noted the existence of eminent families in the Tang and their subsequent disappearance. He considered the phenomenon unique in Chinese history, and the only analogy he could come up with was the Indian caste system. When the early Qing writer Gu Yanwu criticized the rise of imperial autocracy in the preceding Ming dynasty and proposed the revival of feudalism in the form of hereditary local officials as a way to correct this, he cited the Tang aristocracy as a precedent. In the twentieth century, the nature and fate of the great Tang families became a major theme of modern scholarship on China.

During the centuries of division prior to the Sui dynasty, certain families developed great prestige through a history of state service dating back to the Han or the Jin. This status was reinforced by a new obsession with genealogies traced in elaborate written records and by literary or cultural attainments that even the rulers of short-lived dynasties attempted to copy. The situation of the most influential of these families changed after the reunification of China under the Sui. To reduce the number of officials, increase the efficiency of administration, and assure that bureaucrats were obedient to the court, Sui rulers abolished the system of local recommendations for office that had institutionalized hereditary entry-level posts and thus given established families an edge in the competition for offices. The Sui introduced in its place a new process of selection that both looked backward to the Han and forward to the more meritocratic examination system under the Song. Every prefecture in the empire recommended a quota of men, usually three per year, who were sent to the court. There they were interviewed by high officials, who ranked them by talent and character. Some were given posts, while others were offered further training. By the end of the dynasty, examinations to test the candidates' mastery of a single canonical text or their general literary ability were administered in the capital.[40]

The impact of this Sui reform on China's old families was considerable. The ultimate basis of their prestige was their history of imperial service, which distinguished them from wealthy families whose power was merely local, centered on landed estates. Under the new regulations, any significant office was most readily attained by someone in the capital, without regard for his family history. The rise of examinations as a route to Tang office reinforced the privileged position of those in the capital.

In response, ambitious members of the great families took up residence in Chang'an. Those who stayed behind abandoned any claims to political eminence and gradually ceased to figure in family genealogies that certified social status. The genealogies of the great families had never been comprehensive kin lists but were selective records of related people who had attained success in political careers and were thus judged worthy of commemoration. Lines of the family that failed to produce officials for two or three generations were trimmed from the family tree and ceased to be kin. The great families of the Tang did not allow sentiment to interfere with calculations of worldly advantage. Only those who made their way in the world through office or marriage counted as members of the true elite.

Thus, the structure of lineages in the Tang gave social form to the political hierarchy. Easy access to office depended upon lineage membership, but continued membership in the lineage depended upon securing high office. Although many families within the great lineages maintained some local power based on land ownership and the command of large populations of servants, many less prestigious clans could make the same claims. Given the practice of partible inheritance (dividing family land among all legitimate sons), estates inevitably broke up in the course of a couple of generations, so they could not provide an enduring foundation for eminence. Only the interlinked prestige of state service and genealogy could assure social status. Although they were not entirely subject to imperial command, the great clans were enmeshed in the imperial system. Their survival depended on it, and when the Tang dynasty fell, they collapsed along with it.

The reliance of the great Tang families on court position, and the secondary importance of local bases, is revealed in their changing patterns of conduct. During the fourth century, when northern China was divided among rival states, the Cui family of Shandong in the northeast had relied on their local base, intermarrying with other leading northeastern families, assisting nearby kin, and sometimes holding local office. With the reunification of the north under the Wei in the early fifth century, the Cuis resumed their pursuit of official careers, and the majority of Cui men attained posts of the fifth rank or higher. During the civil wars from the middle of the sixth century, the Cui family split over which leader they supported, and more importantly over whether to focus on careers at the capital or the defense of their local base. Virtually all those who would become known in the Tang were descended from family members who, in the second half of the sixth century, chose to serve as officials.[41]

Under the Sui and the early Tang, all politically active members of the Cui lineage departed Shandong, as did most recorded members of other leading families in the northeast. Not all immediately resettled in the capital, but that became their primary target. Other leading families followed the same pattern. During the Tang, the Li family of Zhaojun, another major northeastern lineage that had regularly intermarried with the Cuis, gave up any significant local base and cast their lot entirely with state service in the capital. The tendency of families to abandon old estates in the northeast and move to Chang'an may well have been accelerated by the disruptions of the An Lushan rebellion in the middle of the eighth century.[42]

In addition to holding office, the great families converted their prestige into a political and financial resource. From the sixth century, biographies and inscriptions increasingly rated individuals' status based on their families' centuries of eminence. Members of one elite lineage disparaged those of others, or asserted that their lineage alone was worthy of admiration. With reunification under the Sui and Tang, the pattern of status competition shifted. The oldest families increasingly grouped themselves together as a uniquely exalted class set off against all others through their insistence on exclusive intermarriage and their ability to command generous betrothal gifts. The latter secured not only substantial financial rewards but also alliances with rising families.[43]

These references to "old" versus "rising" families show that the Tang elite consisted of several strata. Uppermost were the few truly prestigious old lineages known throughout the empire and acknowledged as preeminent. This group was in turn divided into four regional subgroups with separate roots. The most exalted were the four great lineages "east of the mountains," that is, from modern Shandong: the Cui lineage of Boling, the Li lineage of Zhaojun, the Lu lineage of Fanyang, and the Zheng lineage of Rongyang. In the early Tang these families married exclusively with one another and regarded even the imperial house as their inferiors. More politically powerful, but less prestigious, were the great families of Guanzhong. These lineages, including the imperial Li family, had risen to eminence under the non-Chinese dynasties of the fifth and sixth centuries. Many of them were related by marriage to earlier imperial lines or had intermarried with leading clans of north China's nomadic rulers, from whose culture they had adopted many of their own practices and values. To the north of the Guanzhong lineages was the third major regional cluster, the great families of Daibei (modern northern Shanxi), who enjoyed a similar history and status. The last regional group was the leading families of the Yangzi drainage basin, who had risen to eminence under the southern dynasties.[44]

Below this pan-imperial elite was a much larger group of wealthy families whose power extended only within their own prefectures or provinces. These families did not figure in the imperial histories, but they have been studied through fragments of state-sponsored genealogical compendia discovered at Dunhuang. These fragments include a list of the prominent clans of Dunhuang and the prominent families of prefectures throughout the empire. One manuscript compiled sometime shortly before 790 lists no fewer than 791 families, including many uncommon surnames that figure in no other historical sources. These texts give some sense of the broader group that formed Tang China's ruling elite, although they still probably constituted only one or two percent of the population.[45]

Thus, the first rulers of the Tang confronted a world with a hierarchy of family pedigrees, but a hierarchy that did not take account of the new state. To correct this, Emperor Taizong in 632 ordered a group of officials who were not from leading old families to create a compendium of genealogies that listed and ranked the empire's major lineages. When the first draft was submitted, one branch of the Cui family was rated above the imperial line, indicating that acceptance of the supreme prestige of old pedigrees was widespread, if not universal. The emperor flew into a rage. The old Shandong families clung to empty reputations, he said, while their actual conditions were so reduced that they sold their daughters for profit. He ordered a revised compendium in which rankings were based on members' positions in the bureaucracy under the Tang. The revised work, entitled the *Record of Clans and Lineages of the Zhenguan Reign Period* (*Zhen guan shi zu zhi*), was submitted in 638. Imperial kin were ranked first, the families of the first two empresses immediately below them, and the Cui family demoted to third rank.[46]

The emperor's new ranking system had little immediate impact. Since many of the highest officials in the early Tang court came from established families, including the head of the Cui family that had been so rudely degraded, the only major shift was to place imperial kin by blood and marriage in the highest ranks, leaving the rest largely unchanged. However, the long-run impact of this compendium was significant. First, it recognized newly risen families, many of local importance or military background, who became active and honored participants in the Tang state. Second, it began to tie the old families inextricably to the dynasty. While the shifting principle of inclusion did not significantly alter the substance of the compendium, it radically changed its form, in that office-holding under the Tang became the *sine qua non* of status. As the established families came to accept this idea, they and the dynasty were drawn together in a mutual dependence benefiting both parties, but at the same time making the survival of the great families contingent on the fate of the dynasty.

In 659 Emperor Gaozong ordered a new genealogical compendium that more rigorously imposed the principle of identifying status with office. Not only was ranking based entirely on level of office, but it included all families of officials who had attained at least the fifth rank (on a scale of one to ten, with one highest), thereby including those of many local officials and military commanders. By setting the standard for inclusion so low, it defined the dynasty's political elite in the broadest sense and ranked all members of that elite in terms of office.

As part of Emperor Xianzong's reassertion of central authority after the An Lushan rebellion, an empire-wide compilation entitled the *Surname Compilation of the Yuanhe Reign Period* (*Yuan he xing zuan*) was issued in 812. However, this work made no attempt to rank lineages but simply listed them by rhyme groups under their respective regions. Thus, by the last century of Tang rule, the very principle of family rankings had ceased to be an issue, at least as far as the state was concerned.[47]

Genealogy played a role not only in defining status but also ethnicity, including that of the imperial lineage itself. Just as Han Chinese sought status by claiming membership in a prestigious lineage, so non-Han individuals and families could advance socially by asserting a genealogy that would make them Han, and preferably Han with some notable ancestor or family line. The simplest genealogical path was to change one's surname and those of one's ancestors, of which the most blatant example was the imperial Li family itself. At least on its female side, and perhaps on the male side as well, the family descended from non-Han people, but it went to great lengths to construct a prestigious Han genealogy and even descent from Laozi.[48]

The practice of changing surnames to reassign ethnic identity for political purposes had figured prominently at least since the Han, when non-Han hostages and surrendered Xiongnu might be given Han surnames. The Tuoba rulers of the Northern Wei adopted the Chinese surname Yuan and granted this as an award to many of their followers. When Emperor Xiaowen of the Wei launched a policy of sinicizing his court, he ordered the Tuoba nobility to take Chinese surnames. The Tang imperial house also granted its surname to nomads who submitted. In Tang times, many leading lineages of non-Han origins sought to efface their tribal roots. They composed genealogies listing only office-holding ancestors who held Chinese surnames, thus editing their lineages according to political principles in much the same way that the Han Chinese elite did. They omitted their more distant ancestors with non-Han surnames and tribal offices and often leaped from the most recent two or three generations back to fictive ancestors in the Han dynasty. One Tang genealogy stated that the Dugu clan—a non-Han family that had helped establish the Northern Zhou and whose women had married into imperial families in the Northern Zhou, Sui, and Tang—once had the surname Liu.

Less dishonest, and more frequent, was the strategy of claiming descent from a highly prestigious alien lineage, such as the ruling house of the Northern Wei. Most of the Guanzhong and Daibei elites followed this practice. An example was the assertion that the early Tang official Zhangsun Wuji descended from the imperial Tuoba house, when his actual ancestors were the lower-ranked Baba clan. A closely related strategy was to acknowledge one's tribal roots but claim descent from a ruling or noble house of the steppes. In status-conscious Tang society, being a tribal noble was more prestigious than having an ethnic Han pedigree. Geshu Han, like several leading Tang generals of non-Han origins, claimed descent from a chiefly clan and pointed out the humbler tribal origins of some of his fellows, including his rival An Lushan. Those who held office in semi-autonomous foreign communities also frequently claimed noble non-Han origins. Given the roles of these men as intermediaries between the Tang state and tribal allies, their non-Han genealogies could have been positively beneficial.

Yet another genealogical strategy was to claim that one's founding ancestor was an ethnic Han who had been captured by alien tribes or for some other reason carried off to the west. The great Tang poet Li Bo, almost certainly of non-Han origins, invented such a genealogy. The ancestor most often chosen for this purpose was the Han dynasty general Li Ling, who was captured by the Xiongnu in 99 B.C. Descent from Li Ling was usually claimed by relatively unassimilated peoples such as the Uighurs and Kirghiz, who asserted this kin tie to assist them in making political alliances with the Chinese. Thus, both the Tang Emperor Wuzong and an allied Uighur leader claimed shared descent from Li Ling as a foundation for their collaboration. Tang writers explained the occasional appearance of black hair among the Kirghiz, who generally had blond or reddish hair, as being the result of intermarriage between Li Ling's soldiers and the ancestors of the Kirghiz.

A final genealogical strategy for dealing across ethnic lines was the occasional practice among non-Han leaders of tracing descent from the legendary Yellow Emperor himself—the founding ancestor of the Han Chinese people—or from the ancient Zhou ruling house. Such claims flattered both those who made them and their Tang recipients, who could thus assert a larger realm for their putative ancestor. The Chinese had linked themselves to more distant peoples through a common origin in the ancient sage-kings at least since the late Warring States and early Han mythic geography, the *Canon of Mountains and Seas* (*Shan hai jing*).[49]

The End of the Great Families

To account for the eclipse of the great families and of the principles that underlay their status, most scholars have appealed to the rise of the examination system. This is a case of turning sequence into cause. At the beginning of the Tang, society was ranked on the basis of genealogy, while in the early Song, some four hundred years later, access to government office and its associated prestige came through the examinations. However, the examination system cannot account for the decline of the great families in the Tang, for a number of reasons.

To begin with, throughout the Tang, examinations were only one route to office among many, and not everyone who passed an examination procured a post. Only around 10 percent of Tang officials were chosen through exams. The primary routes to office were hereditary. Imperial relatives were entitled to enter the bureaucracy at the fourth or fifth rank, while great grandsons, grandsons, and sons of officials of the fifth rank or above were entitled to entry at the seventh, eighth, or ninth rank. This form of privilege accounted for approximately one quarter of all selections.

In addition, Tang rulers established a hereditary "aristocracy" that held archaic noble titles from pre-imperial times. While these titles in themselves conferred no actual power or income, they entitled the recipients to entry-level posts at the fifth, sixth, or seventh rank. By comparison, the vast majority of examination candidates entered at the lowest tenth rank. The Tang also maintained a distinction between "pure" posts, devoted to ritual observance and high-level policymaking, and "turbid" posts, consisting of clerical work. Pure posts most frequently went to those who entered the bureaucracy through hereditary privilege. Thus, following the principles of their genealogical compendia, the early Tang rulers honored the notion of family status but sought to make that status dependent on the emperor's gift.[50]

In an attempt to combat the power of established families who resisted her rise, Empress Wu created large numbers of supernumerary posts that she could fill with her own followers or sell to raise funds. She also used the *jinshi* examination as the privileged route to high office. Gradually, this difficult exam became the most desirable way to begin a career for young men aspiring to the highest posts, so that by the late Tang even those eligible for hereditary access to a post often attempted to pass the *jinshi* examinations.

Yet even the growing prestige of the *jinshi* exam did not lead to the decline of the old families. They proved so adept at mastering the examination that it became a new gateway to perpetual status rather than a roadblock. More than one-third of Tang examination graduates (and more than half the chief ministers and senior officials) came from the ten most prominent surname groups. This domination of high court offices by the leading families continued throughout the dynasty, reaching its statistical peak in the middle of the ninth century.[51] This continuity was due to features of the great families and of the examination system itself—features that help to explain the evolution and ultimate disappearance of the old families.

The old families were highly successful at the examinations because of their longstanding scholarly traditions and their ability to provide their offspring with a first-rate education at home. By contrast, the limited public education available in the Tang declined after the first century of the dynasty. Top educators were concentrated in three metropolitan schools in Chang'an, which were available only to families resident in the capital. By law, the Academy for Sons of the State was reserved for sons or grandsons of men of the third rank or above; the Imperial Academy was reserved for offspring of officials of the fourth and fifth ranks; and the Academy of the Four Gates was restricted to sons or grandsons of sixth- or seventh-rank officials, except for a few slots set aside for offspring of nonofficials. Special academies attached to the Chancellery and the Crown Prince's Palace were reserved for members of the imperial family and selected offspring of third-rank officials and above. Schools in the provinces were clearly inferior to these academies and were largely reserved for sons of local officials or scions of large landholding families.[52] Thus, the established families living in Chang'an had a huge educational edge over other contenders.

The predominance of established families in high office was also due to the nature of the examinations. Like the dynasty's best schools, the examinations themselves were given only in the capital. Although candidates were recruited from outside prefectures, and sending up candidates became an important function of local government after the An Lushan rebellion, there was no system of examinations at the prefectural or provincial levels as there would be in later periods. Consequently, the same offspring of high officials who had privileged access to the best teachers also enjoyed an immediate physical access to the examination sites.[53]

Unlike the examinations of later Chinese dynasties, which relied on written papers whose authorship was concealed from evaluators, Tang examinations required an extended, ritually orchestrated interaction between examiners and candidates, and among the candidates themselves. Long before the formal test, candidates traveled through the capital presenting samples of their writing, sometimes quite voluminous, to potential patrons and even to the examiner. A patron actively campaigned for the candidate of his choice, and in some cases promised him a daughter in marriage. The practice became so routinized that potential patrons frequently stipulated the topics they would consider reading. Writings were stolen, and celebrated writers such as Wen Tingyun reportedly sold poems that the purchaser could circulate as his own.[54]

In 742 the chief examiner allowed all candidates to openly submit their lyrical pieces weeks in advance, and for this he was celebrated as being even-handed. More often, factions and networks formed around particular candidates, and social or political ties were manipulated to secure the desired results. In some years the complete list of selected candidates was drawn up before the papers were even written. As the volume of writing grew overwhelming, ties of family or patronage became the key to the choice of examination clients.[55] No one argued that this state of affairs was wrong in principle, which indicates how the examinations were perceived in the period. This strong social element of the examination process invariably favored the offspring of established families, particularly those in the capital.

The final aspect of the examinations that favored the success of elite families was their actual content. At the beginning of the Tang the *jinshi* examination demanded responses on current affairs, to complement the exam on the exposition of the classics. In 681 the *jinshi* examination was restructured to consist of three parts: canonical knowledge, literary writings, and dissertations on current affairs. However, in practice literary writings formed the core of the examination until the end of the dynasty. The writings circulated in advance consisted entirely of *belles lettres,* sometimes nothing but lyric poetry. Private tuition supplanted public education during the first century of the dynasty primarily because even the capital's schools provided no training in literary composition and hence did not prepare students for the exams. The *jinshi* examination was regularly criticized for its exclusive focus on literary skill, but the failure of such recurrent attacks demonstrates that the *jinshi* exam was widely accepted as a test of compositional abilities.[56]

This focus of the empire's most prestigious exam on poetry requires an explanation, especially for modern people who assume that bureaucracy is a form of rational government, calculated to attain the most efficient and effective performance of a set of specified functions. Under the Northern and Southern Dynasties, the writing and exchange of verse had defined membership in a new social elite where aesthetic accomplishments distinguished true gentlemen from mere landlords. While the link between aesthetic sensibilities and political authority was particularly evident in the south, the southern literary arts enjoyed prestige in the courts of Emperor Yang of the Sui, Taizong of the Tang, and subsequent rulers. The crucial nature of *belles lettres* at the court was demonstrated in great literary entertainments, where more than a hundred poems were composed on a given theme and prizes awarded to the best.[57] The *jinshi* examination formalized and sanctioned this centrality of verse as an elite activity.

To summarize the social and historical role of the Tang examinations, they conferred membership into a group defined by social status rather than office. The tests were only one element in the broader formation of social networks and alliances, in which the presentation of writings and the establishment of patron-client ties culminated in the awarding of degrees. Success in the exams entailed participation in a set of rituals that established lifelong bonds between the examiner and his graduates and among the graduates as a group. In the last half of the dynasty, it also transformed the latest graduates into the most desirable candidates for marriage, comparable to the position of elite daughters in the early years of the dynasty. The examinations themselves, and the circulation of writings that preceded them, continued a tradition from the preceding centuries of defining elite status by skill at literary composition. Rather than merely selecting officials for government work, the examinations helped to create a new "privileged corporation" whose attributes and practices closely mirrored, and in some cases replicated, those that had defined the old aristocratic families. Thus, it is no surprise to find those very families taking pride of place within the new social structure.[58]

However, the old elite's success in transforming itself into this new corporation also carried the seeds of its destruction. The power of the great families of the late Tang, like the families themselves, was based on "little more than an idea." Tied to examinations and offices both for the selective genealogies that defined them and the prestige that exalted them, the late Tang elite was a service aristocracy that had no mode of existence outside the state. Commanding no base of local support, they wielded influence only to the extent that people around them honored their genealogies and offices. Unlike other imperial Chinese elites, who combined local power with state office, they could not survive without the dynasty, and so they perished with the Tang government they had served.[59]

The actual elimination of the old families resulted from a virtual class war, due to the rise of new bases of power outside the imperial bureaucracy. The military governors in the northeast and central plain, and the salt monopoly in the south, recruited men on the basis of military, fiscal, and administrative expertise. Even within the court itself, officials were marginalized by the eunuchs who controlled the armed forces and by academicians who served as the emperor's closest advisers. The Tang elite, defined by its literary accomplishments and social networks, increasingly became the target of hostility and contempt from those who had gained power through the practical skills required in military and financial administration.

Among the men who helped to topple the dynasty were many like the chief rebel Huang Chao, who had repeatedly failed in the examinations and whose contempt for the exam-based elite consequently turned to hatred. When Huang's former subordinate Zhu Wen formally ended the Tang, one of his followers who was also a failed examination candidate urged the murder of the highest Tang officials. Thirty of them, all with eminent surnames, were killed in the sixth month of 905, and they were tossed into the Yellow River so that this political "pure stream" would merge with the "muddy" one. The old elite families might have survived this physical massacre, but they could not survive the revolution in attitudes that underlay it.

8

RELIGION

THE TANG dynasty marked the highpoint of institutional Daoism and Buddhism in imperial China, both in social influence and intellectual prestige. Daoism enjoyed unparalleled political influence owing to the support of the imperial family, and Buddhism emerged during this period as a truly Chinese faith. The court also systematically reworked imperial ritual and burial practices. Finally, the Tang dynasty left us richer documentation than earlier periods about many local religious cults, and it witnessed the emergence of others, most notably the city god cult, that would become fundamental in late imperial Chinese religion.

Daoism in the Tang

Daoist links to the state and the literati had emerged in both the north and south during the centuries of division. With China's reunification under the Sui and Tang, these regional traditions were blended into a common ecumenical religion powerful enough to compete with Buddhism for the support of the court and leading families. This newly constructed intellectual system was called the Teaching of the Way (*Dao jiao*), placing it in parallel with the Teaching of the Buddha (*Fo jiao*) and the Teaching of the Confucian scholars (*Ru jiao*). Its doctrines derived from the earliest Daoist canon assembled by the southerner Lu Xiujing in the fifth century and expanded in the sixth.[1] Because Lu Xiujing was a codifier of the Lingbao tradition, this school provided the framework for synthesizing the various Daoist traditions. It also incorporated major elements of Buddhism into both doctrines and rituals, thus appealing to all classes, from the court and leading official families to the farmers in village communities.[2]

The Tang was also a period of major developments in the patronage of Daoism. Links between Daoism and the Tang imperial house had been forged before the dynasty was established. Emperor Yang of the Sui honored the Shangqing Daoist master Wang Yuanzhi (528–635) as a "teacher of emperors and kings." But when the emperor ignored Wang's advice against moving the Sui capital to Jiangdu on the Yangzi, Wang secretly transmitted Daoist "registers" (indicating high spiritual standing) to the Tang founder, Li Yuan. This assured him of Daoist support for his subsequent founding of the Tang. His son Li Shimin (Emperor Taizong) subsequently honored Wang Yuanzhi in a special imperial decree and also sponsored the writing of calligraphic extracts from Lingbao scriptures by leading court officials.[3]

This Daoist support led the early emperors to decide, in response to a suggestion by Wang Yuanzhi, to recognize Laozi as the ruling family's ultimate ancestor. Laozi was the putative author of the *Canon of the Way and Its Power* (*Dao de jing*), and, since the Han, a recognized divinity who received sacrifice from the state. The Tang emperors' focus on the divinized Laozi began with reports of his miraculous appearances in 617 and 618 to proclaim that the Tang would rule the empire. In 620 Emperor Gaozu pronounced Laozi to be the "sage ancestor" of the Tang imperial house and gave this title to the Louguan Monastery just south of the capital, which had been a historical center for the worship of Laozi. The descent of the imperial line from Laozi was affirmed by Emperor Taizong, and Daoism was declared the highest religion of the realm in 625 and again in 637. While earlier rulers in the north and south had sought legitimation from Daoist masters, the Tang rulers claimed something more: divine support as their inalienable birthright.[4]

Tang support of Daoism continued under Emperor Gaozong and Empress Wu. In 666 Gaozong gave Laozi an even loftier imperial title and set up state-sponsored temples in each of the more than three hundred prefectures of the empire. These temples held ritual feasts called *zhai* during major imperial and Daoist festivals throughout the year. Gaozong also placed the Daoist clergy, along with Buddhist monks, under state auspices by creating legal statutes for their regulation. In 675 he issued the first imperial decree to compile a Daoist canon, and in 678 he made the *Canon of the Way and Its Power* a compulsory text for imperial examinations.

The court invited leading Daoist scholars and thaumaturges (wonder workers)—notably Pan Shizheng (585–682) and Ye Fashan (631–720)—to advise the rulers, provide them with magical talismans, and perform rituals of purification and communication with deities.[5] Ye Fashan served no fewer than five emperors and was honored with inscriptions from Emperor Xuanzong, who praised him for serving the dynasty with both advice and magical powers. The emperor even indicated that his service continued from beyond the human realm:

> Using byways and subtle assistance,
> He transforms spiritually and creates supernaturally . . .
> Subduing rebellions and assisting with pacification,
> He succors completion and seconds the seasons.[6]

Imperial support of Daoism reached its apogee under Xuanzong, who fully mobilized the religion in support of the dynasty. He placed paired statues of himself and Laozi in all state-sponsored Daoist temples, dedicated the Tang ancestral temples in Chang'an and Luoyang to Daoist worship, and ordered the Daoist clergy at all state-sponsored institutions to perform rituals on the empire's behalf. In 743 Xuanzong went so far as to place all Daoists under the Court of the Imperial Clan, thus making them officially kin.

Emperor Xuanzong also summoned to his court Pan Shizheng's leading disciple, Sima Chengzhen (646–735), a descendant of the imperial house of the Jin dynasty who was trained as an official before turning to Daoism at the age of twenty-one and becoming one of the most celebrated calligraphers in Chinese history. In 721 Emperor Xuanzong had the *Canon of the Way* inscribed on stone in three different styles of Sima's calligraphy. In the same year Sima bestowed lay ordination on the emperor and subsequently gave him a magic sword and mirror. Xuanzong also had him perform the Golden Register (*Jin lu*) *zhai* ritual, the greatest of medieval Daoist rites, which aimed to prevent all natural calamities, secure the empire's stability, and prolong the emperor's life. Finally, in 731 Emperor Xuanzong changed the traditional rituals to the five sacred directional peaks of China into Daoist ceremonies devoted to the five Perfected Ones who were supposed to dwell on those mountains.[7] Together with the changes of ritual in the ancestral temple, this reform of the most important nature rites of the dynasty indicated the degree to which Daoism was adopted by the Tang government.

After the An Lushan rebellion, imperial patronage continued in diminished form. However, in association with the rise of regional powers, several regional Daoist centers gained prominence. The most important was the Black Sheep Temple in Chengdu, Sichuan, where Laozi had supposedly met his servant Yin Xi before departing to the west. In 883 the officiant at a sacrificial offering at the temple discovered a miraculous brick that produced a marvelous sound when struck and was inscribed with ancient seal characters indicating that Laozi would bring peace to the world. After this discovery, the temple began to receive substantial imperial largesse.[8]

Daoism also had a significant impact on the literary elite. Tang poetry is full of references to Daoist astronomical beliefs, erotic encounters with immortals, mental flights through the Heavens or the fabulous grottoes that, according to Daoist teachings, linked the great mountain chains, and the pursuit of immortality and liberation from human bonds, which were the religion's central aims. Many leading poets, including Li Bo (Bai) and Li Shangyin, were lay devotees of Daoism and apparently practiced many of the meditative, breathing, dietary, and sexual exercises that aimed at immortality. The work of lesser-known poets, including Cao Tang, was largely devoted to Daoist themes. Many of the literati also made visits to the great Daoist complexes near the capital or at Mao Shan (near modern Nanjing).[9]

In the late Tang, Daoist clergy demonstrated an increasing interest in appealing to the common people. They offered techniques, using spells and talismans inspired by Tantric Buddhism, to secure good fortune in building a house. Daoist texts found at Dunhuang also present early forms of geomancy. Daoists collected miracle tales pertaining to ordinary people and introduced the Ten Worthies Who Rescue from Suffering, a set of new deities said to help ordinary people in distress. These gods first appeared in the Sui but reemerged with more explicitly Daoist names in the Tang. They were modeled on the Buddhas of the Ten Directions and were often conflated with the Ten Kings of Hell, who played a central role in memorial services for the salvation of the dead.[10]

These developments in late Tang Daoism are epitomized in the career of Du Guangting (850–933). After failing the examinations and studying Daoism at Mount Tiantai, he joined the court of Emperor Xizong in 875 as a counselor, drafter of decrees, and ultimately the commissioner of Daoist ritual. In 881, when Huang Chao's forces occupied the capital, he fled with the court to Sichuan, returned to the capital in 885, but then fled again the next year. When the Tang commander in Sichuan, Wang Jian, established his own state of Former Shu in 901, Du Guangting accepted the post of royal tutor. After retiring from the Shu court, he devoted the last decades of his life to writing and editing Daoist texts, an unprecedented number of which are preserved in the Daoist canon.

These works, written when Daoism was under threat, provide a detailed and systematic account of virtually all aspects of that tradition. They cover an extraordinary range of topics, including popular miracles, saints' biographies, rituals and liturgies, sacred geography, inscriptions, commentaries on Daoist classics, official documents, and poetry. Among these voluminous writings is the only substantial work ever devoted exclusively to the activities of women in Daoism.[11]

Daoist Nuns and Priestesses

In Daoism, as in many other aspects of society, the Tang dynasty was an age of unparalleled opportunity and achievement for elite women. According to Du, his primary purpose was to record women saints neglected by other sources, to show their contributions to various religious lineages (above all his own Shangqing tradition), and to demonstrate the multiplicity of paths to the Way. Less explicit but clear is his desire to incorporate local cults (often devoted to women) into Daoism and to dramatize Daoism's superiority to Buddhism, a theme in several of the women's lives.

The most distinctively feminine aspect of Du's biographies was his account of early life leading to religious practice. He wrote of childhood tensions between filial duty and a precocious religious vocation, sometimes featuring early displays of magical powers or the hidden performance of good works. A central theme was the marriage crisis, where the imperative to wed conflicted with an aspiration toward self-perfection through religious devotion. Some women avoided marriage by becoming hermits or wanderers, while others entered a Daoist convent. Concubines of deceased emperors or nobles were often forced to move to a convent, and female children were sometimes given to convents by their parents to save them from illness or starvation. For many women Daoists, entry into a convent was a way to pursue education and a literary career.[12]

Consecration as a Daoist nun to evade an unwanted marriage or to provide a career outside the household also figured among women of the imperial family. The Taiping Princess temporarily became a Daoist nun

212 CHINA'S COSMOPOLITAN EMPIRE

to avoid a forced marriage to the king of Turfan, but the ordination of other princesses had a more religious aspect. The most celebrated was the ordination of two daughters of Emperor Ruizong in 711. This ceremony was celebrated at fabulous expense to the state, and each princess was given her own new monastery with easy access to the palace. In total, around a dozen Tang princesses were ordained, allowing them to escape the court but continue to participate in politics. They traveled extensively, devoted themselves to art and literature, and, according to hostile Confucian sources, led lives of sexual license and self-indulgence. Being ordained as a Daoist nun could also serve to purge the taint of a previous imperial marriage, as in the case of Yang Guifei, whose ordination was an intermediate step between the end of her marriage to a prince and her entry into the emperor's harem. Yang Guifei appears as a posthumous Daoist priestess on one of the Isles of the Immortals in Bo Juyi's celebrated poem "The Song of Lasting Regret."[13]

Several funerary inscriptions also depict the Daoist careers of elite women. One tells of a woman who became a Buddhist nun at the age of eight but was forced to become a Daoist during the persecution of Buddhism in 845. Several of the surviving inscriptions, like those for Buddhist nuns or abbesses, suggest that a woman's religious vocation resulted from the merit and good deeds accumulated over centuries by the great family from which she sprang.[14]

Female Daoist adepts figured as founders of local cults, particularly in southern and eastern regions and along the coast. Huang Lingwei (ca. 640–721, best-known as the Flower Maiden)—like many others, ordained at the age of twelve—devoted years of her life to locating the lost shrine of Lady Wei Huacun (252–334), who was the ultimate ancestor of the Shangqing tradition through her revelation of its scriptures to Yang Xi. Huang revived the shrine, performed the *zhai* rites there, and gathered female disciples, who maintained it for decades. A later priestess, Xue Xuantong, was celebrated at her death by the local governor in a memorial to the emperor in 882. In reply, the emperor sent down a decree declaring that she illuminated her locality and the empire, comparing her achievements to those of Wei Huacun and Huang Lingwei. Perhaps most influential of all was Zu Shu (fl. 889–904). After being ordained in several traditions, she encountered a divine being who instructed her in the techniques of exorcism and the talismans of the Thunder Rites that became hugely influential under the Song. In this capacity she was declared to be the founder of the Pure Subtlety (*qing wei*) tradition.[15]

Many women who were active Daoists left behind no traces in the written record. Yet we can get a sense of their number from the fact that under Emperor Xuanzong there were 1,137 Daoist temples for men and 550 for women. And we can learn something of their activities from the conventions of Tang poetry. Poets wrote about women of their acquaintance, usually in some position at court, who departed secular life to become novices in Daoist temples. These poems usually focused on cutting off the hair, removing makeup, and replacing elaborate court costumes with monastic garb:

> She leaves off combing her thicket of side-locks and washes off her
>   rouge;
> On her head a lotus-blossom crown as she emerges from the Palace
>   of Never-Ending Life.
> As other disciples fetch away the verses and repetitives she sang,
> Other palace women separate and distribute her dancing cloaks and
>   chemises.

They often ended with imagined visions of the new novice soaring off in meditative flights through space. Others referred to the intention of the new nun, often described as a "fallen immortal" (which was the Daoist equivalent of the bodhisattva ideal in Buddhism), to use the powers she would soon acquire to save all living beings.[16]

Many poems described female Daoist masters in terms generally applied to men, except that the poet often hinted at an element of erotic attraction between him and his subject. Most dealt with female "refined masters," charismatic figures who had no administrative tasks in the temples to which their presence brought prestige. The poems described the great age or spiritual attainments of such masters and the paradises to which they could soar. Other poems told of eminent Daoist women who became recluses in the mountains, where the poet traveled to seek them out. They described the women's ascetic practices, such as fasting, which facilitated the lightening of the body and attainment of visions.[17]

Finally, much poetry on "Daoist" women was dedicated to those whom poets depicted as lovers or companions and whose links to religious institutions were unclear. While many women remained celibate to pursue religious goals, Du Guangting accepted marriage as one route to transcendence. Divine marriage between mortal men and goddesses figured in the Shangqing tradition as a central ritual and an aspect of textual revelations. Some poetry on Daoist women as lovers described affairs with them as journeys through the cosmos, as in this quatrain by Li Shangyin addressed to two sisters who were Daoist nuns:

> Stealing peaches [of immortality] and snatching drugs; these are
>   difficult to do together.
> In the middle of the twelve-layered city walls, we locked up the
>   multicolored moon toad.
> We should taste them together with the elixir on the same night,
> Then the jade storied buildings will be nothing but these rock
>   crystal curtains.[18]

Here the poet pretends that in sharing peaches and elixirs of immortality with the sisters, he could transform his bedroom into a celestial paradise.

Finally, the imagery of Daoist goddesses was used to celebrate the beauty of women who had no religious calling. The use of "goddesses" as erotic figures dates back at least to Warring States poems in the *Songs of the South* (*Chu ci*) anthology. The Queen Mother of the West, the archetypal Daoist divinity, similarly became an erotically charged figure in stories of her liaison with Emperor Wu of the Han. In the Tang, this literary tradition fused with the emerging practice of poems by and about courtesans and dancers. The most striking example was a lesbian love poem about three orphaned sisters who became courtesans and famous musicians. It was written by a woman who was herself a celebrated courtesan, Daoist nun, and poet, Yu Xuanji (844–868). Yu invoked references ranging from the classic beauty Xi Shi to Daoist paradises and the Queen Mother to celebrate the three beauties. Other poems used the same images to portray dancers and prostitutes, and a common vocabulary developed between certain sexual practices and techniques of attaining immortality. This overlap between the worlds of the temple and the brothel found expression in the emergence of the Daoist Queen Mother of the West as the patron divinity of the prostitutes and female musicians who filled the pleasure quarters of Tang cities.[19]

The Emergence of a Chinese Buddhism

Although Daoism was officially the highest religion of Tang China, Buddhism remained the most popular and influential faith. Along with Daoism, Buddhism also became a fundamental part of the political order and the economy, sponsored and regulated by the state. Fully established within Chinese society, Tang Buddhism became truly sinicized through the separation of China from Central Asia and India, which made China its own Buddhist heartland, and through the emergence within China itself of new, indigenous Buddhist intellectual and ritual traditions.[20]

To begin at the highest level, Buddhism was a spiritual arm of the state. Its primary instruments were the imperial monasteries established in each prefecture of the empire and the palace chapels established by the ruling family within imperial precincts. The imperial monasteries were inhabited by the intellectual elite of the monastic order and supported by funds from the imperial treasury. These monasteries staged ceremonies for the welfare of the state, including the celebration of imperial birthdays and the observance of memorial services for the spirits of deceased emperors or dowager empresses, who were virtually all devout Buddhists. Laymen would be invited to participate in great vegetarian feasts held in the monasteries, and it was not unheard of for several tens of thousands of people to be fed at a single event. Monasteries also conducted elaborate collective mortuary and memorial rites for the thousands of soldiers who perished in Tang military campaigns. Apart from Emperor Wuzong's attempted suppression and mass confiscation of Buddhist property in 845, which lasted only a year, no emperor ever questioned the place of Buddhism within the Tang state.[21]

In addition to performing ceremonies for the state and the imperial clan, the Buddhist order also assisted in defending the empire. When foreign invasions threatened, emperors who believed in Buddhism ordered the imperial monasteries and palace chapels to chant a sutra entitled *The Scripture for Humane Kings* (*Ren wang jing*). This had been composed, probably in the late fifth century, to invoke spirit armies and other powers to protect the state, and it was credited with miraculously checking invaders. Statues of the Buddhas and bodhisattvas were assembled on a platform and draped with pennants and flowers, and in some cases the emperor himself personally attended the chanting. In 765, when the combined Uighur and Tibetan armies threatened the capital only to fall back when the sudden death of the Uighur ruler ended their alliance, the Buddhists claimed credit for this divine intervention.[22]

Another group of monasteries serving the state were those on Mount Wutai, associated with the cult of the bodhisattva Manjusri (Fig. 24). Any signs of his presence—strange fragrances, lights in the sky, colored clouds appearing out of nowhere—were auspicious for the dynasty and

Fig. 24   Surviving temples at Mount Wutai.

were immediately reported to the court, which then made donations to the monasteries. The Japanese pilgrim Ennin reports the tremendous generosity of these gifts even in the 840s, when the dynasty was financially weakened and the ruler hostile to Buddhism.[23] Mount Wutai was also the site of a putative community of female Daoist immortals who appeared as a feminine version of the utopian community described by Tao Yuanming in his fifth-century prose narrative *Peach Blossom Spring*.[24]

In addition to religious services to the empire, the monasteries also provided hostels or lodgings to people traveling with state sponsorship or protection. The most typical visitors were Buddhist pilgrims who moved from monastery to monastery on their way to important sites, or any monk who was required to travel. State-sponsored monasteries also served as hostels for officials traveling to posts or on other government business, and sometimes even for examination candidates on their way to the capital. Many monasteries turned the provision of rooms into a business and, as Ennin noted, some pilgrims could not obtain rooms because they were all occupied by paying guests. Because of their scenic location in hills or mountains, many monasteries became retreats where officials or other members of the elite took temporary refuge to restore their psychic energy. Journeys into the mountains to stay at Buddhist temples became a standard theme of Tang poetry.[25]

The official Buddhist church was also, according to hostile bureaucrats, the greatest landowner in Tang China, due to the charitable donations of believers. In this capacity the monasteries differed little from other landlords, for they either worked the land with slaves (or special servile Buddhist households, often filled by condemned criminals) or they rented it out in small plots to tenants. The actual scale of Buddhist holdings is difficult to estimate, because many rich families buried their dead in a monastery or established a chapel there and then "donated" land to maintain religious services. This land was actually retained by the donor, but it now escaped taxation since it was registered under the tax-exempt Buddhist church. Buddhist monasteries also frequently owned water-powered mills and oil presses which they rented out to families who produced flour or oil for the monastery.[26]

More significant than the political and economic activities of the Buddhist monasteries were their religious and educational services. Apart from having recourse to monasteries in times of need, the common people regularly encountered Buddhism in the great festivals that marked the calendar and became the chief occasion for fairs and irregular markets in the countryside. The first great celebration of the year was the Lantern Festival, which lasted from the fourteenth to the sixteenth days of the first month. The ward gates of the capital, normally locked at night, were left open so that the populace could go from temple to temple to observe the lavish displays of lanterns and images.

Next came the Buddha's birthday on the eighth day of the fourth month, when Buddha images were bathed and paraded through the streets. In certain years the rarest relics of the Buddha, most notably the famous finger bone (which has now been discovered in a crypt beneath the Famen Monastery, near Chang'an), were carried through the capital in a procession that triggered mass hysteria and the sacrificial burning of heads or arms. In 873 a soldier chopped off his own arm and held it in his other hand as he followed the procession. The last important festival was All Souls' Feast, on the fifteenth day of the seventh month, to commemorate Mulian's rescue of his mother from hell.[27]

The Buddhist church also influenced Tang life through popular lectures in large cities and small towns. These involved story-telling, anecdotes, and parables intended to entertain and enlighten. Both Buddhist and anti-Buddhist accounts suggested that they drew tremendous crowds and deeply influenced many commoners. Distinct from these lectures but equally popular were oral recitations in poetry and prose, often accompanied by pictures, of popular Buddhist stories. These tales eventually became the "transformation texts" that significantly contributed to the emergence of vernacular fiction.[28] The temple fairs that played an important economic role in the Tang countryside were an occasion for theatrical performances that made Buddhist tales and doctrines part of the mental universe of peasants.

Votive inscriptions at Buddhist caves, along with documents discovered at Dunhuang, provide evidence of the impact on Tang society of lay Buddhist societies or clubs under monastic sponsorship. They constructed images, copied scriptures, prepared vegetarian feasts, gathered the faithful for the recitation of sutras, and provided for the burial of members. Often in association with these societies, the monasteries provided hospitals and dispensaries for the sick, kitchens for the hungry, orphanages for abandoned children, havens for the aged, and other charitable services. In short, monasteries and associated clubs played a role as charitable defenders of the poor that would be taken up by rich lineages and guilds in late imperial China. In addition, they built roads, constructed bridges, and widened river channels for navigation.[29]

Buddhism also took the form of wandering monks, often persecuted by the authorities, who mingled with villagers to spread the religion through the countryside. Many acted as village exorcists, magicians, or mediums. One hostile Tang memorial tells of a well that wandering monks claimed could cure disease, but those who would drink from it had to abstain from eating meat and pungent vegetables. The "magic" well thus served to indoctrinate villagers in Buddhist dietary principles.

Sometimes peasants, often children, experienced a form of spirit possession in which they chanted new sutras or wrote texts in strange scripts that were later recognized as Sanskrit or some Central Asian alphabet. These people and the texts they produced became the focus of intense local devotion that sometimes developed into a small-scale religious movement. The Buddhist establishment viewed them with suspicion, and hagiographies tell how eminent monks exorcised the demons that possessed these people.[30] But the opposition of the official church could not prevent these variant forms of "Buddhism" from becoming inextricably intertwined with Chinese popular religion.

One important form of Tang popular piety was the Inexhaustible Treasuries, sponsored by the Sect of the Three Stages. Founded in the Sui, this sect preached that with the inevitable disappearance of the Buddha's law in the world of impermanence, all religious distinctions, including those between monk and layman, had lost meaning. These believers lived apart from other monks in special quarters in certain monasteries, and in place of conventional, institutional Buddhism, they advocated universal reverence for the Buddha nature of all living creatures. They made the classic lay obligation of charity their highest virtue and founded the Inexhaustible Treasuries, which had many regional branches. At the New Year Festival and the Ghost Festival, people donated cash and movable goods to their local branch of the Inexhaustible Treasuries, which lent these resources out at interest and used the income to repair Buddhist buildings and images and to provide relief for the poor. This institution emerged as an empire-wide system of charity until Emperor Xuanzong abolished it in the middle of the eighth century because of the sect's attacks on institutional Buddhism.[31]

The changing international order was likewise significant for the emergence of a Chinese Buddhism. Because Buddhism had originated in India and entered China primarily through Central Asia, scholars from Central Asia had for centuries served as the intellectual masters of Buddhism in China. In the Buddhist worldview, India held pride of place at the center of the world, while China was reduced to a marginal position. This appears most clearly in the writings of the pilgrims who traveled to India to find scriptures and carry them back to China.

Thus, the early pilgrim Faxian translated the name of the Indian state of Madhydesa as "Middle Kingdom" (*zhong guo*) and asserted that its clothing and food were essentially the same as China's. This statement, incorporated into Li Daoyuan's *Commentary to the Classic of Waterways* (*Shui jing zhu*), was not an empirical observation but rather an assertion that the homeland of the Buddha, as the central land of the religion, had to be equivalent to the "central" land of China. This argument defended Buddhism from the charge that it was a barbarian creed that true Chinese should not honor. Although Faxian could not acknowledge that the centrality of India entailed the marginality of China, this point was explicit in both Brahman and Buddhist works, which defined the Chinese as foreigners or barbarians on the same level as the tribes of Central Asia.[32]

This issue was even more explicit in the writings of the great Tang pilgrim Xuanzang (ca. 600–664), who experienced India not merely as a

land where Buddhist writings could be found but as a landscape satu-
rated with traces and stories revealing not just what the Buddha said and
did but above all what a Buddha *was*. Brief references to the current state
of India, often focused on signs of the imminent disappearance of the law,
led to elaborate accounts of events in the Buddha's life that took place at
that site. Thus, India emerged as the most direct and vivid medium for
grasping the truth of Buddhism, which for Xuanzang was the highest
truth. As the site of the Buddha's life and enlightenment, it was the center
not only of the world but of the cosmos.

When monks at Nalanda Monastery urged Xuanzang to stay in India
rather than return to the barbaric land of China where the Buddha had
chosen not to be born, he could only argue that the Buddha would not
"forget those who are not yet enlightened." After listing the virtues of
China's rulers, he concluded plaintively, "How can you then say that the
Buddha did not go to my country because of its insignificance?" At almost the same time, the monk Daoxuan (596–667) calculated that India
was the physical center of the world and asserted that Indian civilization
was superior because, among other things, it had an alphabetic script.[33]

In the eighth century, however, as the international scene shifted, China
emerged as a sacred Buddhist land in its own right, as well as a center for
the dissemination of Buddhist teachings and texts throughout East Asia.
Sui and Tang China became religiously significant realms through claiming to possess physical remains of the Buddha and other Buddhist divinities. Relic veneration had emerged at an early date in Buddhist history, intertwined with the legend of the Mauryan king Asoka. As the
ideal Buddhist monarch, he had set up 84,000 stupas across his realm,
each containing ashes from the Buddha's cremation. This story was well-
known in China by the end of the fifth century. Early Chinese Buddhists
argued that since Asoka had ruled the entire continent of which China
was a part, then diligent searches—aided by magical signs such as glow-
ing lights—would reveal Buddha relics in China. The earliest story of
such a discovery dates from the fifth century, and sources speak of nine-
teen further finds in the fourth and fifth centuries. Such discoveries were
also made in the sixth century in southern China.[34]

The marginal position of China, still implied by the discovery of only
Asokan relics, changed under the Sui. The Sui founder Emperor Wen,
having in 601 reached the significant age of sixty, ordered an empire-wide
distribution of the Buddha's relics, an act that he repeated in 602 and
604. According to Sui sources, monks from India traveled to China to

witness the ceremonies and later to make pilgrimages to China's stupas. One Indian monk is reported to have discovered in his own country a stone inscription prophesying Emperor Wen's establishment of the reliquary stupas. Emperor Wen further ordered the translation of texts describing his actions into Sanskrit, thus symbolically reversing the flow of translations. The three Korean kingdoms sent petitions to the Sui court requesting a share in the relics, although the Sui court may have demanded that they make this request.[35] Thus, Emperor Wen assimilated his status to that of the ideal Buddhist monarch, thereby equating the Sui with the model Buddhist empire and asserting China's status as the central Buddhist realm to which Koreans and even Indians turned in search of Buddhism's holiest sites.

The Chinese also discovered in their empire the realms of other Buddhist divinities, most notably the dwelling place of Manjusri at Mount Wutai. This bodhisattva had become celebrated as one of the most learned and benevolent of beings, who saved people from purgatory or converted all sentient beings. Because he lived on a permanently snow-capped mountain and his original Indian name meant Five Peaks, Chinese commentators argued that he dwelt on Mount Wutai ("Five Peaks") in the northeast (modern Shanxi). Daoxuan states this as a fact, with a list of canonical proofs, in a report written around 664. Mount Wutai thus became the first great site of Buddhist pilgrimage in the Tang empire, where pious Chinese could encounter a landscape full of divine traces without a journey to India.

Visits to the mountain and written endorsements by Central and South Asian monks in the seventh and eighth centuries, many sponsored by Empress Wu, strengthened Mount Wutai's reputation as a sacred Buddhist site. Because Li Yuan began the campaign that founded the Tang from a base in the region of Mount Wutai, the esoteric Master Amoghavajra (Bukong) argued that its bodhisattva was a special protector of the Tang. This led to the practice of sending imperial gifts in response to any sighting of divine manifestations. Ennin's diary, describing a large-scale pilgrimage of Japanese and other monks to the mountain, reports such sightings. Moreover, images from Nepal and formularies in Sanskrit, Tibetan, and Khotanese show that the association of Mount Wutai with the bodhisattva had become widespread throughout Central and South Asia by the eleventh century.[36]

Further support for the Tang claim that China had become the new center of the Buddhist world was provided by the doctrine of the imminent end of the Buddha's *dharma* (teachings). Buddhism taught that the Buddha's teachings, like everything in the physical world, were destined to become corrupt and perish. In China this idea had been elaborated under the influence of Daoist millenarianism and attempted suppressions of Buddhism in 446 and 574. By the fifth and sixth centuries it was widely believed that established Buddhism was nearing extinction. But the resurgence of the Buddhist church under the Sui and Tang led to a reinterpretation of this doctrine as a prophecy that the faith was on the verge of extinction *in India*. This view left China at the center of the Buddhist world.[37]

Another version of this prophecy was employed by Empress Wu to justify her own rule. She cited an apocryphal scripture describing how Maitreya, the future Buddha who would restore the true teaching after its disappearance, would descend from his celestial realm into a "magical city" of great walls and towers. This provided a model for her own Bright Hall complex at Luoyang, which included a giant Maitreya statue. She also sponsored a translation of the *Great Cloud Sutra* with a commentary, the core of which was a prophecy that a female follower of the Buddha would be reborn as a pious ruler of the whole continent, a prophecy that clearly referred to Empress Wu herself. When the new translation was presented at court, one of its authors described the empress as a reincarnation of Maitreya. In 690 it was distributed to all the monasteries of the empire, and two months later Empress Wu proclaimed her own dynasty. Five years later she added the name Maitreya to her title.[38]

The putative decline of Indian Buddhism had a basis in fact, in that Buddhism had disappeared in its old heartland along the Ganges by the ninth century and in Central Asia after the Muslim conquest. However, Buddhism continued to flourish in Bihar, Bengal, and Orissa through the twelfth century. This period also witnessed considerable intellectual vitality, including the elaboration of Tantric Buddhism and its exportation to Tibet, where it became the central teaching.[39] However, when the Northern Song dynasty sponsored a massive project to translate and disseminate Tantric texts, the Chinese Buddhist establishment ignored the project and its publications. This demonstrates the final aspect of China's emergence as the central Buddhist realm under the Tang: the rise to dominance of indigenous intellectual traditions.

Western scholars have proposed a three-stage process for the sinicization of Buddhism. Up to roughly the year 400, Chinese philosophers attempted to explain Buddhism in terms of their own intellectual traditions, above all the Dark Studies (*Xuan xue*) in which the *Master Zhuang* (*Zhuangzi*), the *Master Lao* (*Laozi*), and the *Canon of Change* (*Yi jing*) were reinterpreted to provide a new metaphysical grounding for moral and political authority. During this first phase, Buddhism was made to fit established Chinese categories. The second phase, led by Central Asian scholars, aimed at understanding Buddhist texts in their own terms, free of indigenous Chinese philosophy. This era, beginning with the arrival of Kumarajiva in Chang'an in 401, was devoted to translating the Buddhist canon and mastering the interpretive traditions of India and Central Asia that were needed to gloss it. At the end of the sixth century, in the third stage, Chinese Buddhists began to reject foreign traditions of interpretation and commentary and to produce intellectual traditions without explicit antecedents in Indian Buddhism. While many scholars have criticized this schema on numerous grounds, it remains the only synthetic framework for dealing with the period prior to the Tang.[40]

Buddhist China's indigenous intellectual traditions emerged from this background. The preceding two centuries of translations and commentaries gave Tang scholars confidence in their own understanding of Buddhism. But the overwhelming volume of Indian scriptures, written over centuries and thus laden with contradictions, produced a crisis among Buddhists, who sought a single message in their sacred texts. Moreover, the doctrine of the decline of the *dharma* had led to the belief that many detailed doctrines and regulations in earlier texts were no longer applicable. The new age required new ideas and new practices.

The Buddhism that consequently emerged in the Sui and Tang was embodied in four schools: Tiantai, Huayan, Chan, and Pure Land. These had several features in common: a Chinese "patriarchate" that transmitted authority in teacher-disciple "lineages," emphasis on practice over scholasticism, insistence on the possibility of attaining enlightenment in this life, and a new freedom to interpret scriptures based on personal religious experience rather than recapturing the author's original meaning. These represented a new willingness to discover Buddhism's truths and ultimate ends in personal experience and that of one's compatriots, rather than in the textual legacy of an alien land. A correlate of this new independence was the increased reliance on apocryphal scriptures composed in China to address Chinese concerns.[41]

Fundamental to the rise of charismatic Buddhist teachers and their freedom in interpreting texts was the teaching of "doctrinal classification." This explained contradictions between scriptures by arguing that the Buddha had taught at several levels, adjusting doctrine to the needs of his audience or expounding false ideas that allowed people to advance. Similarly, from the fifth century, Chinese Buddhists argued that different scriptures represented the teachings of the Buddha at various points in his career. Combining these two ideas, Tang Buddhists divided scriptures into "periods" (from earliest to latest) and "teachings" (from the simplest to the most profound). The fullest forms of this approach were found in the Tiantai and Huayan traditions, but virtually all Tang Buddhists employed it to some degree, with each tradition arguing that its favorite body of sutras represented the Buddha's highest teaching. Out of such ideas also arose a hierarchy of practices, in which meditation, visualization, invocation, and other modes of enlightenment were ranked against each other and internally divided into levels of excellence.[42]

The new emphasis on practice, and on deriving philosophy from practice rather than texts, is exemplified in the early history of the Huayan tradition. The putative founder of this tradition, Dushun (557–640) lived among the common people, exorcizing demons and curing diseases with powers gained in meditation. On the basis of meditative "discernments" (guan) rather than speculative arguments, he reinterpreted the "emptiness" (kong) of classic Buddhist doctrine as a "structuring principle" (li) that was inseparable from "phenomena" (shi). This marked an important shift toward affirming the phenomenal world. The second Huayan patriarch, Zhiyan (602–668), studied all the major works of Buddhist speculative thought only to be plunged into despair by their diverse arguments and contradictions. Even after settling on the Huayan Sutra as the key text, he realized the truth only after two months of meditation at the direction of a monk who magically appeared to him and then vanished.[43]

Like the Huayan tradition, the other new Buddhist schools also developed "lineages" of masters. This practice was pioneered by the Tiantai tradition, which had been the first to trace its doctrine from patriarch to patriarch back to the Buddha.[44] However, it was the Chan Buddhists who made master-disciple transmission the foundation of their religious practice. Chan's emphasis on patriarchal transmission originated as an attempt by a marginal group to become orthodox. According to the Continued Biographies of Eminent Monks (Xu gao seng zhuan), five meditation traditions were brought to the capital under the imperial sponsorship of the Sui. Several regional groups who later developed into Chan together created a lineage from Bodhidharma back to the Buddha, in which esoteric doctrines distinct from those in scriptures had supposedly been handed down from master to disciple.[45]

The attempt to gain authority against alternative traditions through this genealogy turned into an internal battle within the emerging Chan school itself, as diverse traditions each claimed to be heirs of the true transmission. The most celebrated case was the split between the northern and southern traditions over who was the legitimate "sixth patriarch," Shenxiu (606–706) or Huineng (d. 713). Because of these rivalries, the compilation of lists of master-disciple transmissions into a fixed history took centuries.[46]

The Chan tradition also claimed uniqueness through its idea of an extra-textual transmission passed from mind to mind through its charismatic patriarchs, quite outside received texts. This made possible rhetorical calls to "burn the scriptures" or "kill the Buddha," which allowed Chan to successfully move from the margins to the center of Chinese Buddhist thought, in the process becoming an "anti-institutional institution" and an "anti-textual textual tradition." The invention of the Chan lineage thus dramatized the appeals to the centrality of personal experience and the possibility of enlightenment in this life that defined Tang Buddhism.[47]

Confucian Ritual in State and Local Cults

The last of the triad of Tang religions was Confucianism, identifiable with imperial and local civic cults and with evolving readings of the state canon. Developments in these fields, together with the philosophical revival of Confucianism in the ninth century, help account for the rise of Neo-Confucianism to intellectual dominance in late imperial China.

The Tang did not introduce new imperial rituals, instead treating the received ritual classics dating from the Han as canonical. The final codification of state ritual, in 732, called the *Rituals of the Great Tang in the Kaiyuan Reign Period (Da Tang kaiyuan li)*, excluded practices from Daoism or Buddhism that had emerged in the centuries since the Han, even though both faiths were employed by the imperial house and the Tang state. This codification included only rituals from earlier empires: accession ceremonies, sacrifices to Heaven at the round suburban altar, worship of imperial ancestors and selected ancestors of the two preceding dynasties, the *feng* and *shan* sacrifices, imperial tours of inspection, the Bright Hall, and the calendar. However, the relative importance of these practices and the meanings attributed to them were significantly altered.[48]

The primary shift was from an emphasis on the dynasty as a construct of biological descent to an emphasis on its public, universal nature. The source of dynastic power became less the potent virtue of the emperor's biological ancestors and more the all-encompassing Heaven (of which the emperor was the son) and the ruler's political virtues. Tang imperial ritual shifted the emphasis from the notion that "all under Heaven is [the affair of] a family" to the idea that "all under Heaven is public." Instead of being the realm of the ruling house, the empire was viewed as a public good that transcended and negated the parochialism of family ties. This emphasis on the emperor as the Son of Heaven extended and sacralized the Han creation of a realm transcending regional cultures and family interests.

Familial rites in the ancestral temple became less important. In the Han, when the crown prince was installed as heir apparent he visited the ancestral temple to express his thanks, and this gesture was repeated after he ascended to the throne. The Tang eliminated this ritual, substituting instead the ceremony by which, during the Northern and Southern Dynasties, one dynasty yielded the mandate to the next. This ritual, in turn, was modeled on a mythic age when the ruler handed the throne not to his son but to the best man in his kingdom. In this way, the Tang ritual of accession negated heredity and stressed virtue or merit. This allowed some selection for talent, or at least for the absence of any perceived threat. Consequently, the oldest son, fully grown and hence likely to be a rival or threat, was rarely chosen. After the eunuchs came to dominate the court, all pretense of selection for talent was abandoned, and only young, weak, or incompetent heirs chosen.[49]

In place of the ancestral temple, outdoor altars to the supreme gods of Heaven and Earth became central. A sacrifice to Heaven was introduced into the ritual installation of an emperor, while rites to the ancestors of the dynastic founder became private, family matters. The cult of Heaven was further emphasized by the elimination of adjunct deities from the ritual, so that Heaven alone received the major sacrifices. The central altar rites were performed outside the capital, on land that belonged to the entire empire, and the emphasis was on the emperor as the protector and embodiment of his people.[50]

The *feng* and *shan* rituals were also transformed. In the Qin and Han,

the *feng* sacrifice on Mount Tai, marking the achievement of universal order, had been carried out in strict secrecy. The emperor alone went to the
summit and performed the ritual in isolation. Jade tablets inscribed with
announcements to the divinity were hidden in a series of caskets and coffers, which were then buried to guarantee that their messages remained
known only to the emperor. Many scholars argued that the sacrifices
helped the emperor attain immortality. In the Tang, by contrast, the *feng*
and *shan* became public rites involving the whole state. Numerous officials accompanied Emperor Gaozong to the summit, and under Empress Wu even the harem figured in the *shan* ceremony. The preserved
text of the announcement to Heaven shows that the ceremonies were carried out in the name of the people. Even the exclusive staging of the ceremony at Mount Tai was abandoned; it was also performed on Mount
Song to demonstrate that no single point in the empire was privileged.[51]

Imperial tombs also emphasized the new public and cosmic conception
of the emperor. Instead of building artificial burial mounds outside the
capital, as the Han had done for their emperors, the Tang buried their
rulers in the sides of natural mountains. This required less labor and was
more imposing. Imperial tombs were surrounded by hundreds of satellite
tombs, where leading officials, generals, and imperial relatives were buried. Satellite tombs had also been built in the Han, so that the tombs of
Emperor Wu's favorite generals lay in the shadow of his mound. But the
scale of the Tang complexes was much greater. Emperor Taizong's burial
site covered 45,000 acres and had about 200 satellite tombs. The promise
of burial in a satellite tomb was a great honor that encouraged loyalty to
the regime and drew the entire political class into the Tang ancestral
cult.[52]

The Tang also dedicated a sacrificial cult to "political ancestors" from
preceding dynasties. Ceremonies honoring the founders of immediately
preceding dynasties had a textual justification in the *Record of Ritual* (*Li
ji*) and had been practiced during the Northern and Southern Dynasties.
However, the Tang radically increased the number of political ancestors,
so that by 748 they were making offerings to the First Emperor of Qin,
the founder of the Western Han, the founder of the Eastern Han, and the
founders of most subsequent dynasties. These offerings drew China's entire imperial past into the Tang sacrifices and marked the Tang's concern
over the lineal succession of the mandate from dynasty to dynasty. They
also stressed the public, cosmic, and ethical character of rule at the expense of kinship and inheritance. Bo Juyi noted in a poem that the incor-

poration of earlier dynasties into Tang rites showed that the empire was not the property of a single family.[53]

The closer ties of the emperor to Heaven and the more public vision of the empire also altered the Chinese calendar. From early times, political power had been inextricably linked to the calendar, which both defined the rituals of the court and demonstrated the unique relation of the ruler to divine powers. Under the Han and the southern dynasties each dynasty proclaimed only one new calendar, or carried forward that of its predecessor. This explicitly identified the calendar with the ruling house. The northern dynasties had altered this practice, sometimes promulgating two or three calendars, perhaps influenced by numerological calculations in apocryphal texts. In the Tang, however, the calendar was changed no fewer than nine times in a constant search for a more precise reckoning based on Arabic and Indian astronomy. This emphasis on the correspondence of the calendar to Heaven, at the expense of loyalty to the dynastic house, again asserted the public and cosmic concerns of Tang emperors.[54]

The new vision of the emperor also led to adding the word "Heaven" (*Tian*) to imperial titles. Emperor Taizong declared himself to be both Heavenly Qaghan and Son of Heaven, Gaozong styled himself the Heavenly Emperor, and Empress Wu called herself the Heavenly Empress. These new titles set Tang emperors apart from earlier rulers, emphasizing claims to universal dominion and cosmic potency. The celestial trappings of authority were enacted in Tang ceremonies, as described by Ennin in his account of a magistrate's receipt of an imperial decree in Dengzhou. The entire population of the town lay prostrate, chanting their submission while the magistrate bowed to receive the document that he alone could touch.[55]

In addition to reforming major state cults, the Tang also developed or consolidated new local cults. The most important of these was the cult of the city god, which had emerged in southern China during the period of division. It was associated with the walls that separated the civilized city from a threatening wilderness represented by the angry, blood-drinking ghosts of people who had died violent deaths or by animal spirits and earth gods. Many stories recounted rivalries between local officials and powerful local spirits, and the officials often lost.[56]

In contrast with malevolent gods who demanded blood sacrifice from the people and threatened the power of local officials, the benignly human city god was an ally of officials and subject to punishment at their hands if he failed to protect local interests. As a moralization or domestication of local religion, the city god cult extended the norms of elite, imperial culture into the frontiers and the countryside, from which it had previously been excluded. It may also have been linked to the spread of Buddhism, which introduced an Indian deity associated with walls and gates.[57] The cult's rise to prominence represented the success of the court in communicating the image of the empire as a divine force that ordered space through its ability to command spirits.

The city god cult also demonstrated the ability of the imperial elite to command ideological support from the new urban classes. The Tang witnessed the emergence of large-scale urban settlements devoted primarily to trade, and thus of a self-consciously urban, mercantile class. The cult of the city god, which flourished primarily in the highly commercialized lower and middle Yangzi regions and along the southeast coast, was at least in part the religious expression of the appearance of a self-conscious urban group who identified their lifestyle and well-being with that of the city as a whole.[58]

While the city god cult became the most important local state cult and probably the sole empire-wide example, the state also embraced cults to regionally eminent divinities. One well-documented example is the cult to Wu Zixu in the lower Yangzi region and along the coast around Hangzhou Bay. Wu Zixu was a celebrated figure in the wars between Chu, Wu, and Yue states in the late sixth and early fifth centuries B.C. There were local temples to him from as early as the Han, and he was described as a "popular divinity" in the Wu region in the third century A.D. Tang inscriptions by local officials recounted the government-supported repair of his temples. One inscription stated that the people appealed to him for rain and that he guaranteed rich harvests. Another attributed to him the creation of the Han Canal, which was the southernmost leg of the Grand Canal, and described how people made offerings to him out of fear that he would stir up great waves. A late Tang inscription described Wu Zixu as the divinity of the Hangzhou tidal bore (high waves produced by a tide moving up a narrowing estuary). This was regularly met by daring feats of swimming that often resulted in de facto human sacrifice.[59]

A final Tang popular cult that merits attention because of its importance in later religion and literature is the one devoted to foxes. This magical beast, which at least since the Northern and Southern Dynasties was noted for its ability to cross over into the human realm, often infested or haunted human habitations, in the manner of poltergeists in Europe. Sometimes the human inhabitants made regular offerings of food to invading foxes, in which case the haunting became a cult. While records from the Tang are sparse, there is one detailed account: "Since the beginning of the Tang, many of the commoners have worshipped fox spirits. They make offerings in their bedchambers to beg for their favor. The foxes share people's food and drink. They [the worshippers] do not serve a single master [each house worshipped its own fox]. At the time there was a saying, 'Where there is no fox demon, no village can be established.'"[60]

Several stories depicted tensions between newly arrived officials and foxes who received such offerings. These tensions were part of the broader phenomenon in which animal spirits embodying local beliefs were combated by representatives of the court and ultimately by the city god. In a couple of stories, including "Ms. Ren," foxes brought wealth to those they favored. Sudden prosperity supernaturally bestowed—a preoccupation perhaps associated with the rise of a money economy where riches seemed to appear magically out of nowhere—became a major theme of later Chinese popular religion. People struck bargains with demonic forces that produced fabulous riches which, because of their illegitimacy, often proved evanescent. And finally, foxes (*hu*) were often associated with non-Han people (*hu* with a different graph), and in many stories they pursued activities that the Chinese linked to foreigners, particularly as Buddhist monks and wealthy merchants.[61]

Rereading the Confucian Canon

In addition to state cults, canonical studies played a major role in Tang Confucianism. The primary repositories for these texts in the centuries of division were the powerful families, who based claims to office and unchallenged social prestige on their transmission of the true Chinese culture created under the Han. Many of these elite families educated each succeeding generation in the interpretation of canonical texts and in the writing of poetry. These intellectual traditions, particularly the ritual texts, continued to shape the social life of elite families into the Tang dynasty, even though most aristocrats were philosophically or religiously committed to the doctrines or practices of Buddhism or Daoism. The great Tang families revered the Confucian canon as the intellectual embodiment of the imperial state and the social hierarchy. While Buddhism or Daoism may have guided their spiritual lives and their views about life and death, Confucian texts remained fundamental to their sense of social order.[62]

Intergenerational transmission of canonical texts particularly distinguished northern families, which were more cohesive than families in the south and consequently more concerned with the rituals that guided family conduct. However, as the great families became tied to the state and the examination system over the course of the Tang dynasty, the nature and social role of these intellectual pursuits began to change. The Confucian canon sanctioned almost all of the important activities in which the state was involved and almost every policy that the dynasty formulated; indeed, the very activity of governing was traced back to canonical sources. They were quoted in the context of politically critical questions, such as the management of barbarians, and for issues central to the prestige of the ruling house, such as the maintenance of the ancestral temple. The classics outlined the principles of political morality that guided the conduct of government officials, from the sovereign to the lowest clerk. The Tang elite operated on the basic assumption that administrative competence was never enough; all matters of government had to be informed with Confucian moral awareness, lest government deteriorate into disorder and tyranny. For this reason, Confucian texts occupied a central place in the education of those who aspired to a political career.

Despite this social prestige and professional importance, canonical studies in the early Tang, as in the Northern and Southern Dynasties, was an intellectual backwater. Focused on preserving continuity with earlier periods and guiding the ritual practice of elite households, such studies showed little concern for rereading the old texts to formulate new intellectual programs. Most scholars studied the canonical texts just enough to secure official posts—which depended only on some memorization for the exams—and to perform necessary rituals at home or in the court. The state was interested in ensuring that standardized versions of the texts were available and that these were read in a manner compatible with the dynasty's interests.[63]

From its inception, the Tang state undertook measures to ensure the textual correctness of the canon and its exegetical literature. In 630 Emperor Taizong, concerned that "the classics are remote from the Sage [Confucius], their texts confused and mistaken," ordered the great scholar Yan Shigu (581–645) to establish definitive texts of the Five Canons: *Change, Documents (Shu), Odes (Shi), Rites, Spring and Autumn Annals (Chun qiu)* with the *Zuo Commentary.* In doing this he was carrying on a work begun under the Sui. After completing the project, Yan defended it in a court debate, defeating his opponents through his quotation of old editions and through the clarity and detail of his citation of authorities. In 633 the text was officially promulgated.[64]

In addition to textual accuracy, the state also sought to ensure interpretive consistency as a sign of imperial order and for the sake of the newly created examination system. However, the Tang did not impose its officially sanctioned interpretation as an unquestionable orthodoxy in the manner of the late imperial states. Debate over the official interpretation was permitted and even encouraged, with the same open-mindedness that allowed the Tang state to combine intellectual commitments to Daoism, Buddhism, and Confucianism. Still, in order to facilitate some agreement on the meaning of the canon, it was necessary to reconcile and harmonize the differences that had emerged during the Northern and Southern Dynasties.

This period is typically portrayed in histories of classical commentary as an age of decline, when political fragmentation resulted in a chasm between north and south. "Northern learning" carried on the historically oriented tradition of Zheng Xuan (127–200), an Eastern Han synthesizer. Scholars provided readings for difficult characters or usages, supplied institutional, geographical, or historical background, and offered elementary interpretive guidance. A major practical concern was to gloss details on rituals and ritual objects, so that they could be successfully performed. "Southern learning," by contrast, was steeped in the doctrines of Buddhism and the metaphysical speculations of Dark Studies. Arguing that words could never fully express meaning, southern writers denied the importance of the specific wording of texts, which they dismissed as exoteric (publicly open) and hence vulgar and provisional. They instead used commentary as an occasion for speculation on metaphysical themes and a wisdom beyond words. Consequently, in contrast to northern learning, they showed little interest in the details of palaces, clothing, and rituals.

Another major development in the commentarial tradition during the Northern and Southern Dynasties was the rise of "explication" (yishu). Under the Han there had been two primary modes of writing commentaries: an "annotation style" based on terse, philologically-oriented notes, and a "chapter-and-verse" style that expounded the text's significance but was notorious for being long and prolix. In the late fourth or early fifth century, a new genre of commentary appeared which resembled the chapter-and-verse commentaries in length and comprehensive treatment but differed from the earlier form in its detailed and systematic analysis of the structure and usage of the text.

This new genre was couched in a question-and-answer form that appears to have reflected the oral-dialogic origins of the commentaries, in which meaning was elaborated through the posing of questions by disciples or rivals that were then answered by a master. This had distant roots in the *Gongyang* commentary on the *Spring and Autumn Annals,* but its flourishing in the Northern and Southern Dynasties most likely reflected the contemporary popularity of a form of Buddhist scriptural exposition (*du jiang*) which involved public dialogues between a master and an interlocutor before an audience of students or at court. Another influence was the popularity among the great southern families of "pure conversation" (*qing tan*), in which men debated set topics such as "Music has neither joy nor sadness" and rivals sought to best each other through skillful argument or clever wordplay.[65]

Confronted with this diversity of interpretations and methods, in 638 Taizong ordered a committee of scholars under Kong Yingda to prepare an authoritative commentary on the recently established text of the Five Canons. For each text the committee selected one existing commentary as the basis on which to add their readings. To prepare these, they exhaustively examined the existing literature, citing hundreds of titles to demonstrate the inclusive nature of their work and to refute all the interpretations that they rejected. The initial draft, presented in 642, was criticized for verbosity and sent back for revisions. Kong Yingda died before completing the work, and in 651 the brother-in-law and favorite minister of the newly deceased Emperor Taizong, Zhangsun Wuji, was appointed to head a committee to finish the task. The completed work, known as the *Correct Meaning of the Five Canons* (*Wu jing zheng yi*), was submitted and approved in 653. This served as the basis for all future standard commentaries on the imperial canon.

The attempt to reconcile the northern and southern commentarial traditions was exemplified in the finished commentary. For the needs of the court, which was interested primarily in principles for policy and the details of ritual performance, the philologically oriented northern tradition provided the clearest guidance. The scholars omitted some of the more mystical readings of the canon that had been prominent in the Northern and Southern Dynasties, and Kong Yingda explicitly noted his decision to set aside Buddhist explanations. However, the synthesis of Confucianism with Dark Studies—expounded by Lu Deming (560–630) under the Sui in the *Explanations of Canonical Texts (Jing dian shi wen)*—figured prominently in several subcommentaries, most notably that to the commentary on the *Change* by Wang Bi, the most celebrated exponent of Dark Studies.[66] The court-sponsored subcommentaries thus aimed to translate the political reunification of north and south China into the canonical realm.

The *Correct Meaning of the Five Canons* made five basic assumptions. First, it held that the canon was the work of sages and prescribed morally paradigmatic attitudes, intentions, and rules. Second, it assumed that the canon was a unique record of the ideal realm of high antiquity and thus was radically distinct from other early texts such as the writings of the philosophers or stone inscriptions. Third, it assumed that although Confucius and his immediate disciples had a transcendent and infallible insight into the meaning of the canon, intellectuals in the Tang did not. Unlike the earlier scholars of the Han, or the subsequent Song commentators, the Tang writers were haunted by a sense of being permanently cut off from the original meaning of the classics. They believed that this had come about in part because Confucius had powers of perception that his later epigones lacked, and in part because the First Emperor's "burning of the books" had created an irreparable rupture in the transmission of the classics, reinforced by the long eclipse of classical scholarship in the Northern and Southern Dynasties. The fourth assumption was that, given this rupture, men of the present day could gain access to the classical texts only through commentaries handed down from earlier times. The final assumption was that, as monolithic compositions, all parts of the canon were of equal value. Every chapter, sentence, phrase, or word merited scrupulous attention.

In the eighth and ninth centuries, this set of assumptions faced a series of challenges. One of the most prominent early criticisms came not from the realm of canonical studies proper but from historiography. In his *Generalizations on History (Shi tong)* of 710, Liu Zhiji included an assessment of the virtues and faults of the *Spring and Autumn Annals* and the *Zuo Commentary.* One major element of his argument, his assertion that the *Zuo Commentary* was superior to its rivals because it provided elaborate historical narratives, jibed with the early Tang consensus that commentaries were critical for reading the canon and that the *Zuo* was the best commentary for this classic. But Liu Zhiji went beyond this consensus in assessing the *Spring and Autumn Annals,* the most influential classic in the early imperial period, as a work of history that should be judged by the standards of history writing.

Thus, he argued that for Confucius to chronicle only the state of Lu when he had available the records of other states, and to omit dramatic portrayals of men and events, were serious historiographic errors. Similarly, Liu criticized Confucius's supposed practice of modifying the historical account or omitting certain events to indicate his moral judgments, traditionally considered the *raison d'être* of the work and the core of its genius, as a failure in history's fundamental task of providing a truthful record. While Liu did not make the connection explicit, his criticisms of Confucius accorded with his savage assault on the censoring of histories in his own day under pressures from rulers and leading officials. In contrast with his criticism of the canonical *Annals*, Liu celebrated the achievements of Zuo Qiuming, putative author of the *Zuo Commentary*, whom Liu implicitly granted a status superior to that of Confucius. Underlying these judgments was the idea that the canon was not a universally normative, transcendent standard of values but rather a work of writing to be judged by the same standards as other texts in the same genre.[67]

Liu Zhiji was atypical both in the fundamental character of his critique and in its timing. He wrote in 710, well before the collapse of the centralized empire after An Lushan's rebellion had led to a more general questioning of court-sponsored official commentaries. Discussion of the canon in the first half of the eighth century focused largely on the choice of texts and commentaries, and above all on criticisms of the purely utilitarian approach of most scholars to the canon as a means of securing a government post. Many writers held forth against the low level of scholarship required by the examinations, which allowed candidates to study only the briefest of texts.

The decline of the central court and the rise of regional powers after the An Lushan rebellion provoked a more general questioning of the officially established texts and commentaries. The most famous of these revisionist approaches, and the most influential on later developments, was a new interpretation of the *Spring and Autumn Annals* developed by Dan Zhu in the 760s and carried on by his followers Zhao Kuang and Lu Chun. These men were based in the southeast, away from the court and the worst effects of militarism, and their ideas spread to the capital only after decades of independent development. Furthermore, none of them were members of the great families who had been the most zealous exponents of canonical studies. The focus on the *Annals* was also significant, because this text had been the political classic par excellence, read as the key to Confucius's theories of kingship and his own role as an uncrowned king and prophet of the Han and its institutions.[68]

The chief importance of these scholars, however, lay in the originality of their ideas. Earlier students of the *Annals* had followed one of the three commentaries established in the Han period, sometimes modifying a point of interpretation or combining elements from several commentaries. Dan Zhu, however, proposed to reject the authority of all three commentaries and return directly to the classic itself to establish through empirical analysis the rules of praise and blame employed by Confucius. He proposed that the canon was "medicine" that could cure the ills of the Tang body politic, but that it would work only through direct and systematic study of the text itself, freed from the intervening layer of commentary and subcommentary. Like Reformation Christians proposing to sweep away the Church Fathers and return directly to the words of the Bible, Dan Zhu and his followers cast aside the cumulative weight of early imperial canonical scholarship to seek the sage directly in his own words. And like Reformation writers, they found in ancient texts a means of justifying their own originality, and a site for discovering the new ideas that were developing in the period.[69]

At one level Liu Zhiji's criticisms were more radical, in that he challenged the position of Confucius as the ultimate standard. But Liu did not systematically elaborate his criticism, and in taking the *Zuo Commentary* as his model he still accepted the early imperial practice of relying on commentaries. Dan Zhu's criticism was more historically significant. His call for a return to the original text was only the first step in a methodical program of textual analysis. Moreover, he asserted his ability to understand a canonical text without the mediation of a commentary. This anticipated the hermeneutic of late imperial China, when Neo-Confucians declared their ability to directly understand the meaning of Confucius on the basis of their own inborn sage-nature. This spanning of the epistemological chasm between the sage and ordinary men, an intellectual feat made possible by a revaluation of previously ignored texts such as the *Mencius,* represented an epochal change in Chinese thought.

This new hermeneutic, aimed at directly recapturing the original meaning of the canon, achieved its fullest expression in the leading figures of the "ancient text" (*gu wen*) revival, Liu Zongyuan (773–819) and Han Yu (768–824). Writing in the first decades of the ninth century, and having in his youth studied the new approach to the *Spring and Autumn An-nals* with Dan Zhu's follower Lu Chun, Liu Zongyuan mocked as ped-ants the great Han scholars Ma Yuan and Zheng Xuan, the embodiments of the philological style of reading the classics that dominated the early Tang. The purpose of classical studies was to read the texts themselves in order to grasp "the mind of the sages" and the "origins of the Way." Rather than write commentaries on the classics, Liu Zongyuan cited them, above all the *Annals,* in essays that articulated his own thought about the political problems of his day. In several essays, particularly "Against the *Discourses of the States*" (*Fei Guo yu*), he denounced the re-ceived commentaries where he thought they disseminated ideas that led to political or moral confusion that obstructed attempts to deal with the crises of the post-rebellion era. Thus, he followed Dan Zhu in downgrad-ing the commentaries and in advocating the direct reading of the canon for political guidance in restoring order to the world.[70]

This new reading of the classics found its most radical expression in the works of Han Yu. With a new understanding of sagehood that was covertly adapted from the Buddhist ideal of the bodhisattva, he asserted the identical nature of the sage and the common man ("Shun was a man; I am also a man.") and thus the potential wisdom in all men.[71] Arguing from this principle, which would become the fundamental assumption of Neo-Confucianism, Han Yu posited that any man with proper care and attention could recapture the meaning of the canonical texts and realize that meaning in his conduct. Writing of his friend Lu Tong, he said:

> The three commentaries of the *Spring and Autumn Annals* left up in
>   the attic,
> He faced the main text alone, investigating it thoroughly.[72]

Han Yu asserted that explanation should proceed from the inside out, seeking key passages in the text, juxtaposing and comparing them, using one passage to explain another. Instead of assigning equal value to all passages, this new approach recognized a hierarchy in which certain key lines became the linchpins of proper thought, to be mulled over and med-itated upon throughout the scholar's life. Following from the principle that scholars should seek the "overall meaning" of the canon, he argued that any ancient text might contain elements of the true Way of antiquity (thereby echoing Liu Zhiji).[73] Thus, one should critically study not only the Five Canons but also the early philosophers, histories such as the

Discourses of the States (Guo yu), and even inscriptions on stone and bronze, such as the Qin stone drum inscriptions, about which Han Yu wrote a poem.

From this program Han Yu pioneered new genres of scholarly inquiry, such as essays "On Reading *Master Mo*," "On Reading *Master Xun*," and so on. These ideas led to the Song canonization of the *Analects* and the *Mencius,* the new concern with paleography (ancient forms of writing) and the physical remains of antiquity, and the comprehensive critical examination of all records of the past that arose in the Song and became the defining hallmarks of late imperial critical studies.[74]

Printing

Closely tied to religion in its origins, printing became the foundation of many of the changes in the economy, technology, and intellectual life that defined late imperial China.[75] Excluding such predecessors as seals, ink squeezes, stencils, and rubbings, the earliest form of printing technology was woodblock, which involved carving a page of text into a piece of wood and then stamping it onto paper. This practice began in the Tang dynasty, although handwritten manuscripts remained the predominant form of disseminating texts for many centuries.[76]

The earliest surviving printed texts are eighth-century samples of Buddhist charms preserved in Korea and Japan. The oldest is a scroll discovered in 1966 in a stone stupa in the Pulguk-sa temple in Kyongju, Korea. Since it includes characters that were introduced during the reign of Empress Wu, was translated in 704, and was found in a temple constructed in 751, this text must date from the first half of the eighth century. A printed version of chapter seventeen of the *Lotus Sutra* discovered in Turfan also contains characters from the reign of Empress Wu, suggesting that it is roughly contemporary with the scroll found in Korea. Another specimen of that same scroll printed between 764 and 770 has been preserved in Japan.[77]

The amount of carving required to produce these miniature scrolls does not approach the scale of a full book. The earliest surviving book is probably a copy of the *Diamond Sutra* dated to 868 that was discovered at Dunhuang in 1907. It consists of seven sheets of white paper pasted together to form a scroll of between seventeen and eighteen feet. It features an illustration at the beginning, a detailed colophon at the end, and high-quality calligraphy. It is thus of much higher quality than the charms found in Japan and Korea, although it is uncertain whether this represents an advance in technique or simply greater effort expended on a more prestigious work. Other printed materials discovered at Dunhuang include scrolls of charms and several calendars.

The fact that the earliest surviving books consist of Buddhist scriptures suggests that print technology was first developed to make multiple copies of sacred works, a meritorious act that could secure blessings for the sponsor and those whom he or she wished to assist. This idea is clearly articulated in the colophon to the *Diamond Sutra,* where the author states that he "reverently made this for blessings to my parents, and for universal distribution." The final phrase indicates the desire to endlessly repeat the production of the text, a desire best fulfilled by printing. It is likely that the aforementioned materials discovered in Japan and Korea were likewise printed for the merit of distribution, rather than to be read, and that they were produced for use as Buddhist "relics" in the form of words.[78]

By the late Tang and the Five Dynasties period printing had spread to many fields outside religion. Late-ninth-century references indicate the existence of printed books on astrology, dream divination, and geomancy, as well as a biography of an eminent Daoist, and lexicographical works, including dictionaries. Examples of the latter were brought back to Japan in 865 by a pilgrim monk, along with Buddhist sutras and printed texts on medicine.[79]

The earliest non-Buddhist printed materials that have survived are calendars. This provoked a clash with the imperial government, which believed that the production of private calendars challenged the emperor's right, as Son of Heaven, to regulate the relationship between the movement of heavenly bodies and earthly activities. In 835 Feng Su observed: "In all the provinces of Sichuan and Huainan printed calendars are on sale in the markets. Every year, before the Imperial Observatory has submitted the new calendar for approval and had it officially promulgated, these printed calendars have flooded the empire. This violates the principle that the calendar is a gift of His Majesty." In 881, when Emperor Huizong took refuge in Sichuan from the Huang Chao rebellion that destroyed the dynasty, he found disputes among merchants because of differences between the official calendar and privately printed ones. By 953 the Later Zhou government had to print its own calendar in order to compete with privately published ones.[80]

The tenth century witnessed the earliest known printed version of a

Daoist text and the first printing of the collected works of an individual author—more than one thousand poems by the monk Guanxiu. Between 932 and 953 the Confucian classics were printed for the first time, and a few years later a printed version of Lu Deming's *Explanation of Terms in Canonical Texts* also appeared. The first printed version of the Daoist canon was produced in 940. At this time several cities emerged as printing centers, including Luoyang and Kaifeng (soon to become the Song capital), which produced most of the texts for northern China, and Chengdu, Nanjing, and Hangzhou in the Yangzi basin. Chang'an also developed a printing industry at this time.[81]

Thus, by the beginning of the Song empire in 960, printing had begun to establish an empire-wide community of standardized scholarly discourse and to disseminate a more popular literate culture. The Song government would avail itself of this new technology to sponsor publication of works on mathematics, medicine, agriculture, the military arts, pharmacology and herbal lore, the Confucian canon with commentaries, dynastic histories, law codes, and writings of major philosophers—all for an expanding literate audience. It also printed complete editions of the Buddhist canon, including the latest state-sponsored translations of Tantric scriptures, which were sent as diplomatic gifts to rulers of neighboring states.[82] Private publishers produced less edifying works for rising urban markets, as written texts began their slow transformation into commodities for the masses.

9

WRITING

THE TANG is the literary dynasty *par excellence* in Chinese history, celebrated for its great writers and, above all, for the excellence of its poetry. The period's leading poets—Wang Wei, Li Bo (Bai), and Du Fu—are almost universally accepted as China's greatest authors.[1] Tang short stories are treated less reverentially in literary histories, but these prose compositions are the first self-consciously artistic fiction written in China, and they introduce into Chinese literature significant aspects of human experience. Given the importance of the novel in later imperial China, Tang stories mark a major literary development, above all in their accounts of romance.

The literary essays pioneered by writers such as Han Yu and Liu Zongyuan provided the models for all subsequent work in this genre. Elaborating the idea that literary style was fundamental to philosophical thought and moral order, these writings embodied more clearly than any others a distinctively Tang vision in which literature, thought, and politics were inextricably intertwined.

Location and Lyric in Early Tang Poetry

In the Han dynasty, poetry was a product of the court, where it assigned praise and blame or revealed the realm's moral state. In the Northern and Southern Dynasties, these moralizing functions were largely ignored. At first, the dissociation of poetry from the state and its ethical standards was liberating. Poets found numerous themes in the dissociation itself, elaborating verses on eremitism (withdrawal from the world), landscape, and Daoist philosophy. However, by the late fifth century, poetry was dominated by the courts and princely salons of south China, where great families with long traditions of literary cultivation were the self-appointed arbiters of style. Most poetry was little more than an elegant diversion and a mode of elite conviviality, where both Confucian moralizing and the independence of the recluse were considered unforgivably boorish.

The poetry of the Sui and the early Tang carried on the courtly tradition of the southern dynasties. It was largely written at the capital or in one of the subsidiary courts of an imperial prince. Rigidly circumscribed with respect to topic, diction, structure, and occasion, it was a mode of social discourse where members of the elite competed to see who could most rapidly compose poems with set themes and rhymes. Winners received prizes, while the slowest paid a forfeit. Sometimes writers derived themes from the stylized imitation of folk lyrics known as Music Bureau poetry, or they celebrated an object or event in the courtier's own life. Vocabulary was limited and marked by recurring elegant terms, and the use of everyday words was considered vulgar. Ornament was preferred to simplicity and indirect suggestion to explicit statement, as in this poem:

> In the springtime garden the moon tarries;
> A bamboo hall opens at nightfall.
> A startled bird cleaves the forest in passage,
> As windblown petals come from across the water.[2]

Rules of prosody dictated the numbers of syllables, the use of parallelism, and, in the so-called "regulated" forms, the patterns of tones.

These rigid formulas transformed poetry into a learnable art that any trained individual could rapidly produce to suit the needs of the moment. However, mastering this skill required protracted study, which privileged the offspring of leading families, who were educated from a young age in the subtleties and decorum of composition as a sign of proper breeding. Poetry was judged entirely on how well the poet operated within the rules, and the expression of a distinctive voice was no virtue. The composition of lines celebrating superiors was an especially effective means of ingratiating oneself with the court. The formulaic nature of court verse encouraged the compilation of encyclopedias of poetic lore and literary references that allowed courtiers to quickly locate lines and ideas suitable to the treatment of any poetic topic.[3]

As verse became enmeshed in the political hierarchy, rulers themselves participated in the evaluation and composition of poems. The last emperors of the southern Chen dynasty and the Sui were well-known poets, and scholars blamed their indulgence in literature and supposed consequent neglect of governing for the fall of their dynasties. However, even Emperor Taizong, one of China's most active rulers, left a large body of poems. A military man from the northwest, he struggled to produce polished verses like those of his cultured officials. He also sometimes exercised his imperial prerogative to incorporate his courtiers' best lines into his own work. Later emperors, though less prolific, were often avid patrons and practitioners of poetry.[4]

Early Tang verse was also written at banquets in inns or private homes to see off a friend or for other social occasions. Such "occasional" verse had been composed and gathered into collections since the third century, and hundreds of such collections were produced in the Tang. The sole surviving example shows that such poetry, produced by aspiring bureaucrats, was much like that of the court, only less skillful.[5]

Another site for writing poetry was the farm or estate, which provided an alternative to the artificiality of the court. One of the earliest Tang poets to find inspiration for verse in the countryside was Wang Ji (590–644). While generally regarded as a minor poet, Wang was the first to take as his model the life and verse of the recluse poet Tao Yuanming (365–427), who gave up an official career to write eremitic poetry about sleeping in his village hut, suffering from poverty, and toiling in his fields. This rediscovery led to Tao's canonization as the greatest poet of the Northern and Southern Dynasties and also anticipated the High Tang's reworking of China's poetic past. In keeping with Tao Yuanming's model, Wang Ji used simple diction, direct syntax, and a sequential, almost narrative unity absent from court poetry.[6]

The introduction of poetic composition into the *jinshi* examination in 680 marked a key moment in the transformation from court poetry to a more lyrical style. Through the examination and her own personal choices, Empress Wu promoted several poets of humble birth who themselves became patrons of others from local elites or even poor families. Under the influence of this broader group of officials, more popular genres, notably seven-syllable songs, became prominent at court.

By the first decade of the eighth century, protracted periods spent in local administrations had also become the occasion for writing a more personal kind of verse. The most celebrated of the "exile" poets—Yang

Jiong, Wang Bo, Lu Zhaolin, and Luo Binwang—became known as the Four Talents of the Early Tang. They used the established techniques of court poetry to express private suffering, and they also availed themselves of earlier genres marked by strong emotions, such as the poems in the Han anthology *Songs of the South* (*Chu ci*). Luo Binwang was noted for adapting the rhetorical and philosophical styles of parallel prose to his poems, making them lengthier and more serious. The emerging genre of "frontier poetry" also allowed writers to vividly dramatize life in the wilds.[7] These developments allowed poetry to become more personal, emotional, and morally serious, thus laying the foundations for High Tang verse.

Emperor Xuanzong's abolition of the courts of imperial princes in 722, in order to reduce the political interference of imperial relatives and palace women, closed off the main route of patronage for aristocratic youths. Consequently, the most ambitious poets among them were forced to seek out a new, wider audience outside the courts. The style they developed has been characterized as "capital poetry," indicating that it evolved from court poetry but was distinguished by the broader social range of its participants and themes.[8] Capital poetry differed from the verse of the preceding period in its emphasis on the tonal system, its interest in Buddhist and eremitic themes, and its reduced sense of poetic decorum, as in this example:

> Hidden by bamboo, hear now and again a well-pulley turning,
> But at his window see only webs of spiders.
> Our host rests ever aloof, though not pleading sickness,
> In a circling wall of tangled growth, one aging scholar.[9]

Capital poetry remained less a fine art than a refined arm of social discourse that helped to establish personal ties among members of the bureaucracy and examination candidates. The emergence of a full-blown, self-conscious poetic artform would be the work of outsiders, just as earlier modifications of court poetry had come from those exiled to the provinces. But the greatness of High Tang verse depended on the prior existence of capital poetry, whose freedom of form and expression allowed poets at the margins of this movement to fully develop their own private voices, and whose popularity prepared a wide audience for the appreciation of the new style.[10]

Besides providing a site for the composition and exchange of verse,

Chang'an and other Tang cities became a major theme of verse in their
own right. Poets celebrated the glories of the capital, meditated on individual loneliness in the midst of bustling crowds, and described the he-
roic young men and beautiful women who filled urban streets and bars:

> A young man of Five Barrows suburb east of the Golden Market,
> Silver saddle and white horse cross the spring wind.
> When fallen flowers are trampled under, where will he roam?
> With a laugh he enters the tavern of a lovely Turkish wench.[11]

The cities also became centers of rival poetic circles or, in the case of
the capital, distinct poetic communities operating independently of one
another in different neighborhoods. Particularly important were the regional capitals of the independent military governors who controlled
much of north China. For prestige or enjoyment, these men surrounded
themselves with skilled poets, and their courts became literary centers ri-
valing Chang'an. This geographic dispersal of composition by the late
Tang makes generalizations about poetry difficult, as each center developed distinct styles and values.[12]

Perhaps most important, cities provided the scene for linking verse and
music, most notably in the performances of the pleasure quarters. Especially important was the courtesans' contribution to the popularity of the
song lyric (ci), which would emerge as a major poetic genre in the decades following the collapse of the dynasty. The Dunhuang documents
include 545 songs, largely of "popular" rather than literati composition,
and thus the sorts of songs performed in the pleasure quarters and related
sites. These deal with themes ranging from romance to history and politics.

Women were also the primary performers of music and song in the imperial court, local government offices, and elite homes. Emperor Xuanzong created a Palace Music School where hundreds of musicians and
singers learned to perform new music, including popular and foreign
songs. The emperor himself composed songs with an irregular number of
characters per line, perhaps reflecting the influence of foreign tunes. After
the fall of the capital to An Lushan, performers who had trained at the
Palace Music School scattered to southern urban centers, where leading
literati composers were also writing song lyrics for, and about, musical
performers.[13]

Nevertheless, the relation between these songs, enjoyed at all levels of

Chinese society, and literati poetry remains unclear. Several conventional verse forms, notably the quatrain and the old Music Bureau poetry, had been set to music. Tang poets wrote pieces identified as lyrics for songs, and prefaces by some early ninth-century poets indicate that they composed new words for popular tunes. About two thirds of the lyrics that have survived and been identified date from the ninth century, and six poets (Wen Tingyun, Huangfu Song, Bo (Bai) Juyi, Liu Yuxi, Xue Neng, and Sikong Tu) account for just under half of those preserved. By far the largest number is attributed to Wen Tingyun, whose fondness for the pleasure quarters seems to have seriously affected his career. Accounts of his life indicate that he relied on the composition of song lyrics to earn money.

The evidence thus suggests that while songs and their lyrics were a major element of Tang popular culture, and some major poets composed them, this activity remained discreditable among literati. Only in the *Collection from among the Flowers* (*Hua jian ji*) anthology, compiled in the post-Tang Shu court in 940, was the song lyric formalized as a distinct literati genre. However, this sanctioning as serious art was accompanied by the narrowing of its themes to romantic topics and the standardization of its form into a two-stanza heteronomic lyric (that is, verse with irregular numbers of syllables per line). The preface to the collection, written by Ouyang Jiong (896–971), carefully distinguished genuine literati works from popular lyrics that were "not only vulgar in style" but also "empty in substance." Thus, while the pleasure quarters were a major setting for Tang lyrical composition and performance, their formative influence on Tang poetry could not be openly acknowledged.[14]

A final urban site of inspiration for verse in the Tang was the garden. Third-century eremitic poets had celebrated the private garden as a privileged space for escape from the pressures of the court and city. In the middle and late Tang, the urban garden provided the setting for the emergence of a private sphere of play, free from the regulated structures of state and family. The poet Bo Juyi—calling himself a "middling hermit," between those lofty spirits who remained aloof while holding office and the lesser hermits who retreated to the hills—lovingly described his garden estate in Luoyang. He thus established it as a model for a bourgeois space where the human spirit could be cultivated along with flowers and fruit.[15] Together with Liu Zongyuan, he also pioneered the idea that truly possessing a garden or any piece of land entailed not simply its purchase but its aesthetic appreciation, as marked through the act of writing about it. In later imperial China, this poetic expropriation became conventional in the practice of inscribing specific garden sites with poetic names and couplets.[16]

High Tang Poetry's Reassimilation of the Past

The Tang dynasty moved away from a moral and political history of poetry, which condemned writing in recent centuries as decadent, to an aesthetic approach in which past writers and styles provided diverse, usable models for contemporary writers. This shift was linked both to the spatial movement of poetry-writing beyond the imperial court, and also to a redefinition of what it meant to be a poet.

The dominant history of poetry in the early Tang derived from several writers in the northern dynasties and the Sui who condemned the parallel prose and ornate verse of their own time, calling for a simpler, more serious language modeled on the classics and Han writings. The tension between two southern anthologies produced under princes of the Liang dynasty in the sixth century highlighted the issues. The classicizing *Selection of Refined Literature* (*Wen xuan*) focused on writing from the Han and the centuries immediately following it as models of literature. The more modernist *New Songs from a Jade Tower* (*Yu tai xin yong*) primarily collected works by recent, often living, authors, although its preface apologized for concentrating on "palace poetry" and other writings on romantic themes. In the same century, the great theoretician of literature Liu Xie (465–522) began his magnum opus by arguing that literature served primarily a socio-political function, so that all serious writing must use the classics as model and standard. Similarly, Pei Ziye (502–556) wrote "An Essay on Insect Carving" that denounced the literature of his day as devoted to pointless craft and ornament.[17]

The triumph of the northern military dynasts amplified calls for a return to serious literature that would preserve moral and political order rather than serve social and aesthetic pleasures. The clearest expression of this attitude was a memorial in 584 from the scholar Li E to Emperor Wen of the Sui:

When the wise kings of antiquity transformed the people, they necessarily changed what they saw and heard. They curbed the people's sensual desires, and they blocked their impulse to abandon themselves to evil . . . The *Songs, Documents, Rites,* and *Change* were the

gate to moral duties . . . All those who presented memorials and offered rhapsodies, composed elegies, and engraved inscriptions did so
to praise virtue and give precedence to wisdom.

Descending to later ages, customs and teachings gradually declined. The three rulers of Wei valued literary elaborations one
more than the other. They ignored the great way of being ruler; they
liked the minor art of "insect carving." Those below followed those
above, much as an echo or a shadow. Competing for ornamented appearance consequently became the custom. In the southeast in Qi
and Liang it spread so completely that noble and base, wise and
foolish, all devoted themselves solely to verse . . . They competed
over the originality of a single poem and contested the cleverness
of a single word. Poem after poem and document after document
never got beyond describing the moon and dew; tables were heaped
and chests filled with nothing more than the appearance of wind
and clouds. Society ranked men by such endeavours, and the court
picked officials on this basis.[18]

However, this critique was a poetics without poetry; it had nothing
to replace the aesthetic it attacked. Certain figures, including Emperor
Taizong, approved calls for a "return to antiquity" (*fu gu,* with antiquity
identified as the classics, which were pre-Han, and Han texts) but nevertheless continued to write in the court style. Others, including Taizong's
adviser Wei Zheng (580–643), took seriously the charge to write simpler
poetry about political concerns but ended up writing didactic verse that
merely stated moral principles rather than dramatizing them. The failure
of this program to elicit appealing verse led to its general abandonment in
the later years of Taizong's reign, when leading poets contented themselves with skillful celebrations of life at court.[19]

Despite these initial failures, poets in the second half of the seventh
century, particularly those outside court circles who could experiment
with more personal expression, developed a simpler, more direct, morally
serious poetic language. Chen Ziang (661–702), the great "outsider"
poet celebrated as the ancestor of the High Tang style, developed his rejection of the contemporary world into a major poetic theme and expressed it in a new style identified with the "return to antiquity." However, the model for his most ambitious poems was not classical or Han
texts but the Jin dynasty poet Ruan Ji, whose "Songs of My Cares" detailed his anguished search for personal meaning, and the abstract Dark
Studies poetry of the fourth century:

I look back, but do not see the ancients;
I look ahead, but can't see those yet to come.
I brood on the endlessness of Heaven and Earth,
Tears streaming down, I stand alone.[20]

By the early eighth century, even some court poets had developed an "ancient style" verse as an alternative to the rigorous parallelism and tonal balances of more regulated court compositions. Chen Ziang was admired and imitated by such leading court poets as Song Zhiwen (656–712) and Zhang Jiuling (678–740). A successful politician and patron known for his imitations of Chen's verse, Zhang blurred the distinction between insider and outsider, bringing "return to antiquity" poetics into the court. Thus, although some High Tang poets proclaimed the "return to antiquity" as what set them apart from their courtly predecessors, they shared many techniques and were quite removed from the moralizing implicit in their slogan.[21]

While the most celebrated figures of the High Tang did not embrace the anti-aesthetic "return to antiquity" movement, there was no alternative historical model for poetry available to them. Thus, in 753 Yin Fan wrote of Wang Changling: "After the Caos, after Liu Zhen, after the Lu brothers and the Xies [all third-century poets], for four hundred years all true affective power and strength disappeared. But now we have Wang Changling."[22] Although Wang Changling himself in no way supported a return to antiquity, Yin Fan saw him as the only poet of merit since the Han dynasty's collapse. Similarly, the great High Tang poet Li Bo, the antithesis of the moralizer, nevertheless began a set of "ancient style" poems with one poem reiterating the established viewpoint that the canonical Odes, the high point of ancient verse, was followed by a gradual decline whose only exception was a last upsurge represented by the Cao family's lyrics at the end of the Han. After that, Chinese poetry was a wasteland until the poetic revival of Li Bo's own day.[23] The didactic "return to antiquity" model provided the only historical framework for Chinese verse.

The divergence between "return to antiquity" as a slogan and as an actual form of verse was demonstrated by the career of Yuan Jie (719–772). While Li Bo and his fellow writers were congratulating themselves for recapturing the glories of antiquity through stylistic modifications and a more personal verse, Yuan Jie denounced them as composers of "lewd and deluding songs of singing boys and dancing girls in private chambers," and set out to write moralizing poetry with an archaic diction borrowed directly from ancient verse. He also wrote prefaces to his poems pointing out their moral lessons. Yet after compiling an anthology of the works of like-minded poets in 760, Yuan Jie began to write in a less radical ancient style, and late in life he turned to landscape and eremitic poetry, abandoning his commitment to public, political verse. He was never widely embraced by the Tang literati, leading him to argue that fame was proof of inferiority, while rejection demonstrated the truth and moral stature of one's writings. Thus, while virtually all High Tang writers embraced "return to antiquity" slogans, the only poet to actually practice them was rendered completely marginal.[24]

This divergence of theory and practice ended soon after the An Lushan rebellion. In the second half of the eighth century the rhetoric of a return to antiquity declined, amid a resurgence of capital poetry and a new celebration of the achievements of the poets of the southern dynasties. One southern poet, Tao Yuanming, had been an object of poetic and personal emulation by Wang Ji at the beginning of the dynasty, but Wang Ji remained a peripheral figure. More important was Wang Wei (ca. 699–761), who eschewed the ethical aspects of a return to antiquity while borrowing from southern dynasties poets such as Xie Lingyun, Bao Zhao, Xie Tiao, and Yu Xin. He also encouraged a revival of Tao Yuanming's work in the 720s and 730s. A poetic prodigy and offspring of a leading family, Wang found a place at court at a young age and mastered the art of court poetry. He then refined it by simplifying its style, elevating its antipathy toward emotions into their complete negation through the Buddhism he espoused, and perfecting the art of the couplet by replacing elaborate ingenuity with simple statements rich in implication:

> Fire on shore, a lone boat spends the night,
> Fisherman's houses, there evening birds return.
> Vast and empty, Heaven and Earth grow dark,
> The heart calm as the broad stream.[25]

He thus emerged as one of the great voices of the High Tang while remaining central to the social circle that practiced capital poetry.

The literary world following the An Lushan rebellion was dominated by men who were socially linked to Wang Wei and imitated his verse. They established a canon of High Tang writers that included the leading court poets of the early eighth century (Shen Quanqi and Song Zhiwen), Wang Wei himself, and some of his lesser followers. Their tastes were captured in a preface written by Dugu Ji, a leading member of the post-rebellion mainstream. He criticized the poets of the third century—models for the "return to antiquity" tradition—for their excessive "unadorned substance" and insufficient ornament. While admitting that poets of the southern dynasties had erred in the opposite direction, he treated this excess of ornament as a hallmark of civilization. This argument that the literary sophistication of recent centuries represented cultural advance rather than moral decay was one of the earliest alternatives to calls for a return to antiquity.[26]

The revaluation of the poetic past practiced by Wang Wei and articulated by Dugu Ji attained full expression in the work of Du Fu (712–770), now generally regarded as China's greatest poet. Yuan Zhen, who along with Han Yu first called attention to Du Fu, argued that his greatness resulted from his comprehensive mastery of his poetic predecessors. In his funerary inscription for Du Fu, Yuan listed the leading poets of the past and concluded that Du Fu had first mastered all of their styles and then surpassed them: "He comprehended all the ancients' styles and sweep, combined each modern's special achievement . . . Since there have been poets, there has never been Du Fu's equal."[27] Such assimilation of past verse as the basis of self-expression characterized poets in the second half of the Tang, for whom earlier literature in all its guises was a resource to draw upon, imitate, and recombine. In the long term, this approach to the past became a burden for Chinese poets, but in the first flush of rediscovery it led to some of the greatest poetry ever produced in China:

> Weeping over battle, many new ghosts,
> In sorrow reciting poems, an old man alone.
> A tumult of clouds sinks downward in sunset,
> Hard-pressed, the snow dances in whirlwinds.
> Ladle cast down, no green lees in the cup,
> The brazier lingers on, fire seems crimson.
> From several provinces, now news has ceased,
> I sit here in sorrow tracing words in the air.[28]

While the poetic incorporation of the entire past began in the High Tang, it found theoretical formulation only later in the works of Jiaoran, a poet-monk active in the southeast during the late eighth century. He argued that good poetry required a balance between "innovation" and "returning to the past"; exclusively privileging either was harmful. He also defended the poetry of the late southern dynasties (the *bête noire* of "return to antiquity" poetics) and denounced the capital poets' lack of literary-historical awareness. In part, this was a battle of regional cultures, as he was not only southern himself but a descendant of the great southern poet Xie Lingyun. Nevertheless, his theory captured the attitude toward the past exemplified in the finest poetry written in the middle and late Tang.[29]

Changing attitudes toward the poetic past also led to an evolving appreciation of Tang verse. Shortly after the An Lushan rebellion, writers were already looking back on the reign of Xuanzong as a golden age of order and power. But only decades later would this period be recognized, or rather mythologized, as the golden age of Chinese verse, and only later still would the modern canon of High Tang poets—Wang Wei, Li Bo, and Du Fu—be fixed. Poets who started composing verse after the 760s perceived themselves as latecomers laboring in the shadow of a vanished greatness, even though the nature and identity of that greatness were not yet defined.

Mainstream capital writers in the second half of the eighth century posited a canon including poets from the early Tang but excluding Li Bo and Du Fu. Not until the early 800s would Han Yu and Yuan Zhen declare these two to represent the height of Chinese poetry, and even in 837 the poet Yao He still began his anthology of favorite verse with Wang Wei. In 900 Wei Zhuang, compiling an anthology as a sequel to Yao He's, began with Du Fu, Li Bo, and Wang Wei joined together in a triumvirate that has endured to the present day. His decision, which combined the early ninth-century radicals' taste for Li Bo and Du Fu with the conservative, court-based elites' taste for Wang Wei, defined the High Tang for the rest of Chinese history. This move was possible only because the social networks of the conservative elite and its court-based culture had been swept away in the cataclysms that were destroying the Tang.[30] Thus, the myth of Tang literary supremacy, like the myth of Tang political supremacy, emerged in response to its two periods of catastrophic collapse.

The Changing Image of the Poet

To the extent that poetry was an aspect of life at court, the poet was simply one face of the courtier or statesman. An emperor or minister in the Tang empire was expected to write poetry just as he was expected to write decrees, memorials, or essays on policy. All these appeared in the *Selection of Refined Literature* that defined the significant literary genres of the period. Reading what appears to be personal verse as political allegory, as was sanctioned by conventions for reading the *Odes,* was part of the same intellectual discourse.

Shifting poetry to new locales and social strata, and challenging the politico-moral discourse of a return to antiquity, carved out a new social role for poets in the Tang. Poetry writing was elevated from a social grace to a matter of supreme importance. The poet became a distinctive character, somewhere between an eccentric and a "genius" of the type celebrated in European romanticism. Verse became a vocation, to the perfection of which the poet devoted his life. Certain authors described poetry writing as a "profession" that generated "property" and granted the poet "ownership" of his work.

This new vision emerged in the writings of Li Bo and Du Fu. For Li Bo, poetry was the means by which a man of genius demonstrated his superiority. For Du Fu, it allowed a man to carve out a place in history:

> Literature is a deed of eternity,
> Whose success or failure is known in the mote of consciousness.

The image of the poet as a hero who supplants the ruler figured in the conclusion of his poem "My Thatched Roof Is Ruined by the Autumn Wind," where Du Fu calls upon Heaven to create for his sake a great roof to shelter all the poor gentlemen of the world.[31] For both Du Fu and Li Bo, and for others who followed, poetry became the highest calling and not just an adjunct to, or poor substitute for, a political career. By the turn of the tenth century, some described poetry as an almost mystical undertaking, a devotional practice paired with Chan Buddhism (the Chinese ancestor of Zen). It was no longer an ornament of one's life but the be-all and end-all of existence, for which a poet like Meng Jiao (751–814) would willingly sacrifice everything:

> His purity scraped out frost and snow's marrow,
> His chanting stirred officers of spirits and gods.
> His whole age, filled with flattering words,
> But no one took this master as his master.
> Thus I know that after my way is done,
> I too will lie cold and still like this.[32]

While the idea that verse expressed the poet's deepest intentions had been a commonplace since the ancient Warring States period, it had been judged according to the fixed standards of morality or politics. Only in the Tang did character as expressed in poetry become the ultimate ground for its evaluation and appreciation. The discovery of character in poetry emerged with the revived interest in Tao Yuanming, whose readers conflated his verse and personality. But the archetypal poet whose personality became the basis for interpreting his verse was Li Bo.[33]

While Du Fu is now treated as China's greatest poet, Li Bo is China's greatest poetic *personality*. Later critics advised people to imitate Du Fu, whose brilliance seemed possible to copy, while Li Bo's greatness was inextricably tied to his being Li Bo.[34] From the beginning, his poetry displayed innovation and excess, a shocking violation of decorum that seemed to directly express his inimitable character. An outsider born in Sichuan to what may have been a Turkish family, he invented a personal mythology of a Chinese family banished to Central Asia, a youthful career as a swordsman and killer, and a pattern of throwing away large fortunes that he almost certainly never had. He attracted the attention of the director of the Imperial Library, who began the practice of treating Li Bo as superhuman by calling him the "banished immortal" and saying that one of his poems "could make gods and ghosts weep." Given a post in the Hanlin Academy in 742 by Emperor Xuanzong, he quickly became the subject of anecdotes about his irreverent behavior. While such conduct could be admired, his extremes led to dismissal two years later, and he spent the last two decades of his life wandering in the south.[35]

Li Bo's contemporaries seem to have regarded him more as a subject of amazement than as a serious poet. Interest in his work emerged in the last decades of the eighth century, when writers around Han Yu and Bo Juyi (772–846) paired him with Du Fu as the two greatest poets of the preceding period. Even these appreciations of his poetry, however, tended to turn into accounts of the person, his verse being read through the myth of the man. He thus resembled Lord Byron, whose poetic heroes were always interpreted as versions of Byron himself and whose personal myth has for most readers swallowed up the poems. Meditating on fleeting glories, describing the difficulty of the road to Sichuan, or celebrating swordsmen, Li Bo always evinced a signature energy and excess. Even his celebrated songs about drinking revolved around the drinker:

> Here among the flowers a single jug of wine,
> No close friends here, I pour alone
> And lifting cup to bright moon, ask it to join me,
> Then face my shadow, and we become three.

Similarly, his poems on immortals became "advertisements for himself":

> Westward I climbed to Lotus Blossom Peak,
> Far in the distance I saw the bright star:
> In her pale hand she held a lotus,
> Stepping in emptiness, pacing pure ether.
> Her rainbow robes trailed broad sashes,
> Then fluttering in wind, she rose up to Heaven.
> She invited me to climb Cloud Terrace Peak,
> On high to salute Wei Shuqing, the immortal.[36]

After Li Bo, the practice of discovering an imagined poet in his verse and reading the verse to find the man became conventions of Chinese poetic interpretation. Thus, Bo Juyi's descriptions of his own wild behavior often echoed the accounts of Li Bo. More distinctively, Bo Juyi's writing in a careless and common style facilitated his claims to behaving and composing "naturally" and encouraged his image as a man close to the people, who supposedly tested his verse by seeing if it could be understood when recited to an old woman.[37] Once again, style was the key to the person, and the person to the style. This focus on personality as the basis for interpretation stimulated a new genre of anecdotes telling how the poet's circumstances led to the composition of a poem.[38]

The idea that poetry was a vocation to which the practitioner devoted his life in the tireless perfection of his craft took several forms during the Tang. A notable early example was Meng Jiao, who together with his friend Han Yu did much to shape mid-Tang poetry. Meng Jiao argued that constant suffering was the hallmark of the true poet, the proof of his moral superiority. Enduring cold and hunger was a positive value, diametrically opposing the poet to the complacency of the rich and powerful. His writings featured lines such as: "The poet suffers making poems," "The old man, hungry from poetry, is not bitter," or "Poets are usually pure and rugged, Die from hunger, cling to desolate mountains." The poet's life as suffering is epitomized in his "Going Out East Gate":

> During my life I've woven
> A thousand poems in the diction of the Great Odes.
> My road is as though spun from a silkworm,
> Round and round as my twisted, knotted guts.[39]

The next generation developed a different vision of poetry as vocation. In place of the suffering poet as moral exemplar, Jia Dao (779–843) and Yao He (ca. 779–ca. 849) embodied the idea of the poet as the tireless collector and polisher of couplets. Closely linked with the discipline and asceticism of Chan Buddhism, poetry became the purpose of life to which the writer sacrificed everything. This ideal of the poet working obsessively at his art was epitomized in the phrase *ku yin*, literally "bitter chanting," which celebrated "painstaking composition" as the poet's greatest virtue.[40]

Like Meng Jiao, Jia Dao lived in poverty, but the most celebrated anecdotes about him highlighted not his suffering but his absorption in composition. In these stories, he rode through the streets on a mule, totally focused on completing a couplet. He bumped into or obstructed some high official, who, depending on the story, either threw him in prison or helped him finish the line. Devotion to art obliterated hierarchy, and indeed these poets were noted for observing a rough social equality. This vision was sketched in a couplet by the poet Zhou Pu addressed to the Chan monk Dawei:

> For Chan it is Dawei, for poetry Zhou Pu,
> With the Great Tang's Son of Heaven, just three people.[41]

Here the monk, the poet, and the emperor constitute three distinct and separate realms, each devoted to its own cause.

This late Tang vision defined poetry as a craft to be mastered through endless toil. Early Chinese lyric theory had described a poem as the spontaneous, true response of a person to an actual scene. By contrast, the late Tang poets celebrated a poem as the product of protracted reflection detached from any experience that supposedly elicited it. The most celebrated account of this mode of composition dealt with the poet Li He (790–816), who despite his early death left over two hundred poems. According to Li Shangyin (813–858), a poet greatly influenced by Li He, the latter carried a brocade bag wherever he rode, and whenever he had an idea for a line or couplet he jotted it down and threw it in the bag. Upon his return, he took out these snatches of ideas and worked them into poems. This anecdote expressed the widespread belief that the poet "got" (*de*) an idea through a flash of inspiration or a dream revealing a hidden idea of which he was scarcely conscious. Such happy discoveries formed the brilliant couplets at the core of a poem, around which the writer laboriously fashioned his verse, like a jeweler mounting a precious gem. This model combined the image of poetry as a learned craft with the idea that the poet was a man possessed, both a vehicle for divine inspiration and an obsessive for whom composing poetry was a "disease" or "addiction."[42]

The idea of poetry as a lifetime vocation led poets to collect and edit their own works. Through careful selection and arrangement, weeding out inferior pieces and assembling in sequence what remained, the poet turned the work of a lifetime into a crafted expression of his character and industry. The inclusion of "exchange" poems, essentially correspondence with other poets, also demonstrated the range and eminence of a writer's social contacts. An all-inclusive collection, like that of Bo Juyi, became a poetic diary that could document, reconstruct, and publicize an entire lifetime. Indeed, it became conventional in late imperial China to write chronological biographies of poets based on their collected verse. While this approach to collection was only emerging in the Tang, it was sufficiently established that when Li Shen compiled an anthology of his poems written between 820 and 836, most of the poems were actually composed between 836 and 838. Persuaded of the need to document a life in verse but not having had the time to do so, he filled in the years from 820 to 836 with new work.[43]

Related to the idea of poetry writing as a lifelong vocation was the emerging image of the Tang poet as a "professional" who used his talent to acquire property. From its introduction in 680 as the core of the *jinshi* examination, poetry writing became the high road to lucrative office. But less exalted professional uses developed as well. Wen Tingyun supposedly supported himself by selling lyrics in the pleasure quarters. Wang Dingbao in his *Collected Statements from the Tang (Tang zhi yan)* said that Wen "considered literary works as commercial goods, and therefore discerning men scorned him."[44] However, Wen was probably not the only poet to derive an income from his skills, and many reputable poets, treating their verse as a form of wealth, developed new notions of literary property and ownership of their work. The most conspicuous was once again Bo Juyi, who described his writings as a quantifiable legacy:

> I broke up a cypress to make a bookcase,
> The case sturdy, the cypress strong.
> Whose collection is stored there?
> The heading says Bo Letian [Juyi].

My lifetime's capital/inheritance is in writing
From childhood to old age.
Seventy scrolls from beginning to end,
In size, three thousand pieces.
I know well that at last they will be scattered,
But I cannot bear to rashly throw them away . . .
I can only entrust it to my daughter
To keep and pass on to my grandchild.[45]

Apart from poems as a form of wealth that the poet created and hoarded, poetry and aesthetic appreciation became the means of claiming possession of a physical space. In one poem of the *Wang Stream Collection,* Wang Wei noted that there had been earlier owners and would be future ones, but by capturing the sites in his verse he made the estate uniquely his own. Similar claims to truly possessing gardens or hills by purchasing them and then capturing them in verse became a standard theme of later Tang writing.[46]

Romantic Fictions

In the early twentieth century, the great writer Lu Xun argued that the Tang classical short stories now called *chuanqi* ("transmissions of the remarkable") were the first examples of self-conscious fiction in China. In fact, the stories' conventional inclusion of detailed chronologies, accurate layouts of cities, and even real people suggests that no one acknowledged they were writing fiction, in the modern sense of a story accepted as an invention. Yet in its etymological sense of "devised" or "crafted," "fiction" does describe what is new in the Tang stories. In contrast with earlier "records of the strange" (*zhi guai*), the Tang stories did not simply provide information and entertainment, but were crafted literary forms to be aesthetically appreciated for the manner in which they were told.[47]

This conscious artistry in the creation of a literary text is expressed in at least four ways. First, Tang writers devised a range of literary techniques to render simple, familiar stories more complex or interesting. Many of their short stories had been previously recorded as accounts of strange phenomena, so in reworking the narrative the writers focused attention on the manner of the telling rather than the plot. This highlighted the fact that the new story was a crafted work.[48]

Second, dreams played a central role in several narratives such as "The

World in a Pillow" and "Grand Commander of Nanke." Both of these told of ambitious young scholars who dreamed entire lives of struggle and political success, only to awaken and discover that it had all been a dream lasting a few minutes. These stories were literary successors of the celebrated "butterfly dream" in which the Warring States philosopher Zhuang Zhou dreamt he was a butterfly, only to become unsure that he was not actually a butterfly dreaming of being Master Zhuang. Besides challenging the distinction between reality and fiction—a role that dreams would play in Chinese literature down through the *Dream of the Red Chamber* in the mid-eighteenth century—dreams also allowed the introduction of fantastic elements into the narrative without losing the story's grounding in reality. Tang poets from Chen Ziang through Li Bo and beyond used dream accounts in verse to introduce spirit journeys and other fictional imaginings while still remaining within lived experience. Dreams played the same role in short stories, while emphasizing the crafted nature of the tale.[49]

Third, authors highlighted the literary nature of the stories by manipulating received narrative conventions. A notable example is "Ms. Ren," which adapted the established fox-spirit story into a new form, the "fox romance." This was done in part by humanizing the fox-spirit heroine of the tale and turning her into a moral exemplar. However, adapting the established genre was also essential to the story's telling. It begins with a man encountering a mysterious beauty on the streets of Chang'an, spending the night with her in her splendid house on the outskirts of the city, discovering the next morning that the "house" is an abandoned lot, and being told by a local vendor that the beauty is a local fox-spirit. This exactly recapitulates the classic fox story, which would have ended there. Instead, the author, Shen Jiji (a noted official historian of the late eighth century), used this simply as the starting point for an elaborate romantic triangle that gradually reveals the characters of its participants, only to end in Ms. Ren's tragic death. Similarly, the seeming realism of "Li Wa" thinly veils elements drawn from conventional tales of liaisons between men and spirits.[50] Authors of classical short stories thus critically manipulated or deconstructed structural conventions of earlier stories to create their new narratives.

The last method by which Tang authors highlighted the literary nature of their stories was to include other literary modes: poems, letters, historiographical techniques, and quotations from received works. Most important were the verse exchanges between men and women in romances or the insertion of poems as comments by characters acting as observers. This was already a major feature of one of the earliest Tang classical short stories, "Wandering in the Immortals' Cave," which told a conventional story of a man who has a sexual liaison with a goddess. In the Tang story, however, the narrative serves only as the occasion for extended exchanges of verse between the author/hero and the spirit women. The most celebrated Tang story is Yuan Zhen's "Yingying's Story," which both refers to and "quotes" at length poems and letters attributed to the two chief figures, as well as poems by friends of the hero, including one from the author himself.[51] The prominent role of such crafted texts inserted into the stories turns many of the short stories into texts about the performance of texts, or stories on the powers of narrative.

Literary texts inserted into stories also provide models to guide characters' actions and give meaning to events. This is particularly true of Yingying, who in the course of the narrative adopts virtually every role granted to women in the Chinese literary tradition: innocent maiden, stern moralist, passionate goddess, and abandoned woman. While less versatile in his roles, Scholar Zhang in turn justifies his abandonment of Yingying with references to earlier texts. The two protagonists present their own texts and speeches in order to take control of the story and make it their own. In addition, the author who writes the encompassing narrative inserts his own vision of the story, derived from earlier poetic accounts of goddesses.[52] Thus, "Yingying's Story" contains three distinct versions of itself. This multiplicity of embedded authors and points of view highlights the literary character of the tale.

All these techniques for crafting a literary story emerged in the Tang because, particularly after the An Lushan rebellion, leading writers—including Han Yu, Liu Zongyuan, Yuan Zhen, Shen Jiji, and Bo Xingjian (brother of Bo Juyi)—began to use fiction to explore their own situation. At the same time, Bo Juyi, Wei Zhuang, and other major poets wrote long narrative ballads dealing with themes related to the stories, and sometimes paired a poem with a prose version or preface telling the same tale.

Not only were the authors of the stories literati, but so were the leading male characters, both fictive and real. The actual poet Li Yi was the leading man in "The Story of Huo Xiaoyu," which served to explain his notorious jealousy. Furthermore, the stories revolved around major events in the lives of the literati: going to the capital for examinations, passing the exam, or taking up a first post. Thus, the themes in the stories were those that concerned late Tang literati in their everyday lives, from the aspirations attained in their dreams to the fears that haunted their nightmares. There may have also been a female audience for the stories, notably among the courtesans who were described as literate in the *Record of the Northern Hamlet (Bei li zhi)* and assumed to be so in the stories themselves.

Since literati were both authors and audience, it is notable that among the most important themes were romance and sex. This focus on male-female relations in a manner not seen in earlier Chinese writing can be explained in several ways. First, and least interesting, is the fact that people are always interested in sex, and the rise of prose fiction in China, as in the West, gave a central focus for that interest. The close linkage of fiction with sex is suggested by the Ming scholar Hu Yinglin (1551–1602), one of the first Chinese to systematically study fiction, and the first to call the Tang tales in the classical language *chuanqi*: "As for gentlemen of great taste, they know the absurdity [of fiction] in their heart, but they rush to speak of fiction with their mouths. In the daylight they repudiate it as erroneous, but in the dark they quote and use it. It is like licentious sounds and beauty in women; people hate it but cannot stop loving it. The more people love it, the more they speak of it. And the more they speak of it, the more authors write it."[53] Hu treated fiction as dark and shameful, a textual equivalent of eroticism and sensuality, which people morally condemn but obsessively pursue. Indeed, the repetitive character of the passage suggests that the author was prey to the same fascination he observed in others, which doubtless motivated Tang writers, too.

Second, and more significant, were the links of romance to new private spaces where scholars could escape the constraints of career and family. Earlier Chinese accounts of romantic liaisons imagined similar escapes from the conventional world in encounters with goddesses, ghosts, or fox-spirits. The new fascination with human romance was the interpersonal equivalent of the literati's passion for gardens. The romantic bond in literature offered a prototype for elective personal associations based on shared taste and refined sensibilities, a dream of escape from the destiny of an arranged marriage. This dream originated in the literary and emotional bonds a scholar enjoyed with courtesans during his years of preparation for the examinations, and which he might preserve as a lingering echo in relations with a favorite concubine. Thus, while many heroines of Tang romantic stories were not explicitly courtesans, their behavior, the manner in which they were introduced to the scholar, and the brevity of the relationship were patterned on what literati authors and audience knew from visits to the pleasure quarters.[54]

Another innovation in Tang short stories was a thinly concealed fascination with the power of money. While the passionate romance foregrounded the elective equality of the lovers, most of the stories also noted the monetary conditions that made such "free" choice only temporarily possible. The major turning point in many romantic relationships was caused by the exhaustion of the financial resources of one or the other party, or an event, such as passing an exam, that transformed the worldly prospects of the man. The hidden power of money most commonly appeared as pressure from the man's family, upon whom he was ultimately dependent. This pressure demanded his submission to an arranged marriage that spelled the end of the brief period of romance. The ultimate power of the familial order, which swallowed up men and excluded courtesans, probably also explains why in these tales the male protagonists, who faced the same circumstances as the author and his friends, are generally weak, passive, and without character, while the women are active, decisive, and the emotional center of the story.

The tension between romance and family paralleled that between true ownership based on spiritual appreciation of a site or object and mere economic possession based on purchase. The tension common to these two themes suggests a final aspect of Tang interest in romances. In early imperial China, emotions were considered a danger, which the ruler or scholar mastered to secure his position and stabilize the world. Although this attitude started to change during the Northern and Southern Dynasties, emotions remained suspect as a guide to conduct. However, by the Ming dynasty many writers would argue that being "sentimental" or "full of emotion" (*duo qing*) distinguished the cultivated person from an uncultured boor. While Tang stories did not yet evince a full-blown cult of feelings, the tentative celebration of freely chosen romance and the condemnation in some stories of the unfaithful male lover's lack of feeling marked a first step toward the literary psychology that became prominent in later imperial China.[55]

Critical Essays

The classical prose essay (*gu wen*) is conventionally regarded as the definitive intellectual achievement of the late Tang and a high point of Chinese literature. However, these essays were just one genre within a

broader range of prose writings about politics and culture in the after-
math of the An Lushan rebellion, including prefaces to literary anthologies, personal letters, and other forms of critical prose. The classical essay
can be understood only within this broader context.

The Tang essayists emerged from the convergence of two intellectual
programs: calls for a "return to antiquity" as the model for writing, and
attempts to restore dynastic power following the An Lushan rebellion.
When Li E was writing his memorial to the Sui emperor advocating a
simpler writing style patterned on the classics and Han texts, Wang Tong
tried to revive classical models for writing history through the imitation
of Confucius. Several early Tang historians also promoted a more classical style that "balanced substance and adornment," though they justified
this by appealing to utility in government rather than to the classics. Liu
Zhiji (661–721) denounced as anachronistic the copying of older styles
but called instead for a more "genuine" and "pure" utilitarian style.
Writing just before the An Lushan rebellion, Li Hua (ca. 710–767) identified the canon as the timeless literary Way (dao) and the standard for
judging all writing. This formulation served as the foundation for later
advocacy of classical prose.[56]

The classical prose movement also grew out of the debate over how to
restore the Tang dynasty after the An Lushan rebellion. Restoration of
the pre-rebellion order, already nostalgically recalled as a golden age, became the focus of Tang writers. Most prose authors in the late eighth and
early ninth centuries, exemplified by Quan Deyu (759–818) and Liang Su
(753–793), shared a conservative "restorationist" consensus committed
to two ideas: that power should be concentrated in the central government and that access to positions of authority should be through proven
literary mastery.[57] The power of the regional military governors, the rise
of the salt monopoly, and the new role of eunuchs in the court's military
establishment all challenged these ideas. The center had lost administrative, military, and fiscal power to the provinces, so that expertise in business and in the command of armies challenged literary skill as the accepted avenue to power. Even at court the influence of literary men was
surpassed by that of eunuchs. The problem was to demonstrate that literary attainments could facilitate the recentralization of power and the restoration of the earlier Tang order. This required a new theory of the respective roles of literature and politics.

The model of literature elaborated by most exponents of restoration
was a variant of the call for a return to antiquity. In this model, literature

(*wen*) was a fundamental and guiding aspect of culture (also *wen*). However, whereas the writing of the canon had been exemplary and authoritative, subsequent periods had witnessed either the separation of scholarly from literary writings—with the former becoming artless and hence
without influence, while the latter lost all morality and substance—or the
gradual triumph of empty adornment (also *wen*) over moral substance.
Literature hit its low point with the stylized, erotic palace poetry of
the last two southern dynasties. The writings of early Tang officials attempted to reverse this trend by recombining the moral seriousness of the
north with the literary accomplishments of the south.[58]

Writing after the rebellion, scholars suggested that the early Tang,
rather than ending the literary failings of the late southern dynasties, had
instead continued to emphasize literary embellishments at the expense of
moral or political purpose. The rebellion itself had resulted in part from
the political failures of literary stylists at court. Essayists such as Li Hua
(710–767), Xiao Yingshi (706–758), and Jia Zhi (718–772) argued that
this trend could be reversed only by adopting the classics as literary models and reducing or eliminating *belles lettres* in the examinations. Their
ultimate literary ideal was "balance" or "completeness." "Balance" combined principle (*li*) with linguistic ornament (*wen*) so that writing was
both morally correct and efficacious. "Completeness" entailed mastering
the full range of genres and styles, so that writing could be adjusted to the
demands of the moment.[59]

Another idea, suggested first by Liang Su and elaborated by Bo Juyi
and Liu Yuxi (772–842), was that literature influenced people because
the writer infused it with his own spirit energies (*qi*). The later writers argued that literary men enjoyed purer and more plentiful energies than ordinary people, either through their cultivation of literature or through a
special endowment from Heaven. This idea justified the employment of
writers as officials and charged their writing with a numinous power.[60]

The political program of the restorationists focused on recreating an
idealized court culture patterned on the early years of the reigns of emperors Taizong and Xuanzong. Aiming to recentralize power, they insisted that the emperor was the ultimate source of order and values
but that his functioning depended on literary men, for several reasons.
First, proper government required clear communication between ruler
and ruled. This meant that literary men must both proclaim the emperor's decisions in edicts and present the situation of the people to the
emperor, in memorials, political poetry, and folk songs they collected.
Second, literary men, with their repertoire of historical examples and

their persuasive powers, were uniquely qualified to advise and guide the emperor in his decision-making. Third, literary texts were powerful tools for displaying the character of the writer, which justified their use in examinations and made graduates better officials than eunuchs or fiscal experts. Fourth, literary education cultivated civil virtues, enabling its recipients to defend the people's interests and making them superior leaders to military men, whose stock in trade was violence.[61]

Much of the restorationist program was shared by the classical prose movement that emerged at the end of the eighth century, but the latter offered new theories of literary style, the uses of the past, individuality, and relations with the court. The classical prose writers, above all Han Yu (768–824), are celebrated in Chinese literary history for transforming what had been utilitarian or minor forms of writing—the essay, the preface, the letter, the inscription—into major artistic genres. In Song times this idea was expressed in the formula that Han Yu had "taken his prose and made it verse" (yi wen wei shi), while his verse was "merely rhymed prose." These remarks assumed that the major genres were clearly distinguished and that poetry was the most linguistically refined and purest literary form, the ultimate vehicle for self-expression. To make a morally serious language that recaptured the purity and power of ancient works, Han Yu tried to break down the literary boundaries that had developed over the centuries. He stripped away the conventions that had come to characterize each genre and used the techniques of one to reinvigorate the other. In this program, the "ancient" (gu) was not simply another set of conventions to be copied but a radical negation of contemporary practice to achieve a stylistic revolution.[62]

The clearest account of this revolution is Han Yu's letter to the examination candidate Li Yi. In response to Li Yi's inquiries about the nature of writing, Han Yu described how he had fashioned his writing style and, in the process, himself. He stated that both the true Way and the literature that expressed it had declined for centuries. Anyone hoping to match the ancient masters consequently required a long apprenticeship during which he had to abandon all thought of worldly success. Han Yu himself had spent more than twenty years reading only the classics and the works of the Han dynasty, seeking to expunge from his mind the accumulated clichés and set phrases of recent centuries.

How excruciatingly difficult it was, full of creaking and squeaking! As to how I looked to others, I was impervious to their ridicule. I went on like this for many years, still unchanging. After that, I was

able to distinguish the genuine from the false in the ancient works
... Then, when I selected from my mind ideas to express through my
pen, they came flowing forth. As to how I looked to others, I was
happy when they laughed at me, and I was troubled when they
praised me, for I was afraid that I still harboured some of their ideas.

He asserted that he would have to continue this process of searching and
purging to the end of his days.[63]

This letter shows the key elements of Han Yu's program. First, he established a new corpus of study and memorization. *Jinshi* candidates typically prepared for the examinations by devoting themselves to studying
poems canonized in the major anthologies, above all the *Selection of
Refined Literature*. Han Yu challenged the exams as a legitimate target of
study, calling on students to abandon the standard poems and their conventional idioms. In their place, he offered a "classic" corpus of pre-
imperial and Han writings, whose free and flexible rhythms were superior to the set numbers of characters per line demanded by the rigid
parallelism that had defined proper prose for centuries.

However, the classic corpus was not itself a body of texts to be imitated. Instead, as Han Yu argued in a fictional dialogue in his "Letter to
Liu Chengfu," one should study the texts of the sages in order to "take
their *ideas* as your model, not their diction." Ancient writings were superior because "in antiquity all phrases came from the men themselves."
Rather than copying phrases from ancient texts, he advocated a total absorption in them until one had internalized the thinking of the ancient
sages and could spontaneously write new lines in the manner of the old.

This development of a new vocabulary through rediscovering an old
one paralleled his program of systematically purging poetic language.
Han Yu first stripped away everything that Tang writers considered "poetic," producing a style that struck his contemporaries as "barren" and
"hard." In place of the conventional phrases and binomes, he used his
thorough knowledge of the classics to retrieve the true, early sense of individual graphs, which he then recombined to form original phrases.[64]
Only gradually, through numerous poetic "failures," did he develop a
new style in which he expressed his own character and individuality, although his verse was never aesthetically pleasing to his contemporaries.[65]

Han Yu's account of his self-formation also introduced the themes of
antiquity and individuality. For Han Yu, as for Liu Zongyuan and others,
"antiquity" was not a corpus of writings that allowed scholars to escape

post-Han developments by imitating earlier styles but was rather a "spiritual state" to be achieved through a lifetime of self-cultivation. By protracted study and self-criticism, one stripped away the decadence of the contemporary world that had led to political collapse and transformed oneself into an embodiment of the classical Way of the sages. Internalizing antiquity in this manner required both constant reading of ancient texts and reshaping oneself through the discipline of writing. "Study," as Han Yu remarked, "is how one perfects the Way, while writing (*wen*) is how one perfects normative patterns." Writing in this "classical" manner achieved a "mental style" based on internalizing the values of the ancients, rather than merely following the rules in canonical texts. It was the literary parallel to Han Yu's philosophical ideal of living so as to recapture "the Way of the sage."[66]

Individuality figured in the writings of Han Yu and Liu Zongyuan as an explicit ideal and an implicit value. It appeared explicitly in the repeated use by Han Yu and his followers of the epithets "remarkable" (*qi*) and "strange" (*guai*) as high praise. The insistence that good literature must be unusual and could be created only by a distinctive talent fashioned through protracted study was the correlate of the necessity of escaping from convention:

Men take no notice of the hundred and one objects they see day and night. But when they see something extraordinary, they notice it and talk about it. How could literature be any different? Many men of the Han dynasty were competent in letters, but only Sima Xiangru, Sima Qian, Liu Xiang, and Yang Xiong were considered outstanding. This is because it is those who apply themselves long and hard who are remembered by posterity. As to those who drift with the times without any distinction or originality, they may not be criticized by their contemporaries, but their names will certainly not be perpetuated by later generations.[67]

This insistence that good literature was distinctive and personal extended Han Yu's denial of the possibility of achieving real style through imitation. Since education aimed at fashioning a new self that produced its own original phrases, the true writer had to develop a unique, individual voice. By assimilating the sages' values, the writer became his own man, standing apart from contemporary society and rejecting all established models. This ideal was also central to the literary thought of Liu

Zongyuan and figured in his rejection of the idea that he could be a teacher, since each student had to fashion his own style.[68]

Han Yu's insistence on individuality entailed political choices. This is clearest in his essay "In Praise of Boyi." Boyi and his brother were famous for rejecting as criminal the Zhou rebellion against the Shang in the eleventh century B.C. and for starving themselves to death rather than live under the rebels, despite the supposed universal approval of the virtuous Zhou rulers' elimination of the monstrous Shang king at the behest of Heaven. As Han Yu wrote: "Scholars who stand alone and act independently, with the sole purpose of complying with the principles of righteousness, without regard to the views of others, are outstanding men . . . There is only one in a hundred or a thousand years who presses forward and is not beset by doubts despite the objections of the whole world. A man like Boyi went so far as to disregard even Heaven and Earth and the judgment of numberless generations after him." Despite Boyi's rejection of Heaven and the sages, and the fact that he was ultimately wrong, Han Yu celebrated Boyi's act because it provided the supreme measure of the self-reliant judgment that was necessary to stand against accepted conventions. Political heroism could derive only from such defiance of Heaven and the entire world.[69]

This affirmation of individuality led to the idea that the writer who was truly good, both artistically and morally, would invariably be ignored or rejected by society. The most notable exponent of this idea was Han Yu's friend and fellow poet Meng Jiao, who in several poems asserted the inevitable isolation, and often poverty, of the true poet:

> Bad poets all win public office,
> The good poet only clings to the hills.
> Clings to the hills, shivering cold,
> Grieving in misery all the day through.
> A poet, what's more, wins their spite,
> Swords and pikes grow out of their teeth.

While the occasional early writer had celebrated a rejected singularity, only in the late Tang did this become an explicit value shared by a group of intellectuals who regarded themselves as an elite of exceptional men rejected by the herd of conventional literati. What Han Yu and his friends celebrated as a moral and artistic repudiation of exhausted values that had led to the collapse of the Tang state developed, among some subse-

quent poets, into the idea of "singularity as an inner compulsion" bordering on madness that marked the isolated genius almost in the manner
of European romanticism.[70]

In addition to their stylistic revolution, their new approach to the past,
and their cult of individuality, the group around Han Yu also developed
new attitudes toward the ruler and the court. This change may have resulted from the careers of these men, most of whom spent much of their
time in local administrations far from the imperial center. This encouraged them to insist on the fundamental importance of the self-cultivation
of scholar-officials (*shi*) for creating social order, and their denial of the
central role of the ruler. Han Yu articulated this in his most important essay, "Finding the Origin of the Way." This essay adapted his literary
model to a political history in which the ancient sage kings had established an ideal order that since the Han had been corrupted by Daoism
and Buddhism. Because sages had not ruled since before Confucius, self-
cultivation by scholar-officials had become the key to restoring political
and moral order. Instead of a state in which Confucianism dealt with
family matters and public order, while Daoism or Buddhism provided a
spiritual or cosmic dimension, Han Yu advocated an integrated Confucian morality that reunited the private and public spheres.[71]

Liu Zongyuan also reduced the importance of the ruler, arguing that
the human and natural worlds were separate, so Heaven was not a moral
agent that used natural phenomena such as floods or famine to communi-
cate its judgments about rulers. In the classical theory, the Son of Heaven
linked Heaven and Earth, so unusual phenomena were interpreted as
Heaven's praise or blame of his conduct, and his rituals were supposed
to maintain the natural order. While some earlier writers, notably Xun
Kuang in the third century B.C. and Wang Chong in the first century A.D.,
had denied all connection between natural phenomena and human conduct, the affirmation of such links had become conventional in the Chinese model of emperorship. Liu Zongyuan denied this ruler-centered universe in at least three separate essays. The poet and thinker Liu Yuxi,
while disputing Liu Zongyuan's thoroughgoing skepticism, agreed that
Heaven did not act as a guarantor of morality in the world.[72]

In another innovation, Han Yu called for the restoration of the exalted
position of teacher. Although teacher-disciple relations had been important in the Warring States and Han, during the Northern and Southern
Dynasties education had become largely a family matter, so that the
status of teaching as a profession seriously declined. In the Tang, the so-

cial links between examiners and candidates, while paralleling the old teacher-disciple ties of earlier times to some extent, contributed to the relative eclipse of the professional teacher. In his essay "On the Teacher," Han Yu insisted that in antiquity all men, including the sages, had studied with teachers, who underpinned the social order. He also styled himself as a teacher in his relations with younger scholars, probably influenced by Chan Buddhism's insistence on forming a lineage through face-to-face, oral transmission. However, this innovation was not followed even by contemporary admirers such as Liu Zongyuan.[73]

One last aspect of Han Yu's thought is his attitude toward Buddhism. Most Tang intellectuals regarded Daoism or Buddhism, or both, as major fields of study or as spiritual guides. However, in "Finding the Origin of the Way" and in the celebrated "Memorial on the Bone of the Buddha," which railed against the adoration of the Buddha's finger-bone relic, Han Yu denounced the institutional religions as destroyers of the true Way and called for their suppression. The only writing in the period that is comparable in its attempt to install a dominant Confucianism in place of the conventional division of labor among the three religious doctrines is Li Ao's essay "On Returning to One's Nature." In it, Li tried to disentangle Tang Confucianism from its syncretic accretions of Buddhist doctrine.[74] When Song Neo-Confucians constructed their intellectual lineage, they fixed upon these two authors. Han Yu was celebrated as their intellectual ancestor, while Li Ao was condemned for supposedly introducing Buddhist ideas into his understanding of Confucian teachings. Both of these readings were anachronistic, and the latter was inaccurate. In any case, the ideas of these two authors regarding Buddhism were marginal to Tang intellectual history.

In conclusion, developments in the role of writing during the Tang have a few common features that underpin the exalted place this dynasty has traditionally held in Chinese literary history. All the new forms of writing were linked to the emergence of a distinctive urban culture, which provided both new settings where writing was pursued and new themes for literary treatment. The emergence of this new urban culture shifted the literary center of gravity away from the courts, where it had been since the Han, and thereby encouraged the move away from the socio-political grounding of literature. The rise of a more urban, mercantile society also facilitated the emergence of new private or semiprivate spaces as both setting and subject for literature. The themes of the social role of money, either veiled or explicit, and of literary possession also emerged from this new context. Most important, all these developments converged in a new model of the writer and his place in society. Whether discovering the significance of poetry in the genius or character of its author, insisting on a unique personal style created through decades of endeavor as definitive of the essayist, or making the romantic travails of the young writer the central topic of a new genre of fiction, the Tang literary world translated individual character and literary genius into socially celebrated attributes.

CONCLUSION

THE SACK of Chang'an by the troops of the rebel and military man Huang Chao in 881 brought an end not only to the last remnants of Tang imperial power but also to more than a millennium in which Chang'an had often been China's capital and always an important strategic center. A few days after they occupied the capital, the rebel troops ran amok, looting the houses of wealthy families and slaughtering their inhabitants. The looters aimed to kill officials, in particular. However, as so often in Chinese verse, the poet Wei Zhuang, who immortalized the event in his "Lament of the Lady of Qin," focused on the plight of female victims, who stood in for the massacred courtiers with whom they were conventionally linked:

> In house after house blood flows like boiling fountains;
> In place after place victims scream: their screams shake the earth.
> Dancers and singing girls have all disappeared,
> Babies and young girls are abandoned alive . . .
> My neighbor in the west had a daughter, lovely as a goddess;
> Her lustrous eyes flashed from side to side cutting the autumn
>   waters like an inch of sword blade.
> Her toilet completed, all she did was gaze at the reflection of spring
>   in her mirror,
> So young she didn't know what happened outside her doors.
> Some thug leaps up her golden staircase,
> Rips the dress to bare half her shoulder, about to shame her,

But dragged by the clothes she refuses to go through the vermilion
   gate,
So with rouge powder and perfumed cream on her face
   she's stabbed down till she's dead.[1]

To the north, south, east, and west, Wei Zhuang traced out a mandala of
violated women and burned houses that symbolized the apocalypse in
which the Tang state perished. Presaging China's future development, the
poem concluded with a vision that in the midst of universal disorder
southern China alone was "as clear as water and as smooth as a whet-
stone."[2]

   After the Tang's collapse, north and south China split apart, with each
half in turn divided into competing states (Map 17). Like the earlier,
longer periods of division—the Warring States (481–221 B.C.) and the
Northern and Southern Dynasties (A.D. 220–581)—this period, known
as the Five Dynasties (907–960), was a time of major changes. The
first was the disappearance of the great families who had dominated
Tang government and society and had defined a style or ideal against
which the elite measured itself. The unquestioned supremacy of these
families came to an end because they had linked themselves completely to
high offices in the Tang imperial court. Having abandoned their local
bases and physically moved to the capitals of Chang'an and Luoyang,
where they bought up new properties, they had no place of retreat in
times of disaster. The pillaging of the capitals resulted not only in the
deaths of the leading members of the great families and the end of the dynasty to which they were tied but also the destruction of their material
wealth.

   A second and less obvious factor in the decline and disappearance of
the great families was the proliferation of offspring over the centuries. A
large percentage of the provincial elites in late Tang and tenth-century
China, as shown in funerary inscriptions, were members of less successful
lines of the great families and were not of local origin. The leading families of the Tang, like their predecessors in the Northern and Southern
Dynasties, composed genealogies that acknowledged kin ties only with
branches that continued to produce officials in the capitals. Less successful lines were excluded. They did not disappear, however, but seem to
have sought new avenues of advancement with the military governors in
the northeast or as local officials or businessmen in the south.[3] Thus,

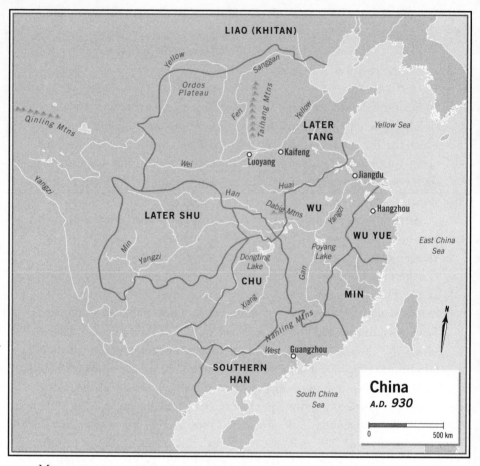

MAP 17

while pride in genealogy continued into the eleventh century, as shown in the histories composed under the Song dynasty, the choronyms (surnames tagged with a place of origin) of the greatest families no longer distinguished members of the imperial elite from their provincial counterparts.

A related major change was the rise of a new ethic of merit, in which talent became generally accepted as the basis of social status. In accounts of Chinese history, this change in focus from genealogy to talent is often described as a central aspect of the transition from the Tang to the Song, but in fact it began during the Tang. The examination system had introduced merit or talent into the selection of Tang officials, even though the nature of the exams and the rituals in which they were embedded helped preserve the dominance of established families. More important, the staffs of the military governors who dominated the northeast and of the commissioners who administered the salt monopoly in the south, which was the fiscal foundation of the late Tang state, both emphasized talent in making appointments. These offices thus provided channels through which brilliant men of humble background could rise to positions of real power. Their courts even provided alternative avenues of advancement for leading poets in the last century of the Tang.

The new emphasis on talent developed further in the tenth century, as competing regimes emerged across the north and south. Leaders of the Five Dynasties in the north (Later Liang, Later Tang, Later Jin, Later Han, and Later Zhou), who were largely military men, and leaders of the Ten Kingdoms in the south (Wu, Wu Yue, Min, Chu, Southern Han, Former Shu, Later Shu, Jingnan, Southern Tang, Northern Han) depended on the recruitment of subordinates with genuine military, fiscal, and administrative ability. When warlords from the northeast captured major northern cities such as Luoyang and Kaifeng and made them their new capitals, the provincial soldiers and administrators who had served them relocated *en masse* to these new sites. The most significant importation of provincial talent was a Turkish-led invasion in 923 that placed men from the northeast in a dominant position in the new bureaucracy in Luoyang. This movement into the old imperial centers of men who had risen to power in the more meritocratic courts of the military governors changed the bureaucratic culture of major cities, making it more talent-based. This is demonstrated in a 996 funerary inscription by Liu Kai, a bureaucrat from the northeast who had accompanied the founding emperor of the Later Tang dynasty to Luoyang:

At the end of the Tang, when bandits overturned the two capitals, the genealogies of the officials were burned and destroyed. Using one's surname to masquerade as the descendant of a famous old family, this is to muddy things and fail to make distinctions. How can I imitate this practice? If through ability a peddler or a servant becomes useful to his generation and serves as minister to the prince, is he necessarily the son of a famous old family? As for somebody with no ability, even if he is the son of a famous family, what does it matter now?[4]

The emergence of competing political centers in the tenth century affected the conduct and values not only of the rulers but also of members of the elite for whom these centers offered new career opportunities. A high degree of geographic mobility had characterized the Tang elite, as successful family members moved into the capital while their less eminent branches drifted toward the provinces, either to serve northeastern military governors or to make their fortunes in the economically developing south. Those who rose to office in the south often converted their salary income into land or commercial capital as their families resettled in the new region. Large numbers of ninth-century inscriptions in the south focus on the property of the deceased, suggesting that many southern families were no longer, or had never been, tied to the state. These inscriptions often emphasized the geomantic virtues of the tomb that would enhance the family's wealth: "As for his tomb, to the east it looks upon the edge of the ford; to the west it abuts on the long embankment; in front, it faces the Red Spirit; to the rear, it borders on the mounds and hills. The tomb is peaceful at this location. For ten thousand generations and one thousand years, children and descendants will from early years amass glory and fortune."[5]

As a multiplicity of local regimes emerged throughout China in the tenth century, each new political center increasingly monopolized the resources in its immediate vicinity, so that members of the elite often had to secure their positions by obtaining government posts. Those who could not obtain a position with one local ruler might have greater success with another, and consequently families moved from one local capital to the next as opportunities arose. More and more rulers copied the northeastern military governors in appointing their leading officials by decree rather than through the examinations and other bureaucratic procedures that had stabilized the old elite. Appointments by decree thus became a major tool for opening up top positions to men whose talents would have been concealed by literary examinations. Thus, although the Tang examination system established at least the idea of appointments based on merit, and the Song exams would institutionalize a new form of meritocracy, in the tenth century those who bestowed offices on the basis of merit deliberately circumvented the exam system.[6]

The extension of meritocratic values from their old centers in the northeast throughout all of China altered the makeup of the tenth-century elite. In funerary inscriptions, military servicemen celebrated one set of values, civil servants endorsed a second set, and wealthy families with no government contacts held yet a third. While late-Tang families had most often married within their own type, in the tenth century they began to opt for a strategy of diversification. This entailed educating each son to enter a different profession and arranging marriages with different types of elite families in order to extend their social networks and multiply the political and social niches into which they might fit.

A typical example was Wang Xuxian, a civil bureaucrat who sought to ingratiate himself with a local warlord by offering younger kinsmen to serve in both civil and military posts: "My son Qian likes to study and is conscientious and meticulous; he can be employed in your service. My younger brother's son Ren has integrity; he can become a general." This pattern had first emerged in the militarized culture of the northeast, where military and civil careers were closely linked and where there was no tradition of denigrating military service. As military regimes divided up the Tang empire in the tenth century, and as central military commands or rulers' personal armies emerged as the centers of political power from which the next generation of leaders emerged, such diversification of occupations within the family spread throughout the Chinese elite.[7]

Along with new patterns of political service and geographic mobility among elites, the late Tang and the tenth century also witnessed the continuing southward shift of Chinese civilization. This long-term trend had begun in the fourth century, accelerated during the southern dynasties, and continued under the Tang. In the first centuries of the dynasty, the longstanding appeal of good land and more reliable rainfall in the south was reinforced by the development of more efficient water transport over the region's rivers and by the Grand Canal that linked the most productive southern regions to northern markets. Following the An Lushan rebellion, the pull of southern prosperity was reinforced by a push from northern devastation. This migration did not lead to a demographic decline in the north, where the population continued to grow, but rather to an extraordinary increase of the southern population. Between 742 and 1080 (two years for which comprehensive census records have survived), the population in the north increased by only 26 percent, while that in the south increased by 328 percent.[8] At the end of this process, the majority of the Chinese population lived in the south, and the demographic dominance of this region would increase over the rest of Chinese history.

The continued economic development of the south in the late Tang, and the chaos in the north, meant that the less successful lines of leading families, as well as any ambitious families without a background of imperial service, opted to move to the Yangzi drainage basin in search of greater opportunities. Textual evidence suggests that a rapid north-to-south demographic transition began in the ninth century and accelerated in the tenth. Inscriptions also show that elite migration accelerated significantly after the Huang Chao rebellion, both as a means to escape the chaos in the north and to seek employment opportunities with newly founded southern dynasties. The majority of officials in the southern courts for whom we have evidence were emigrants from the north. Thus, the temporary appearance of multiple southern courts in the tenth century added yet another inducement for elites to move into the Yangzi basin, thereby intensifying the established, long-term trend.

A final significant point is that these new waves of wealthier immigrants tended to push the earlier great families who had moved south during the southern dynasties and early Tang away from the major towns along the lower Yangzi and the Grand Canal and into regional peripheries. Thus, the population expansion of the south in the ninth and tenth centuries was a process of filling in what had been more marginal regions, while the already developed areas around major cities remained relatively unchanged. Inscriptional materials confirm that the majority of southern elites were more recent immigrants rather than long-established families and that the latter appeared increasingly in marginal towns.[9]

In conclusion, following the disappearance over the course of the Tang dynasty of the landholding patterns, urban design, and commercial constraints that had defined the reunited state under the Sui and early Tang, multiple changes in the tenth century—the end of the great families, the rise of a meritocratic ethos, and the permanent shift of China's demographic and economic centers of gravity to the south—set the stage for new geographic, social, economic, and political institutions that would define not just the Song dynasty but all of later imperial China.

DATES AND DYNASTIES

PRONUNCIATION GUIDE

NOTES

BIBLIOGRAPHY

ACKNOWLEDGMENTS

INDEX

DATES AND DYNASTIES

734   Li Linfu becomes chief minister

737   Fullest version of legal code promulgated; formal shift to full
        reliance on professional soldiers at the frontier

742   Frontier formally divided into ten military commands; An Lushan
        takes command in the northeast

749   Formal abolition of the regimental army

751   Arabs defeat the Tang at the Talas River, beginning Islam's
        conquest of Central Asia

752   Li Linfu dies, breaking links of An Lushan to court

755   An Lushan rebels; takes Chang'an in 756

763   An Lushan rebellion ends

780   Double tax system formally introduced

781   First war with the military governors, ending in 786 with
        recognition of their powers

790   Major defeat at hands of Tibet, ending Tang power in Central
        Asia

801   Alliance with Nanzhao to defeat Tibet ends fifty years of war in
        the west

814   Resumption of war with the military governors, ending in 819
        with court dominant but bankrupt

821   Beginning of factional struggle between Niu Sengru and Li Deyu

835   Sweet Dew Incident results in eunuch control of the court

845   Brief suppression of Buddhism, ending the next year

858   Rebellions and banditry begin to sweep the south

875   Huang Chao's rebellion begins, ending with his death in 884

880   Huang Chao occupies Luoyang and Chang'an, ending Tang's
        power; warlords carve up China

907   Tang dynasty formally replaced

CHINESE DYNASTIES

Shang	ca. 1600–1027 B.C.
Zhou	1027–256 B.C.
Western Zhou	1027–771 B.C.
Eastern Zhou	771–256 B.C.
Spring and Autumn Period	722–481 B.C.
Qin	221–206 B.C.
Western (Former) Han	206 B.C.–A.D. 8
Xin	8–23

Eastern (Later) Han	23–220
Three Kingdoms (Wei, Sui, Wu)	220–280
Western Jin	265–317
Northern and Southern Dynasties	317–589
Sui	589–618
Tang	618–907
Five Dynasties	907–960
Song	960–1279
Northern Song	960–1126
Southern Song	1126–1279
Yuan	1279–1368
Ming	1368–1644
Qing	1644–1912

PRONUNCIATION GUIDE

Pronunciation is as in English unless noted below.

c   as *ts* in *nets*
ch   as in *chat*
g   as in *girl*
j   as in *jingle*
q   as *ch* in *cheese*
x   as *sh* in *sheer*
y   as in *year*
z   as *dz* in *adze*
zh   as *j* in *John*
a   as *e* in *pen* for yan, jian, qian, xian; otherwise as *a* in *father*
ai   as in *aye*
ang   as *ong* in *wrong*
ao   as *ow* in *now*
e   as *e* in *yet* in the combinations ye, -ie, -ue; otherwise as *e* in *the*
ei   as in *neigh*
en   as *un* in *fun*
eng   as *ung* in *rung*
er   pronounced as *are*
i   as in the *i* of *sir* after c, s, z; as in the *ir* of *sir* after ch, sh, zh, r
ie   as *ye* in *yet*
iu   as *yo* in *yoyo*
ong   as *ung* in German *Achtung*
ou   as in *oh*
u   after j, q, x, and y as *ui* in *suit;* otherwise as *u* in *rule*
ua   after j, q, x, and y as *ue* in *duet;* otherwise as *wa* in *water*
uai   as in *why*
ue   as *ue* in *duet*
ui   as in *way*
uo   similar to *o* in *once*

NOTES

1. The Geography of Empire

1. Somers, "Time, Space and Structure in the Consolidation of the T'ang Dynasty (A.D. 617–700)"; Wang, "The Middle Yangtze in Tang Politics"; Schafer, *The Vermilion Bird*; Schafer, *The Empire of Min*.

2. The economic privileging of the Chinese imperial capital regions, with an emphasis on water control, was pointed out in Wittfogel, *Wirtschaft und Gesellschaft Chinas*, esp. pp. 273ff. See also Chi, *Key Economic Areas in Chinese History*. While both works are dated, the basic thesis remains of fundamental importance.

3. *Han shu*, as quoted in Chi, *Key Economic Areas*, pp. 79–83. On privileging the capital through investment in water and transport, see also Shi, *Zhongguo gu du he wenhua*, ch. 5.

4. Chi, *Key Economic Areas*, pp. 84–88. On the later history of the Zhengguo Canal, see Elvin, *The Retreat of the Elephants*, p. 122; Will, "Clear Waters versus Muddy Waters: The Zheng-Bai Irrigation System of Shaanxi in the Late-Imperial Period"; Shi, *Tang dai lishi dili yanjiu*, pp. 88–90.

5. Chi, *Key Economic Areas*, pp. 89–95.

6. Lewis, *China Between Empires*, chs. 1, 5.

7. On these military men and their relations to Zhou rulers, see Dien, "The Role of the Military in the Western Wei/Northern Chou State"; Dien, "The Bestowal of Surnames under the Western Wei-Northern Chou: A Case of Counter-Acculturation."

8. See Shi, *Tang dai lishi dili yanjiu*, pp. 63–87; Shi, *Huangtu gaoyuan lishi dili yanjiu*, sections 1–5; Shi, *Zhongguo gu du he wenhua*, pp. 277–285, 439–443, 537–540. In English, see Elvin, "Introduction," pp. 16–17, in *Sediments of Time*.

9. Quoted in Elvin, *The Retreat of the Elephants*, p. 19. On Liu Zongyuan, see Chen, *Liu Tsung-yüan and Intellectual Change in T'ang China, 773–819*.

10. Elvin, *The Retreat of the Elephants*, pp. 24–26.

11. Shi, *Tang dai lishi dili yanjiu*, pp. 104–106, 111–130; Yan, *Tang dai jiaotong tong kao*, pp. 1589–1628.

12. Quoted in Shi, *Tang dai lishi dili yanjiu*, p. 318.

13. Shi, *Tang dai lishi dili yanjiu*, pp. 470–490; Chen, "Lun Sui mo Tang chu suowei 'Shandong haojie'"; Chen, *Tang dai zhengzhi shi shulun gao*, pp. 176–196. On the manner in which these forts may have affected Tang kinship patterns, see Ebrey, "Early Stages in the Development of Descent Group Organization," pp. 29–34.

14. Graff, *Medieval Chinese Warfare*, pp. 161–163, 171–178; Graff, "Dou Jiande's Dilemma."

15. Shi, *Tang dai lishi dili yanjiu*, pp. 98–104; Aoyama, *Tō Sō jidai no kōtsū to chishi chizu no kenkyū*, pp. 267–271.

16. Abramson, *Ethnic Identity in the Tang*, pp. 109–110; Hartman, *Han Yü*, p. 330n77.

17. Yan, "Tang Wudai shiqi de Chengdu," pp. 207–211, 236–239, 244 (quoting the Du Fu poem); Yan, *Tang dai jiaotong tong kao*, vol. 4.

18. Benn, *China's Golden Age*, pp. 182–184; Elvin, *The Pattern of the Chinese Past*, pp. 131–134.

19. Elvin, *The Retreat of the Elephants*, pp. 55, 64.

20. Elvin, *The Pattern of the Chinese Past*, p. 132; *The Retreat of the Elephants*, pp. 55, 64.

21. Van Slyke, *Yangtze*, pp. 19–24.

22. Schafer, *The Empire of Min*.

23. Backus, *The Nan-chao Kingdom and T'ang China's Southwestern Frontier*.

24. Schafer, *The Vermilion Bird: T'ang Images of the South*.

25. Shi, *Tang dai lishi dili yanjiu*, pp. 133–136, 138–139.

26. Ibid., pp. 139–140.

27. Twitchett, "Monasteries and China's Economy in Medieval Times," pp. 532–533. On the regional variations of irrigation, see Needham and Bray, *Science and Civilisation in China*, vol. 6, *Biology and Biological Technology*, pt. 2, *Agriculture*, pp. 109–113.

28. Graff, "Dou Jiande's Dilemma," pp. 86–98.

29. Elvin, *The Pattern of the Chinese Past*, pt. 2. Ch. 10 examines the revolution in water transport.

30. On the canals, see Xiong, *Emperor Yang of the Sui Dynasty*, pp. 86–93; Wright, *The Sui Dynasty*, pp. 177–181. On the granaries, see Xiong, *Emperor Yang of the Sui Dynasty*, pp. 175–180. On the Grand Canal in later Chinese history, see van Slyke, *Yangtze*, ch. 6; Tregear, *Geography of China*, pp. 78–80; Chi, *Key Economic Areas in Chinese History*, pp. 113–121.

31. Elvin, *The Retreat of the Elephants*, pp. 120, 130–136, 140, 437.

32. Cited in Elvin, *The Pattern of the Chinese Past*, p. 136–137. These superlatives about the huge number of boats in use are confirmed by specific figures scattered in eighth-century records of thousands of craft destroyed by fires or storms. On the numbers of boats and their speeds, see Benn, *China's Golden Age,* pp. 164–165.

33. Twitchett, "Merchant, Trade, and Government in Late T'ang," pp. 81–87; Elvin, *The Pattern of the Chinese Past*, p. 136.

34. Shi, *Tang dai lishi dili yanjiu*, pp. 313–341. For references in poetry and histories to the diverse routes passing through Yangzhou (Jiangdu), see p. 317.

35. Lewis, *The Construction of Space*, pp. 247–273; Abramson, *Ethnic Identity*, pp. 119–121.

36. Abramson, *Ethnic Identity*, p. 220n96.

37. Ibid., pp. 109–114. The quotation is on pp. 110–111.

38. Ibid., pp. 114–119. The quotation is on pp. 118–119.

39. Ibid., pp. 141–149; Lewis, *The Construction of Space*, chs. 4–5.

40. Abramson, *Ethnic Identity*, pp. 122–125.

2. From Foundation to Rebellion

1. Rouzer, *Writing Another's Dream: The Poetry of Wen Tingyun*, pp. 123–128. Chapter 4 discusses the history poems of Wen Tingyun. For poems of Li Shangyin (813–858) on the same theme, see Owen, *An Anthology of Chinese Literature*, pp. 515–517; Owen, *The Late Tang: Chinese Poetry of the Mid-Ninth Century*, pp. 427–430.

2. On Xiang Yu's decision to return to Chu, see Lewis, *The Construction of Space in Early China*, p. 176; Lewis, *The Early Chinese Empires: Qin and Han*, pp. 19, 60–61. On Emperor Yang's decision to move south, and how Guanzhong was crucial to Li Yuan's success, see Chen, *Tangdai zhengzhi shi shulun gao*, p. 201.

3. English narratives are Bingham, *The Founding of the T'ang Dynasty*; Graff, *Medieval Chinese Warfare*, ch. 8; Somers, "Time, Space and Structure in the Consolidation of the Tang Dynasty"; Wechsler, "The Founding of the T'ang Dynasty"; Wechsler, "T'ai-tsung (reign 626–649) the Consolidator."

4. Graff, *Medieval Chinese Warfare*, pp. 162–165.

5. Ibid., pp. 165–178. On omens and rituals, see Wechsler, *Mirror to the Son of Heaven*, pp. 31–32; Wechsler, *Offerings of Jade and Silk*, ch. 3. On Daoist support, see Bokenkamp, "Time After Time: Taoist Apocalyptic History and the Founding of the T'ang Dynasty"; Seidel, "The Image of the Perfect Ruler in Early Taoist Messianism."

6. Somers, "Time, Space and Structure," pp. 374–378.

7. Wechsler, "Founding of the T'ang," pp. 168–181.

8. Graff, *Medieval Chinese Warfare,* pp. 185–188; Wechsler, "Founding of the T'ang," pp. 181–182, 220–224.

9. Wechsler, "T'ai-tsung," pp. 189–200, 231–235; Graff, *Medieval Chinese Warfare,* pp. 195–201.

10. Somers, "Time, Space and Structure," pp. 380–389. See also Graff, *Medieval Chinese Warfare,* pp. 190–191; Wechsler, "T'ai-tsung," pp. 208–210. On the thesis of region-based factions struggling for power in the early Tang court, see Chen, *Tangdai zhengzhi shi shulun gao,* pp. 170ff; Gu, "An-Shi luan qian zhi Hebei dao."

11. Twitchett and Wechsler, "Kao-tsung and the Empress Wu," pp. 273–287.

12. Ibid., pp. 244–257 (these narrate Wu Zhao's rise to power, with unexamined horror stories and slander intact); Guisso, "Reigns of the Empress Wu, Chung-tsung and Jui-tsung (684–712)," pp. 294–300, 303–304, 308, 312, 315–316 (here the modern historian accepts an account of the aged empress's liaison with a pair of young half-brothers, in which her taking aphrodisiacs allows her to grow new teeth), pp. 318–319, 320. The same charges of "lewdness," "ambition," and domination of her husband are made against Empress Wei, the wife of the next emperor, see pp. 322, 325. On the biases of the sources on her reign, see Guisso, *Wu Tse-t'ien and the Politics of Legitimation,* ch. 2, appendix A. For an old but readable narrative history, see Fitzgerald, *The Empress Wu.* For a more recent and sympathetic account, see Dien, *Empress Wu Zetian in Fiction and in History.* On the bias against women in politics, see Yang, "Female Rulers in Imperial China."

13. Twitchett and Wechsler, "Kao-tsung and the Empress Wu," pp. 257–258; Guisso, "Reigns of the Empress Wu, Chung-tsung and Rui-tsung," pp. 291–293, 307, 319. Accepting the traditional Chinese contempt for women as prone to superstition, Twitchett and Guisso argue that Wu Zhao moved the capital for fear of the ghosts of those whom she had killed. On the economic advantages of Luoyang, and later Tang emergency shifts there, see Twitchett, "Hsüan-tsung," pp. 355–356, 357, 388, 395, 397, 399–400.

14. Guisso, *Wu Tse-t'ien and the Politics of Legitimation,* ch. 7.

15. Guisso, "Reigns of Empress Wu, Chung-tsung and Rui-tsung," pp. 309–311; Twitchett, "Hsüan-tsung," pp. 349–351. For a table listing all Tang chief ministers and their terms from the foundation of the dynasty to the end of the Empress Wu's reign, see Guisso, *Wu Tse-t'ien and the Politics of Legitimation,* appendix B. On the "Scholars of the Northern Gate," see Guisso, "Reigns of the Empress Wu, Chung-tsung and Jui-tsung," pp. 310–311; Twitchett and Wechsler, "Kao-tsung and the Empress Wu," p. 263; Guisso, *Wu Tse-t'ien and the Politics of Legitimation,* p. 134. On the similar "Academy of Assembled Worthies" and the Hanlin scholars under Xuanzong, see Twitchett, "Hsüan-tsung," pp. 378, 450; Bischoff, *La Forêt des Pinceaux;* Chiu-Duke, *To Rebuild the Empire: Lu Chih's Confucian Pragmatist Approach to the Mid-T'ang Predicament,* pp. 33–36; Ikeda, "Sei Tō no Shuken'in."

16. Twitchett, "Hsüan-tsung," pp. 362–370; Guisso, *Wu Tse-t'ien and the Politics of Legitimation,* ch. 8.

17. Guisso, "Reigns of the Empress Wu, Chung-tsung and Rui-tsung," pp. 321–328; Twitchett, "Hsüan-tsung," pp. 333–345.

18. This follows the analysis of Denis Twitchett in his chapter "Hsüan-tsung" in the *Cambridge History of China.*

19. Twitchett, "Hsüan-tsung," pp. 382–395; Chen, *Tangdai zhengzhi shi shulun gao,* pp. 170, 199–200.

20. Pulleyblank, *The Background of the Rebellion of An Lu-shan,* ch. 3, pp. 49–50; Twitchett, "Hsüan-tsung," pp. 384–387, 395, 397, 399–400, 419–420, 445, 447, 449, 457; Twitchett, *Financial Administration under the T'ang Dynasty,* pp. 12–16, 27.

21. For translations of the Tang biography of An Lushan, see Levy, *Biography of An Lushan;* Des Rotours, *Histoire de Ngan Lou-chan.* See also Pulleyblank, *The Background of the Rebellion of An Lu-shan,* ch. 2.

22. Pulleyblank, *Background of the Rebellion of An Lu-shan,* chs. 4, 7 (the first chapter traces the emergence of Li Linfu's dictatorship, and the second his relation to An Lu-shan); Twitchett, "Hsüan-tsung," pp. 427–430, 444–453.

23. Pulleyblank, "The An Lu-shan Rebellion and the Origins of Chronic Militarism in Late T'ang China," pp. 40–54; Twitchett, "Hsüan-tsung," pp. 447–461; Graff, *Medieval Chinese Warfare,* pp. 216–223.

24. Chen, *Sui Tang zhidu yuan yuan lüelun gao.* See also his "Lun Sui mo Tang chu suowei 'Shandong haojie'" and "Ji Tang dai zhi Li, Wu, Wei, Wang hunyin jituan."

25. On a Tang-dynasty text by a commander describing the organization and conduct of expeditionary forces, see Graff, *Medieval Chinese Warfare,* pp. 192–195.

26. Guisso, "Reigns of Empress Wu, Chung-tsung, and Jui-tsung," pp. 313–318; Twitchett, "Hsüan-tsung," pp. 362–365. On foreign difficulties during the dictatorship of Li Linfu, see ibid., pp. 430–447. On the geographic distribution of units, see Graff, *Medieval Chinese Warfare,* pp. 190–191.

27. Graff, *Medieval Chinese Warfare,* pp. 205–209; Twitchett, "Hsüan-tsung," pp. 415–418.

28. Graff, *Medieval Chinese Warfare,* pp. 208–210, 212–213.

29. Ibid., p. 210; Peterson, "Court and Province in Mid- and Late T'ang," pp. 464–468.

30. Graff, *Medieval Chinese Warfare,* p. 211; Twitchett, "Hsüan-tsung," pp. 366–369.

31. Graff, *Medieval Chinese Warfare,* pp. 211–212; Twitchett, "Hsüan-tsung," pp. 369–370.

32. Ebrey, *The Aristocratic Families of Early Imperial China: A Case Study of the Po-ling Ts'ui Family;* Johnson, *The Medieval Chinese Oligarchy.* The bibliographies of these works include the major earlier works in Chinese and Japanese.

See also Lewis, *China Between Empires: The Northern and Southern Dynasties*, ch. 2; Twitchett, "Composition of the T'ang Ruling Class," pp. 83–85.

33. Twitchett, "Composition of the T'ang Ruling Class." For a translation of Shen Gua's discussion, see pp. 54–56. See also p. 76.

34. Wechsler, "T'ai-tsung," pp. 212–213; Twitchett and Wechsler, "Kao-tsung and the Empress Wu," pp. 260–261; Twitchett, "Hsüan-tsung," pp. 382–383; Twitchett, "Composition of the T'ang Ruling Class," pp. 62–66, 73.

35. Twitchett, "Composition of the T'ang Ruling Class," pp. 67–68, 73–74.

36. Translated with substantial introductions in Johnson, *The T'ang Code*, vol. 1, *General Principles* and *The T'ang Code*, vol. 2, *Specific Articles*. Because the Tang code provided the model for the early Japanese state, Japanese scholars have been particularly active in studying Tang law. Some of their major works are listed in the bibliography to Volume 1 of Johnson's translation.

37. Hansen, *Negotiating Daily Life in Traditional China: How Ordinary People Used Contracts, 600–1400*, chs. 2–3. See also Johnson, *The T'ang Code*, vol. 2, pp. 464–466.

38. Wright, "The Sui Dynasty," pp. 103–106; *The Sui Dynasty*, ch. 5, esp. pp. 116–119.

39. All levels below the code were preserved only in their Japanese adaptations. See Twitchett, "The Fragment of the T'ang Ordinances of the Department of Waterways Discovered at Tun-huang"; Twitchett, "A Note on the Tunhuang Fragments of the T'ang Regulations"; Inoue, "The *Ritsuryō* System in Japan."

40. Wechsler, "The Founding of the T'ang Dynasty," pp. 178–179; Wechsler, "T'ai-tsung," pp. 206–207; Twitchett and Wechsler, "Kao-tsung and the Empress Wu," pp. 273–274; Twitchett, "Hsüan-tsung," pp. 354–355, 414–415. For an early collection of legal cases that describe court-room proceedings, see van Gulik, *T'ang-yin-pi-shih: Parallel Cases from under the Pear-tree*. For an example of deciding a case, see Wallacker, "The Poet as Jurist: Po Chü-I and a Case of Conjugal Homicide."

41. Johnson, *The T'ang Code*, vol. 1, pp. 14–17; McKnight, *The Quality of Mercy*, ch. 3.

42. Johnson, *The T'ang Code*, vol. 1, pp. 17–21. On theft, see *The T'ang Code*, vol. 2, p. 6, articles 270–280.

43. Johnson, *The T'ang Code*, vol. 1, pp. 23–29.

44. On hierarchy in the codes, see Johnson, *The T'ang Code*, vol. 2, pp. 9–11.

45. Johnson, *The T'ang Code*, vol. 2, p. 4.

46. Des Rotours, *Traité des Fonctionnaires et Traité de l'Armée, tr. de La Nouvelle Histoire des T'ang (chap. XLVI–L)*.

47. On the pre-Tang forms, see Crowell, "Government Land Policies and Systems in Early Imperial China," pp. 303–308; Xiong, *Emperor Yang of the Sui Dynasty*, pp. 180–182; Wright, "The Sui Dynasty," pp. 93–96. On the Tang system, see Xiong, "The Land-Tenure System of T'ang China."

48. Twitchett, *Financial Administration under the T'ang Dynasty*, pp. 1–11;

Twitchett, "Introduction," pp. 24–28; Twitchett, "Lands under State Cultivation during the T'ang Dynasty."

49. Twitchett, *Financial Administration under the T'ang Dynasty,* pp. 24–26.

50. Ibid., pp. 28–34.

51. Ibid., pp. 16–23.

3. Warlords and Monopolists

1. Peterson, "P'u-ku Huai-en and the T'ang Court"; Peterson, "Court and Province," pp. 474–486, 490–491; Dalby, "Court Politics in Late T'ang Times," pp. 561–567, 569–570. On Pugu Huaien's diplomatic role, see Peterson, "Court and Province," p. 483; Dalby, "Court Politics," p. 567.

2. Mackerras, "The Uighurs"; Mackerras, *The Uighur Empire According to the Tang Dynastic Histories;* de la Vaissière, *Sogdian Traders,* pp. 215–225, 306–309; Peterson, "Court and Province," pp. 480, 483–484; Graff, *Medieval Chinese Warfare,* pp. 221–222, 227–228; Dalby, "Court Politics," pp. 565, 567–569, 677–678 (on the Tang loss of pasturelands to Tibet and reliance on the Uighur horse trade).

3. Pulleyblank, "The An Lu-shan Rebellion and the Origins of Chronic Militarism," pp. 45, 55; Graff, *Medieval Chinese Warfare,* p. 222, 229; Dalby, "Court Politics," pp. 566–567.

4. Dalby, "Court Politics," pp. 567–568; Pulleyblank, "The An Lu-shan Rebellion and the Origins of Chronic Militarism," pp. 47–50; Peterson, "Court and Province," pp. 484–485, 493–494.

5. Dalby, "Court Politics," pp. 571–574, 576, 578–579; Peterson, "Court and Province," pp. 512–514; Graff, *Medieval Chinese Warfare,* pp. 233, 243.

6. Dalby, "Court Politics," pp. 574–576; Twitchett, *Financial Administration under the T'ang Dynasty,* chs. 3, 6; Twitchett, "The Salt Commissioners after the Rebellion of An Lu-shan."

7. Twitchett, *Financial Administration,* ch. 2, esp. pp. 34–48, 157–164; Peterson, "Court and Province," pp. 498–500.

8. Dalby, "Court Politics," pp. 582–586; Graff, *Medieval Chinese Warfare,* pp. 235–236; Peterson, "Court and Province," pp. 500–507. On the career of Lu Zhi, see Twitchett, "Lu Chih (754–805): Imperial Adviser and Court Official"; Chiu-Duke, *To Rebuild the Empire: Lu Chih's Confucian Pragmatist Approach to the Mid-T'ang Predicament;* McMullen, *State and Scholars in T'ang China,* pp. 239–243.

9. Dalby, "Court Politics," pp. 586–589, 598–599; Peterson, "Court and Province," pp. 512–514.

10. Dalby, "Court Politics," pp. 586–589, 594–598; Chiu-Duke, *To Rebuild the Empire,* pp. 34–61.

11. Peterson, "Court and Province," pp. 509, 511–512; Dalby, "Court Politics," pp. 593, 594, 600–601, 633; Peterson, "The Restoration Completed: Em-

peror Hsien-tsung and the Provinces," pp. 153–154; Somers, "The End of the T'ang," pp. 687, 703, 754.

12. Dalby, "Court Politics," pp. 607–611.

13. Peterson, "Court and Province," pp. 522–535; Dalby, "Court Politics," pp. 611–616; Graff, *Medieval Chinese Warfare,* pp. 326–328; Peterson, "The Restoration Completed"; Peterson, "Regional Defense against the Central Power."

14. Peterson, "Court and Province," pp. 499, 526–527; Dalby, "Court Politics," pp. 616–619.

15. Peterson, "Court and Province," pp. 535–537, 554–555; Dalby, "Court Politics," pp. 619–620.

16. Peterson, "Court and Province," pp. 535, 544–545; Dalby, "Court Politics," pp. 623, 633–636.

17. Peterson, "Court and Province," pp. 538–541, 547–552; Dalby, "Court Politics," pp. 636–638; Reischauer, *Ennin's Travels in T'ang China,* ch. 7, esp. pp. 270–271; Ennin, *Ennin's Diary,* year 845, XI, 3.

18. All Chinese accounts of the period are dominated by this theme. In English, see Dalby, "Court Politics," pp. 639–654; Mair, "Scroll Presentation in the T'ang Dynasty."

19. Dalby, "Court Politics," pp. 640–641. On the examinations and patronage, see Herbert, *Examine the Honest, Appraise the Able,* pp. 27–31, 91–106; McMullen, *State and Scholars in T'ang China,* pp. 61–66.

20. Dalby, "Court Politics," pp. 645–654.

21. Moore, *Rituals of Recruitment in T'ang China,* pp. 91–100, 141–149, 161–163, 181–182, 198–218; Moore, "The Ceremony of Gratitude," pp. 211–212, 220–236; Des Rotours, *La Traité des Examens,* pp. 198–205. On the symbolism of the bowl and robe, see Kieschnick, *The Impact of Buddhism on Chinese Material Culture,* pp. 103–112.

22. Dalby, "Court Politics," pp. 654–659.

23. Ibid., pp. 659–669. On the suppression of Buddhism under Wuzong, see Chen, "The Economic Background of the Hui-ch'ang Suppression of Buddhism"; Ch'en, *Buddhism in China,* pp. 226–233; Weinstein, *Buddhism under the T'ang,* pp. 114–136.

24. Somers, "End of the T'ang," pp. 684–692, 729; Graff, *Medieval Chinese Warfare,* pp. 241–242.

25. Somers, "End of the T'ang," pp. 695–700, 727–750, 756–762; Yates, *Washing Silk,* pp. 8–17. For a poetic account by Wei Zhuang (836–910) of the sack of Chang'an, see Yates, *Washing Silk,* pp. 108–122. See also Graff, *Medieval Chinese Warfare,* pp. 242–243; Wang, "The Middle Yangtse in T'ang Politics," pp. 220–226.

26. Somers, "End of the T'ang," pp. 720–726; Peterson, "Court and Province," pp. 543, 559–560.

27. Somers, "End of the T'ang," pp. 702–712, 714–717, 730–741, 744–745, 748–750, 754–755. On suspicion between the court and its commanders in the late Tang, see also Pulleyblank, "The An Lu-shan Rebellion and the Origins of Chronic Militarism," pp. 54–60; Graff, *Medieval Chinese Warfare*, pp. 233–234; Wang, *The Structure of Power in North China During the Five Dynasties*, pp. 17–19.

28. For the peripatetic lives of the late Tang rulers, see Somers, "End of the T'ang," pp. 748–750, 754–755, 766–781; Yates, *Washing Silk*, pp. 17–35; Graff, *Medieval Chinese Warfare*, pp. 242–244.

29. Twitchett, "Varied Patterns of Provincial Autonomy," pp. 91–93.

30. Twitchett, "Varied Patterns of Provincial Autonomy," pp. 94–95.

31. Pulleyblank, "The An Lu-shan Rebellion and the Origins of Chronic Militarism," pp. 53–56.

32. Somers, "End of the T'ang," pp. 762–781.

33. Twitchett, "Provincial Autonomy and Central Finance in Late T'ang"; Twitchett, "Varied Patterns of Provincial Autonomy," pp. 98–99; Graff, *Medieval Chinese Warfare*, pp. 229–230.

34. Pulleyblank, *The Background of the Rebellion of An Lu-shan*, ch. 6; Pulleyblank, "The An Lu-shan Rebellion and the Origins of Chronic Militarism," pp. 50–53; Chen, "Lun Sui mo Tang chu suowei 'Shandong haojie'"; Chen, "Lun Tang dai zhi fanjiang yu fubing," pp. 671–674; Chen, *Tang dai zhengzhi shi shulun gao*, pp. 170–172, 178–200; Shi, *Tang dai lishi dili yanjiu*, pp. 468–495.

35. Twitchett, "Varied Patterns of Provincial Autonomy," pp. 99–100; Shi, *Huangtu gaoyuan*, pp. 548–579; Peterson, "Court and Province," pp. 494–495.

36. Twitchett, "Varied Patterns of Provincial Autonomy," pp. 100–101. On the difference between the middle and lower Yangzi, see Wang, "The Middle Yangtse in T'ang Politics," pp. 194–195, 203–204, 208–220.

37. Peterson, "Court and Province," pp. 497–500, 509–510, 516–521; Wang, *Structure of Power in North China During the Five Dynasties*, pp. 14–16. On non-payment of taxes by loyal provinces, see Nunome, *Chūgoku no rekishi*, vol. 4, *Zui Tō teikoku*, pp. 333–334.

38. Peterson, "Court and Province," pp. 514–516, 540–543, 552; Graff, *Medieval Chinese Warfare*, pp. 231–233, 238–241, 244.

39. Nunome, *Chūgoku no rekishi*, vol. 4, *Zui Tō teikoku*, pp. 324–332. See also McMullen, "The Cult of Ch'i T'ai-kung and T'ang Attitudes to the Military."

40. Wang, *Structure of Power in North China During the Five Dynasties*, pp. 51–54, 65–72, 77, 94–97, 101–104, 143–148, 158–164, 169–171, 187–188, 205–207; Lorge, *War, Politics and Society in Early Modern China*, ch. 1; Davis, *Court and Family in Sung China*, pp. 8–9; Worthy, "The Founding of Sung China."

41. Nunome, *Chūgoku no rekishi,* vol. 4, pp. 414–422; Abramson, *Ethnic Identity,* pp. 155, 158.

42. Peterson, "Court and Province," pp. 515–516; Dalby, "Court Politics," p. 593; Somers, "End of the Tang," pp. 691, 729, 750–754.

43. Twitchett, *Financial Administration,* ch. 2.

44. Ibid., pp. 31–32, 34, 38, 40, 44–45, 52, 58, 62–65, 118, 122.

45. Ibid., pp. 49–62.

46. Ibid., ch. 6, esp. pp. 109–123; Twitchett, "The Salt Administrators after the Rebellion of An Lu-shan."

47. Twitchett, "Varied Patterns of Provincial Autonomy," pp. 103–105.

48. Hartwell, "Financial Expertise, Examinations, and the Formulation of Economic Policy in Northern Sung China"; Hartwell, "Demographic, Political, and Social Transformations of China, 750–1550," pp. 365–426.

49. Twitchett, *Financial Administration,* pp. 118–123.

50. Dalby, "Court Politics," p. 571; Abramson, *Ethnic Identity in Tang China,* p. 95; *Wen yuan ying hua* (Beijing: Zhongua, 1966), ch. 489, p. 2500a.

4. Urban Life

1. On the principles underlying the building of the city, and the tension between textual classicism and *fengshui,* see Xiong, *Sui-Tang Chang'an,* ch. 2. On the canonical inadequacy of Han Chang'an, see Lewis, *The Early Chinese Empires: Qin and Han,* ch. 2, section 2.

2. On the largely symbolic and ideological program in the site and structure of the city, see Kiang, *Cities of Aristocrats and Bureaucrats,* pp. 2–5. Such archaizing appeals to a vanished past as a means of superseding an unsatisfactory present had begun in the sixth century, when both the Liang dynasty in the south and the Zhou dynasty in the north had appealed to the classic *Rituals of Zhou* as a model for a strong state. See Pearce, "Form and Matter: Archaizing Reform in Sixth-Century China."

3. For a translation of the poem and comments on its problems, see Owen, *The Poetry of the Early T'ang,* pp. 54–56.

4. Shi, *Zhongguo gu du he wenhua,* pp. 451–453; Benn, *China's Golden Age,* p. 50; Wright, "The Sui Dynasty," pp. 79–80.

5. For detailed accounts of the Palace City and the Imperial City, see Xiong, *Sui-Tang Chang'an,* ch. 3, 5; Thilo, *Chang'an: Metropole Ostasiens und Weltstadt,* vol. 1, chs. 3–4.

6. Kiang, *Cities of Aristocrats and Bureaucrats,* p. 53n20. Actually scaling the walls of the Imperial City was punished with a three-year imprisonment. This rigorous separation of officials and populace was described by an Arab visitor in the ninth century. See Kiang, p. 1.

7. Kiang, *Cities of Aristocrats and Bureaucrats,* pp. 17–18; Benn, *China's Golden Age,* pp. 48–50; Shi, *Zhongguo gu du he wenhua,* pp. 454–458.

8. Thilo, *Chang'an*, vol. 1, pp. 107–112; Xiong, *Sui-Tang Chang'an*, pp. 208–210; Kiang, *Cities of Aristocrats and Bureaucrats*, pp. 39–40.

9. Kiang, *Cities of Aristocrats and Bureaucrats*, pp. 23–25; Benn, *China's Golden Age*, p. 51; Shi, *Zhongguo gu du he wenhua*, pp. 458–468.

10. Xiong, *Sui-Tang Chang'an*, pp. 211–214; Kiang, *Cities of Aristocrats and Bureaucrats*, pp. 25–27; Shi, *Zhongguo gu du he wenhua*, pp. 468–480.

11. Benn, *China's Golden Age*, pp. 51–52, 68–69; Xiong, *Sui-Tang Chang'an*, pp. 217–233, map 8.2; Thilo, *Chang'an*, vol. 2, pp. 130–139, 258–260.

12. Thilo, *Chang'an*, vol. 1, pp. 210–211; vol. 2, pp. 73–75, 80–84, 86–88; Abramson, *Ethnic Identity*, pp. 175–176.

13. Benn, *China's Golden Age*, p. 52.

14. Xiong, *Sui-Tang Chang'an*, ch. 9, map 9.1; Thilo, *Chang'an*, vol. 2, pp. 305–363; Shi, *Zhongguo gu du he wenhua*, pp. 480–490; Benn, *China's Golden Age*, pp. 59–64; Kohn, *Monastic Life in Medieval Daoism*, pp. 66–67. On Tang imperial princesses becoming Daoist nuns, see Benn, *The Cavern-Mystery Transmission*.

15. Owen, *The Great Age of Chinese Poetry*, p. 178.

16. Xiong, *Sui-Tang Chang'an*, ch. 6; Thilo, *Chang'an*, vol. 2, pp. 293–305. For an account of Tang rituals, see Wechsler, *Offerings of Jade and Silk*; McMullen, "Bureaucrats and Cosmology: The Ritual Code of T'ang China."

17. Xiong, *Sui-Tang Chang'an*, ch. 7; Benn, *China's Golden Age*, pp. 53–58; Kiang, *Cities of Aristocrats and Bureaucrats*, pp. 19–23; Thilo, *Chang'an*, vol. 2, pp. 260–280.

18. Although some modern scholars have attempted to equate these lanes with later trade associations or guilds (also called "hang"), evidence suggests that they were simply regulated lines of shops. On the importance of these lines of shops in early imperial markets, see Lewis, *The Early Chinese Empires: Qin and Han*, ch. 3. For an assessment of their status in the Sui and Tang, see Xiong, *Sui-Tang Chang'an*, pp. 174–179; Katō, "On the Hang or Association of Merchants in China."

19. Xiong, *Sui-Tang Chang'an*, pp. 166–168. Page 168 has a table showing the years in which the markets existed.

20. Xiong, *Sui-Tang Chang'an*, pp. 183–192; Benn, *China's Golden Age*, pp. 56–57.

21. Cited in Bingham, *Founding of the T'ang Dynasty*, p. 14.

22. Kiang, *Cities of Aristocrats and Bureaucrats*, pp. 29–33; Xiong, *Emperor Yang of the Sui Dynasty*, ch. 4; Shi, *Zhongguo gu du he wenhua*, pp. 493–539. On the contrast in the markets, see pp. 507–509.

23. For literary references to the names of the pleasure districts in Han dynasty Chang'an and Luoyang, see Mather, *The Poet Shen Yüeh*, p. 81.

24. There are two translations of the *Record*: Levy, "Records of the Gay Quarters"; and des Rotours, *Courtisanes Chinoises à la fin des T'ang*. The latter is much better annotated and more accurate. For accounts of the text and the soci-

ety that it chronicles, see Benn, *China's Golden Age,* pp. 64–67; Rouzer, *Articulated Ladies,* ch. 7; Xiong, "*Ji*-Entertainers in Tang Chang'an," pp. 152–160; Levy, "The Gay Quarters of Chang-an"; Thilo, *Chang'an,* vol. 2, pp. 67–71.

25. Reed, *A Tang Miscellany,* p. 110. On Yu Xuanji, see Idema and Grant, *The Red Brush,* pp. 189–195; van Gulik, *Sexual Life in Ancient China,* pp. 172–175.

26. Dudbridge, *The Tale of Li Wa;* Rouzer, *Articulated Ladies,* pp. 240–247; Dai, "Notes sur le Li-wa-tchouan."

27. Cited in Rouzer, *Articulated Ladies,* pp. 271–273. On the Tang practice of setting poems to music, see Rouzer, *Writing Another's Dream,* ch. 2.

28. Rouzer, *Articulated Ladies,* pp. 243, 263; Moore, *Rituals of Recruitment in Tang China,* ch. 7. On the Apricot Garden, see pp. 254, 259, 263–265. On the sharing of anecdotes by Sun Qi and Wang Dingbao, see p. 248.

29. Cited in Rouzer, *Articulated Ladies,* p. 274.

30. Moore, *Rituals of Recruitment in Tang China,* pp. 252–254.

31. Yates, *Washing Silk,* p. 235. For similar images to describe successful candidates, compare the poem on pp. 162–163.

32. Rouzer, *Articulated Ladies,* pp. 252–265, 275–281.

33. Levy, *Translations from Po Chü-yi's Collected Works,* vol. 1, p. 130. For an extended work attributed to Bo Juyi on the pleasure quarters, see vol. 2, pp. 18–20.

34. Xiong, "*Ji*-Entertainers in Tang Chang'an," pp. 150–152. On the female performers of transformation texts, see Mair, *T'ang Transformation Texts,* pp. 152–156. On acrobats, see Benn, *China's Golden Age,* pp. 159–160.

35. Owen, *The Great Age of Chinese Poetry,* pp. 130, 301; Sun, *Li Po: A New Translation,* pp. 132, 198, 240–242, 244, 248, 326; Yates, *Washing Silk,* pp. 96, 166–167; Owen, *The Late Tang,* pp. 241–243 (a set of poems on a popular erotic dance), 264–266, 269–270, 272–277, 290, 293, 310–311, 313, 321, 528–529, 551–552. For the anecdote, see Owen, *The Great Age of Chinese Poetry,* pp. 91–94.

36. Thilo, *Chang'an,* vol. 2, pp. 506–509.

37. Goody, *The Culture of Flowers,* pp. 358–359. On the anthology, see Shields, *Crafting a Collection: The Cultural Contexts and Poetic Practice of the Huajian ji.* On the erotics of flowers in China, see Barnhart, *Peach Blossom Spring: Gardens and Flowers in Chinese Paintings,* pp. 84–85.

38. Thilo, *Chang'an,* vol. 2, p. 551.

39. Goody, *Culture of Flowers,* pp. 368–369. On the peony craze, see Schafer, "The Last Years of Ch'ang-an," p. 152. On the peony's nickname, see Bartholomew, "Botanical Puns in Chinese Art from the Collection of the Asian Art Museum of San Francisco," pp. 23–24.

40. Thilo, *Chang'an,* vol. 1, p. 254; vol. 2, pp. 551–553.

41. Goody, *The Culture of Flowers,* p. 386n149.

42. Thilo, *Chang'an*, vol. 2, p. 258; Chen, *Images and Ideas in Chinese Classical Prose*, p. 99.

43. Goody, *The Culture of Flowers*, pp. 385–386.

44. On the distinction between trade in the markets and that outside, see Xiong, *Sui-Tang Chang'an*, pp. 179–192.

45. Twitchett, "The Tang Market System," pp. 230–232; Kiang, *Cities of Aristocrats and Bureaucrats*, p. 71.

46. Kiang, *Cities of Aristocrats and Bureaucrats*, p. 72; Benn, *China's Golden Age*, pp. 48–49.

47. Twitchett, "The T'ang Market System," p. 232–233; Kiang, *Cities of Aristocrats and Bureaucrats*, pp. 71–72.

48. Kiang, *Cities of Aristocrats and Bureaucrats*, pp. 72–83; Shi, *Tang dai lishi dili yanjiu*, pp. 234–249, 314–318.

49. Reischauer, *Ennin's Diary*, pp. 16–20, 23. Remarks on the night markets and lanterns of Jiangdu by Du Mu, Wang Jian, and Li Shen are quoted in Kiang, *Cities of Aristocrats and Bureaucrats*, p. 82.

50. Shi, *Tang dai lishi dili yanjiu*, pp. 324–326; Kiang, *Cities of Aristocrats and Bureaucrats*, p. 82.

51. On Kaifeng, see Kiang, *Cities of Aristocrats and Bureaucrats*, pp. 87–90; Shi, *Tang dai lishi dili yanjiu*, pp. 319–321. On Chengdu and Sichuan, see Shi, *Tang dai lishi dili yanjiu*, pp. 330–333; Yan, "Tang Wu Dai shiqi de Chengdu." For the poem on Damask City, see Yates, *Washing Silk*, p. 195. For other poems on the city, see pp. 227, 228.

52. Twitchett, *Financial Administration under the T'ang Dynasty*, pp. 52, 58, 118, 122–123; Twitchett, "Merchant, Trade and Government in Late T'ang," pp. 78–80; Twitchett, "The T'ang Market System," pp. 240–242; Sen, *Buddhism, Diplomacy, and Trade*, pp. 153–154.

53. Hou, *Monnaies d'offrande et la notion de trésorerie dans la religion Chinoise*, pp. 3–17; Dudbridge, *Religious Experience and Lay Society in T'ang China*, pp. 54–55, 94–97, 99, 101, 106.

54. Elvin, *Pattern of the Chinese Past*, ch. 11.

55. Ibid., pp. 172–174.

5. Rural Society

1. Han, *Sui Tang Wu dai shi gang*, pp. 158–161, 167–169, 291; Wang, *Sui Tang Wu dai shi*, pp. 252–254, 270–272; Elvin, *The Pattern of the Chinese Past*, pp. 61–63.

2. Han, *Sui Tang Wu dai shi gang*, pp. 164–166; Wang, *Sui Tang Wu dai shi*, pp. 230, 301.

3. Pulleyblank, *The Background of the Rebellion of An Lu-shan*, pp. 29–32.

4. Han, *Sui Tang Wu dai shi gang*, pp. 289–291.

5. Nunome, *Chūgoku no rekishi,* vol. 4, *Zui Tō teikoku,* pp. 297–298; Schafer, "Tang," pp. 89–90, 92–93; Needham and Bray, *Agriculture,* p. 461.

6. Gernet, *Buddhism in Chinese Society,* pp. 142–150; Ch'en, *The Chinese Transformation of Buddhism,* pp. 151–156.

7. Nunome, *Chūgoku no rekishi,* vol. 4, *Zui Tō teikoku,* pp. 298–299; Gernet, *Buddhism in Chinese Society,* pp. 145–146; Han, *Sui Tang Wu dai shi gang,* pp. 159, 164, 304.

8. Han, *Sui Tang Wu dai shi gang,* p. 298.

9. Wang, *Sui Tang Wu dai shi,* pp. 307–310; Elvin, *The Pattern of the Chinese Past,* pp. 80–82.

10. Reischauer, tr., *Ennin's Diary,* pp. 202–203.

11. Wang, *Sui Tang Wu dai shi,* p. 308.

12. Ibid., p. 312.

13. Owen, *The Great Age of Chinese Poetry,* pp. 31–32; Owen, *An Anthology of Chinese Literature,* pp. 392–395.

14. Needham and Bray, *Agriculture,* pp. 245–251.

15. Li, *Tang dai Jiangnan nongye de fazhan,* p. 95.

16. Elvin, *The Pattern of the Chinese Past,* pp. 119–120; Li, *Tang dai Jiangnan nongye de fazhan,* p. 95; Needham and Bray, *Agriculture,* pp. 289–298.

17. Li, *Tang dai Jiangnan nongye de fazhan,* pp. 50–51, 90–93.

18. Needham and Bray, *Agriculture,* pp. 171, 180–185; Elvin, *The Pattern of the Chinese Past,* pp. 118–119; Li, *Tang dai Jiangnan nongye de fazhan,* pp. 88–95.

19. Needham and Bray, *Agriculture,* pp. 111, 499.

20. Elvin, *The Pattern of the Chinese Past,* p. 119; Needham and Bray, *Agriculture,* pp. 223–229, 234–236.

21. Li, *Tang dai Jiangnan nongye de fazhan,* p. 89.

22. Elvin, *The Pattern of the Chinese Past,* pp. 121–123; Li, *Tang dai Jiangnan nongye de fazhan,* pp. 95–97; Needham and Bray, *Agriculture,* pp. 426, 465, 491–495.

23. Elvin, *The Pattern of the Chinese Past,* pp. 122–123.

24. Needham and Bray, *Agriculture,* pp. 109–111.

25. Ibid., pp. 110–111, 113–121; Elvin, *The Pattern of the Chinese Past,* p. 125.

26. Needham and Bray, *Agriculture,* pp. 123–126; Li, *Tang dai Jiangnan nongye de fazhan,* pp. 75, 85.

27. Li, *Tang dai Jiangnan nongye de fazhan,* pp. 73–86.

28. Needham and Wang, *Science and Civilisation in China,* vol. 4, *Physics and Physical Technology,* pt. 2: *Mechanical Engineering,* pp. 330–362; Elvin, *The Pattern of the Chinese Past,* pp. 126–127.

29. Elvin, *The Pattern of the Chinese Past,* pp. 113–116.

30. Li, *Tang dai Jiangnan nongye de fazhan,* pp. 129–141.

31. Elvin, *The Pattern of the Chinese Past,* pp. 128–129.

32. Ibid., pp. 131–133.

33. Ibid., p. 134. Passage quoted is on this page.

34. Ibid., pp. 139–144.

35. Twitchett, "The T'ang Market System," pp. 233–234; Twitchett, "Merchant, Trade and Government in Late T'ang," p. 77.

36. Twitchett, "The T'ang Market System," pp. 234–237.

37. Ibid., pp. 235–236. On the hierarchy of market centers, see the articles by William Skinner cited in ch. 1, note 1.

38. Twitchett, "The T'ang Market System," pp. 238–239.

39. Ibid., pp. 240–241.

40. Needham and Huang, *Science and Civilisation in China,* vol. 6, *Biology and Biological Technology,* pt. 5: *Fermentations and Food Science,* pp. 503–519; Needham and Bray, *Agriculture,* pp. 428–429; Kieschnick, *The Impact of Buddhism on Chinese Material Culture,* pp. 262–265; Needham and Daniels, *Agro-Industries,* pp. 477–478.

41. Kieschnick, *The Impact of Buddhism on Chinese Material Culture,* pp. 262–275; Needham and Huang, *Fermentations and Food Science,* p. 515.

42. Kieschnick, *The Impact of Buddhism on Chinese Material Culture,* pp. 265–266; Needham and Huang, *Fermentations and Food Science,* pp. 515–517.

43. Kieschnick, *The Impact of Buddhism on Chinese Material Culture,* p. 265; Wang, *Tea and Chinese Culture,* pp. 21–22; Needham and Bray, *Agriculture,* pp. 17–20. On large numbers of merchants specializing in the tea trade, see Dudbridge, *Religious Experience and Lay Society in T'ang China,* p. 88.

44. Needham and Huang, *Fermentations and Food Science,* pp. 519–523, 555–557.

45. Needham and Bray, *Agriculture,* pp. 426, 601–602; Mazumdar, *Sugar and Society in China,* ch. 1. For a complete treatment of the history and technology of Chinese sugar manufacture, see Needham and Daniels, *Agro-Industries: Sugarcane Technology.*

46. Mazumdar, *Sugar and Society in China,* pp. 20–28, 123–126, 193–194; Kieschnick, *The Impact of Buddhism on Chinese Material Culture,* pp. 249–262.

6. The Outer World

1. Wechsler, "The Founding of the T'ang Dynasty: Kao-tsu," pp. 150–152; Barfield, *The Perilous Frontier,* pp. 139–140, 141–142; Pan, *Son of Heaven and Heavenly Qaghan,* pp. 180–181, 181–182.

2. Pan, *Son of Heaven and Heavenly Qaghan,* pp. 133–138, 166, 171–176.

3. Barfield, *The Perilous Frontier,* pp. 132–138, describes the structure of this first Turkish empire and traces the series of succession disputes that plagued it.

4. Pan, *Son of Heaven and Heavenly Qaghan*, pp. 167–170, 172–173, 176; Barfield, *The Perilous Frontier*, pp. 139, 140–144; Graff, *Medieval Chinese Warfare*, pp. 185–186.

5. Graff, *Medieval Chinese Warfare*, pp. 186–188.

6. Ibid., pp. 175–176; Barfield, *The Perilous Frontier*, p. 141.

7. Barfield, *The Perilous Frontier*, pp. 139–144; Pan, *Son of Heaven and Heavenly Qaghan*, p. 181.

8. The quotation is in Pan, *Son of Heaven and Heavenly Qaghan*, p. 182; Pulleyblank, "The An Lu-shan Rebellion and the Origins of Chronic Militarism," pp. 37–38.

9. Pan, *Son of Heaven and Heavenly Qaghan*, pp. 180–181, 287–296.

10. Ibid., pp. 197–202.

11. Ibid., pp. 190–197; Barfield, *The Perilous Frontier*, pp. 145–146; Graff, *Medieval Chinese Warfare*, p. 195.

12. Barfield, *The Perilous Frontier*, pp. 145–146.

13. Graff, *Medieval Chinese Warfare*, pp. 205–207; Barfield, *The Perilous Frontier*, pp. 147–150; Pan, *Son of Heaven and Heavenly Qaghan*, ch. 8.

14. Wang, *Ambassadors from the Islands of Immortals*, ch. 2; Holcombe, *The Genesis of East Asia*, pp. 53–60.

15. Pan, *Son of Heaven and Heavenly Qaghan*, ch. 6; Holcombe, *The Genesis of East Asia*, ch. 7.

16. The most detailed account is Wang, *Ambassadors from the Islands of Immortals*. See also Holcombe, *The Genesis of East Asia*, pp. 79–83, ch. 8.

17. Holcombe, *The Genesis of East Asia*, ch. 6, esp. pp. 156–164.

18. Backus, *The Nan-chao Kingdom and T'ang China's Southwestern Frontier*, ch. 3, pp. 78–81.

19. Holcombe, *The Genesis of East Asia*, pp. 94–108.

20. Ibid., pp. 60–77.

21. Ibid., pp. 38–52.

22. Pan, *Son of Heaven and Heavenly Qaghan*, chs. 6, 8.

23. Beckwith, *The Tibetan Empire in Central Asia*, ch. 2; Pan, *Son of Heaven and Heavenly Qaghan*, ch.7; Sen, *Buddhism, Diplomacy, and Trade*, pp. 16–34. For a translation of Xuanzang's account of his journey through Central Asia and northern India, see Xuanzang, *The Great Tang Dynasty Record of the Western Regions*.

24. Beckwith, *The Tibetan Empire in Central Asia*, pp. 143–156; Pan, *Son of Heaven and Heavenly Qaghan*, chs. 9–10; Backus, *The Nan-chao Kingdom and T'ang China's Southwestern Frontier*, pp. 77–81.

25. Drompp, *Tang China and the Collapse of the Uighur Empire*, provides a detailed study of the causes of the Uighur collapse and the Chinese response.

26. Beckwith, *The Tibetan Empire in Central Asia*, pp. 155–158, 163–172; Pan, *Son of Heaven and Heavenly Qaghan*, pp. 337–344; Backus, *The Nan-chao Kingdom*, pp. 98–100.

27. Backus, *The Nan-chao Kingdom*, ch. 6.

28. Beckwith, *The Tibetan Empire in Central Asia*, chs. 3, 5, and pp. 87–90, 93–97, 147–148, 152, 157–163.

29. Drompp, *Tang China and the Collapse of the Uighur Empire*, ch. 7; Sen, *Buddhism, Diplomacy, and Trade*, ch. 2–3.

30. Schafer, *The Golden Peaches of Samarkand*, pp. 13–14; Sen, *Buddhism, Diplomacy, and Trade*, pp. 212–213.

31. Sen, *Buddhism, Diplomacy, and Trade*. The reconfiguration of the Sino-Indian trade after the fall of the Tang is described in chs. 4–5.

32. Liu, *Ancient India and Ancient China: Trade and Religious Exchanges*, AD 1–600; Sen, *Buddhism, Diplomacy, and Trade*, pp. 37–44, 102–110, 160–165, 169–176, 185–192, 203–211, 237–240.

33. Sen, *Buddhism, Diplomacy, and Trade*, pp. 165–167. On the axiomatic wealth of Persians, see Abramson, *Ethnic Identity*, p. 20.

34. Schafer, *The Golden Peaches of Samarkand*, pp. 11–13.

35. Needham, Wang, and Lu, *Science and Civilisation in China*, vol. 4, *Physics and Physical Technology*, pt. 3: *Civil Engineering and Nautics*, pp. 458–460; Hourani, *Arab Seafaring in the Indian Ocean in Ancient and Early Medieval Times*, pp. 88–95.

36. Sen, *Buddhism, Diplomacy, and Trade*, pp. 182–185.

37. Hartwell, "Foreign Trade, Monetary Policy and Chinese 'Mercantilism,'" pp. 453–488; Clark, *Community, Trade, and Networks: Southern Fujian Province from the Third to the Thirteenth Century*, chs. 5–6.

38. Wallerstein, *The Modern World-System*, pp. 15–17. The details of the theory are worked out through three volumes published between 1974 and 1988. The model is also elaborated in Wallerstein, "The Rise and Future Demise of the World Capitalist System." The cited definition is elaborated on pp. 5–6. See also Frank, *ReOrient: Global Economy in the Asian Age*; Frank and Gillis, "The 5,000-Year World System"; Adshead, *T'ang China: The Rise of the East in World History*; Adshead, *China in World History*, chs. 2–3. The most useful treatment is Abu-Lughod, *Before European Hegemony*. China is discussed in detail in chapter 10, and the world system of the period and its decline synthesized in chapter 11. A good synopsis focused on China is Sen, *Buddhism, Diplomacy, and Trade*, pp. 197–202.

39. Wright and Twitchett, "Introduction," p. 1. The most detailed consideration of the place of foreigners in Tang China, or more accurately within Tang thinking, is Abramson, *Ethnic Identity in Tang China*.

40. Schafer, *The Golden Peaches*, pp. 25–28.

41. Schafer, *The Golden Peaches*. Attitudes to foreigners are sketched on pp. 22–25.

42. Cited in Abramson, *Ethnic Identity*, pp. 86–87. On the *Comprehensive Institutions* and its ideas about China and the outer world, see McMullen, *State and Scholars*, pp. 203–205.

43. Schafer, *The Golden Peaches,* pp. 11–13.

44. Holcombe, *The Genesis of East Asia,* pp. 87–89, 153–154, 158–159; Schafer, *The Golden Peaches,* pp. 14–16.

45. Schafer, *The Golden Peaches,* pp. 17–19; Shi, *Tang dai lishi dili yanjiu,* pp. 234–249.

46. Benn, *China's Golden Age,* pp. 53–56; Schafer, *The Golden Peaches,* p. 20; Pan, *Son of Heaven and Heavenly Qaghan,* pp. 296–301.

47. Schafer, *The Golden Peaches,* pp. 50–57; Owen, *An Anthology of Chinese Literature,* pp. 455–456; Abramson, *Ethnic Identity,* pp. 20–21. On types of dancing in Tang China, see Benn, *China's Golden Age,* pp. 167–169.

48. On the introduction of Tantrism and its limits, as an aspect of Chinese foreign relations, see Sen, *Buddhism, Diplomacy, and Trade,* ch. 3. The best evidence of the scale and regularity of foreign pilgrimages is Reischauer, tr., *Ennin's Diary.* On pilgrims from India, see Sen, *Buddhism, Diplomacy, and Trade,* pp. 79–86.

49. The most thorough discussion of Buddhism as a foreign faith in the Tang is Abramson, *Ethnic Identity,* ch. 3.

50. Cited in ibid., pp. 59–60.

51. Cited in ibid., pp. 65–66.

52. Benn, *Burning for the Buddha.*

53. Abramson, *Ethnic Identity,* pp. 72–75; Ch'en, *Buddhism in China,* pp. 231–232; Kieschnick, *The Eminent Monk,* ch. 2. On the links of distant places with magical powers, see Helms, *Ulysses' Sail,* and Helms, *Craft and the Kingly Art.*

7. Kinship

1. Ebrey, "Women, Marriage, and the Family," pp. 207–210, 216–221.

2. Wright, *The Sui Dynasty,* pp. 59, 64–65, 67, 71–73, 80–81, 89, 157–158; Xiong, *Emperor Yang of the Sui Dynasty,* pp. 22, 164; Tung, *Fables for the Patriarchs,* pp. 69, 97–98.

3. Wright, *The Sui Dynasty,* pp. 158, 163; Xiong, *Emperor Yang of the Sui Dynasty,* pp. 18–19, 23, 26, 255.

4. Tung, *Fables for the Patriarchs,* p. 59.

5. Guisso, "The Empress Wu, Chung-tsung, and Jui-tsung," pp. 326–328.

6. Rouzer, *Articulated Ladies,* ch. 5, esp. pp. 180–200.

7. Tung, *Fables for the Patriarchs,* ch. 2, "Fate of the Imperial Daughters." The full history of the Taihe Princess can be reconstructed from the narrative and documents in Drompp, *Tang China and the Collapse of the Uighur Empire,* the relevant pages of which are listed in the index entry on p. 362.

8. Tung, *Fables for the Patriarchs,* pp. 46–50.

9. Yen, *Family Instructions for the Yen Clan,* p. 20.

10. Ebrey, "Shifts in Marriage Finance from the Sixth to the Thirteenth Century," pp. 98–102.

11. Bo, "The Song of Lasting Regret," in Wang, ed., *Images of Women in Chinese Thought and Culture*, p. 424.

12. Ebrey, "Shifts in Marriage Finance," pp. 112–123; Tung, *Fables for the Patriarchs*, pp. 14, 220n20.

13. A useful survey is Karetzky, *Court Art of the Tang*. See illustrations 11–14, 26–28, 39, 43, 45–46, 70–71, 81, 85, 90, 93, 96–98, 107; Tung, *Fables for the Patriarchs*, cover, pp. 20–21, 27, 74, 85, 128, 142.

14. Song and Song, "The Analects for Women," in Wang, ed., *Images of Women in Chinese Thought and Culture*, pp. 327–340. The passage quoted is on p. 333. For a translation of Ban Zhao's work, see Wang, ed., *Images of Women in Chinese Thought and Culture*, pp. 177–188. For a partial translation of the *Canon of Women's Filial Piety*, see Ebrey, tr., "The *Book of Filial Piety for Women* Attributed to a Woman Née Zheng (ca. 730)." See also Tung, *Fables for the Patriarchs*, pp. 91–94.

15. Owen, *The End of the Chinese "Middle Ages,"* pp. 130–138.

16. Ebrey, "Concubines in Sung China"; Ebrey, *The Inner Quarters*, ch. 12.

17. Mair, *Tun-huang Popular Narratives*, pp. 96, 97.

18. Tung, *Fables for the Patriarchs*, pp. 94–97, 229n22.

19. On the ritual strictures, see Ebrey, "Concubines in Sung China," pp. 40–44. On concubines in Tang law, see "Concubines in Sung China," pp. 44–46. For translations of all the legal articles pertaining to concubines, see the entries listed in Johnson, tr., *The T'ang Code*, vol. 2, *Specific Articles*, p. 584.

20. Ebrey, "Concubines in Sung China," pp. 52–61.

21. Ibid., pp. 45, 60–61.

22. These women are studied together in Tung, *Fables for the Patriarchs*, ch. 3–4.

23. Wright, *The Sui Dynasty*, p. 157.

24. On the shrew in Chinese literature, see Wu, *The Chinese Virago*. For the Tang, see pp. 30, 33, 41, 43, 57–59, 61, 70–79, 82–86, 89–91. See also Tung, *Fables for the Patriarchs*, pp. 10, 48, 93–99, 105, 108, 143, 144, 215; Benn, *China's Golden Age*, p. 248.

25. Both cited in Tung, *Fables for the Patriarchs*, p. 98.

26. Ebrey, "Early Stages in the Development of Descent Group Organization," p. 21, including the quote. For a sketch of the Tang festival calendar, see Benn, *China's Golden Age*, pp. 149–154.

27. Johnson, *The Medieval Chinese Oligarchy*, p. 97.

28. Teiser, *The Ghost Festival*, pp. 48–56. On the mythic background of the story, see pp. 113–139.

29. Teiser, *The Ghost Festival*, pp. 87–91. For a complete translation, see Mair, *Tun-huang Popular Narratives*, pp. 87–121.

30. Mair, *T'ang Transformation Texts,* describes the genre, its origins, and its public performances.

31. On the mother-son tie in the story, see Teiser, *The Ghost Festival,* pp. 130–134, ch. 7. On later evolution, see Cole, *Mothers and Sons in Chinese Buddhism;* Lai, "Father in Heaven, Mother in Hell: Gender Politics in the Creation and Transformation of Mulian's Mother." On the figure of Mulian in contemporary Daoist rituals, see Lagerwey, *Taoist Ritual in Chinese Society and History,* ch. 13, "The Attack on Hell." For ritual visits to the underworld patterned on the story, see Ahern, *The Cult of the Dead in a Chinese Village,* pp. 228–244. On ritual plays, see Johnson, ed., *Ritual Opera, Operatic Ritual: "Mu-lien Rescues his Mother" in Chinese Popular Culture;* Johnson, "Mu-lien in Pao-chüan."

32. Mair, *Tun-huang Popular Narratives,* p. 93. Other passages on the inefficacy of conventional ancestor worship are on pp. 95–96, 97, 109, 110, 111 (sacrifice to ancestors as the crime of killing animals), 116. A passage on p. 102 even insists on the limited value of Buddhist good works for redeeming parents when conducted outside the Ghost Festival, that is, without the intervention of the assembled monks.

33. On Tang funerals and ideas about the afterlife, see Benn, *China's Golden Age,* ch. 12.

34. Teiser, *The Scripture on the Ten Kings,* ch. 16; Dudbridge, *Religious Experience and Lay Society,* pp. 51–52, 69.

35. Teiser, "The Growth of Purgatory," pp. 115, 117–118, 121–122, 128–132. Pages 125–128 cite evidence from the Song and Yuan dynasties.

36. Hou, *Monnaies d'offrande et la notion de trésorerie dans la religion chinoise,* pp. 5–6, 130. See also Brokaw, *The Ledgers of Merit and Demerit.*

37. Dudbridge, *Religious Experience and Lay Society,* pp. 104–116, 154–160; van Gulik, *Sexual Life in Ancient China,* pp. 208–210.

38. Dudbridge, *Religious Experience and Lay Society,* pp. 161–173. Notes on pp. 165–166 list the major studies on the practice in later periods. See also Benn, *China's Golden Age,* p. 244. Pages 243–248 describe marriage in Tang China.

39. In addition to pages cited in the preceding notes, see Dudbridge, "The Tale of Liu Yi and Its Analogues" on links between the two types of stories. For the parallel methods of enrichment by service to a god or sexual liaison with a fox, see "The Tale of Liu Yi and Its Analogues," p. 65; Shen Jiji, "Ren's Story," in Owen, ed., *Anthology of Chinese Literature,* pp. 523–524.

40. Wright, *The Sui Dynasty,* pp. 100–104; Ebrey, *The Aristocratic Families of Early Imperial China,* pp. 81–83.

41. Ebrey, *The Aristocratic Families of Early Imperial China,* pp. 55–81; Chen, *Liu Tsung-yüan and Intellectual Change in T'ang China,* pp. 33–40; Chiu-Duke, *To Rebuild the Empire,* ch. 1, esp. p. 20.

42. Johnson, "The Last Years of a Great Clan," pp. 18–20, 32–40, 47, 98–100.

43. Ebrey, *The Aristocratic Families of Early Imperial China*, pp. 85–88.

44. Twitchett, "Composition of the T'ang Ruling Class," pp. 50–51.

45. Ibid., pp. 61–62, 69–76.

46. Ibid., pp. 62–63; Ikeda, "Decline of the T'ang Aristocracy," pp. 36–38.

47. Twitchett, "Composition of the T'ang Ruling Class," pp. 63–67; Ikeda, "Decline of the T'ang Aristocracy," pp. 40–42.

48. On the ethnic use of genealogies, see Abramson, *Ethnic Identity*, pp. 150–156.

49. Lewis, *The Construction of Space*, pp. 296–300.

50. Ikeda, "Decline of the T'ang Aristocracy," pp. 44–49.

51. Ibid., p. 102; Johnson, *The Medieval Chinese Oligarchy*, pp. 134, 136, 138, 139, 140.

52. On Tang education, see McMullen, *State and Scholars in T'ang China*, ch. 1. On the educational predominance of the capital, see pp. 35–43.

53. Moore, *Rituals of Recruitment*, ch. 3, elaborates this point, and traces the first developments of local exams in the second half of the Tang.

54. On the creation of an "examination society" and the rituals that shaped it, see Moore, *Rituals of Recruitment*.

55. Ibid., pp. 139–152, 160.

56. Ibid., pp. 13–18, 153; McMullen, *State and Scholars*, pp. 39–40, 206–210, 213–217, 229–232, 241–244.

57. On the pivotal role of literary composition in the Tang elite, see McMullen, *State and Scholars*, ch. 6. On the extension of the "southern" model to the Tang court and thus to society at large, and the importance of literary celebrations at court, see pp. 212–217, 223–227.

58. Moore, *Rituals of Recruitment*, pp. 22–23.

59. Johnson, "Last Years of a Great Clan," p. 96–101. On the pivotal role of this combination of local bases with state service in allowing elites to survive dynastic collapse, see Lewis, *Writing and Authority*, "Conclusion."

8. Religion

1. Yamada, "The Lingbao School," pp. 230–238; Kohn, "The Northern Celestial Masters," p. 297.

2. Kirkland, *Taoism*, pp. 92–93; Robinet, *Taoism: Growth of a Religion*, pp. 194–211.

3. On Daoist links to the Tang founding, see Bokenkamp, "Time After Time: Taoist Apocalyptic History and the Founding of the T'ang Dynasty"; Kirkland, *Taoism*, pp. 152–153; Kohn and Kirkland, "Daoism in the Tang (618–907)," pp. 340–342; Reiter, *The Aspirations and Standards of Taoist Priests in the Early T'ang Period*, part 1.

4. Kohn and Kirkland, "Daoism in the Tang," pp. 341–342; Kirkland, "Di-

mensions of T'ang Taoism," pp. 86–88; Kirkland, *Taoism,* pp. 153–154; Kohn, *God of the Dao,* pp. 22–23, 311–328.

5. Barrett, *Taoism Under the T'ang,* pp. 29–45; Kohn and Kirkland, "Daoism in the Tang," pp. 342–345; Ch'en, *Chinese Transformation of Buddhism,* pp. 95–102.

6. Kirkland, *Taoism,* pp. 158–159; Kohn and Kirkland, "Daoism in the Tang," pp. 342–343; Kirkland, "Tales of Thaumaturgy: T'ang Accounts of the Wonder-Worker Yeh Fa-shan."

7. On the Daoist policies of Xuanzong, see Benn, "Taoism as Ideology in the Reign of Emperor Hsüan-tsung"; Benn, "Religious Aspects of Emperor Hsüan-tsung's Taoist Ideology." See also Kohn and Kirkland, "Daoism in the Tang," pp. 345–348, 369–370; Kirkland, *Taoism,* pp. 156–158. On Sima Chengzhen's thought, see Kohn, *Seven Steps to the Tao: Sima Chengzhen's "Zuowang Lun."* On Daoists at the high Tang court, see Kirkland, "Taoists of the High T'ang." On the *Jin lu zhai* ritual, see Benn, "Ordinations and *Zhai* Rituals," pp. 310–311, 320–321.

8. Kohn and Kirkland, "Daoism in the Tang," p. 349; Chen, Chen, and Zeng, eds., *Daojia jin shi lüe,* pp. 186–192. On the symbolism of the black sheep in relation to Laozi, and the myth of Yin Xi, see Kohn, *God of the Dao,* pp. 255–289.

9. The Daoist poetry of Tang China is the topic of numerous works by Edward H. Schafer. See *Mirages on the Sea of Time: The Taoist Poetry of Ts'ao T'ang;* "The Capeline Cantos: Verses on the Divine Loves of Taoist Priestesses"; "Wu Yün's 'Cantos on Pacing the Void'"; "Wu Yün's Stanzas on 'Saunters in Sylphdom'"; *Mao Shan in T'ang Times.*

10. Kohn and Kirkland, "Daoism in the Tang," pp. 348–351, 373–375. On Daoist miracle collections, see Verellen, "Evidential Miracles in Support of Taoism." On the rising role of Daoist magic in local communities, see Dudbridge, *Religious Experience and Lay Society,* pp. 72–75.

11. Verellen, *Du Guangting (850–933): Taoiste de cour à la fin de la Chine médiévale.* In English, see Bell, "Du Kuang-t'ing"; Barrett, *Taoism Under the T'ang,* pp. 94–98; Kohn, "Taoist Scholasticism"; Cahill, *Divine Traces of the Daoist Sisterhood,* pp. 12–14.

12. Cahill, *Divine Traces of the Daoist Sisterhood,* pp. 12–20. The biographies of Tang saints are translated with commentary on pp. 103–193. See also Despeux and Kohn, *Women in Daoism,* pp. 118–133; Baptandier, *The Lady of Linshui.*

13. Despeux, "Women in Daoism," pp. 388–390. On the ordination of the two princesses, see Benn, *The Cavern-Mystery Transmission.* For poems dedicated to the princesses, see Cahill, *Transcendence and Divine Passion,* pp. 216–218. On accounts of the liberated lives of imperial princesses, see Tung, *Fables for the Patriarchs,* ch. 2. On Yang Guifei as a posthumous priestess in Bo Juyi's poem, see "The Song of Lasting Regret," tr. Paul Kroll, in Wang, ed., *Images of Women in Chinese Thought and Culture,* p. 428.

14. See examples translated in Wang, ed., *Images of Women in Chinese Thought and Culture*, pp. 308–315.

15. Kirkland, *Taoism*, pp. 139–143; Cahill, *Divine Traces of the Daoist Sisterhood*, pp. 119–126, 186–193; Despeux, "Women in Daoism," pp. 387–388, 390–391; Boltz, *Survey of Taoist Literature*, pp. 38–41, 47, 69–70, 71–73, 81–83, 96–97, 118–119; Boltz, "Not by the Seal of Office Alone," pp. 269–286.

16. Cahill, *Transcendence and Divine Passion*, pp. 218–223.

17. Ibid., pp. 223–230.

18. Ibid., pp. 230–234.

19. On the literary history of erotically charged goddesses, see Rouzer, *Articulated Ladies*, ch. 2. On "Daoist" poems for courtesans and performers, see Cahill, *Transcendence and Divine Passion*, pp. 234–238.

20. On the leading schools of Tang Buddhism, see Ch'en, *Buddhism in China*, ch. 11–12. On the Song invention of Tang schools, see Faure, *The Will to Orthodoxy*, "Introduction"; Faure, "The Concept of One-Practice Samādhi in Early Ch'an," pp. 118–125; Getz, "Siming Zhili and Tiantai Pure Land in the Sung Dynasty"; Getz, "T'ien-t'ai Pure Land Societies and the Creation of the Pure Land Patriarchate"; Gimello, "Mārga and Culture"; Gregory, *Tsung-mi and the Sinification of Buddhism*; McRae, *The Northern School and the Formation of Early Ch'an Buddhism*, "Introduction" and ch. 4; McRae, *Seeing Through Zen*, ch. 1.

21. Ch'en, *Buddhism in China*, pp. 275–278; Ch'en, *Chinese Transformation of Buddhism*, pp. 105–112; Reischauer, *Ennin's Travels in T'ang China*, pp. 168–170. On the attitudes and policies of Tang emperors, see Weinstein, *Buddhism Under the T'ang*.

22. Orzech, *Politics and Transcendent Wisdom: The Scripture for Humane Kings in the Creation of Chinese Buddhism*, pp. 77–78, 142–143, 191–203; Weinstein, *Buddhism Under the T'ang*, p. 78.

23. Reischauer, *Ennin's Travels*, ch. 6; Dudbridge, *Religious Experience and Lay Society*, pp. 77, 81–84; Birnbaum, *Studies on the Mystery of Mañjuśrī* .

24. Dudbridge, *Religious Experience and Lay Society*, pp. 76–79.

25. Ch'en, *Chinese Transformation of Buddhism*, pp. 171–177.

26. Gernet, *Buddhism in Chinese Society: An Economic History from the Fifth to the Tenth Centuries*. For a more compact treatment, see Ch'en, *Chinese Transformation of Buddhism*, ch. 4.

27. Ch'en, *Buddhism in China*, pp. 278–285. For accounts of relic worship at the Famen Monastery and the recent archaeological discoveries there, see Sen, *Buddhism, Diplomacy, and Trade*, pp. 64–74.

28. Mair, *T'ang Transformation Texts*; Mair, *Painting and Performance: Chinese Picture Recitation and Its Indian Genesis*; Mair, tr., *Tun-huang Popular Narratives*; Ch'en, *Buddhism in China*, pp. 285–289.

29. Gernet, *Buddhism in Chinese Society*, pp. 217–228, 259–277; Ch'en, *Chi-*

nese Transformation of Buddhism, pp. 281–303; Ch'en, *Buddhism in China*, pp. 290–296.

30. Kieschnick, *The Eminent Monk*, ch. 2; Dudbridge, *Religious Experience and Lay Society*, p. 102.

31. On the Inexhaustible Treasuries, see Gernet, *Buddhism in Chinese Society*, pp. 210–217. On the Sect of the Three Stages, see Hubbard, *Absolute Delusion, Perfect Buddhahood*. On the sect's suppression, see Lewis, "Suppression of the Three Stages Sect."

32. On China's position in a Buddhist world, see Sen, *Buddhism, Diplomacy, and Trade*, pp. 6–12; Abramson, *Ethnic Identity*, pp. 75–76. On Faxian, see Ch'en, *Buddhism in China*, pp. 89–93. For the passage in the *Commentary to the Classic of Waterways*, see Petech, *Northern India According to the Shui-ching-chu*, p. 20. For the passage in Faxian's account, see Legge, tr., *Record of Buddhistic Kingdoms*, pp. 42–43.

33. Eckel, *To See the Buddha*, pp. 51–65; Strong, *The Legend of King Aśoka*, p. 8. On the Buddha's Diamond Seat as the unmoving spot at the center of the cosmos, see Xuanzang, *The Great Tang Dynasty Record of the Western Regions*, pp. 244–245. On Xuanzang's conversation on China's place in the world, see Forte, "Hui-chih," p. 125; Needham, *Science and Civilisation in China*, vol. 1, pp. 209–210. Needham notes that Xuanzang defends Chinese civilization largely for its achievements in astronomy and cosmology. On Daoxuan's arguments, see Sen, *Buddhism, Diplomacy, and Trade*, p. 9.

34. Zürcher, *Buddhist Conquest of China*, pp. 277–280. On the legend of Aśoka and the relics, see Strong, *Legend of King Aśoka*, pp. 109–119; Strong, *Relics of the Buddha*, ch. 5.

35. On Emperor Wen's Buddhist policies, see Wright, *The Sui Dynasty*, pp. 126–138; Chen, *Monks and Monarchs, Kinship and Kingship*. On Emperor Wen's stupa-building campaign and its international ramifications, see Wright, *Sui Dynasty*, pp. 134–138; Chen, *Monks and Monarchs*, ch. 2; Sen, *Buddhism, Diplomacy, and Trade*, pp. 62–64.

36. Sen, *Buddhism, Diplomacy, and Trade*, pp. 79–86; Cartelli, "The Poetry of Mt. Wutai."

37. Sen, *Buddhism, Diplomacy, and Trade*, pp. 86–101.

38. The textual and building campaigns of the empress are described in Forte, *Political Propaganda and Ideology in China at the End of the Seventh Century*; Forte, *The Mingtang and Buddhist Utopias*; Forte, "The Maitreyist Huaiyi (d. 695) and Taoism."

39. Sen, *Buddhism, Diplomacy, and Trade*, ch. 3.

40. The three-stage model, with different dates, was presented in Wright, *Buddhism in Chinese History*, chs. 2–4. For more recent formulations, see Buswell, *The Formation of Ch'an Ideology in China and Korea*, pp. 15–16; Gregory, *Tsung-mi and the Sinification of Buddhism*, pp. 3–5, 110–111; Gregory, *Inquiry*

into the Origin of Humanity, pp. 25–28. For critiques, see Scharf, *Coming to Terms with Chinese Buddhism,* pp. 4–25; Gimello, "Random Reflections on the 'Sinicization' of Buddhism." The model is criticized for reifying (treating as concrete objects) entities such as "Indian Buddhism" and "Chinese culture," confusing sectarian polemics with intellectual history, and reading post-Tang categories back into earlier periods. It takes at face value the sequential polemics of Chinese and Japanese Buddhists. Thus the translators of the fifth and sixth centuries dismissed their predecessors' work as distortion, only to be attacked in turn as text-bound scholastics by Tang Buddhists, who were then placed in "lineages" constituted after the fact by Song writers and sectarian polemicists in Japan.

41. Weinstein, "Imperial Patronage in the Formation of T'ang Buddhism," pp. 272–273. On the apocrypha, see Buswell, *The Formation of Ch'an Ideology in China and Korea,* ch. 1; Buswell, ed., *Chinese Buddhist Apocrypha.*

42. On doctrinal classification in China and its emergence in Huayan, see Gregory, *Tsung-mi and the Sinification of Buddhism,* chs. 3–4, esp. pp. 104–115; Gregory, *Inquiry into the Origin of Humanity,* pp. 4–8. On its place in Tiantai, see Chappell, ed., *T'ien-t'ai Buddhism,* esp. pp. 21–42; Chen, *Making and Remaking History,* pp. 14–18, 127–132, 154. On the ranking of practices as modeled on the ranking of scriptures, see Chappell, "From Dispute to Dual Cultivation," pp. 184–194.

43. Gregory, *Tsung-mi,* pp. 5–12. For the link of philosophy to practice in the third Huayan "patriarch," see Chen, *Philosopher, Practitioner, Politician: The Many Lives of Fazang.* On links of practice to doctrine in later Huayan, see Gimello, "Li T'ung-hsüan and the Practical Dimensions of Hua-yen." For a synthesis of the school's teachings, see Cook, *Hua-yen Buddhism.*

44. Jia, *The Hongzhou School of Chan Buddhism,* p. 2.

45. Faure, *Rhetoric of Immediacy,* p. 11; Faure, *Will to Orthodoxy,* p. 9; Jia, *Hongzhou School,* p. 9; Chen, "An Alternative View of the Meditation Tradition in China," pp. 345–367, 384–385.

46. On the disputed formation of the Chan lineage, in addition to the works in the preceding notes and Gregory's *Tsung-mi,* see McRae, "The Ox-head School of Chinese Ch'an Buddhism"; McRae, "Shen-hui and the Teaching of Sudden Enlightenment in Early Ch'an Buddhism"; Adamek, *The Mystique of Transmission;* Yampolsky, *The Platform Sutra of the Sixth Patriarch;* Powell, tr., *The Record of Tung-shan.*

47. Faure, *Rhetoric of Immediacy,* ch. 1. The phrases quoted are on p. 18.

48. Wechsler, *Offerings on Jade and Silk: Ritual and Symbol in the Legitimation of the T'ang Dynasty.* See also McMullen, "Bureaucrats and Cosmology: The Ritual Code of T'ang China"; McMullen, *State and Scholars,* ch. 4.

49. Wechsler, *Offerings of Jade and Silk,* ch. 4.

50. Ibid., ch. 5.

51. Ibid., ch. 9.

52. Ibid., ch. 7. For a reconstruction of the only documented imperial funeral ritual, see McMullen, "The Death Rites of Tang Daizong." On the tombs, see Eckfeld, *Imperial Tombs in Tang China*. On the Han debate over the significance of the sacrifices, see Lewis, "The *Feng* and *Shan* Sacrifices of Emperor Wu of the Han."

53. Wechsler, *Offerings of Jade and Silk*, pp. 135–141.

54. Ibid., ch. 11. On the relations of the Tang court to the calendar, see Schafer, *Pacing the Void*, ch. 2.

55. Ennin, *Ennin's Diary*, pp. 180–182.

56. Johnson, "The City God Cults of T'ang and Sung China," pp. 365–388, 402–409, 425–433; Lewis, *China Between Empires*, pp. 219–220.

57. Hansen, "Gods on Walls: A Case of Indian Influence on Chinese Lay Religions?"

58. Johnson, "City God Cults"; Dudbridge, *Religious Experience and Lay Society*, pp. 70, 99, 136.

59. Johnson, "The Wu Tzu-hsü *Pien-wen* and Its Sources: Part II," pp. 480–487.

60. Huntington, *Alien Kind*, pp. 130–131. For Tang accounts of foxes as poltergeists, see Huntington, *Alien Kind*, pp. 91, 94, 98–99, 104, 125. On poltergeists and foxes, see also Dudbridge, *Religious Experience and Lay Society in T'ang China*, pp. 55nn12–13, 133–135, 146, 160n17, 226–231. See Kang, *The Cult of the Fox*.

61. Huntington, *Alien Kind*, pp. 135–136, 144–145; von Glahn, *The Sinister Way*, ch. 6–7; Taussig, *The Devil and Commodity Fetishism in South America*. On foxes as foreigners, see Kang, "The Fox *(hu)* and Barbarian *(hu)*"; Blauth, *Altchinesische Geschichte über Fuchsdämonen* (translation with commentary of fox stories from the *Taiping guang ji*); Abramson, *Ethnic Identity*, pp. 28, 33, 74.

62. Chen, *Liu Tsung-yüan and Intellectual Change in Tang China*, pp. 21–24.

63. McMullen, *State and Scholars*, pp. 67–69, 79.

64. Ibid., pp. 72–73.

65. Makeham, *Transmitters and Creators: Chinese Commentators and Commentaries on the Analects*, chs. 2–3.

66. McMullen, *State and Scholars*, pp. 73–79. On the reconciliation of north and south, see pp. 71, 72, 76; Barrett, *Li Ao*, pp. 15–16.

67. Pulleyblank, "Chinese Historical Criticism: Liu Chih-chi and Ssu-ma Kuang," pp. 142–149; McMullen, *State and Scholars*, pp. 90–91.

68. Chen, *Liu Tsung-yüan and Intellectual Change*, pp. 59–60.

69. Pulleyblank, "Neo-Confucianism in T'ang Intellectual Life," pp. 88–91; Chen, *Liu Tsung-Yüan and Intellectual Change*, pp. 28–30; McMullen, *State and Scholars*, pp. 101–103.

70. Chen, *Liu Tsung-yüan and Intellectual Change*, pp. 59–61, 134–144. On the focus of Liu's thought on politics, see pp. 89–97.

71. Liu, tr., *Classical Chinese Prose*, pp. 30–33.

72. Cited in Chen, *Liu Tsung-yüan and Intellectual Change*, p. 143.

73. On "antiquity" as a rubric for the political and spiritual ideal represented by the early sages culminating in Confucius, see Chen, *Liu Tsung-yüan and Intellectual Change*, pp. 84–89; Hartman, *Han Yü and the T'ang Search for Unity*, pp. 217–218.

74. Hartman, *Han Yü and the T'ang Search for Unity*, pp. 174–187.

75. On the printing industry and its impact in late imperial China, see Brokaw and Chow, eds., *Printing and Book Culture in Late Imperial China*; Brokaw, *Commerce in Culture*; Chow, *Publishing, Culture, and Power*; Chia, *Printing for Profit*; Zeitlin and Liu, eds., *Writing and Materiality in China*, Part II; Chia, "*Mashaben*: Commercial Publishing in Jianyang from the Song to the Ming"; Widmer, *The Beauty and the Book*, ch. 8; McDermott, *A Social History of the Chinese Book*. The "Bibliographical Notes" at the end of McDermott's book provide a thorough coverage of works in Chinese, Japanese, and European languages. The religious background to the rise of printing has been laid out most systematically in Barrett, "The Rise and Spread of Printing: A New Account of Religious Factors"; Barrett, *The Woman Who Discovered Printing*.

76. On the scope and form of handwritten texts, see Drège, *Les Bibliothèques en Chine au temps des manuscrits*. On the incomplete nature of the supplanting of handwriting by printing, see McDermott, *A Social History of the Chinese Book*. On the evolving technology of woodblock carving, see McDermott, *A Social History of the Chinese Book*, ch. 1.

77. Needham and Tsien, *Science and Civilisation in China*, vol. 5, *Chemistry and Chemical Technology*, pt. 1: *Paper and Printing*, pp. 146–150; McDermott, *A Social History of the Chinese Book*, pp. 9–12. Dated but still useful studies of printing in China include Carter, *The Invention of Printing in China*; Pelliot, *Les Débuts de l'imprimerie en Chine*.

78. Barrett, *The Woman Who Discovered Printing*.

79. Needham and Tsien, *Paper and Printing*, pp. 151–153.

80. Barrett, "The Rise and Spread of Printing: A New Account of Religious Factors"; Elvin, *The Pattern of the Chinese Past*, p. 181; Thilo, *Chang'an*, vol. 2, pp. 256–257.

81. Needham and Tsien, *Paper and Printing*, pp. 154–159; Seo, "The Printing Industry in Chang'an's Eastern Market."

82. Sen, *Buddhism, Diplomacy, and Trade*, pp. 110–132.

9. Writing

1. Owen, *The Poetry of the Early T'ang*; *The Great Age of Chinese Poetry*; *The Poetry of Meng Chiao and Han Yü*; *The Late T'ang*. On individual Tang poets, see Warner, *A Wild Deer Amid Soaring Phoenixes: The Opposition Poetics of*

Wang Ji; Yang, *The Chan Interpretations of Wang Wei's Poetry;* Barnstone and Barnstone, *Laughing Lost in the Mountains: Poems of Wang Wei,* "Introduction"; Varsano, *Tracking the Banished Immortal: The Poetry of Li Bo and Its Critical Reception;* Stočes, *La ciel pour couverture, la terre pour oreiller: La vie et l'oeuvre de Li Po;* Chou, *Reconsidering Tu Fu;* Davis, *Tu Fu;* McCraw, *Du Fu's Laments from the South;* Hung, *Tu Fu;* Tu, *Li Ho;* Rouzer, *Writing Another's Dream: The Poetry of Wen Tingyun;* Liu, *The Poetry of Li Shang-yin;* Yates, *Washing Silk.*

2. Owen, *The Poetry of the Early T'ang,* p. 50.

3. Ibid., pp. 7–12, 33, 46–49, 234–255, 257.

4. Ibid., pp. 52–59. Jack Chen has a forthcoming monograph on Taizong's poetry. See also Owen, *The Late Tang,* pp. 24–29, on Emperor Wenzong's (r. 827–840) passion for poetry.

5. Owen, *Poetry of the Early T'ang,* pp. 274–280.

6. Warner, *A Wild Deer Amid Soaring Phoenixes.*

7. Owen, *Poetry of the Early T'ang,* chs. 7–8, 10–11; Owen, *The Great Age of Chinese Poetry,* pp. 23–26, 76, 82, 88–89, 110–112, 114–118, 136, 144, 148, 155, 216, 294, 308.

8. Owen, *Poetry of the Early T'ang,* chs. 20–23.

9. Owen, *The Great Age of Chinese Poetry,* p. 55.

10. On "capital poetry," see ibid., pp. xii–xiv, 4–5, 19–26, 52–70, 226–227, 253–280. On the tension between poetry as social discourse and poetry as art, see also Owen, *Poetry of the Early T'ang,* pp. 379, 399–400.

11. Owen, *The Great Age of Chinese Poetry,* p. 130.

12. Owen, *Poetry of the Early T'ang,* pp. 55–59, 67–68, 103–122, 361–362, 404–405; *The Great Age of Chinese Poetry,* pp. 47, 69, 130, 172–173, 186, 195–196, 203, 212, 281–282, 296, 299; *The Late Tang,* pp. 6, 23, 27–28, 31, 33, 34, 41–42, 44.

13. Lin, "The Formation of a Distinct Generic Identity for *Tz'u,*" pp. 6–19; Rouzer, *Writing Another's Dream,* ch. 2; Chang, *The Evolution of Chinese Tz'u Poetry,* pp. 5–15; Wagner, *The Lotus Boat,* ch. 2–3; Schaab-Hanke, *Die Entwicklung des höfischen Theaters in China zwischen dem 7. und 10. Jahrhundert.*

14. Shields, *Crafting a Collection,* ch. 1; Chang, *The Evolution of Chinese Tz'u Poetry,* pp. 15–32; Wagner, *The Lotus Boat,* ch. 5. On Wen Tingyun, see also Rouzer, *Writing Another's Dream,* ch. 3; Owen, *The Late Tang,* pp. 534–539, 560–565.

15. Owen, *End of the Chinese "Middle Ages,"* pp. 83–89.

16. Yang, *Metamorphosis of the Private Sphere,* chs. 1–4, esp. ch. 1. On Liu Zongyuan, see Owen, *The End of the Chinese "Middle Ages,"* pp. 24–33, 57–64. On the poetic inscription of space, see Owen, *Remembrances,* ch. 1. On the garden as lyric site in late imperial China, see Xiao, *The Chinese Garden as Lyric Enclave.*

17. Owen, *Poetry of the Early T'ang*, pp. 15–16.

18. Chen, *Images and Ideas in Classical Chinese Prose*, pp. 1–6. For a translation, see Bol, "*This Culture of Ours*," pp. 90–91. Pages 84–92 and 102–104 examine the debate over ornament *vs.* simplicity.

19. Owen, *Poetry of the Early T'ang*, chs. 2–4, 6.

20. Ibid., chs. 12–13, esp. pp. 153–155, 165–167, 170–171, 184–187, 200, 207, 213–215, 218–219, 227, 236, 270, 301. The poem cited is on p. 175.

21. Owen, *Poetry of the Early T'ang*, pp. 344–347, 383–384, 394–395, 409–423.

22. Owen, *The Great Age of Chinese Poetry*, pp. 96–97. On the Caos and Liu Zheng as exemplary poets, see Lin, "The Decline and Revival of *Feng-ku* (Wind and Bone)."

23. Varsano, *Tracking the Banished Immortal*, ch. 3.

24. Owen, *Great Age of Chinese Poetry*, pp. 225–246.

25. Ibid., ch. 4 (the poem is on p. 46); Yang, *The Chan Interpretation of Wang Wei's Poetry*, ch. 1.

26. Owen, *Great Age of Chinese Poetry*, pp. 254–256.

27. Quoted in McCraw, *Du Fu's Laments from the South*, p. ix. See also Chou, *Reconsidering Tu Fu*, pp. 33–34; Owen, *Great Age of Chinese Poetry*, pp. xv, 183–185; Owen, *The Late Tang*, p. 16.

28. Owen, *Great Age of Chinese Poetry*, p. 201.

29. Ibid., pp. 287–295.

30. Ibid., pp. xi–xv, 166, 170, 303–316; Owen, *Late Tang*, pp. 2–8, 102–104.

31. Owen, *Great Age of Chinese Poetry*, pp. 115–118, 203, 207–209; Owen, *Late Tang*, pp. 98–99.

32. Owen, *Late Tang*, pp. 123–124.

33. Tian, *Tao Yuanming and Manuscript Culture*.

34. Owen, *Great Age of Chinese Poetry*, pp. 109–110.

35. Ibid., ch. 8.

36. Varsano, *Tracking the Banished Immortal*, ch. 1–2.

37. Owen, *Late Tang*, pp. 56–61, 88–89.

38. Ibid., pp. 131–132.

39. Owen, *Poetry of Meng Chiao and Han Yü*, ch. 9. The lines quoted are on pp. 157, 158, 163. Han Yu wrote how Heaven had sent Li Bo and Du Fu to earth to suffer so that they could write beautiful poems. See Owen, *Late Tang*, p. 161.

40. Owen, *Late Tang*, pp. 58, 90, 93, 121, 123, 160, 162, 186, 452, 493–494.

41. Ibid., pp. 9, 90–99, 119–126.

42. Owen, *End of the Chinese "Middle Ages,"* pp. 107–129. On Li Shangyin's story, see Owen, *Late Tang*, pp. 159–163. On Li He, see also Wu, *The Poetics of Decadence*, ch. 3.

43. Owen, *Late Tang*, pp. 9, 29, 34, 38–39, 43–44, 53–55, 77–80 (the discussion of Li Shen), 91, 156–159.

44. Ibid., pp. 155, 238–239; Wagner, *The Lotus Boat,* pp. 120–121. On the *Collected Statements,* see Moore, *Rituals of Recruitment,* ch. 2.

45. Owen, *Late Tang,* pp. 50–55.

46. Owen, *End of the Chinese "Middle Ages,"* pp. 24–33; Yang, *Metamorphosis of the Private Sphere,* ch. 1; Tian, *Tao Yuanming,* ch. 1.

47. Lu, *From Historicity to Fictionality,* pp. 114–125; Gu, *Chinese Theories of Fiction,* pp. 67–82; Nienhauser, "Some Preliminary Remarks on Fiction, the Classical Tradition and Society in Late Ninth-Century China."

48. Kao, "Aspects of Derivation in Chinese Narrative." See also Chang, "The *Yang Lin* Story Series."

49. On dream stories in the Tang, see Lu, *From Historicity to Fictionality,* pp. 116–117, 120–127. On dreams in Tang poetry, see Owen, *Poetry of the Early T'ang,* pp. 197–199; *Great Age of Chinese Poetry,* pp. 122–126; Varsano, *Tracking the Banished Immortal,* pp. 107–108. On "dream narratives," see Knechtges, "Dream Adventure Stories in Europe and T'ang China."

50. Huntington, *Alien Kind,* pp. 225–228; Levi, *La Chine Romanesque,* pp. 261–275.

51. On "Wandering in the Immortals' Cave," see Rouzer, *Articulated Ladies,* pp. 204–216, 313–354. On the incorporated genres in "Yingying," see Yu, ed., *Ways With Words,* pp. 182–201; Owen, *End of the Chinese "Middle Ages,"* pp. 161–162, 163, 165–169.

52. Owen, *End of the Chinese "Middle Ages,"* pp. 149–173.

53. Quoted in Lu, *From Historicity to Fictionality,* pp. 51–52.

54. Owen, *End of the Chinese "Middle Ages,"* pp. 130–134; Hsieh, *Love and Women in Early Chinese Fiction.*

55. On emotions in the *chuanqi,* see Bol, "Perspective on Readings of *Yingying zhuan,*" in Yu, ed., *Ways With Words,* pp. 198–201.

56. Chen, *Images and Ideas in Classical Chinese Prose,* pp. 1–6; Bol, "*This Culture of Ours,*" pp. 84–92, 102–104; McMullen, "Historical and Literary Theory," pp. 333–341.

57. DeBlasi, *Reform in the Balance: The Defense of Literary Culture in Mid-Tang China.* See also DeBlasi, "Striving for Completeness: Quan Deyu and the Evolution of the Tang Intellectual Mainstream"; Bol, "*This Culture of Ours,*" pp. 108–125, 131.

58. Bol, "*This Culture of Ours,*" ch. 3; McMullen, *State and Scholars,* pp. 213–217.

59. Bol, "*This Culture of Ours,*" pp. 110–118; DeBlasi, *Reform in the Balance,* pp. 24–30, 34–39; McMullen, *State and Scholars,* pp. 241–244.

60. DeBlasi, *Reform in the Balance,* pp. 30–31, 45–61; Bol, "*This Culture of Ours,*" pp. 118–121.

61. DeBlasi, *Reform in the Balance,* pp. 28–30, 65–78; Chiu-Duke, *To Rebuild the Empire,* ch. 8.

62. Hartman, *Han Yü and the T'ang Search for Unity,* pp. 212–218, 224–225, 239–241, 257–273; Bol, *"This Culture of Ours,"* pp. 132–133. For another view of Han Yu, see McMullen, "Han Yu: An Alternative Picture," esp. pp. 650–657.

63. For translations, see Chen, *Images and Ideas,* pp. 8–10; Hartman, *Han Yü,* pp. 242–244.

64. Hartman, *Han Yü,* pp. 248–252. The quotations appear on pp. 248, 254.

65. Owen, *Poetry of Meng Chiao and Han Yü,* pp. 36–54.

66. On "antiquity" and the "Way of the sage" in Han Yu's thought, see Bol, *"This Culture of Ours,"* pp. 125–131. The quotation is on p. 125. On "antiquity" in the writings of Liu Zongyuan, see Chen, *Liu Tsung-yüan and Intellectual Change,* ch. 4. On the necessity of constant study to create the exemplary moral and literary man, and the consequent identification of writing and self-cultivation, with particular emphasis on Liu Zongyuan, see DeBlasi, *Reform in the Balance,* pp. 117–137.

67. Chen, *Images and Ideas,* pp. 17–18.

68. Hartman, *Han Yü,* pp. 254–257; Bol, *"This Culture of Ours,"* pp. 133–138; Chen, *Images and Ideas,* ch. 2; DeBlasi, *Reform in the Balance,* pp. 120–126.

69. Han Yu, "In Praise of Po-i [Boyi]," translated in Liu, *Chinese Classical Prose,* pp. 39–41. The quotation is on p. 39.

70. Owen, *End of the Chinese "Middle Ages,"* ch. 1. The quotation is on p. 14.

71. This de-centering of the ruler went further in Liu Zongyuan's "Critique of the *Discourses of the States*" *(Fei Guo yu),* which insisted that officials' sense of moral responsibility took precedence over loyalty to the ruler. See DeBlasi, *Reform in the Balance,* pp. 117, 137–144; Hartman, *Han Yü,* pp. 145–160, esp. pp. 147, 150–152; Bol, *"This Culture of Ours,"* pp. 128–131.

72. Chen, *Liu Tsung-yüan,* ch. 5; Owen, *End of the Chinese "Middle Ages,"* pp. 48–53; DeBlasi, *Reform in the Balance,* pp. 86–88; Lamont, "An Early Ninth Century Debate on Heaven."

73. Hartman, *Han Yü,* pp. 160–166; Han Yu, "On the Teacher," in Liu, *Classical Chinese Prose,* pp. 35–37; Chen, *Liu Tsung-yüan,* pp. 54, 145–148.

74. Bol, *"This Culture of Ours,"* pp. 126–131, 137–140, 162–185; Hartman, *Han Yü,* pp. 84–93; McMullen, "Han Yu," pp. 645–650; Chen, *Images and Ideas,* pp. 15–16, 19–22, 46, 57, 69; Barrett, *Li Ao,* esp. ch. 4; Emmerich, *Li Ao,* pp. 281–310.

Conclusion

1. Yates, *Washing Silk,* pp. 111–112. For background, see pp. 16–17.

2. Ibid., p. 122.

3. Tackett, "Transformation of Medieval Chinese Elites," ch. 2.

4. Ibid., ch. 5. The inscription is on pp. 97–98.

5. Ibid., pp. 33–41, esp. p. 39. The inscription is on p. 36.

6. Ibid., ch. 4.

7. Ibid., chs. 1, 3 (the quotation is on p. 109); Wang, *Structure of Power in North China during the Five Dynasties.*

8. Hartwell, "Demographic, Political and Social Transformations," p. 369, Table 1. See also Shiba, "Urbanization and the Development of Markets in the Lower Yangtze Valley," pp. 15–20.

9. Hartwell, "Demographic, Political and Social Transformations," pp. 389–391; Tackett, "Transformation," pp. 83–85, 162–167.

BIBLIOGRAPHY

Abramson, Marc S. *Ethnic Identity in Tang China*. Philadelphia: University of Pennsylvania Press, 2008.

Abu-Lughod, Janet L. *Before European Hegemony: The World System A.D. 1250–1350*. Oxford: Oxford University Press, 1989.

Adamek, Wendi L. *The Mystique of Transmission: On an Early Chan History and Its Contents*. New York: Columbia University Press, 2007.

Adshead, S. A. M. *China in World History*. Basingstoke: MacMillan, 1988.

———. *T'ang China: The Rise of the East in World History*. Basingstoke: Palgrave MacMillan, 2004.

Ahern, Emily. *The Cult of the Dead in a Chinese Village*. Stanford: Stanford University Press, 1973.

Aoyama, Sadao. *Tō Sō jidai no kōtsū to chishi chizu no kenkyū*. Tokyo: Yoshikawa Kobunkō, 1963.

Backus, Charles. *The Nan-chao Kingdom and T'ang China's Southwestern Frontier*. Cambridge: Cambridge University Press, 1981.

Ban, Zhao. "Lessons for Women (*Nüjie*)." In *Images of Women in Chinese Thought and Culture*. Ed. Robin R. Wang. Indianapolis: Hackett, 2003.

Baptandier, Brigitte. *The Lady of Linshui: A Chinese Female Cult*. Tr. Kristin Ingrid Fryklund. Stanford: Stanford University Press, 2008.

Barfield, Thomas J. *The Perilous Frontier: Nomadic Empires and China*. Cambridge: Basil Blackwell, 1989.

Barnhart, Richard M. *Peach Blossom Spring: Gardens and Flowers in Chinese Paintings*. New York: Metropolitan Museum of Art, 1983.

Barnstone, Tony, and Willis Barnstone. "Introduction." In *Laughing Lost in the Mountains: Poems of Wang Wei*. Hanover, N.H.: University Press of New England, 1991.

Barrett, Timothy. *Li Ao: Buddhist, Taoist, or Neo-Confucian?* Oxford: Oxford University Press, 1992.

———. "The Rise and Spread of Printing: A New Account of Religious Factors." Working Papers in the Study of Religions. London: School of Oriental and African Studies, University of London, 2001.

———. *Taoism under the T'ang.* London: Wellsweep Press, 1996.

———. *The Woman Who Discovered Printing.* New Haven: Yale University
Press, 2008.

Bartholomew, T. T. "Botanical Puns in Chinese Art from the Collection of the
Asian Art Museum of San Francisco." *Orientations* 16 (September, 1985):
18–24.

Beckwith, Christopher I. *The Tibetan Empire in Central Asia: A History of the
Struggle for Great Power among Tibetans, Turks, Arabs, and Chinese during the Early Middle Ages.* Princeton: Princeton University Press, 1987.

Benn, Charles D. *The Cavern-Mystery Transmission: A Taoist Ordination Rite
of A.D. 711.* Honolulu: University of Hawai'i Press, 1991.

———. *China's Golden Age: Everyday Life in the Tang Dynasty.* Oxford: Oxford University Press, 2002.

———. "Daoist Ordinations and *Zhai* Rituals in Medieval China." In *Daoism
Handbook.* Ed. Livia Kohn. Leiden: E. J. Brill, 2000.

———. "Religious Aspects of Emperor Hsüan-tsung's Taoist Ideology." In *Buddhist and Taoist Practice in Medieval Chinese Society.* Ed. David W.
Chappell. Honolulu: University of Hawai'i Press, 1987.

———. "Taoism as Ideology in the Reign of Emperor Hsüan-tsung." Ph.D.
diss., University of Michigan, 1977.

Benn, James. A. *Burning for the Buddha: Self-Immolation in Chinese Buddhism.*
Honolulu: University of Hawai'i, 2007.

Bielenstein, Hans. "The Chinese Colonization of Fukien until the End of the
T'ang." In *Studia Serica Bernhard Karlgren Dedicata.* Ed. Soren Egerod.
Copenhagen: Ejnar Munksgard, 1959.

Bingham, Woodridge. *The Founding of the T'ang Dynasty: The Fall of the Sui and
Rise of the T'ang.* Baltimore: American Council of Learned Societies, 1941.

Birnbaum, Raoul. *Studies on the Mystery of Manjuśri.* Boulder: Society for the
Study of Chinese Religions, Monograph 2, 1983.

Bischoff, F. A., tr. *La Forêt des Pinceaux: Étude sur l'Academie du Han-lin sous
la Dynastie des T'ang et traduction du Han lin tche.* Paris: Presses
Universitaires de France, 1963.

Blauth, Birthe. *Altchinesische Geschichte über Fuchsdämonen.* Frankfurt am
Main: Peter Lang, 1996.

Bokenkamp, Stephen. "Time After Time: Taoist Apocalyptic History and the
Founding of the T'ang Dynasty." *Asia Major,* Third Series 7 (1994): 59–88.

Bol, Peter. *"This Culture of Ours": Intellectual Transitions in T'ang and Sung
China.* Stanford: Stanford University Press, 1992.

Boltz, Judith M. "Not by the Seal of Office Alone: New Weapons in Battles with the Supernatural." In *Religion and Society in T'ang and Sung China*. Ed. Patricia Buckley Ebrey and Peter N. Gregory. Honolulu: University of Hawai'i Press, 1993.

———. *A Survey of Taoist Literature: Tenth to Seventeenth Centuries*. Berkeley: Institute of East Asian Studies, Center for Chinese Studies, University of California, 1987.

Brokaw, Cynthia. *Commerce in Culture: The Sibao Book Trade in the Qing and Republican Periods*. Cambridge: Harvard University Press, 2007.

———. *The Ledgers of Merit and Demerit: Social Change and Moral Order in Late Imperial China*. Princeton: Princeton University Press, 1991.

Brokaw, Cynthia, and Kai-wing Chow, eds. *Printing and Book Culture in Late Imperial China*. Berkeley: University of California Press, 2005.

Buchanan, Keith. *The Transformation of the Chinese Earth*. London: G. Bell and Sons, 1970.

Buswell, Robert E., Jr. *The Formation of Ch'an Ideology in China and Korea: The Vajrasamāmadhi-Sūtra, a Buddhist Apocryphon*. Princeton: Princeton University Press, 1989.

———, ed. *Chinese Buddhist Apocrypha*. Honolulu: University of Hawai'i Press, 1990.

Cahill, Suzanne E. *Divine Traces of the Daoist Sisterhood: "Records of the Assembled Transcendents of the Fortified Walled City" by Du Guangting (850–933)*. Magdalena, N.M.: Three Pines Press, 2006.

———. "Smell Good and Get a Job: How Daoist Women Saints Were Verified and Legitimatized during the Tang Dynasty (618–907)." In *Presence and Presentations: Women in the Chinese Literati Tradition*. Ed. Sherry J. Mou. London: MacMillan, 1999.

———. *Transcendence and Divine Passion: The Queen Mother of the West in Medieval China*. Stanford: Stanford University Press, 1993.

Cartelli, Mary Anne. "The Poetry of Mt. Wutai: Chinese Buddhist Verse from Dunhuang." Ph.D. diss., Columbia University, 1999.

Carter, Thomas. *The Invention of Printing in China and Its Spread Westward*. New York: Columbia University Press, 1925; 2nd ed. rev. by L. C. Goodrich. New York: Ronald Press, 1955.

Chang, Han-liang. "The *Yang Lin* Story Series." In *China and the West: Comparative Literature Studies*. Ed. William Tay, Ying-hsiung Chou, and Heh-hsiang Yuan. Hong Kong: The Chinese University Press, 1980.

Chang, Kang-i Sun. *The Evolution of Chinese Tz'u Poetry: From Late T'ang to Northern Sung*. Princeton: Princeton University Press, 1980.

Chappell, David. "From Dispute to Dual Cultivation: Pure Land Responses to Ch'an Critics." In *Traditions of Meditation in Chinese Buddhism*. Ed. Peter N. Gregory. Kuroda Institute Studies in East Asian Buddhism, No. 4. Honolulu: University of Hawai'i Press, 1986.

———, ed. *T'ien-t'ai Buddhism: An Outline of the Fourfold Teachings*. Tokyo: Daiichi Shobō, 1983.

Chen, Jinhua. "An Alternative View of the Meditation Tradition in China: Meditation in the Life and Works of Daoxuan (596–667)." *T'oung Pao* 88:4–5 (2002): 332–395.

———. *Making and Remaking History: A Study of Tiantai Sectarian Historiography*. Tokyo: International Institute for Buddhist Studies, International College for Advanced Buddhist Studies, 1999.

———. *Monks and Monarchs, Kinship and Kingship: Tanqian in Sui Buddhism and Politics*. Kyoto: Scuolo Italiana di Studi sull'Asia Orientale, 2002.

———. *Philosopher, Practitioner, Politician: The Many Lives of Fazang 643–712*. Leiden: E. J. Brill, 2007.

Chen, Jo-shui. "Empress Wu and Proto-Feminist Sentiments in T'ang China." In *Imperial Rulership and Cultural Change in Traditional China*. Ed. Frederick P. Brandauer and Chun-chieh Huang. Seattle: University of Washington Press, 1994.

———. *Liu Tsung-yüan and Intellectual Change in T'ang China, 773–819*. Cambridge: Cambridge University Press, 1992.

Ch'en, Kenneth K. S. *Buddhism in China: A Historical Survey*. Princeton: Princeton University Press, 1964.

———. *The Chinese Transformation of Buddhism*. Princeton: Princeton University Press, 1973.

———. "The Economic Background of the Hui-ch'ang Suppression of Buddhism." *Harvard Journal of Asiatic Studies* 19 (1956): 67–105.

Chen, Yinke. "Ji Tang dai zhi Li, Wu, Wei, Wang hunyin jituan." In *Chen Yinke Xiansheng lunwen ji*. Vol. 1. Taipei: San Ren Xing, 1974.

———. "Lun Sui mo Tang chu suowei 'Shandong haojie.'" In *Chen Yinke Xiansheng lunwen ji*. Vol. 1. Taipei: San Ren Xing, 1974.

———. "Lun Tang dai zhi fanjiang yu fubing." In *Chen Yinke Xiansheng lunwen ji*. Vol. 1. Taipei: San Ren Xing, 1974.

———. *Sui Tang zhidu yuan yuan lüelun gao*. In *Chen Yinke Xiansheng lunwen ji*. Vol. 1. Taipei: San Ren Xing, 1974.

———. *Tang dai zhengzhi shi shulun gao*. In *Chen Yinke Xiansheng lunwen ji*. Vol. 1. Taipei: San Ren Xing, 1974.

Chen, Yuan, Chen Zhizhao, and Zeng Qingying, eds. *Daojia jin shi lüe*. Beijing: Wenwu, 1988.

Chen, Yu-shih. *Images and Ideas in Chinese Classical Prose: Studies of Four Masters*. Stanford: Stanford University Press, 1988.

Chi, Ch'ao-ting. *Key Economic Areas in Chinese History as Revealed in the Development of Public Works for Water-Control*. London: George Allen and Unwin, 1936.

Chia, Lucille. "*Mashaben*: Commercial Publishing in Jianyang from the Song to the Ming." In *The Song-Yuan-Ming Transition in Chinese History*. Ed. Paul

Jakov Smith and Richard von Glahn. Cambridge: Harvard University Press, 2003.

————. *Printing for Profit: The Commercial Publishers of Jianyang, Fujian (11th–17th Centuries)*. Cambridge: Harvard University Press, 2002.

Chiu-Duke, Josephine. *To Rebuild the Empire: Lu Chih's Confucian Pragmatist Approach to the Mid-T'ang Predicament*. Albany: State University of New York Press, 2000.

Chou, Eva Shan. *Reconsidering Tu Fu: Literary Greatness and Cultural Context*. Cambridge: Cambridge University Press, 1995.

Chow, Kai-wing. *Publishing, Culture, and Power in Early Modern China*. Stanford: Stanford University Press, 2004.

Clark, Hugh R. *Community, Trade, and Networks: Southern Fujian from the Third to the Thirteenth Century*. Cambridge: Cambridge University Press, 1991.

Cole, Alan. *Mothers and Sons in Chinese Buddhism*. Stanford: Stanford University Press, 1998.

Cook, Francis H. *Hua-yen Buddhism: The Jewel Net of Indra*. University Park: Pennsylvania State University Press, 1977.

Crowell, William G. "Government Land Policies and Systems in Early Imperial China." Ph.D. diss., University of Washington, 1979.

Dalby, Michael. "Court Politics in Late T'ang Times." In *Cambridge History of China*. Vol. 3, *Sui and T'ang China, Part I*. Ed. Denis Twitchett and John K. Fairbank. Cambridge: Cambridge University Press, 1979.

Davidson, Ronald M. *Tibetan Renaissance: Tantric Buddhism in the Rebirth of Tibetan Culture*. New York: Columbia University Press, 2005.

Davis, A. R. *Tu Fu*. New York: Twayne, 1971.

DeBlasi, Anthony. *Reform in the Balance: The Defense of Literary Culture in Mid-Tang China*. Albany: State University of New York Press, 2002.

————. "Striving for Completeness: Quan Deyu and the Evolution of the Tang Intellectual Mainstream." *Harvard Journal of Asiatic Studies* 61:1 (2001): 5–36.

de Crespigny, Rafe. *Generals of the South: The Foundation and Early History of the Three Kingdoms State of Wu*. Canberra: Australian National University Press, 1990.

de la Vaissière, Étienne. *Sogdian Traders: A History*. Tr. James Ward. Leiden: E. J. Brill, 2005.

————, ed. *Les Sogdiens en Chine*. Paris: École Française d'Extrême Orient, 2005.

Despeux, Catherine. "Women in Daoism." In *Daoism Handbook*. Ed. Livia Kohn. Leiden: E. J. Brill, 2000.

Despeux, Catherine, and Livia Kohn. *Women in Daoism*. Magdalena, N.M.: Three Pines Press, 2003.

Des Rotours, Robert, tr. *Courtisanes Chinoises à la Fin des T'ang (entre circa*

789 et le 8 janvier 881): *Pei-li tche (Anecdotes du quartier du Nord).* Paris: Presses Universitaires de France, 1968.

———, tr. *Histoire de Ngan Lou-chan.* Paris: Presses Universitaires de France, 1962.

———, tr. *Traité des Examens, Traduit de la Nouvelle Histoire des T'ang (chap. XLIV, XLV).* Paris: E. Leroux, 1932.

———, tr. *Traité des Fonctionnaires et Traité de l'Armée, tr. de la Nouvelle Histoire des T'ang (chap. XLVI–L).* Leiden: E. J. Brill, 1947–48.

Dien, Albert E. "The Bestowal of Surnames under the Western Wei–Northern Chou: A Case of Counter-Acculturation." *T'oung Pao* 63 (1977): 137–177.

———. "The Role of the Military in the Western Wei/Northern Chou State." In *State and Society in Early Medieval China.* Ed. Albert E. Dien. Stanford: Stanford University Press, 1990.

Dien, Dora Shu-fang. *Empress Wu Zetian in Fiction and in History: Female Defiance in Confucian China.* New York: Nova Science Publishers, 2003.

Drège, Jean-Pierre. *Les Bibliothèques en Chine au temps des manuscrits (jusqu'au Xe siècle).* Paris: École Française d'Extrême-Orient, 1991.

Drompp, Michael R. *Tang China and the Collapse of the Uighur Empire.* Leiden: E. J. Brill, 2005.

Dudbridge, Glen. *Religious Experience and Lay Society in T'ang China: A Reading of Tai Fu's Kuang-i chi.* Cambridge: Cambridge University Press, 1995.

———. *The Tale of Li Wa: Study and Critical Edition of a Chinese Story from the Ninth Century.* London: Ithaca Press, 1983.

———. "The Tale of Liu Yi and Its Analogues." In *Paradoxes of Traditional Chinese Literature.* Ed. Eva Hung. Hong Kong: Chinese University of Hong Kong Press, 1994.

Ebrey, Patricia B. *The Aristocratic Families of Early Imperial China: A Case Study of the Po-ling Ts'ui Family.* Cambridge: Cambridge University Press, 1978.

———, tr. "The *Book of Filial Piety for Women* Attributed to a Woman Née Zheng (ca. 730)." In *Under Confucian Eyes: Writings on Gender in Chinese History.* Ed. Susan Mann and Yu-yin Cheng. Berkeley: University of California Press, 2001.

———. "Concubines in Sung China." Reprinted in *Women and the Family in Chinese History.* London: Routledge, 2003.

———. "The Early Stages in the Development of Descent Group Organization." In *Kinship Organization in Late Imperial China, 1000–1940.* Ed. Patricia Buckley Ebrey and James L. Watson. Berkeley: University of California Press, 1986.

———. *The Inner Quarters: Marriage and the Lives of Chinese Women in the Sung Period.* Berkeley: University of California Press, 1993.

———. "Shifts in Marriage Finance from the Sixth to the Thirteenth Century."

In *Marriage and Inequality in Chinese Society*. Ed. Rubie S. Watson and Patricia Buckley Ebrey. Berkeley: University of California Press, 1991.

———. "Women, Marriage, and the Family." In *Heritage of China: Contemporary Perspectives on Chinese Civilization*. Ed. Paul S. Ropp. Berkeley: University of California Press, 1990.

Eckel, Malcolm David. *To See the Buddha: A Philosopher's Quest for the Meaning of Emptiness*. Princeton: Princeton University Press, 1992.

Eckfeld, Tonia. *Imperial Tombs in Tang China, 618–907*. London: Routledge Curzon, 2005.

Elvin, Mark. "Introduction." In *Sediments of Time: Environment and Society in Chinese History*. Ed. Mark Elvin and Liu Ts'ui-jung. Cambridge: Cambridge University Press, 1998.

———. *The Pattern of the Chinese Past*. Stanford: Stanford University Press, 1973.

———. *The Retreat of the Elephants: An Environmental History of China*. New Haven: Yale University Press, 2004.

Emmerich, Reinhard. *Li Ao (ca. 772–ca. 841)*. Wiesbaden: Harrassowitz Verlag, 1987.

Ennin. *Ennin's Diary: The Record of a Pilgrimage to China in Search of the Law*. Tr. Edwin Reischauer. New York: Ronald Press, 1955.

Faure, Bernard. "One-Practice Samādhi in Early Ch'an." In *Traditions of Meditation in Chinese Buddhism*. Ed. Peter N. Gregory. Kuroda Institute Studies in East Asian Buddhism, No. 4. Honolulu: University of Hawai'i Press, 1986.

———. *The Rhetoric of Immediacy: A Cultural Critique of Chan/Zen Buddhism*. Stanford: Stanford University Press, 1991.

———. *The Will to Orthodoxy: A Critical Genealogy of Northern Chan Buddhism*. Stanford: Stanford University Press, 1997.

Finnane, Antonia. *Speaking of Yangzhou: A Chinese City, 1550–1850*. Cambridge: Harvard University Press, 2004.

Fitzgerald, C. P. *The Empress Wu*. London: Cresset Press, 1956.

Forte, Antonino. "Hui-chih (fr. 676–703 A.D.), a Brahmin Born in China." *Estratto da Annali dell'Istituto Universitario Orientale* 45 (1985): 106–134.

———. "The Maitreyist Huaiyi (d. 695) and Taoism." *Tang yanjiu* 4 (1998): 15–29.

———. *The Mingtang and Buddhist Utopias in the History of the Astronomical Clock: The Tower, Statue, and Armillary Sphere Constructed by Empress Wu*. Paris: École Française d'Extrême-Orient, 1988.

———. *Political Propaganda and Ideology in China at the End of the Seventh Century: Inquiry into the Nature, Authors and Function of the Tunhuang Document S.6502 Followed by an Annotated Translation*. Naples: Istituto Universitario Orientale, 1976.

Frank, Andre Gunder. *ReOrient: Global Economy in the Asian Age.* Berkeley: University of California Press, 1998.

Frank, Andre Gunder, and Barry K. Gillis. "The 5,000-Year World System." In *The World System: Five Hundred Years or Five Thousand?* London: Routledge, 1993.

Gentzler, Jennings M. "A Literary Biography of Liu Tsung-yüan, 733–819." Ph.D. diss., Columbia University, 1966.

Gernet, Jacques. *Buddhism in Chinese Society: An Economic History from the Fifth to the Tenth Centuries.* Tr. Franciscus Verellen. New York: Columbia University Press, 1995.

Getz, Daniel Aaron, Jr. "Siming Zhili and Tiantai Pure Land in the Song Dynasty." Ph.D. diss., Yale University, 1994.

———. "T'ien-t'ai Pure Land Societies and the Creation of the Pure Land Patriarchate." In *Buddhism in the Sung.* Ed. Peter N. Gregory and Daniel A. Getz, Jr. Kuroda Institute Studies in East Asian Buddhism, No. 13. Honolulu: University of Hawai'i Press, 1999.

Gimello, Robert M. "Chih-yen (602–668) and the Foundations of Hua-yen Buddhism." Ph.D. diss., Columbia University, 1976.

———. "Li T'ung-hsüan and the Practical Dimensions of Hua-yen." In *Studies in Ch'an and Hua-yen.* Ed. Robert M. Gimello and Peter N. Gregory. Kuroda Institute Studies in East Asian Buddhism, No. 1. Honolulu: University of Hawai'i Press, 1983.

———. "Mārga and Culture: Learning, Letters and Liberation in Northern Song Ch'an." In *Paths to Liberation: The Mārga and Its Transformations in Buddhist Thought.* Ed. Robert Buswell, Jr., and Robert Gimello. Kuroda Institute Studies in East Asian Buddhism, No. 7. Honolulu: University of Hawai'i Press, 1992.

———. "Random Reflections on the 'Sinicization' of Buddhism." *Society for the Study of Chinese Religions Bulletin* 5 (1978): 52–89.

Goody, Jack. *The Culture of Flowers.* Cambridge: Cambridge University Press, 1993.

Graff, David A. "Dou Jiande's Dilemma: Logistics, Strategy, and State Formation in Seventh-Century China." In *Warfare in Chinese History.* Ed. Hans van de Ven. Leiden: E. J. Brill, 2000.

———. *Medieval Chinese Warfare: 300–900.* London: Routledge, 2002.

———. "The Sword and the Brush: Military Specialisation and Career Patterns in Tang China, 618–907." *War and Society* 18:2 (October 2000): 9–21.

Gregory, Peter N. *Inquiry into the Origins of Humanity: An Annotated Translation of Tsung-mi's Yüan jen lun with a Modern Commentary.* Honolulu: University of Hawai'i Press, 1995.

———. *Tsung-mi and the Sinification of Buddhism.* Princeton: Princeton University Press, 1991.

Gregory, Peter N., and Daniel A. Getz, Jr., eds. *Buddhism in the Sung.* Kuroda

Institute Studies in East Asian Buddhism, No. 13. Honolulu: University of Hawai'i Press, 1999.

Gu, Jiguang. "An-Shi luan qian zhi Hebei dao." In *Yanjing Xuebao* 19 (1936): 197–209.

———. *Fubing zhidu kaoshi*. Shanghai: Shanghai Renmin Chubanshe, 1962.

Gu, Mingdong. *Chinese Theories of Fiction: A Non-Western Narrative System*. Albany: State University of New York Press, 2006.

Guisso Richard W. "Reigns of the Empress Wu, Chung-tsung and Jui-tsung (684–712)." In *Cambridge History of China*. Vol. 3, *Sui and T'ang China, Part I*. Ed. Denis Twitchett and John K. Fairbank. Cambridge: Cambridge University Press, 1979.

———. *Wu Tse-t'ien and the Politics of Legitimation in T'ang China*. Bellingham: Western Washington University Press, 1978.

Han, Guopan. *Sui Tang Wu dai shi gang*. Rev. ed. Beijing: Renmin Chubanshe, 1979.

Hansen, Valerie. "Gods on Walls: A Case of Indian Influence on Chinese Lay Religion?" In *Religion and Society in T'ang and Sung China*. Ed. Patricia Buckley Ebrey and Peter N. Gregory. Honolulu: University of Hawai'i Press, 1993.

———. *Negotiating Daily Life in Traditional China: How Ordinary People Used Contracts, 600–1400*. New Haven: Yale University Press, 1995.

Hartman, Charles. "*Alienloquium*: Liu Tsung-yüan's Other Voice." *Chinese Literature: Essays, Articles, Reviews* 4 (1982): 23–73.

———. *Han Yü and the T'ang Search for Unity*. Princeton: Princeton University Press, 1986.

Hartwell, Robert M. "Demographic, Political and Social Transformations of China, 750–1550." *Harvard Journal of Asiatic Studies* 42:2 (1982): 365–442.

———. "Financial Expertise, Examinations, and the Formulation of Economic Policy in Northern Sung China." *Journal of Asian Studies* 30:2 (1971): 281–314.

———. "Foreign Trade, Monetary Policy and Chinese 'Mercantilism.'" In *Collected Studies on Sung History Dedicated to James T. C. Liu in Celebration of his Seventieth Birthday*. Ed. Kinugawa Tsuyoshi, 453–488. Kyoto: Doshosha, 1989.

Helms, Mary W. *Craft and the Kingly Ideal: Art, Trade, and Power*. Austin: University of Texas Press, 1993.

———. *Ulysses' Sail: An Ethnographic Odyssey of Power, Knowledge, and Geographical Distance*. Princeton: Princeton University Press, 1988.

Herbert, P. A. *Examine the Honest, Appraise the Able: Contemporary Assessments of Civil Service Selection in Early Tang China*. Faculty of Asian Studies Monographs, n.s., 10. Canberra: Australia National University Press, 1988.

Hino Kaisaburō. "Tō dai no senran to sanpyō." In Hino, *Tōyō shigaku ronshū*. Vol. 1, *Tō dai hanchin no shihai taisei*. Tokyo: San'ichi Shobō, 1980.

Holcombe, Charles. *The Genesis of East Asia, 221 B.C.–A.D. 907*. Honolulu: University of Hawai'i Press, 2001.

Hou, Ching-lang. *Monnaies d'offrande et la notion de trésorerie dan la religion chinoise*. Paris: Mémoires de l'Institut des Hautes Études Chinoises, 1975.

Hourani, F. George. *Arab Seafaring in the Indian Ocean in Ancient and Early Medieval Times*. Revised and expanded by John Carswell. Princeton: Princeton University Press, 1995.

Hsieh, Daniel. *Love and Women in Early Chinese Fiction*. Hong Kong: The Chinese University Press, 2008.

Hsu, Cho-yun. *Han Agriculture: The Formation of Early Chinese Agrarian Economy (206 B.C.–A.D. 220)*. Seattle: University of Washington Press, 1980.

Hubbard, Jamie. *Absolute Delusion, Perfect Buddhahood: The Rise and Fall of a Chinese Heresy*. Honolulu: University of Hawai'i Press, 2001.

Hung, William. *Tu Fu: China's Greatest Poet*. Cambridge: Harvard University Press, 1952.

Huntington, Rania. *Alien Kind: Foxes and Late Imperial Chinese Literature*. Cambridge: Harvard University Press, 2003.

Hymes, Robert P. *Statesmen and Gentlemen: The Elite of Fu-Chou, Chiang-Hsi, in Northern and Southern Sung*. Cambridge: Cambridge University Press, 1986.

Idema, Wilt, and Beata Grant. *The Red Brush: Writing Women of Imperial China*. Cambridge: Harvard University Asia Center, Harvard University Press, 2004.

Ikeda, On. "The Decline of the T'ang Aristocracy." Unpublished draft chapter for the unpublished Volume 3 of the *Cambridge History of China*.

———. "Sei Tō no Shuken'in." *Hokkaidō Daigaku Bungakubu Kiyō* 19:2 (1971): 45–98.

Inoue, Mitsusada. "The *Ritsuryō* System in Japan." *Acta Asiatica* 31 (1977): 83–112.

Jia, Jinhua. *The Hongzhou School of Chan Buddhism in Eighth- through Tenth-Century China*. Albany: State University of New York Press, 2006.

Johnson, David G. "The City-God Cults of T'ang and Sung China." *Harvard Journal of Asiatic Studies* 45:2 (1985): 363–457.

———. "The Last Years of a Great Clan: The Li Family of Chao chun in Late T'ang and Early Sung." *Harvard Journal of Asiatic Studies* 37:1 (June, 1977): 5–102.

———. *The Medieval Chinese Oligarchy*. Boulder: Westview, 1977.

———. "Mu-lien in Pao-chüan: The Performance Context and Religious Meaning of the *Yu-ming Pao-ch'uan*." In *Ritual and Scripture in Chinese Popular*

Religion: Five Studies. Ed. David Johnson. Berkeley: Publications of the
Chinese Popular Culture Project, 1995.

———, ed. *Ritual Opera, Operatic Ritual: "Mu-lien Rescues his Mother" in
Chinese Popular Culture.* Berkeley: Publications of the Chinese Popular
Culture Project, 1989.

———. "The Wu Tzu-hsü *Pien-wen* and Its Sources, Parts I and II." *Harvard
Journal of Asiatic Studies* 40:1–2 (1980): 93–156, 465–505.

Johnson, Wallace, tr. *The T'ang Code.* Vol. 1, *General Principles.* Princeton:
Princeton University Press, 1979.

———, tr. *The T'ang Code.* Vol. 2, *Specific Articles.* Princeton: Princeton University Press, 1997.

Johnson, Wallace, and Denis Twitchett, "Criminal Procedure in T'ang China."
Asia Major, third series, 6:2 (1993): 113–146.

Kang, Xiaofei. *The Cult of the Fox: Power, Gender, and Popular Religion in
Late Imperial and Modern China.* New York: Columbia University Press,
2006.

———. "The Fox (*hu*) and the Barbarian (*hu*): Unraveling Representations of
the Other in Late Tang Tales." *Journal of Chinese Religions* 27 (1999): 35–
67.

Kao, Karl K. S. "Aspects of Derivation in Chinese Narrative." *Chinese Literature: Articles, Essays, Reviews* 7 (1985): 1–36.

Karetzky, Patricia Eichenbaum. *Court Art of the Tang.* Lanham, N.Y.: University
Press of America, 1996.

Katō, Shigeshi. "On the Hang or Association of Merchants in China." *Memoirs
of the Tōyō Bunko* 8 (1936): 45–83.

Kiang, Heng Chye. *Cities of Aristocrats and Bureaucrats.* Honolulu: University
of Hawai'i Press, 1999.

Kieschnick, John. *The Eminent Monk: Buddhist Ideals in Medieval Chinese Ha-
giography.* Kuroda Institute Studies in East Asian Buddhism, No. 10. Honolulu: University of Hawai'i Press, 1997.

———. *The Impact of Buddhism on Chinese Material Culture.* Princeton:
Princeton University Press, 2003.

Kirkland, Russell. "Dimensions of Tang Taoism: The State of the Field at the
End of the Millennium." *T'ang Studies* 15–16 (1998): 79–123.

———. "Tales of Thaumaturgy: T'ang Accounts of the Wonder-Worker Yeh Fa-
shan." *Monumenta Serica* 40 (1992): 47–86.

———. *Taoism: The Enduring Tradition.* New York: Routledge, 2004.

———. "Taoists of the High T'ang: An Inquiry into the Perceived Significance of
Eminent Taoists in Medieval Chinese Society." Ph.D. diss., Indiana University, 1986.

Knechtges, David R. "Dream Adventure Stories in Europe and T'ang China."
Tamkang Review 4 (1973): 101–119.

Kohn, Livia. *God of the Dao: Lord Lao in History and Myth*. Ann Arbor: Center for Chinese Studies, University of Michigan, 1998.

———. *Monastic Life in Medieval Daoism: A Cross-Cultural Perspective*. Honolulu: University of Hawai'i Press, 2003.

———. "The Northern Celestial Masters." In *Daoism Handbook*. Ed. Livia Kohn. Leiden: E. J. Brill, 2000.

———. *Seven Steps to the Tao: Sima Chengzhen's "Zuowang Lun."* Nettetal: Steyler Verlag, 1987.

Kohn, Livia, and Russell Kirkland. "Daoism in the Tang (618–907)." In *Daoism Handbook*. Ed. Livia Kohn. Leiden: E. J. Brill, 2000.

Kuhn, Dieter. *The Age of Confucian Rule: The Song Transformation of China*. Cambridge: Harvard University Press, 2009.

Lagerwey, John. *Taoist Ritual in Chinese Society and History*. New York: MacMillan, 1987.

Lai, Sufen Sophia. "Father in Heaven, Mother in Hell: Gender Politics in the Creation and Transformation of Mulian's Mother." In *Presence and Presentation: Women in the Chinese Literati Tradition*. Ed. Sherry J. Mou. London: MacMillan, 1999.

Lamont, H. G. "An Early Ninth Century Debate on Heaven: Liu Tsung-yüan's *T'ien shuo* and Liu Yü-hsi's *T'ien lun,* An Annotated Translation and Introduction." *Asia Major,* n.s., Part I, 18:2 (1973): 181–208; Part II, 19:1 (1974): 37–85.

Legge, James, tr. *A Record of Buddhistic Kingdoms: Being an Account of the Chinese Monk Fa-hien of his Travels in India and China (A.D. 399–414) in Search of the Buddhist Books of Discipline*. New York: Dover, 1965.

Levi, Jean. *La Chine Romanesque: Fictions d'Orient et d'Occident*. Paris: Seuil, 1995.

Levy, Howard S. *The Biography of An Lu-shan*. Berkeley: University of California Press, 1960.

———. "The Gay Quarters of Chang'an." *Oriens/West* 7 (1962): 93–105.

———. "Records of the Gay Quarters." *Oriens/West* 8 (1962): 121–128; 8:6 (1963): 115–122; 9:1 (1964): 103–110.

———, tr. *Translations from the Collected Works of Po Chü-yi*. 2 vols. New York: Paragon Book Reprint, 1971.

Lewis, Mark Edward. *China between Empires: The Northern and Southern Dynasties*. Cambridge: Harvard University Press, 2009.

———. *The Construction of Space in Early China*. Albany: State University of New York Press, 2006.

———. *The Early Chinese Empires: Qin and Han*. Cambridge: Harvard University Press, 2007.

———. "The *Feng* and *Shan* Sacrifices of Emperor Wu of the Han." In *State and*

Court Ritual in China. Ed. Joseph P. McDermott. Cambridge: Cambridge University Press, 1999.

———. "The Suppression of the Three Stages Sect: Apocrypha as a Political Issue." In *Chinese Buddhist Apocrypha.* Ed. Robert E. Buswell, Jr. Honolulu: University of Hawai'i Press, 1990.

———. *Writing and Authority in Early China.* Albany: State University of New York Press, 1999.

Li, Bozhong. *Tang dai Jiangnan nongye de fazhan.* Beijing: Nongye Chubanshe, 1990.

Lin, Shuen-fu. "The Formation of a Distinct Generic Identity for *Tz'u.*" In *Voices of the Song Lyric in China.* Ed. Pauline Yu. Berkeley: University of California Press, 1994.

Lin, Wen-yüeh. "The Decline and Revival of *Feng-ku* (Wind and Bone): On the Changing Poetic Styles from the Chien-an Era through the High T'ang Period." In *The Vitality of the Lyric Voice.* Ed. Shuen-fu Lin and Stephen Owen. Princeton: Princeton University Press, 1986.

Liu, James J. Y. *The Poetry of Li Shang-yin.* Chicago: University of Chicago Press, 1969.

Liu, Shi Shun, tr. *Chinese Classical Prose: The Eight Masters of the Tang-Sung Period.* Hong Kong: Renditions, The Chinese University Press, 1979.

Liu, Xinru. *Ancient India and Ancient China: Trade and Religious Exchanges, A.D. 1–600.* Delhi: Oxford University Press, 1988.

Lorge, Peter. *War, Politics and Society in Early Modern China, 900–1795.* London: Routledge, 2005.

Lu, Sheldon Hsiao-peng. *From Historicity to Fictionality: The Chinese Poetics of Narrative.* Stanford: Stanford University Press, 1994.

Mackerras, Colin. *The Uighur Empire According to the Tang Dynastic Histories.* Columbia: University of South Carolina Press, 1973.

———. "The Uighurs." In *The Cambridge History of Early Inner Asia.* Ed. Denis Sinor. Cambridge: Cambridge University Press, 1990.

Mair, Victor H. *Painting and Performance: Chinese Picture Recitation and Its Indian Genesis.* Honolulu: University of Hawai'i Press, 1988.

———. "Scroll Presentation in the T'ang Dynasty." *Harvard Journal of Asiatic Studies* 38:1 (1978): 35–60.

———. *T'ang Transformation Texts: A Study of the Buddhist Contribution in the Rise of Vernacular Fiction and Drama in China.* Cambridge: Harvard University Press, 1989.

———, tr. *Tun-huang Popular Narratives.* Cambridge: Cambridge University Press, 1983.

Makeham, John. *Transmitters and Creators: Chinese Commentators and Commentaries on the Analects.* Cambridge: Harvard University Press, 2004.

Marks, Robert B. *Tigers, Rice, Silk, and Silt: Environment and Economy in Late Imperial South China*. Cambridge: Cambridge University Press, 1998.

Marmé, Michael. *Suzhou: Where the Goods of All the Provinces Converge*. Stanford: Stanford University Press, 2005.

Mather, Richard B. *The Poet Shen Yüeh (441–513): The Reticent Marquis*. Princeton: Princeton University Press, 1988.

Mazumdar, Sucheta. *Sugar and Society in China: Peasants, Technology, and the World Market*. Cambridge: Harvard University Press, 1998.

McCraw, David R. *Du Fu's Laments from the South*. Honolulu: University of Hawai'i Press, 1992.

McDermott, Joseph P. *A Social History of the Chinese Book: Books and Literati Culture in Late Imperial China*. Hong Kong: Hong Kong University Press, 2006.

McKnight, Brian E. *The Quality of Mercy: Amnesties and Traditional Chinese Justice*. Honolulu: University of Hawai'i Press, 1981.

McMullen, David. "Bureaucrats and Cosmology: The Ritual Code of Tang China." In *Rituals of Royalty: Power and Ceremonial in Traditional Societies*. Ed. David Cannadine and Simon Price. Cambridge: Cambridge University Press, 1987.

———. "The Cult of Ch'i T'ai-kung and T'ang Attitudes to the Military." *T'ang Studies* 7 (1989): 59–103.

———. "Han Yü: An Alternative Picture." *Harvard Journal of Asiatic Studies* 49:2 (1989): 603–657.

———. "Historical and Literary Theory in the Mid-Eighth Century." In *Perspectives on the T'ang*. Ed. Arthur F. Wright and Denis Twitchett. New Haven: Yale University Press, 1973.

———. *State and Scholars in T'ang China*. Cambridge: Cambridge University Press, 1988.

———. "Views of the State in Du You and Liu Zongyuan." In *Foundations and Limits of State Power in China*. Ed. Stuart R. Schram. London: School of Oriental and African Studies, University of London, 1987.

McRae, John R. *The Northern School and the Formation of Early Ch'an Buddhism*. Kuroda Institute Studies in East Asian Buddhism, No. 3. Honolulu: University of Hawai'i Press, 1986.

———. "The Ox-head School of Chinese Ch'an Buddhism: From Early Ch'an to the Golden Age." In *Studies in Ch'an and Hua-yen*. Ed. Robert M. Gimello and Peter N. Gregory. Kuroda Institute Studies in East Asian Buddhism, No. 1. Honolulu: University of Hawai'i Press, 1983.

———. *Seeing Through Zen: Encounter, Transformation, and Genealogy in Chan Buddhism*. Berkeley: University of California Press, 2003.

———. "Shen-hui and the Teaching of Sudden Enlightenment in Early Ch'an

Buddhism." In *Sudden and Gradual: Approaches to Enlightenment in Chinese Thought*. Ed. Peter N. Gregory. Kuroda Institute Studies in East Asian Buddhism, No. 5. Honolulu: University of Hawai'i Press, 1987.

Meyer-Fong, Tobie. *Building Culture in Early Qing Yangzhou*. Stanford: Stanford University Press, 2003.

Miller, James. *Daoism: A Short Introduction*. Oxford: Oneworld, 2003.

Miyazaki, Ichisada. "Bukyoku kara denko e: Tō Sō no aida shakai henkaku no ichi men." In *Ajia shi ronkō*, vol. 2. Tokyo: Asahi Shinbun, 1978.

Moore, Oliver. "The Ceremony of Gratitude." In *State and Court Ritual in China*. Ed. Joseph P. McDermott. Cambridge: Cambridge University Press, 1999.

———. *Rituals of Recruitment in T'ang China: Reading an Annual Programme in the Collected Statements by Wang Dingbao (870–940)*. Leiden: E. J. Brill, 2004.

Needham, Joseph. *Science and Civilisation in China*. Vol. 1, *Introductory Orientations*. Cambridge: Cambridge University Press, 1965.

Needham, Joseph, and Francesca Bray. *Science and Civilisation in China*. Vol. 6, *Biology and Biological Technology*, Part 2, *Agriculture*. Cambridge: Cambridge University Press, 1984.

Needham, Joseph, Christian Daniels, and Nicholas K. Menzies. *Science and Civilisation in China*. Vol. 6, *Biology and Biological Technology*, Part 3, *Agro-Industries: Sugarcane Technology, Agro-Industries and Forestry*. Cambridge: Cambridge University Press, 1996.

Needham, Joseph, and H. T. Huang. *Science and Civilisation in China*. Vol. 6, *Biology and Biological Technology*, Part 5, *Fermentations and Food Science*. Cambridge: Cambridge University Press, 2000.

Needham, Joseph, and Tsien Tsuen-hsuin. *Science and Civilisation in China*. Vol. 5, *Chemistry and Chemical Technology*, Part 1, *Paper and Printing*. Cambridge: Cambridge University Press, 1985.

Needham, Joseph, and Wang Ling, *Science and Civilisation in China*. Vol. 4, *Physics and Physical Technology*, Part 2, *Mechanical Engineering*. Cambridge: Cambridge University Press, 1965.

Needham, Joseph, Wang Ling, and Lu Gwei-djen. *Science and Civilisation in China*. Vol. 4, *Physics and Physical Technology*, Part 3, *Civil Engineering and Nautics*. Cambridge: Cambridge University Press, 1971.

Nienhauser, William H., Jr. "Some Preliminary Remarks on Fiction, the Classical Tradition and Society in Late Ninth-Century China." In *Critical Essays on Chinese Fiction*. Ed. Winton L. Y. Yang and Curtis P. Adkins. Hong Kong: The Chinese University Press, 1980.

Nunome, Chōfu. *Chūgoku no rekishi*. Vol. 4, *Zui Tō teikoku*. Tokyo: Kodansha, 1974.

Orzech, Charles D. *Politics and Transcendent Wisdom: The Scripture for Humane Kings in the Creation of Chinese Buddhism.* University Park: Pennsylvania State University Press, 1998.

Owen, Stephen, ed. and tr. *An Anthology of Chinese Literature: Beginnings to 1911.* New York: W. W. Norton, 1996.

———. *The End of the Chinese "Middle Ages": Essays in Mid-Tang Literary Culture.* Stanford: Stanford University Press, 1996.

———. *The Great Age of Chinese Poetry: The High T'ang.* New Haven: Yale University Press, 1981.

———. *The Late Tang: Chinese Poetry of the Mid-Ninth Century (827–860).* Cambridge: Harvard University Press, 2006.

———. *The Poetry of the Early T'ang.* New Haven: Yale University Press, 1977.

———. *The Poetry of Meng Chiao and Han Yü.* New Haven: Yale University Press, 1975.

———. *Remembrances: The Experience of the Past in Chinese Literature.* Cambridge: Harvard University Press, 1986.

Pan, Yihong. *Son of Heaven and Heavenly Qaghan.* Bellingham: Western Washington University Press, 1997.

Pearce, Scott. "Form and Matter: Archaizing Reform in Sixth-Century China." In *Culture and Power in the Reconstitution of the Chinese Realm, 200–600.* Ed. Scott Pearce, Audrey Spiro, and Patricia Ebrey. Cambridge: Harvard University Press, 2001.

Pelliot, Paul. *Les Débuts de l'imprimerie en Chine.* Paris: Imprimerie National, 1953.

Petech, Luciano. *Northern India According to Shui-ching-chu.* Serie oriental Roma, 2. Rome: Istituto Italiano per il Medio ed Estremo Oriente, 1950.

Peterson, Charles A. "The Autonomy of the Northeastern Provinces in the Period Following the An Lu-shan Rebellion." Ph.D. diss., University of Washington, 1966.

———. "Court and Province in Mid- and Late T'ang." In *Cambridge History of China.* Vol. 3, *Sui and T'ang China, Part I.* Ed. Denis Twitchett and John K. Fairbank. Cambridge: Cambridge University Press, 1979.

———. "P'u-ku Huai-en and the T'ang Court: The Limits of Loyalty." *Monumenta Serica* 29 (1970–71): 423–455.

———. "Regional Defense against the Central Power: The Huai-hsi Campaign, 815–817." In *Chinese Ways in Warfare.* Ed. Frank A. Kierman, Jr., and John K. Fairbank. Cambridge: Harvard University Press, 1974.

———. "The Restoration Completed: Emperor Hsien-tsung and the Provinces." In *Perspectives on the T'ang.* Ed. Arthur F. Wright and Denis Twitchett. New Haven: Yale University Press, 1973.

Powell, William F., tr. *The Record of Tung-shan.* Honolulu: University of Hawai'i Press, 1986.

Pulleyblank, E. G. "The An Lu-shan Rebellion and the Origins of Chronic Mili-
    tarism in Late T'ang China." In *Essays on T'ang Society: The Interplay of
    Social and Political and Economic Forces*. Ed. J. C. Perry and Bardwell L.
    Smith. Leiden: E. J. Brill, 1976.

———. *The Background of the Rebellion of An Lu-Shan*. London: Oxford Uni-
    versity Press, 1955.

———. "Chinese Historical Criticism: Liu Chih-chi and Ssu-ma Kuang." In *His-
    torians of China and Japan*. Ed. W. G. Beasley and E. G. Pulleyblank. Lon-
    don: Oxford University Press, 1961.

———. "Neo-Confucianism and Neo-Legalism in T'ang Intellectual Life, 755–
    805." In *The Confucian Persuasion*. Ed. Arthur F. Wright. Stanford: Stan-
    ford University Press, 1960.

Reed, Carrie E. *A Tang Miscellany: An Introduction to Youyang zazu*. New
    York: Peter Lang, 2003.

Reischauer, Edwin O. *Ennin's Diary*. New York: Ronald Press, 1955.

———. *Ennin's Travels in T'ang China*. New York: Ronald Press, 1955.

Reiter, Florian. *The Aspirations and Standards of Taoist Priests in the Early
    T'ang Period*. Wiesbaden: Harrassowitz, 1988.

Robinet, Isabelle. *Taoism: Growth of a Religion*. Tr. Phyllis Brooks. Stanford:
    Stanford University Press, 1997.

Rogers, Michael C. *The Chronicle of Fu Chien: A Case of Exemplar History*.
    Chinese Dynastic Histories Translation, 10. Berkeley: University of Califor-
    nia, 1968.

Rouzer, Paul F. *Articulated Ladies: Gender and the Male Community in Early
    Chinese Texts*. Cambridge: Harvard University Press, 2001.

———. *Writing Another's Dream: The Poetry of Wen Tingyun*. Stanford: Stan-
    ford University Press, 1993.

Sage, Steven F. *Ancient Sichuan and the Unification of China*. Albany: State Uni-
    versity of New York Press, 1992.

Schaab-Hanke, Dorothee. *Die Entwicklung des höfischen Theaters in China
    zwischen dem 7. und 10. Jahrhundert*. Hamburg: Hamburg Sinologische
    Schriften, 2001.

Schafer, Edward H. "The Capeline Cantos: Verses on the Divine Loves of Taoist
    Priestesses." *Asiatische Studien* 32 (1978): 5–65.

———. *The Empire of Min*. Rutland, Vt.: C. E. Tuttle, 1954.

———. *The Golden Peaches of Samarkand: A Study of T'ang Exotics*. Berkeley:
    University of California Press, 1963.

———. "The Last Years of Ch'ang-an." *Oriens Extremus* 10 (1963): 133–179.

———. *Mao Shan in T'ang Times*. Monograph No. 1. Boulder, Co.: Society for
    the Study of Chinese Religions, 1980.

———. *Mirages on the Sea of Time: The Taoist Poetry of Ts'ao T'ang*. Berkeley:
    University of California Press, 1985.

———. *Pacing the Void: T'ang Approaches to the Stars*. Berkeley: University of California Press, 1977.

———. "T'ang." In *Food in Chinese Culture: Anthropological and Historical Perspectives*. Ed. K. C. Chang. New Haven: Yale University Press, 1977.

———. *The Vermilion Bird: T'ang Images of the South*. Berkeley: University of California Press, 1967.

———. "Wu Yün's 'Cantos on Pacing the Void.'" *Harvard Journal of Asiatic Studies* 41 (1981): 377–415.

———. "Wu Yün's Stanzas on 'Saunters in Sylphdom.'" *Monumenta Serica* 33 (1981–83): 1–37.

Scharf, Robert H. *Coming to Terms with Chinese Buddhism: A Reading of the Treasure Store Treatise*. Kuroda Institute Studies in East Asian Buddhism, No. 14. Honolulu: University of Hawai'i Press, 2002.

Seidel, Anna. "The Image of the Perfect Ruler in Early Taoist Messianism." *History of Religions* 9 (1969): 216–247.

Sen, Tansen. *Buddhism, Diplomacy, and Trade: The Realignment of Sino-Indian Relations, 600–1400*. Honolulu: University of Hawai'i Press, 2003.

Seo, Tatsuhiko. "The Printing Industry in Chang'an's Eastern Market." *Memoirs of the Tōyō Bunko* (2004): 1–42.

Shi, Nianhai. *Huangtu gaoyuan lishi dili yanjiu*. Zhengzhou: Huang He Shuili Chubanshe, 2001.

———. *Tang dai lishi dili yanjiu*. Beijing: Zhongguo Shehui Kexue Chubanshe, 1998.

———. *Zhongguo gu du he wenhua*. Beijing: Zhonghua, 1996.

Shiba, Yoshinobu. "Urbanization and the Development of Markets in the Lower Yangtze Valley." In *Crisis and Prosperity in Sung China*. Ed. John Winthrop Haeger. Tucson: University of Arizona Press, 1975.

Shields, Anna M. *Crafting a Collection: The Cultural Contexts and Poetic Practice of the Huajian ji*. Cambridge: Harvard University Press, 2006.

Shiratori, Kurakichi. "Chinese Ideas Reflected in the Ta-ch'in Accounts." *Memoirs of the Research Department of the Toyo Bunko* 15 (1956): 25–72.

Skinner, G. William. "Cities and the Hierarchy of Local Systems." In *The City in Late Imperial China*. Ed. G. William Skinner. Stanford: Stanford University Press, 1977.

———. "Marketing and Social Structures in Rural China," 3 parts. *Journal of Asian Studies* 24:1 (1964): 3–44; 24:2 (1964): 195–228; 24:3 (1965): 363–399.

———. "Regional Urbanization in Nineteenth-Century China." In *The City in Late Imperial China*. Ed. G. William Skinner. Stanford: Stanford University Press, 1977.

Smith, Paul J. *Taxing Heaven's Storehouse: Horses, Bureaucrats, and the Destruction of the Sichuan Tea Industry, 1074–1224*. Cambridge: Harvard University Press, 1991.

Somers, Robert M. "The End of the T'ang." In *Cambridge History of China.*
Vol. 3, *Sui and T'ang China, Part I.* Ed. Denis Twitchett and John K.
Fairbank. Cambridge: Cambridge University Press, 1979.

———. "Time, Space and Structure in the Consolidation of the T'ang Dynasty."
In *State and Society in Early Medieval China.* Ed. Albert E. Dien. Stanford:
Stanford University Press, 1990.

Song, Ruoxin, and Song Ruozhao. "The Analects for Women (*Nü lunyü*)." In
Images of Women in Chinese Thought and Culture. Ed. Robin R. Wang. Indianapolis: Hackett Publishing, 2003.

Stočes, Ferdinand. *La ciel pour couverture, la terre pour oreiller: La vie et
l'oeuvre de Li Po.* Mas de Vert: Philippe Picquier, 2003.

Strickmann, Michel. "The *Consecration Sūtra:* A Buddhist Book of Spells." In
Chinese Buddhist Apocrypha. Ed. Robert J. Buswell, Jr. Honolulu: University of Hawai'i Press, 1990.

Strong, John S. *The Legend of King Aśoka: A Study and Translation of the
Aśokāvadāna.* Princeton: Princeton University Press, 1983.

———. *Relics of the Buddha.* Princeton: Princeton University Press, 2004.

Sun, Yu, tr. *Li Po: A New Translation.* Hong Kong: Commercial Press, 1982.

Tackett, Nicholas Oliver. "Great Clansmen, Bureaucrats, and Local Magnates:
The Structure and Circulation of the Elite in Late-Tang China." *Asia Major,*
third series, 21:2 (2008): 101–152.

———. "The Transformation of Medieval Chinese Elites (850–1000 C.E.)."
Ph.D. diss., Columbia University, 2006.

Tai, Wang-chou. "Notes sur le Li-wa-tchouan." In *Mélanges Sinologiques.*
Beijing: French Institute of Peking, 1951.

Taussig, Michael. *The Devil and Commodity Fetishism in South America.* Chapel Hill: University of North Carolina Press, 1980.

Teiser, Stephen F. *The Ghost Festival in Medieval China.* Princeton: Princeton
University Press, 1988.

———. "The Growth of Purgatory." In *Religion and Society in T'ang and Sung
China.* Ed. Patricia Buckley Ebrey and Peter N. Gregory. Honolulu: University of Hawai'i Press, 1993.

———. *The Scripture on the Ten Kings and the Making of Purgatory in Medieval Chinese Buddhism.* Kuroda Institute Studies in East Asian Buddhism,
No. 9. Honolulu: University of Hawai'i Press, 1994.

Thilo, Thomas. *Chang'an: Metropole Ostasiens und Weltstadt des Mittelalters,
583–904.* 2 vols. Wiesbaden: Otto Harrassowitz, 1997–2006.

Tian, Xiaofei. *Tao Yuanming and Manuscript Culture: The Record of a Dusty
Table.* Seattle: University of Washington Press, 2005.

Tietze, Klaus-Peter. *Ssuch'uan vom 7. bis 10. Jahrhundert: Untersuchungen zur
Frühen Geschichte einer Chinesischen Provinz.* Wiesbaden: Franz Steiner
Verlag, 1980.

Tregear, T. R. *A Geography of China.* Chicago: Aldine, 1965.

Tu, Kuo-ch'ing. *Li Ho*. Boston: Twayne, 1979.

Tuan, Yi-fu. *China*. Chicago: Aldine, 1969.

Tung, Jowen R. *Fables for the Patriarchs: Gender Politics in Tang Discourse*. London: Roman and Littlefield, 2000.

Twitchett, Denis. *The Birth of the Chinese Meritocracy: Bureaucrats and Examinations in T'ang China*. The China Society Occasional Papers, 18. London: The China Society, 1976.

———. "Chinese Biographical Writing." In *Historians of China and Japan*. Ed. W. G. Beasley and E. G. Pulleyblank. London: Oxford University Press, 1961.

———. "The Composition of the T'ang Ruling Class: New Evidence from Tunhuang." In *Perspectives on the T'ang*. Ed. Arthur F. Wright and Denis Twitchett. New Haven: Yale University Press, 1973.

———. *Financial Administration under the T'ang Dynasty*. Cambridge: Cambridge University Press, 1975.

———. "The Fragment of the T'ang Ordinances of the Department of Waterways Discovered at Tun-huang." *Asia Major*, n.s., 6:1 (1957): 23–79.

———. "Hsüan-tsung (reign 712–56)." In *Cambridge History of China*. Vol. 3, *Sui and T'ang China, Part I*. Ed. Denis Twitchett and John K. Fairbank. Cambridge: Cambridge University Press, 1979.

———. "The Implementation of Law in Early T'ang China." *Civiltà Veneziana Studi* 34 (1978): 57–84.

———. "Introduction." In *Cambridge History of China*. Vol. 3, *Sui and T'ang China, Part I*. Ed. Denis Twitchett and John K. Fairbank. Cambridge: Cambridge University Press, 1979.

———. "Kao-tsung (reign 649–83) and the Empress Wu: The Inheritor and the Usurper." In *Cambridge History of China*. Vol. 3, *Sui and T'ang China, Part I*. Ed. Denis Twitchett and John K. Fairbank. Cambridge: Cambridge University Press, 1979.

———. *Land Tenure and the Social Order in T'ang and Sung China*. Inaugural Lecture, School of Oriental and African Studies, University of London, 1961.

———. "Lands under State Cultivation during the T'ang Dynasty." *Journal of the Economic and Social History of the Orient* 2:2 (1959): 162–203; 2:3 (1959): 335–336.

———. "Lu Chih (754–805): Imperial Adviser and Court Official." In *Confucian Personalities*. Ed. Arthur F. Wright and Denis Twitchett. Stanford: Stanford University Press, 1962.

———. "Merchant, Trade, and Government in Late T'ang." *Asia Major*, n.s. 14:1 (1968): 63–95.

———. "The Monasteries and China's Economy in Medieval Times." *Bulletin of the School of Oriental and African Studies* 19:3 (1957): 526–549.

———. "Monastic Estates in T'ang China." *Asia Major*, n.s. 5 (1956): 123–145.

———. "A Note on the Tunhuang Fragments of the T'ang Regulations (*ko*)." *Bulletin of the School of Oriental and African Studies* 30:2 (1967): 369–381.

———. "Provincial Autonomy and Central Finance in Late T'ang." *Asia Major*, n.s. 11:2 (1965): 211–232.

———. "The Salt Commissioners after the Rebellion of An Lu-shan." *Asia Major*, n.s. 4 (1954): 60–89.

———. "Some Remarks on Irrigation under the T'ang." *T'oung Pao* 48:1–3 (1961): 175–194.

———. "The T'ang Market System." *Asia Major*, n.s. 12:2 (1966): 202–248.

———. "Varied Patterns of Provincial Autonomy in the T'ang Dynasty." In *Essays on T'ang Society*. Ed. John Curtis Perry and Bardwell L. Smith. Leiden: E. J. Brill, 1976.

Van Gulik, R. H. *Sexual Life in Ancient China*. Leiden: E. J. Brill, 1961; new ed., 2003.

Van Slyke, Lyman P. *Yangtze: Nature, History, and the River*. Reading, Mass.: Addison-Wesley, 1988.

Varsano, Paula M. *Tracking the Banished Immortal: The Poetry of Li Bo and Its Critical Reception*. Honolulu: University of Hawai'i Press, 2003.

Verellen, Franciscus. *Du Guangting (850–933): Taoiste de cour à la fin de la Chine médiévale*. Paris: Collège de France, Institut des Hautes Études Chinoises, 1989.

———. "Evidential Miracles in Support of Taoism: The Inversion of a Buddhist Apologetic Tradition." *T'oung Pao* 78 (1992): 217–263.

Von Glahn, Richard. *The Country of Streams and Grottoes: Expansion, Settlement, and the Civilizing of the Sichuan Frontier in Song Times*. Cambridge: Harvard University Press, 1987.

———. *The Sinister Way: The Divine and the Demonic in Chinese Religious Culture*. Berkeley: University of California Press, 2004.

Wagner, Marsha L. *The Lotus Boat: The Origins of Chinese Tz'u Poetry in T'ang Popular Culture*. New York: Columbia University Press, 1984.

Wallacker, Benjamin E. "The Poet as Jurist: Po Chü-I and a Case of Conjugal Homicide." *Harvard Journal of Asiatic Studies* 41:1 (1981): 507–526.

Wallerstein, Immanuel. *The Modern World-System I: Capitalist Agriculture and the Origins of the European World-Economy in the Sixteenth Century*. New York: Academic Press, 1974.

———. "The Rise and Future Demise of the World Capitalist System: Concepts for Comparative Analysis." Reprinted in *The Capitalist World-Economy: Essays by Immanuel Wallerstein*. Cambridge: Cambridge University Press, 1979.

Wang, Gungwu. "The Middle Yangtze in Tang Politics." In *Perspectives on the*

T'ang. Ed. Arthur F. Wright and Denis Twitchett. New Haven: Yale University Press, 1973.

———. *The Structure of Power in North China During the Five Dynasties*. Stanford: Stanford University Press, 1963.

Wang, Ling. *Tea and Chinese Culture*. San Francisco: Long River Press, 2005.

Wang, Robin R., ed. *Images of Women in Chinese Thought and Culture: Writing from the Pre-Qin Period through the Song Dynasty*. Indianapolis: Hackett, 2003.

Wang, Zhenping. *Ambassadors from the Islands of Immortals: China-Japan Relations in the Han-Tang Period*. Honolulu: University of Hawai'i Press, 2005.

Wang, Zhongluo. *Sui Tang Wu dai shi*. 2 vols. Shanghai: Renmin Chubanshe, 2003.

Warner, Ding Xiang. *A Wild Deer amid Soaring Phoenixes: The Opposition Poetics of Wang Ji*. Honolulu: University of Hawai'i Press, 2003.

Wechsler, Howard J. "The Confucian Teacher Wang T'ung (584?–617): One Thousand Years of Controversy." *T'oung pao* 63 (1977): 225–272.

———. "Factionalism in Early T'ang Government." In *Perspectives on the T'ang*. Ed. Arthur F. Wright and Denis Twitchett. New Haven: Yale University Press, 1973.

———. "The Founding of the T'ang Dynasty: Kao-tsu (reign 618–26)." In *Cambridge History of China*. Vol. 3, *Sui and T'ang China, Part I*. Ed. Denis Twitchett and John K. Fairbank. Cambridge: Cambridge University Press, 1979.

———. *Mirror to the Son of Heaven: Wei Cheng at the Court of T'ang T'ai-tsung*. New Haven: Yale University Press, 1974.

———. *Offerings of Jade and Silk: Ritual and Symbol in the Legitimation of the T'ang Dynasty*. New Haven: Yale University Press, 1985.

———. "T'ai-tsung (reign 626–649) the Consolidator." In *Cambridge History of China*. Vol. 3, *Sui and T'ang China, Part I*. Ed. Denis Twitchett and John K. Fairbank. Cambridge: Cambridge University Press, 1979.

Weinstein, Stanley. *Buddhism under the T'ang*. Cambridge: Cambridge University Press, 1987.

———. "Imperial Patronage in the Formation of T'ang Buddhism." In *Perspectives on the T'ang*. Ed. Arthur F. Wright and Denis Twitchett. New Haven: Yale University Press, 1973.

Widmer, Ellen. *The Beauty and the Book: Women and Fiction in Nineteenth-Century China*. Cambridge: Harvard University Press, 2006.

Wiens, Herold. *China's March into the Tropics*. Washington, D.C.: Office of Naval Research, U.S. Navy, 1952.

Will, Pierre-Étienne. "Clear Waters versus Muddy Waters: The Zheng-Bai Irrigation System of Shaanxi Province in the Late-Imperial Period." In *Sediments of Time: Environment and Society in Chinese History*. Ed. Mark Elvin and Liu Ts'ui-jung. Cambridge: Cambridge University Press, 1998.

Wittfogel, Karl. *Wirtschaft und Gesellschaft Chinas: Versuch der wissenschaftlichen Analyse einer grossen asiatischen Agrargesellschaft.* Leipzig: C. L. Hirschfield, 1931.

Worthy, Edmund H. "The Founding of Sung China, 950–1000: Integrative Changes in Military and Political Institutions." Ph.D. diss., Princeton University, 1976.

Wright, Arthur F. *Buddhism in Chinese History.* Stanford: Stanford University Press, 1959.

———. "The Sui Dynasty (581–617)." In *Cambridge History of China.* Vol. 3, *Sui and T'ang China, Part I.* Ed. Denis Twitchett and John K. Fairbank. Cambridge: Cambridge University Press, 1979.

———. *The Sui Dynasty: The Unification of China, A.D. 581–617.* New York: Alfred A. Knopf, 1978.

Wright, Arthur, and Dean Twitchett. "Introduction." In *Perspectives on the T'ang.* New Haven: Yale University Press, 1973.

Wu, Fusheng. *The Poetics of Decadence: Chinese Poetry of the Southern Dynasties and Late Tang Periods.* Albany: State University of New York Press, 1998.

Wu, Yenna. *The Chinese Virago: A Literary Theme.* Cambridge: Harvard University Press, 1995.

Xiao, Chi. *The Chinese Garden as Lyric Enclave: A Generic Study of the Story of the Stone.* Ann Arbor: Center for Chinese Studies, University of Michigan, 2001.

Xiong, Victor Cunrui. *Emperor Yang of the Sui Dynasty: His Life, Times, and Legacy.* Albany: State University of New York Press, 2006.

———. "*Ji*-Entertainers in Tang Chang'an." In *Presence and Presentation: Women in the Chinese Literati Tradition.* Ed. Sherry J. Mou. London: MacMillan, 1999.

———. "The Land-tenure System of Tang China: A Study of the Equal-field System and the Turfan Documents." *T'oung Pao* 85 (1999): 328–390.

———. *Sui-Tang Chang'an.* Ann Arbor: Center for Chinese Studies, University of Michigan, 2000.

Xu, Yinong. *The Chinese City in Space and Time: The Development of Urban Form in Suzhou.* Honolulu: University of Hawai'i Press, 2000.

Xuanzang. *The Great Tang Dynasty Record of the Western Regions.* Tr. Li Rongxi. Berkeley: Numata Center for Buddhist Translation and Research, 1996.

Yamada, Toshiaki. "The Lingbao School." In *Daoism Handbook.* Ed. Livia Kohn. Leiden: E. J. Brill, 2000.

Yampolsky, Philip B. *The Platform Sutra of the Sixth Patriarch.* New York: Columbia University Press, 1967.

Yan, Gengwang. *Tang dai jiaotong tong kao.* 6 vols. Taipei: Academia Sinica, 1985–2003.

————. *Tang shi yanjiu cong gao*. Hong Kong: Xinya Yanjiusuo Chubanshe, 1969.

————. "Tang Wudai shiqi de Chengdu." In *Yang Gengwang shi xue lunwen xuanji*. Taipei: Academia Sinica, 1991.

Yan, Zhitui. *See* Yen, Chih-t'ui.

Yang, Chung-i. "Evolution of the Status of 'Dependents.'" In *Chinese Social History: Translations of Selected Studies*. Ed. E-tu Zen Sun and John De Francis. New York: Octagon Books, 1972.

Yang, Jingqing. *The Chan Interpretations of Wang Wei's Poetry*. Hong Kong: The Chinese University Press, 2007.

Yang, Lien-sheng. "Female Rulers in Imperial China." *Harvard Journal of Asiatic Studies* 23 (1960–61): 47–61.

————. "Notes on the Economic History of the Chin Dynasty." *Harvard Journal of Asiatic Studies* 9 (1945–47): 107–185. Reprinted in *Studies in Chinese Institutional History*. Cambridge: Harvard University Press, 1961.

Yang, Xiaoshan. *Metamorphosis of the Private Sphere: Gardens and Objects in Tang-Song Poetry*. Cambridge: Harvard University Press, 2003.

Yates, Robin. *Washing Silk: The Life and Selected Poetry of Wei Chuang (834?–910)*. Cambridge: Harvard University Press, 1988.

Yen, Chih-t'ui. *Family Instructions for the Yen Clan*. Tr. Teng Ssu-yü. Leiden: E. J. Brill, 1968.

Yu, Pauline. "Song Lyrics and the Canon: A Look at Anthologies of Tz'u." In *Voices of the Song Lyric in China*. Ed. Pauline Yu. Berkeley: University of California Press, 1994.

Yu, Pauline, Peter Bol, Stephen Owen, and Willard Peterson, eds. *Ways With Words: Writings about Reading Texts from Early China*. Berkeley: University of California Press, 2000.

Zeitlin, Judith, and Lydia Liu, eds. *Writing and Materiality in China: Essays in Honour of Patrick Hanan*. Cambridge: Harvard University Press, 2003.

Zürcher, Erik. *The Buddhist Conquest of China*. 2 vols. Leiden: E. J. Brill, 1959.

ACKNOWLEDGMENTS

I would like to express my appreciation to all the scholars whose research I have drawn upon in writing this history of the Tang dynasty. Their names can be found in the notes and bibliography. I also wish to acknowledge my gratitude to Timothy Brook, general editor of the History of Imperial China, for support and useful advice, and to Kathleen McDermott of Harvard University Press for conceiving and sponsoring the series. I would like to thank Don and Ellen Wallace for having suggested improvements to the first draft, and Dieter Kuhn and an anonymous reader for having done the same for a later version. Maps 4, 5, 6, 7, 8, 9, and 17 were adapted from maps in David Graff, *Medieval Chinese Warfare, 300–900*. A Humboldt Foundation award, made possible by Reinhard Emmerich, gave me the time to complete the final version of both this and the preceding volume in the series. Above all, I would like to thank my wife, Kristin Ingrid Fryklund, for her work on the manuscript at every stage.

INDEX

Daoism *(continued)*
thaumaturges, 209; Thunder Rites, 212;
women as nuns, 211–212, 213, 214;
women as priestesses, 182, 212
Daoxuan, 220, 221
Dark Studies (*Xuan xue*), 223, 232, 234,
248–249
Daxingcheng, 10, 22, 31, 85, 87
Deforestation, 10–11, 14, 17–18, 76
Dengzhou, 228
Desertification, 76
Dezong, Emperor, 15, 61, 62–64, 78, 80–
81
Di Renjie, 27
Dikes, 20, 134, 135; breaches, 11–12
Directorate for the Education of the Sons
of the State, 102
Discourses of the States (Guo yu), 238
Documents (Shu), 231, 247–248
Dou Jiande, 13–14
Dream of the Red Chamber, 259
Dreams, 258–259
Du Fu: on Chang'an, 89; in modern canon,
4, 241, 252; "My Thatched Roof Is
Ruined by the Autumn Wind," 253; on
poetry, 253; on Sichuan, 15, 17
Du Guangting, 210–211, 213
Du Mu, 12, 109
Du Xunhe, 117
Du You: *Comprehensive Institutions (Tong
dian)*, 167–168
Dugu Ji, 250–251
Dujiangyan irrigation project, 17
Dunhuang, 143, 151, 158, 170; caves at,
88, 89; documents and scrolls from, 49,
55, 192, 193, 199, 218, 238–239, 245
Dushun, 224
Dzumgarian basin, 158–159

Eastern Wei dynasty, 13
Eastern Zhou dynasty, 14
Emotions, 262
End of Tang dynasty, 18, 37, 70–72, 73,
155, 183, 252; and great families, 197,
206; and Huang Chao's destruction of
Chang'an, 70–71, 72, 272–273
Ennin, 66, 93, 116, 141, 216, 221, 228
Equal-field system, 2, 32–33, 54–57, 58,
61, 80, 121–124
*Essential Methods of the Common People
(Qi min yao shu)*, 129, 136, 143
Eunuchs, 63, 69, 70, 71, 72, 79–80, 83–84,
226; role in military system, 60–61, 62,
65–66, 68, 79, 206, 263
Examination system, 83, 84, 153; and

Chang'an's pleasure quarter, 101, 102,
103–104, 105–106, 261–262; and Confucian canon, 231, 232, 235; and
Daoism, 208; and factionalism, 67–68;
and great families, 3, 37, 106–107, 196,
202, 203–206, 231, 274–275; Han Yu
on, 265–266; and marriage, 106–107,
204, 205; and merit, 274–275, 276; and
poetry, 106–107, 204, 205, 243, 244,
257, 266; and short stories, 260–261;
and Empress Wu, 37, 40, 49, 103–104,
203, 243; and Emperor Xuanzong, 40–
41; and Emperor Xuanzong(2), 69
Executions, 97
*Explanations of Canonical Texts (Jing dian
shi wen)*, 234, 240

Factionalism, 66–72
Famen Monastery, 217
Fanyang, 46, 198
Faxian, 219
Fen River valley, 5, 8, 10
Feng Su, 239
Fictional narratives. *See* Short stories
Fictive kinship, 79–80, 84
First Emperor, 26, 28, 29, 227, 234
Fish, farm-raised, 137
Five Dynasties period: Bianzhou during,
117; economic conditions during, 121;
great families during, 50; Kaifeng during,
117, 275; military system during, 78, 79,
80, 140, 275; as period of division, 273,
275; vs. Tang dynasty, 78, 79, 80, 84,
121, 140, 239
Flower Maiden, 212
Foot-binding, 179
Former Shu, kingdom of, 211, 246, 275
Founding of Tang dynasty, 13–14, 31–33,
51, 180, 195, 208, 221
Four Talents of the Early Tang, 244
Fox cult, 229–230
Frame fields, 135
Free commoners vs. base persons, 53, 127–
128
Fruit trees, 126
Fu Yi, 173–175
Fujian province, 18–19, 19, 25, 83, 133,
135, 137, 143
Fuzhou, 170

Ganges valley, 157
Gan River, 18
Gansu province, 25, 28, 33, 46, 157, 158,
170
Gao Lishi, 60, 83